The Complete
Social Scientist

The Complete Social Scientist

A Kurt Lewin Reader

Edited By
Martin Gold

AMERICAN PSYCHOLOGICAL ASSOCIATION
WASHINGTON, DC

Published by
American Psychological Association
750 First Street, NE
Washington, DC 20002

Copies may be ordered from
APA Order Department
P.O. Box 92984
Washington, DC 20090-2984

In the United Kingdom, Europe, Africa, and the Middle East, copies may be ordered from
American Psychological Association
3 Henrietta Street
Covent Garden, London
WC2E 8LU England

Typeset in Century Schoolbook by EPS Group Inc., Easton, MD
Printer: United Book Press, Baltimore, MD
Cover Designer: Minker Design, Bethesda, MD
Technical/Production Editor: Anne Woodworth

Library of Congress Cataloging-in-Publication Data
Lewin, Kurt, 1890–1947.
    The complete social scientist : a Kurt Lewin reader / edited by
Martin Gold.
        p.   cm.
    Includes bibliographical references and index.
    ISBN 1-55798-532-4
    1. Psychology.   2. Social psychology.   I. Gold, Martin, 1931–   .
II. Title.
BF121..L4395   1999
150—dc21   98-48619
                                                                          CIP

British Library Cataloguing-in-Publication Data
A CIP record is available from the British Library.

Printed in the United States of America
First edition

for the
Research Center for Group Dynamics
celebrating its 50th year at the University of Michigan

Contents

Preface

I am pleased to participate in the American Psychological Association's efforts to make the works of Kurt Lewin more accessible to contemporary readers. This anthology is a companion volume to the recently issued one-volume edition of two previous anthologies of Lewin's writings, *Resolving Social Conflicts* and *Field Theory in Social Science*. This anthology includes 15 more articles difficult to obtain either because their original sources are now out-of-print and often absent from the current collections of all but major research libraries or because, in the case of two of the articles, they have never before been available in English.

Scholars engaged in a broad range of disciplines should find this anthology useful. I selected the articles to display the many facets of Lewin's intellectual interests: philosophy of science; social, developmental, personality, motivational, cognitive, and clinical psychology; social organization; social problems; and scientific methodology. Scholars may also find in the compleat social scientist, thus revealed, a model to which they may aspire, if only in part, in considering the directions of their own careers.

Readers in disparate fields will find it illuminating to read Lewin's articles in fields related to but not their own. I have endeavored to help make the connections among the various articles more apparent with some commentary and with a brief intellectual biography of Lewin that speculates on the common sources of his many creative ideas.

Lewin's writing is easily comprehensible to advanced undergraduates and certainly to graduate students and professionals in the several relevant fields. The translator of the two articles from the German, Dr. Anja Spindler, and I have tried to render these articles in English as comprehensible as the German originals while at the same time retaining something of their German accent.

The opportunity to create this anthology has come to me at an especially significant time, when I can dedicate it to the 50th anniversary of the Research Center for Group Dynamics at the University of Michigan. Founded by Lewin at the Massachusetts Institute of Technology in 1945, the Center moved to Michigan in 1948, after Lewin's untimely death, to become part of the University's Institute for Social Research. The Center became my professional home in 1954 and, for me, happily has remained so ever since.

There I have been fortunate to study and work with many of Lewin's students and colleagues. They, and the people I have come to know in the Society for the Advancement of Field Theory, have helped me to gain access to and better understand the whole corpus of Lewin's work. Indeed, many of them have generously entrusted me with their collections of offprints and books by Lewin, some of them once Lewin's own and bearing his signature. So the creation of this anthology is for me the handing on of an invaluable intellectual inheritance.

Martin Gold
Ann Arbor, Michigan

Acknowledgments

I want to acknowledge the many kinds of generous assistance I received in creating this anthology. This was by no means a solo project.

First and foremost, I want to thank Miriam Lewin, who encouraged me to undertake this anthology of her father's work and advised me at every stage of its creation. Other friends, colleagues, and enthusiasts of K. Lewin who advised me include Rudolph Arnheim, Kurt W. Back, David Bargal, Joseph DeRivera, Robert Kleiner, Albert Pepitone, Carol W. Slater, and Hans Toch.

Dr. Anja M. Spindler is the primary translator of "'Two Fundamental Types of Life Processes'" (Selection 5) and "Socializing the Taylor System" (Selection 12). I am fortunate that she was pursuing post-doctoral studies at the Research Center for Group Dynamics at an opportune time.

The Center provided its customary skilled and energetic secretarial services in the persons of Paulette Gadson, Kent Montane, and the ever-helpful Laura Reynolds.

I found much encouragement and assistance at the publishers from Ted Baroody, Beth Beisel, Julia Frank-McNeil, Andrea Phillippi, Mary Lynn Skutley, Gary R. VandenBos, and Anne Woodworth with the wise editorial pen.

Finally, I am indebted to the following holders of current copyrights of articles for permission to reprint them here. The original sources are listed with the titles of the articles in the text.

Selection 2: "The Conflict Between Aristotelian and Galileian Modes of Thought in Contemporary Psychology." This translation reprinted by permission of Nancy Adams Malone, Ann Zener, Julian Zener, and Karl A. Zener.

Selection 4: "Intention, Will, and Need." Reprinted by permission of Miriam Lewin.

Selection 6: "Level of Aspiration." Reprinted by permission of Mrs. George M. (Hunt) Epple and Judith A. Hunt.

Selection 8: "Patterns of Aggressive Behavior in Experimentally Created 'Social Climates.'" Reprinted by permission of Heldref Publications.

Selection 10: "Group Decision and Social Change." Reprinted by permission of Holt, Rinehart & Winston.

Martin Gold
Ann Arbor, Michigan

The Complete
Social Scientist

Introduction

Kurt Lewin continues to be one of the most frequently cited authors in the social sciences. Although his last publication originally appeared in 1949, the *Social Science Citation Index* lists over 180 citations to Lewin's work just in the first 9 months of 1997. The relevance of Lewin's thought and research to contemporary social science—indeed, to contemporary world culture—is clear.

Unfortunately, despite its currency, a great deal of Lewin's work has over time become largely inaccessible to contemporary scholars. The many recent citations are to only a limited set of the more accessible writings. Important early work was published in German, some in journals that were destroyed by the Nazis and, in any case, are now to be found only in remote storage sites of major research universities. These have been gathered recently by Graumann (1981) and Metraux (1981) in Europe. Other works by Lewin, translated into English or written in English after Lewin immigrated to the United States in 1933, are scattered in edited books that have gone out of print or in back issues of journals, many of these now removed from the current collections of all but the largest academic libraries.

To begin to make more of Lewin's work easily accessible again, the American Psychological Association has reissued in one volume two frequently cited but out-of-print anthologies, *Resolving Social Conflicts* and *Field Theory in Social Science* (Lewin, 1997). The present anthology continues that effort, bringing together 15 significant but hard-to-obtain articles, including 2 never before available in English.

These 15 articles were selected not only because each of them still stands as a relevant contribution to the world's culture but also because together, they reflect the extraordinary range over which Kurt Lewin's intellectual activity remains relevant. Witness the range of fields in which recent citations to Lewin have been made: in psychology, including social psychology, of course (e.g., on group leadership, group decision making, group development, attitudes, and beliefs), and also developmental psychology, motivation, clinical psychology, research methods, and psychological theory; in disciplines somewhat afield from psychology proper, including sociology, political science, cultural anthropology, communication sciences, law, medicine, education, and business administration; and in articles on such varied topics as computer programming, sports, nursing, the environment, farm management, death and dying, and tourism. (Citations have appeared in articles written in Croatian, Czech, German, and Japanese as well as, of course, in English.)

The breadth of the fields and interests to which Lewin's thought contributes testifies both to the fundamental nature of many of his ideas and to his breadth as a social scientist. I have grouped the selections in this anthology so that they display the many facets of Lewin as an intellectual—philosopher of science, research psychologist, applied psychologist, and sage.

The first several selections present Lewin as a philosopher of science. In these, Lewin presents the principles that guided him as a research and an applied psychologist—constructing theory, deriving hypotheses, analyzing practical problems, designing studies, and interpreting data—and that provided the scientific orientation from which he replied sagely to requests for advice on many social problems.

The next section includes original reports by Lewin of programs of research that he and his students, or colleagues (Lewin hardly made this distinction), carried out on key theoretical problems in motivational, developmental, and social psychology. In these, readers will find the sources of many of the now-familiar principles on which contemporary scientific psychology rests and, perhaps, feel the excitement of their discovery. This is the work that, more than any other, made Lewin prominent.

Following is a selection of articles that Lewin wrote as an applied psychologist. These studies were driven not so much by theory as they were by current social problems, which Lewin, well-known for his eagerness to make social science useful, was frequently asked to address. In addressing them, Lewin still marshaled his philosophical orientation to science, psychological field theory, innovative experimental methods, and the relevant psychological principles. This sample of work in applied psychology is on wartime food shortages, industrial productivity, and education of minority children.

Last are selections in which Lewin responded to requests for advice from policymakers and community leaders. Lewin permitted himself a more discursive style in these articles, relating his arguments less to specific social scientific theory and data. In these pieces, the substance is more obviously infused with Lewin's social values, although one can find social values implied in Lewin's scientific writings as well. The value that Lewin placed on democratic procedure, individual freedom, and social responsibility provides the framework for the selection and interpretation of the social research he drew on implicitly when he wrote as a sage—in these particular selections on the function psychological science should play in guiding industrial organization in post World War I Germany, on teaching, on the way one should respond as a victim of prejudice, and on the role of social science in war and peace.

Inasmuch as the 15 selections anthologized here were written over a span of 30 years—years of literally revolutionary changes in psychology, the social and physical sciences, and in world culture—some of the most significant contributions of these articles can be grasped only in the context of their times. Therefore, being more familiar than most with the body of Lewin's work, I have presumed to provide commentaries on the selections that mainly locate them in their intellectual and social milieus. For the same purpose, I have also written a brief intellectual biography of Lewin that aims to identify the conditions and the events that shaped his extraordinary, many-faceted mind.

I hope that the reader will recognize that my commentary is not an archivist's notes nor this anthology a museum exhibition. Rather, this whole effort is to make some more of what remains one of the most useful bodies of social scientific writing more accessible intellectually and physically to current scholars. The ideas contained herein are fundamental, stimulating, and heuristic. Further, as Kleiner and Maguire have noted, "Lewin was a complete psychologist—a theorist, a methodologist, and a practitioner" (1986, p. 18)—and more. That is, Kurt Lewin is a unique standing model for what contemporary social scientists can be.

References

Graumann, C. F. (Ed.). (1981). *Kurt Lewin: Werkausgabe, Vol. 1*. Bern, Switzerland: Hans Huber.

Kleiner, R., & Maquire, F. (1986). Lewin's sphere of influence from Berlin. In E. H. Stivers & S. A. Wheelan (Eds.), *The Lewin legacy* (pp. 12–20). New York: Springer-Verlag.

Lewin, K. (1997). *Resolving social conflicts and Field theory in social science*. Washington, DC: American Psychological Association. (Original works published 1948 and 1951)

Metraux, A. (Ed.). (1981). *Kurt Lewin: Werksausgabe, Vols. 2 and 3*. Bern, Switzerland: Hans Huber.

The Making of a Compleat Social Scientist: A Brief Intellectual Biography

Lewin would have acknowledged that he, like everyone else, was a unique event. Lewin was also extraordinary. Few social scientists today follow anything resembling Lewin's model of a compleat social scientist. Few ever have. Following Lewin, who was adamant that scientists should make special efforts to understand the unusual, one may wonder what in Lewin's experience made him such an unusual social scientist. Learning about his formative experiences not only is intrinsically interesting but also helps illuminate the underlying integration of Lewin's social scientific identity.

Thus, before presenting the selections themselves, I identify what I think are some of the significant experiences in Lewin's life that motivated and enabled him to produce the body of works from which these selections come. In doing this, I work on the assumption that for most people, intellectual character—and that is the only aspect of Lewin's character with which I am concerned here—is formed largely in late adolescence and early adulthood.

Philosopher of Science

Lewin's interest in the philosophy of science was not unusual among psychologists at the time and place of his early professional education; in fact, it was normative at the University of Berlin in 1910, when Lewin matriculated there. Wilhelm Wundt, a foremost psychologist of his time, prescribed "that no one should be allowed to teach in psychology 'who is a mere experimenter and not at the same time a psychologically and philosophically educated man, filled with philosophical interests'" (Ash, 1985, p. 289) The man who was to become Lewin's thesis advisor, Carl Stumpf, also regarded attention to philosophical issues as vital to psychological science (Ash, 1995, p. 34ff.) Accordingly, it was common for psychologists, along with other social scientists, to be members of departments or schools of philosophy, rather than of separate departments of psychology, and to concern themselves with philosophical matters.

In Lewin's youth, psychologists were striving to free psychology from its speculative philosophical entanglements and to make of it an empirical and experimental science. Psychologists aspired to the model of the biological sciences, whose objects were directly observable and mostly tangible. Consequently, they confined their research to observable behavior. Nevertheless, their subject matter impelled many thoughtful psychologists to interpret their observations in terms of intangible thoughts, motives, and feelings, and they regularly even skirted close to the spiritual. Their very vocabulary was ambiguous. For example, Lewin, his German instructors, and his classmates read, heard, and wrote about "Seele"—"soul"— in discussions that attempted to deal with ineffable aspects of the mind. D. K. Adams and K. E. Zener, early translators of some of Lewin's German writings, made special note of this confusion in their Translators' Preface to the Lewin anthology, *A Dynamic Theory of Personality* (K. Lewin, 1935). At the same time, the Gestalt psychologists—Wertheimer, Koffka, Köhler—who were prominent among Lewin's mentors in psychology, and later as his colleagues, consistently hypothesized a physical basis in brain structure for the perceptual phenomena they observed. To be scientific in those days, one confined oneself to what one could directly observe and impute a tangible cause.

While negotiating these crosscurrents of ideas as a graduate student, Lewin was fortunate to encounter Ernst Cassirer. Cassirer and other neo-Kantians challenged this kind of literal empiricism with the idea of the idea: If one can only conceive of something, it has a kind of reality, an existence. Scientific theorizing need not be confined to the directly observed. If a concept is useful for constructing a causal hypothesis, create it, define it, describe it, and be mindful that eventually, if the concept is to be fully scientific, one must create a way to measure it—the sooner the better.

The influence of Cassirer's neo-Kantian philosophy is apparent in all of Lewin's philosophical and scientific writing. It seems to me that this influence was, first of all, a liberating force. For Lewin, who was eager to advance psychology as a science but was particularly interested in the insubstantial likes of needs, motives, and intentions, neo-Kantian idealism gave his thinking free flight. Furthermore, this philosophy permitted one to conceive not only of realities unseen but also of the even more intangible coexisting pattern of these. Then, treating ideas as a kind of reality, one could proceed to construct theory—that is, to formulate universal laws that specified the relationships among constructs and the effects of relationships among constructs. In this way, psychology could become a more mature science, that is, one that not only described but also predicted and that used not merely induction from observed regularities but, rather, logical deduction from theory.

Lewin's early exposure to the philosophy of Ernst Cassirer left a deep and indelible impression. He attended Cassirer's seminar in his first year at Berlin, when he was 20 years old, and thereafter became recognized as a scholarly exponent of Cassirer's philosophy, particularly Cassirer's philosophy of science. In 1946, when P. A. Schilpp began to assemble the volume on Cassirer for Open Court's series entitled Library of Living Philosophers, he turned to Lewin for "Cassirer's Philosophy of Science and the Social Sciences" (K. Lewin, 1949; i.e., Selection 1 in this volume). The article was published posthumously, both for Lewin and for Cassirer.

Lewin credited Cassirer not only with legitimating constructivism, the scientific use of constructs or ideas as real objects for study, but also with impressing on him the centrality of relationships and the use of logic in scientific theory (K. Lewin, 1949). In such common use now that social scientists use them without reflection, constructivism, attribution of causality to relationships, and logical deduction from theory were revolutionary and contested in Lewin's student and early professional days.

The idea of relations among parts being causative in a system was central to the physical and the psychological theories being developed at the University of Berlin and elsewhere as Lewin began his professional training and when he became a young professional after World War I. In psychology, the idea of holism—the significance of the total set of conditions—was intrinsic to Gestalt theory. This theory asserted that spatial and temporal relationships among elements were the effective conditions that gave rise to perceptual phenomena such as the phi phenomenon, movement perceived when lights at a certain distance apart blinked on and off in a certain interval of time. Lewin incorporated holism into his explanations of how the relationships among such psychological conditions as needs, wishes, intentions, and opportunities affected behavior. He and his Gestalt colleagues at Berlin became dissatisfied, however, merely to refer to relationships; as espoused at the time in the humanities and by scientists other than Gestalt psychologists, holism often seemed to consist only of waving one's arm broadly in explanation of a puzzling phenomenon. Influenced by Cassirer's attribution of the successes of contemporary physics to its specific formulations, Lewin aimed to express effective psychological relationships as well in precise, logical forms; hence, formulas such as $cons(A) = F(Po(S^A))$, or "the constructiveness of play in Situation A is a function of the potency of the situation (S) related to the activity (A)" appeared in Lewin's writings. (See Selection 7, "Frustration and Regression: An Experiment With Children," pp. 183–225, for the context of this formula.)

Although Cassirer seems to have been the major influence on Lewin as a philosopher of science, he was not the sole influence. Philosophizing permeated the students' milieus at the University of Berlin at the time. Metraux (1992) noted that Lewin "borrowed from phenomenology, logical positivism, Marxism, and the neo-Kantian movement" (p. 379). One of the ideas that marked the neo-Kantians as followers of Immanuel Kant was Kant's phenomenalism, or the belief that sensate organisms are not directly in touch with reality but know it only indirectly through the perceptual processes by which they interpret the input of their senses. The message of logical positivism that circulated mostly from Vienna was that the only statements of fact worthy of attention were those whose truth could be tested by observation. And Marxism, then triumphant in the new Soviet Union, not only directed social scientists to base their theories on who controlled the means of production but also alerted them to consider who controlled their science as well.

Thus, the practice of philosophy was vital and not at all unusual among scientists at the University of Berlin in the 1920s. Lewin was simply unusually good at it.[1]

Research Psychologist

Gestalt psychology was blooming at the University of Berlin when Lewin arrived there as a student in 1910. Its major founders—Wertheimer, Koffka, and Köhler—were there. Gestaltism colored all of Lewin's psychological research thereafter.

Although for this reason he is often regarded as a Gestalt psychologist, Lewin did not swallow Gestalt psychology whole. He accepted its holistic emphasis but did not dwell on physicalistic explanations. As mentioned, neo-Kantianism liberated him from having to think in terms of tangible objects; so, unlike his Gestalt associates, he did not concern himself with whether brain structure and neural currents ultimately explained the phenomena he was interested in. The idea of holism, however—of the "total situation," of "fields of force"—appealed to him.

The appeal of holism was widespread in the intellectual culture of Lewin's youth. German humanists were as much taken with it as were the physicists and Gestalt psychologists. However, for the humanists, holism was a kind of Luddite reaction to intellectual industrialism. Modern science and technology were viewed as turning people into mere machine animals: no more than oxen turning grindstones. Prominent German psychologists partly shared this perspective and regarded stimulus–response behaviorists as dehumanizers. It was this group of psychologists whom the head of Berlin's Institute of Psychology, Carl Stumpf, had in mind when he "decried American 'narrowness and pragmatism'" (Ash, 1995, p. 35). The way was wide open, then, for Lewin to adopt the orientation of the physicists and psychologists around him and to think in terms of patterns of relationships.

Soon going beyond his mentors' and colleagues' interests in perceptual phenomena, Lewin brought the Gestalt orientation to bear on problems of memory and of behavior. Taking up the opposition to associationism, Lewin's early research investigated the effects of motives and intentions on responses to stimuli. He and his students demonstrated that an external stimulus by itself could hardly account for people's responses to it and that what people brought to their encounter with a stimulus had to be

---

[1]It is worth noting here that Lewin seems to have taken Cassirer as a model mentor as well. Although the style of academic decorum in Germany at the time was stiffly formal and authoritarian, Cassirer was quite informal and egalitarian. He encouraged discussion among his students and led them to develop their ideas. Lewin did the same.

In at least one respect, however, Lewin's teaching style differed from Cassirer's. Cassirer is described as having been "serene" in the classroom. As a teacher, Lewin has never been described as "serene." He could not hold his seat long, leapt to the chalkboard, paced about the room, and spoke as though his tongue could not keep up with his thoughts.

taken into account as well. Lewin's account was represented as fields of force that included characteristics of stimuli and of the person.

Lewin then extended the reach of this approach to child and industrial psychology, maintaining that the needs, interests, and skills of the young child and the adult worker inextricably combined with environmental stimuli to determine behavior. Attending to children and workers while they went about their lives rather than to participants in brief laboratory sessions added another dimension to consider. Because the person was never psychologically the same from one moment to the next, one could not expect that responses even to "identical" stimuli would be the same; one had to take into account how the ever-changing person construed the stimulus environment to understand the person's behavior.[2] The totality of the situation became, as Lewin meant it, the totality of the situation as the person experienced it at that moment in time, an idea that was expressed shortly in the concept of life space.

The rigors of scientific method strained a research psychologist's commitment to holism. Lewin's education in a neo-Kantian philosophy of science and in biological research methods converged on controlled experiment as the best way to test the truth of deductions from theory. But how was one to capture the "total situation" in a laboratory experiment? It seems that Lewin's early response to this dilemma was to closely observe experimental participants' reactions and to record them in detail. Especially in experiments with children, the total situation and the participants' responses were often recorded on film, a medium for which Lewin had an early and lifelong enthusiasm. These observations served at least two related purposes: They helped to explain behavior that was exceptional to prediction, and they were a source of further hypotheses. Later in his career, Lewin and his colleagues ingeniously carried the experimental method out of the laboratory into ongoing real-life settings in which the situation was more plausibly "total." This innovation was particularly useful in Lewin's work as an applied psychologist.

Widespread intellectual enthusiasm for holism, the amazing discoveries of field theoretical physics, and, in particular, the concentration of Gestalt psychology at the University of Berlin immediately after World War I set Lewin's research off on a lifelong vector. This environment directed the character of his scientific thinking about whatever psychological and social problems Lewin chose to consider.

Applied Psychologist

In his youth, Lewin was already keenly interested in social problems. He ultimately turned his professional attention to the welfare of children, the

---

[2]Note that in the previous sentence, I have used a device used regularly by Lewin of putting a word—"identical"—in quotation marks. This, and his use of the term "quasi," acknowledge the imprecision of the expression and also the desirability of getting on with the discourse without being sidetracked. In this instance, e.g., external stimuli are never absolutely "identical."

humanization of industry, the psychological condition of oppressed peoples, the proper form of human governance, and other troublesome aspects of human relations. It was not his personal experience with Nazism and the Holocaust that first led Lewin to conduct scientific research for the purpose of ameliorating social problems. Howevermuch experiences in his 40s fueled the urgency of his efforts, Lewin began devoting his talents to "action research" early in his career, marshaling theory, previous findings, and rigorous methods to resolve social conflicts. There were reasons enough in his youth and early adulthood for him to become, in Marrow's phrase, a "practical theorist."

To begin with, Lewin was a Jew growing up in a pervasively anti-Semitic culture. He spent the first 15 years of his life in East Prussia, a part of Germany that was even more anti-Semitic than the rest.

The Lewins lived in the small town of Mogilno, and for several years, Kurt boarded during the week with a Jewish family in the nearby city of Posen to attend a better school. Divided nationalism was a major source of conflict in this region at the time. The territory had belonged to Poland until 1815, and the culture of Eastern Europe was still pervasive. In 1885, 5 years before Lewin's birth, to "Prussian-ize" the area, many Poles were expelled and the central government took charge of the schools. The loyalties of Jews, even those who had been German for generations, was similarly suspect, and to testify to their loyalty, many Jews converted to Christianity or assimilated in less drastic ways. Inasmuch as Kurt's father was a leading figure in the local Jewish congregation, one can surmise that the Lewin family was not among the assimilationists. The precariousness of being Jews can be seen in the tenuousness of their property rights: Kurt's father, a storekeeper, also owned and personally worked a farm on the outskirts of Mogilno, but according to Kurt's daughter Miriam (personal communication, 1997), ownership had to be in a Christian's name. In 1908, just 3 years after the Lewins moved from Mogilno to Berlin, the Prussian Landstag authorized the expropriation of all expatriate Polish property, and much property belonging to Jews fell under this edict.

The Lewins' move to Berlin in 1905 was largely motivated to secure a better education for their four children, of whom 15-year-old Kurt was the oldest of three sons and was now ready to enter a secondary school (or *gymnasium*). Theirs was part of a large stream of migration from rural to urban areas that was taking place throughout industrializing Europe and especially among Jews. The Jewish population of the Posen area dropped from over 76,000 to about 35,000 between 1847 and 1900 (Schorsch, 1972, p. 164). Although anti-Semitism was somewhat muted in Berlin, Kurt had by no means left it behind. A Jewish schoolboy in Berlin must have felt uncomfortable with the Christian education that occupied part of the curriculum of all the state-supported gymnasia, and he must have been quite aware that he was barred from most of his classmates' groups in the German Youth Movement. This same exclusion not only carried over into the participation of university students in the Youth Movement but it also governed most of the university students' societies. Indeed, there were acknowledged Jewish quotas on admission to German universities, and Jews were virtually barred from professorial appointments. Lewin experienced anti-Semitism more intensely again in the German artillery when World War I interrupted his education (M. Lewin, 1992).

Thus, "marginality" did not suddenly spring fully formed as a powerful explanatory concept from the head of a mature psychological theorist. Lewin experienced marginality from his earliest days. Lewin's Jewishness was his personal social problem, and it made him generally sensitive to social problems.

Lewin's efforts to ameliorate social problems began in his student days at the University of Berlin in 1910. The nature of his efforts and their sociopolitical orientation were influenced then, and to some degree throughout his life, by the Korsches: Karl and Hedda. Lewin fell in with the Korsches when he met Hedda, née Gagliardi, in his university classes. Lewin joined Hedda and other students in organizing evening courses and discussion groups for and with working people, an activity that itself was organized regionally by Karl Korsch, whom Hedda had known for about 2 years.

Karl and Kurt had much in common. Although Karl was not Jewish and was not himself reared in Posen, his father's family, like Kurt's, farmed there. For both, their chosen academic professions ran against their fathers' wishes: Kurt was supposed to have become a physician, Karl a lawyer. (When they met, Karl, 4 years Kurt's senior, was completing his dissertation and was about to become a member of the law faculty at the University of Jena.) Karl had also studied philosophy with neo-Kantians and was deeply influenced by them. (A decade later, he would begin to write philosophically about Marxism from a neo-Kantian point of view.)

When Kurt first met him, Karl was a leader of the Free Students, an organization of German university students formed in opposition to the heavy-drinking, sometimes dueling, and mostly anti-Semitic traditional student organizations. He edited the Free Students' newsletter and toured campuses speaking on behalf of the organization. He almost certainly represented the Free Students at the Woodstock of the German Youth Movement on the Hohe Meissner (October 11–13, 1913), where Kurt probably joined him after representing the Free Students at a conference on educational reform (Stafseng & Kleiner, 1992).

Lewin's and the Korsches' lives remained entwined. Lewin's first marriage was to Hedda's best friend, and after World War I, when Kurt returned to the University of Berlin and Karl became a member of the Reichstag in the Weimar Republic, the Lewins and the Korsches lived close to one another in a Berlin suburb. Both fled Nazi Germany in 1933, Lewin directly to the United States, the Korsches first to England and then to the United States in 1938; they stayed in contact with Kurt until his death in 1947.

Karl Korsch's social democratic sociopolitical orientation appealed to Lewin. Although Korsch was a Marxist philosophically, he was marginal to the Communists politically. His relationship to the Communist Party was unstable. Lewin was never a Marxist, but he was a social democrat, and Korsch was happy to have him contribute an article expressing a social democratic view of the Taylor System to a journal that he edited (see Selection 12).

Although social democratic views, association with the Free Students, and participation in the working people's night school were frowned on generally by the faculty at the University of Berlin, Lewin was not entirely alone on the left, even before World War I. For example, one of his most prominent mentors and later colleagues, Max Wertheimer, was an active Social Democrat. Then, when Lewin returned to the university in the turbulent aftermath of World War I, much of the university, with the significant exception of most of the senior faculty, had moved to the left. Student councils claimed control; they held the Rector captive for a few days until he was ordered released by the Social Democratic minister on the intercession of Wertheimer, Albert Einstein, and several other prominent academic leftists. It was significant that amidst all this change, the likelihood of professional advancement for a young Jewish docent increased greatly. It seems natural then that Lewin's personal experiences as a young adult should have made him a social democrat.

Actually, however, Lewin did not engage much in applied psychology in his early professional years. In Germany, Lewin published only two articles in applied psychology, the one on the Taylor System (1920) and one he had presented to a conference on the Montessori method of teaching (1931). Although his experiences in his youth seemed to incline him to become a practical theorist, Lewin's development and practice of "action research" occurred later, in the United States. Then, the impression of earlier influences showed in the problems that he worked on and the nature of his applications and of his sage counsel—on the psychological problems of oppressed minorities, particularly Jews; on prejudice in intergroup relations; on democratic modes of child rearing and education; and, again, on industrial organization.

It would hardly be appropriate to attribute the many facets of Lewin's engagement as a mature social psychologist to his experiences as a youth. Lewin would insist that his later activities be accounted for by the motives and resources he possessed at the time and by the situations to which he brought himself. He would agree, however, that his motives and resources can be understood as contemporary precipitates of his past experience and that these also played a part in his making and choosing situational opportunities.

What was the intellectual character of the mature Lewin that made him so many faceted—as a wellspring of important ideas for so many people in so many fields and as an abiding influence on world culture? Lewin remained broadly interested in the development of science; Donald Adams (Marrow, 1969, pp. 235–236) reported that to the end of his life, Lewin intended to devote himself, when he found the time, to a comparative study of science. Ever thoughtful about the nature of science, he practiced science on the theoretical and methodological cutting edge—indeed, his creative field theory and innovative experimental procedures made him a cutting edge. He recognized the place of science in the culture, as both subject to and causal of change. This broad grounding in science and the liberal social conscience he developed as a member of an oppressed minority were, I think, the early life precipitates that most distinguished the mature Kurt Lewin.

One must not ignore the situation that this individual encountered. It is ironic that the Nazis' intention to destroy the Jews thrust him prominently onto what became the liveliest stage of scientific and general cultural development of Lewin's age. It is, of course, impossible to say with any certainty what would have become of Lewin had the Nazis not come to power in Germany and had Lewin not fled to the United States. It is reasonable, nevertheless, to suppose that the egalitarian, democratic, highly competitive, and relatively well-endowed American institution of science fit Lewin's predispositions to a tee.

Twenty years ago, Mary Henle (1977), a student of Lewin in the 1940s, wrote that social science was then advancing toward where Kurt Lewin had been 60 years before. It seems to me that social psychologists must still catch up. I hope this reintroduction to the original hastens us on our way.

References

Ash, M. G. (1985). Gestalt psychology: Origins in Germany and reception in the United States. In C. E. Buxton (Ed.), *Points of view in the modern history of psychology* (pp. 295–344). Orlando, FL: Academic Press.

Ash, M. G. (1995). *Gestalt psychology in German culture: 1890–1967*. Cambridge, England: Cambridge University Press.

Henle, M. (1977). The influence of Gestalt psychology in America. *Annals of the New York Academy of Sciences, 291*, 3–13.

Lewin, K. (1935). *A dynamic theory of personality*. New York: McGraw-Hill.

Lewin, K. (1949). Cassirer's philosophy of science and the social sciences. In P. A. Schilpp (Ed.), *The philosophy of Ernst Cassirer* (pp. 269–288). La Salle, IL: Open Court.

Lewin, M. (1992). The impact of Kurt Lewin's life on the place of social issues in his work. *Journal of Social Issues, 48*, 15–29.

Marrow, A. J. (1969). *The practical theorist: The life and work of Kurt Lewin*. New York: Basic Books.

Metraux, A. (1992). Kurt Lewin: Philosopher–psychologist. *Science in Context, 5*, 373–384.

Schorsch, I. (1972). *Jewish reactions to German anti-Semitism, 1870–1914*. New York: Columbia University Press.

Stafseng, O., & Kleiner, R. (1992). *Kurt Lewin in the youth and educational reform movements in Germany*. Paper presented at the Fifth International Kurt Lewin Conference of the Society for the Advancement of Field Theory, Philadelphia.

Bibliography

Back, K. (1996). *Roger Boskovich and Kurt Lewin: Pioneering in field theory in physics and psychology*. Paper presented at the Seventh International Kurt Lewin Conference of the Society for the Advancement of Field Theory, Los Angeles.

Becker, H. (1946). *German youth: Bond or free?* London: Kegan Paul, Trench, & Trubner.

Deutsch, M. (1968). Field theory in social psychology. In G. Lindzey & E. Aronson (Eds.), *The handbook of social psychology* (2nd ed., pp. 412–487). Reading, MA: Addison-Wesley.

Eng, E. (1978). Looking back on Kurt Lewin: From field theory to action research. *Journal of the History of the Behavioral Sciences, 14*, 228–232.

Feuer, L. S. (1974). *Einstein and the generations of science.* New York: Basic Books.

Frank, J. D. (1978). Kurt Lewin in retrospect—a psychiatrist's view. *Journal of the History of the Behavioral Sciences, 14*, 223–227.

Gallin, A. (1986). *Midwives to Nazism.* Macon, GA: Mercer University Press.

Gawronsky, D. (1948). Ernst Cassirer: His life and his work. In P. A. Schilpp (Ed.), *The philosophy of Ernst Cassirer* (pp. 1–37). LaSalle, IL: Open Court.

Goode, P. (1979). *Karl Korsch: A study in western Marxism.* London: Macmillan Press.

Halliday, F. (1972). Memories of Karl Korsch: Interview with Hedda Korsch. *New Left Review, 76*, 34–45.

Harrington, A. (1996). *Reenchanted science: Holism in German culture from Wilhelm II to Hitler.* Princeton, NJ: Princeton University Press.

Henle, M. (1978). Kurt Lewin as metatheorist. *Journal of the History of the Behavioral Sciences, 14*, 233–235.

John, M., Eckardt, G., & Hiebsch, H. (1989). Kurt Lewin's early intentions. *European Journal of Social Psychology, 19*, 163–169.

Lewin, K. (1937). Carl Stumpf. *Psychological Review, 44*, 189–194.

Magill, S. (1979). Defense and introspection: German Jewry, 1914. In D. Bronsen (Ed.), *Jews and Germans from 1860 to 1933: The problematic symbiosis* (pp. 209–233). Heidelberg, Germany: Carl Winter Universitätsverlag.

McClelland, C. E. (1981). *State, society, and university in Germany: 1700–1914.* Cambridge, England: Cambridge University Press.

Paulsen, F. L. (1906). *The German universities and university studies* (F. Thilly & W. W. Elwang, Trans.). New York: Scribner. (Original work published 1902)

Reinharz, J. (1975). *Fatherland or promised land: The dilemma of the German Jew, 1893–1914.* Ann Arbor: University of Michigan Press.

Scholem, G. (1979). On the social psychology of the Jews in Germany: 1900–1933. In D. Bronsen (Ed.), *Jews and Germans from 1860 to 1933: The problematic symbiosis* (pp. 9–32). Heidelberg, Germany: Carl Winter Universitätsverlag.

Scholem, G. (1980). *From Berlin to Jerusalem: Memories of my youth* (H. Zohn, Trans.). New York: Schocken Books. (Original work published 1977)

Stackura, P. D. (1981). *The German youth movement: 1900–1945.* London: Macmillan.

Tolman, E. C. (1948). Kurt Lewin: 1890–1847. *Psychological Review, 55*, 1–4.

van Elteren, M. (1992). Karl Korsch and Lewinian social psychology: Failure of a project. *History of the Human Sciences, 5*, 33–61.

Part I

Philosopher of Science

Introduction

The primary cause of Lewin's philosophy of science was to promote the scientific status first of psychology and then of the social sciences generally. His philosophical tools were neo-Kantian idealism and logical positivism; his model was contemporary physics. The following selections from Lewin's work bearing directly on this subject present his thinking from the general to the specific.

The first selection, Lewin's contribution to a volume on the philosophy of Ernst Cassirer, provides a broad overview of Lewin's understanding of his teacher's philosophy of science. It emphasizes method—first, and most important, the constructive methods by which scientific theories should be formulated, showing the influence of neo-Kantian idealism; second, the empirical methods by which scientific assertions should be tested, showing the influence of logical positivism.

In the second selection, Lewin drew implications of his philosophy of science specifically for methods of theory construction in psychology and touched briefly on experimental methods for testing theory. This discussion is organized, on the one hand, by a comparison of the conceptual structures of Aristotle's and Galileo's theories and, on the other hand, by a parallel comparison of theories in physics and in psychology in the 1920s.

The third selection is the most specific. Here Lewin compared his field theory with psychoanalytic theory against the standards of his philosophy of science as applied to psychology, finding relative strengths in both theories. Here, too, the focus is on methods of theorizing, with only brief attention given to methods of testing theory. Particular attention is given to how the two theories take individuals' life histories into account to explain their current experience and behavior.

Cassirer's Philosophy of Science and the Social Sciences (Selection 1)

An essential problem for social science, as compared with biology, for example, is the intangibility of its concepts, such as intentions and emotions. The basic data of modern science are shared observations. Concepts might be useful for theorizing, but they are ultimately useless scientifically if they cannot be realized clearly, if indirectly, by observables—that is, "op-

erationalized." Contemporary physics was dealing with the same problem
(and still is); not even the bubble chamber and the electron microscope
had been invented yet. Nor was the problem fundamentally one of the
"infinitesimal" size of hypothetical entities; theoretically causative relationships among entities are inherently not directly observable but must
be inferred. Lewin devoted most of his review of Cassirer's contributions
to social science (Selection 1) to this problem of "reality," of "existence."

Lewin hoped that a more modern scientific psychology would become
a more powerful psychology, one that might approach contemporary physics in the latter's awesome discoveries. He therefore urged psychology to
heed the conclusions to which Cassirer came in his comparative studies
of science, that scientific power resided in the method of deduction from
logical theory and submission of deduced hypotheses to rigorous experimental test. With these powerful methods, psychology would not only be
able to explain every unique case but it would also be able to generate and
predict events that rarely, if ever, had occurred.

The Conflict Between Aristotelian and Galileian Modes of Thought in Contemporary Psychology (Selection 2)

In his article entitled "The Conflict Between Aristotelian and Galileian
Modes of Thought in Contemporary Psychology" (Selection 2), Lewin compares the scientific status of psychology in 1930 to that of contemporary
physics. The general terms for the comparison were adopted from Cassirer's observations on the conceptual advances made by Galileo over Aristotle. Lewin focuses on several related differences: (a) assuming the existence of universal laws covering all the phenomena in question versus
supposing that some phenomena were indeterminate; (b) explanation by
deduction rather than induction; (c) attributing causation to the totality
of the situation, including the environment of the focal object and not to
only the nature of the object itself; (d) recognizing that the nature of objects is multivarious, their characteristics differentially relevant to any
particular explanation, rather than classifying objects according to certain
significant common characteristics; and (e) testing explanations with experiments, which most nearly realize the idealized conditions for a phenomenon, rather than with observation under common conditions. Lewin
found psychology wanting. The most advanced psychology he found was
in the work on perception by his Gestalt colleagues, and he mentioned his
own efforts to extend this approach beyond perception to motivation, emotion, and child development.

Psychoanalysis and Topological Psychology (Section 3)

The Galilean model is the implicit touchstone of Lewin's comparison of
psychoanalytic to topological (field) theory (Selection 3). Lewin takes this
opportunity to dwell primarily on the difference between historical and

ahistorical—"concrete"—explanation. Perhaps he had in mind the modern physical principle of "no action at a distance."

Lewin acknowledges the superiority of psychoanalytic observation over experimentation for capturing the richness of the total situation. Not only do psychoanalysts explore the current state of the person exhaustively but they also delve extensively into the past. Lewin also points out the shortcomings of this method, compared to the experimental method, for testing laws.

The major shortcoming of historical explanation, according to Lewin, is the incommensurability of conditions in the past with their effective presence. Consistent with the proposition that past experience continues to matter, the psychological characteristics of a past event change with succeeding events. Therefore, a valid explanation of current thoughts, feelings, and actions must be in terms of the "concrete" (i.e., the contemporaneous precipitates of the past).

Lewin expressed some impatience with the reaction that he imagined he would get to this criticism from psychoanalytic theorists: that it goes without saying that psychoanalytic theory adheres to this "principle of concreteness." He believed that one's theoretical foundations, in the broadest sense, must be made explicit and kept in mind lest the science get sloppy. This point of view is apparent in all of Lewin's scientific writing.

1

Cassirer's Philosophy of Science and the Social Sciences

The following remarks[1] on the relation between Cassirer's views on the development of science and the recent history of psychology are the expression of a person who has always felt the deep gratitude of a student to his teacher.

During the period from 1910, when, as a graduate student, I listened to the lectures of the then *Privatdocent* Cassirer, to 1946, psychology has undergone a series of major changes related to basic issues of Behaviorism, Gestalt psychology, Psychoanalysis, Field Theory and the present problem of an integrated social science. The experiment has reached out from "psycho-physics" into any number of areas including motivation, personality, and social psychology. The mathematical problems of representing psychological fields and treating data statistically have proceeded step by step to new levels. Techniques of interviewing, observation, and other forms of fact-finding have grown into a rich and well-established methodology. The scientific infant of 1910, which had hardly cut his cord to mother philosophy and was looking with astonished eyes and an uneasy heart to the grown-up sciences, not knowing whether he should try to copy them or whether he ought to follow his own line—this scientific infant has perhaps not yet fully developed into maturity, but has certainly reached a stage of strength and progress which makes the psychologies of 1910 and 1946 rather different entities. Still, throughout this period, scarcely a year passed when I did not have specific reason to acknowledge the help which Cassirer's views on the nature of science and research offered.

The value of Cassirer's philosophy for psychology lies, I feel, less in his treatment of specific problems of psychology—although his contribution in this field and particularly his recent contributions are of great interest—than in his analysis of the methodology and concept-formation of the natural sciences.

To me these decades of rapid scientific growth of psychology and of the social sciences in general have provided test after test for the correct-

From P. A. Schilpp, Ed., 1949. *The philosophy of Ernst Cassirer*, pp. 269–288.
[1]Some sections of this paper are also published in Lewin, 1947.

ness of most of the ideas on science and scientific development expressed in his *Substanzbegriff und Funktionsbegriff*. Since the primitive discussions of the psychologists of 1910 about whether or not psychology ought to try to include not only qualitative but also quantitative data, and Cassirer's general discussions of the problem of quality and quantity—up to the present problems of research in personality, such as the treatment of biographical data, and Cassirer's discussion of the interdependence of "historical" and "systematic" problems—, I have felt with increasing strength the power and productivity of his basic approach to science.

It is not easy to point in Cassirer's work to a specific concept or any specific statement which provides a striking new insight and solves a previously insoluble problem. Still, as "participant observer" of the recent history of psychology, I may be permitted to state that Cassirer's approach seems to me a most illuminating and constructive help for making those decisions about methods and about the direction of the next step, upon which it depends whether a concrete piece of research will be a substantial contribution to a living science or a well polished container of nothing.

Theory of Science and Empirical Research

The relation between logic and theory of science on the one hand and the progress of empirical science on the other is not a simple one and is not easily transformed into a mutually productive state of affairs.

Since Kant philosophers have tried more or less successfully to avoid telling the empirical scientist what he "ought" to do or not to do. They have learned, with a few exceptions, to regard science as an object they should study rather than rule. This laudable and necessary removal of philosophy from the authoritarian place of the boss or the judge over science has led to a tendency of eliminating all "practical" relations between philosophy and the empirical sciences, including the perhaps possible and fruitful position of philosophy as a consultant to science. As the scientist tries to progress into the eternal frontier of the unknown, he faces highly complex and intricate problems of methods, concepts, and theory formation. It would seem natural that he should turn to the philosophical study of the nature of science for information and help on the methodological and conceptual aspects of the pressing problems he is trying to solve.

There are certain lines along which such help might be forthcoming and certain dangers involved in the all around cooperation of scientists and philosophers on the theory and practice of such an "applied theory of science." To start with the latter: as a rule, the philosopher can hardly be expected to have the detailed knowledge of an active research worker in a specific branch of an empirical science. As a rule, therefore, he should not be expected to make direct contributions to empirical theories. The tragi-comic happening of half a decade ago, when a certain group of philosophers tried to revive good old classical behaviorism just after it had fulfilled its usefulness for psychology and was happily dying, should be a warning against such inappropriate overstepping of boundaries. On the other hand, such danger should not minimize the essential advantages which a closer cooperation between the philosopher and the scientist should offer to both.

As far as I can see, there are two main lines along which valuable and more than accidental help for the empirical and particularly the social sciences may emerge from a closer relation to philosophy. One has to do with mathematical logic, the other with comparative theory of science.

The development of mathematical logic has proceeded considerably beyond what Cassirer had to offer. Mathematical logic seems to provide a fruitful possibility of assistance for specific problems of measurement for basic mathematical questions regarding qualitative data, for general mathematical problems of representing social and psychological fields, and so on. The insight provided by mathematical logic could probably have avoided some of the past headaches and should be of considerable potential assistance to the social scientist in the coming period of the quantitative measurement of social forces.

Mathematical logic has, however, not been of much avail and, in my judgment, is not likely to be of much avail for guiding the psychologist or social scientist through certain other major methodological perplexities.

The logician is accustomed to deal with problems of correct conclusions or other aspects of science and concepts which are "timeless," which hold as much for the physics of Copernicus as for modern physics. These problems are doubtless of great interest to the research-worker. They make up, however, only a small section of the problems of scientific strategy which are the concern of the daily struggle of progressing into the unknown. The main problems, which the scientist has to face and for which he has to find a solution, are inevitably bound to the particular state of development of his science, even if they are problems of method rather than content.

It is unrealistic and unproductive for an empirical scientist to approach problems of scientific method and procedure in a way which does not take cognizance of the basic fact that, to be effective, scientific methods have to be adjusted to the specific state of affairs at a given time. This holds for the techniques of fact-finding, for the process of conceptualization and theorizing, in short, for more or less all aspects of research. Research is the art of taking the next step. Methods and concepts, which may represent a revolutionary progress today, may be outmoded tomorrow. Can the philosopher gain insight into the development of science in a way useful for these vital time-bound aspects of scientific labor?

The logician may be inclined to place these problems outside the realm of a theory of science. He may be inclined to view them not as philosophical problems but as questions which should be dealt with by historians. Doubtless the researcher is deeply influenced by the culture in which he lives and by its technical and economic abilities. Not these problems of cultural history, however, are in question when the social psychologist has to make up his mind whether or not "experiments with groups" are scientifically meaningful, or what procedure he may follow for developing better concepts of personality, of leadership, or of other aspects of group life. Not historical, but conceptual and methodological problems are to be answered, questions about what is scientifically right or wrong, adequate or inadequate; although this correctness may be specific to a special developmental stage of a science and may not hold for a previous or a later stage. In other words, the term "scientific development" refers to levels of scientific maturity, to levels of concepts and theories in the sense of philosophy rather than of human history or psychology.

It is this approach to science as emerging systems of theorems and concepts to which Cassirer has contributed so much. Whenever Cassirer discusses science, he seems to perceive both the permanent characteristics of scientific systems and procedures and the specific conceptual form.

Philosophy of science can come to an insight into the nature of science only by studying science. It is, therefore, in permanent danger of making the science of the past a prototype for all science and of making past methodology the standard by which to measure what scientific methods "ought" to be used or not to be used. Cassirer has in most cases successfully avoided this danger by looking at the scientific methods of the past in the way in which the research-worker at that time would perceive them. He discloses the basic character of science as the eternal attempt to go beyond what is regarded scientifically accessible at any specific time. To proceed beyond the limitations of a given level of knowledge the researcher, as a rule, has to break down methodological taboos which condemn as "unscientific" or "illogical" the very methods or concepts which later on prove to be basic for the next major progress. Cassirer has shown how this step by step revolution of what is "scientifically permissible" dominates the development of mathematics, physics, and chemistry throughout their history.

A second reason why I feel Cassirer's approach is so valuable to the social scientist is his comparative procedure. Although Cassirer has not fully developed what might be called a systematic *comparative theory of the sciences*, he took important steps in this direction. His treatment of mathematics, physics, and chemistry, of historical and systematic disciplines is essentially of a comparative nature. Cassirer shows an unusual ability to blend the analysis of general characteristics of scientific methodology with the analysis of a specific branch of science. It is this ability to reveal the general rule in an example, without destroying the specific characteristics of a particular discipline at a given stage of development, which makes the comparative treatment of some branches of mathematics and of the natural sciences so illuminating for research in the social sciences. This comparative approach opens the way to a perception of similarities between different sciences and between apparently unrelated questions within the same science.

We shall discuss here only one type of problem as an example of the structural similarities between the conceptual problems of the present social sciences and problems of mathematics and the physical sciences at certain stages of development, namely that of "existence."

The Problem of "Existence" in an Empirical Science

Arguments about "existence" may seem metaphysical in nature and may therefore not be expected to be raised in empirical sciences. Actually, however, opinions about existence or non-existence are quite common in the empirical sciences and have greatly influenced scientific development in both a positive and a negative way. Labeling something as "non-existing" is equivalent to declaring it "out of bounds" for the scientist. Attributing "existence" to an item automatically makes it a duty of the scientist to consider this item as an object of research; it includes the necessity of considering its properties as "facts," which cannot be neglected in the total system of theories; finally, it implies that the terms by which one refers to the item are accepted as scientific "concepts" (rather than regarded as "mere words").

The problem of "existence" is, therefore, one of the most illuminating examples for the way in which facts, concepts, and methods are closely interdependent aspects of an empirical science. To demonstrate the way in which this interdependence is functioning in every phase of science is the central theme of this aspect of Cassirer's philosophy.

Cassirer follows the steps by which mathematics is gradually transformed. Geometry and the theory of numbers, for instance, changes from a study of separate forms or entities, which are to be described and analyzed one by one—with the objective of finding "permanent properties"—into a discipline which deals with problems of interrelations and transformations (Cassirer, 1923, p. 68).

> Geometry, as the theory of invariants, treats certain unchangeable relations; but this unchangeableness cannot be defined unless we understand, as its conceptual background, certain fundamental changes relative to which they hold. The unchanging geometrical properties are not such in and for themselves, but only in relation to a system of possible transformations that we implicitly assume. Constancy and change thus appear as thoroughly correlative moments, definable only through each other (Cassirer, 1923, p. 90; wording changed by K. Lewin, in line with the German original).

In physics an equivalent change occurs on the basis of an increasingly close interdependence of fact finding and theory.

> It has been shown, in opposition to the traditional logical doctrine, that the course of the mathematical construction of concepts is defined by the procedures of the *construction of series*. We have not been concerned with separating out the common element from a plurality of similar impressions but with establishing a principle by which their diversity should appear. The unity of the concept has not been found in a fixed group of properties, but in the rule, which represents the mere diversity as a sequence of elements according to law (Cassirer, 1923, p. 148).

In truth, no physicist experiments and measures with the particular instrument that he has sensibly before his eyes; but he substitutes for it an ideal instrument in thought, from which all accidental defects, such as necessarily belong to the particular instrument, are excluded. For example, if we measure the intensity of an electric current by a tangent-compass, then the observations, which we make first with a concrete apparatus, must be related and carried over to a general geometrical model before they are physically applicable. We substitute for a copper wire of a definite strength a strictly geometrical circle without breadth; in place of the steel of the magnetic needle, which has a certain magnitude and form, we substitute an infinitely small, horizontal magnetic axis, which can be moved without friction around a vertical axis; and it is the totality of these transformations, which permits us to carry the observed deflection of the magnetic needle into the general theoretical formula of the strength of the current, and thus to determine the value of the latter. The corrections, which we make and must necessarily make with the use of every physical instrument, are themselves a work of mathematical theory; to exclude these latter, is to deprive the observation itself of its meaning and value (Cassirer, 1923, p. 144).

Until relatively recently psychology, sociology, and anthropology were dominated by a methodology which regarded science as a process of "collecting facts." This methodology showed all the earmarks of early Greek mathematics and pre-Galilean physics. During the last ten years the hostility to theorizing has greatly diminished. It has been replaced by a relatively wide-spread recognition of the necessity for developing better concepts and higher levels of theory.

This change has its corollary in certain changes regarding what is considered "existing." Beliefs regarding "existence" in social science have changed in regard to the degree to which "full reality" is attributed to psychological and social phenomena, and in regard to the reality of their "deeper," dynamic properties.

At the beginning of this century, for instance, the experimental psychology of "will and emotion" had to fight for recognition against a prevalent attitude which placed volition, emotion, and sentiments in the "poetic realm" of beautiful words, a realm to which nothing corresponds which could be regarded as "existing" in the sense in which the scientist uses the term. Although every psychologist had to deal with these facts realistically in his private life, they were banned from the realm of "facts" in the scientific sense. Emotions were declared to be something too "fluid" and "intangible" to be pinned down by scientific analysis or by experimental procedures. Such a methodological argument does not deny existence to the phenomenon, but it has the effect of keeping the topic outside the realm of empirical science.

Like social taboos, a scientific taboo is kept up not so much by a rational argument as by a common attitude among scientists: Any member of the scientific guild who does not strictly adhere to the taboo is looked upon as queer; he is suspected of not adhering to the scientific standards of critical thinking.

The Reality of Social Phenomena

Before the invention of the atom bomb the average physical scientist was hardly ready to concede to social phenomena the same degree of "reality" as to a physical object. Hiroshima and Nagasaki seem to have caused many physical scientists to change their minds. This change was hardly based on philosophical considerations. The bomb has driven home with dramatic intensity the degree to which social happenings are both the result of and the conditions for the occurrence of physical events. The period during which the natural scientist thought of the social scientist as someone interested in dreams and words (rather than as an investigator of facts which are not less real than physical facts and which can be studied no less objectively) has gradually been coming to an end.

The social scientists themselves, of course, have had a stronger belief in the "reality" of the entities they were studying. Still this belief was frequently limited to the specific narrow section with which they happened to be familiar. The economist, for instance, finds it a bit difficult to concede to psychological, to anthropological, or to legal data that degree of reality which he gives to prices and other economic data. Some psychologists still view with suspicion the reality of those cultural facts with which the anthropologist is concerned. They tend to regard only individuals as real and they are not inclined to consider a "group atmosphere" as something which is as real and measurable as, let us say, a physical field of gravity. Concepts like that of "leadership" retained a halo of mysticism even after it had been demonstrated that it is quite possible to measure and not only to "judge" leadership performance.

The denial of existence of a group or of certain aspects of group life is based on arguments which grant existence only to units of certain size, or which concern methodologic–technical problems, or conceptual problems.

Reality and Size

Cassirer (1923) discusses how, periodically throughout the history of physics, vivid discussions have occurred about the reality of the atom, the electron, or whatever else was considered at that time to be the smallest particle of physical material. In the social sciences it has usually been not the part but the whole whose existence has been doubted.

Logically, there is no reason for distinguishing between the reality of a molecule, an atom, or an ion, or more generally between the reality of a whole or its parts. There is no more magic behind the fact that groups have properties of their own, which are different from the properties of their subgroups or their individual members, than behind the fact that molecules have properties, which are different from the properties of the atoms or ions of which they are composed.

In the social as in the physical field the structural properties of a dynamic whole are different from the structural properties of their subparts. Both sets of properties have to be investigated. When one and when the other is most important, depends upon the question to be answered. But there is no difference of reality between them.

If this basic statement is accepted, the problem of existence of a group loses its metaphysical flavor. Instead we face a series of empirical problems. They are equivalent to the chemical question of whether a given aggregate is a mixture of different types of atoms, or whether these atoms have formed molecules of a certain type. The answer to such a question has to be given in chemistry, as in the social sciences, on the basis of an empirical probing into certain testable properties of the case in hand.

For instance, it may be wrong to state that the blond women living in a town "exist as a group" in the sense of being a dynamic whole that is characterized by a close interdependence of their members. They are merely a number of individuals who are "classified under one concept" according to the similarity of one of their properties. If, however, the blond members of a workshop are made an "artificial minority" and are discriminated against by their colleagues, they may well become a group with specific structural properties.

Structural properties are characterized by *relations* between parts rather than by the parts or elements themselves. Cassirer emphasizes that, throughout the history of mathematics and physics, from Anaxagoras and Aristotle to Bacon, Boscovich, Boltzman and the present day, problems of constancy of relations rather than of constancy of elements have gained importance and have gradually changed the picture of what is considered essential.

> The meaning of the mathematical concept cannot be comprehended, as long as we seek any sort of presentational correlate for it in the given; the meaning only appears when we recognize the concept as the expression of a *pure relation*, upon which rests the unity and continuous connection of the members of a manifold. The function of the physical concept also is first evident in this interpretation. The more it disclaims every independent perceptible content and everything pictorial, the more clearly its logical and systematic function is shown. . . . All that the "thing" of the popular view of the world loses in properties, it gains in relations; for it no longer remains isolated and dependent on itself alone, but is connected inseparably by logical threads with the totality of experience. Each particular concept is, as it were, one of these threads, on which we string real experiences and connect them with future possible experiences. The objects of physics: matter and force, atom and ether, can no longer be misunderstood as so many new realities for investigation, and realities whose inner essence is to be penetrated—when once they are recognized as instruments produced by thought for the purpose of comprehending the confusion of phenomena as an ordered and measurable whole (Cassirer, 1923, p. 166).

Reality, Methods, and Experience

If recognition of the existence of an entity depends upon this entity's showing properties or constancies of its own, the judgment about what is real or unreal should be affected by changes in the possibility of demonstrating social properties.

The social sciences have considerably improved their techniques for reliably recording the structure of small or large groups and of registering the various aspects of group life. Sociometric techniques, group observation, interview techniques, and others are enabling the social scientist more and more to gather reliable data on the structural properties of groups, on the relations between groups or subgroups, and on the relation between a group and the life of its individual members.

The taboo against believing in the existence of a social entity is probably most effectively broken by handling this entity experimentally. As long as the scientist merely describes a leadership form, he is open to the criticism that the categories used reflect merely his "subjective views" and do not correspond to the "real" properties of the phenomena under consideration. If the scientist experiments with leadership and varies its form, he relies on an "operational definition" which links the concept of a leadership form to concrete procedures of creating such a leadership form or to the procedures for testing its existence. The "reality" of that to which the concept refers is established by "doing with" rather than "looking at," and this reality is independent of certain "subjective" elements of classification. The progress of physics from Archimedes to Einstein shows consecutive steps, by which the "practical" aspect of the experimental procedure has modified and sometimes revolutionized the scientific concepts regarding the physical world by changing the beliefs of the scientists about what is and what is not real.

To vary a social phenomenon experimentally the experimenter has to take hold of all essential factors, even if he is not yet able to analyze them satisfactorily. A major omission or misjudgment on this point makes the experiment fail. In social research the experimenter has to take into consideration such factors as the personality of individual members, the group structure, ideology and cultural values, and economic factors. Group experimentation is a form of social management. To be successful it, like social management, has to take into account all of the various factors that happen to be important for the case in hand. Experimentation with groups will therefore lead to a natural integration of the social sciences, and it will force the social scientist to recognize as reality the totality of factors which determine group life.

Social Reality and Concepts

It seems that the social scientist has a better chance of accomplishing such a realistic integration than the social practitioner. For thousands of years kings, priests, politicians, educators, producers, fathers and mothers—in fact, all individuals—have been trying day by day to influence smaller or larger groups. One might assume that this would have led to accumulated wisdom of a well integrated nature. Unfortunately nothing is further from the truth. We know that our average diplomat thinks in very one-sided terms, perhaps those of law, or economics, or military strategy. We know that the average manufacturer holds highly distorted views about what makes a work-team tick. We know that no one can answer today even such relatively simple questions as what determines the productivity of a committee meeting.

Several factors have come together to prevent practical experience from leading to clear insight. Certainly, the man of affairs is convinced of the reality of group life, but he is usually opposed to a conceptual analysis. He prefers to think in terms of "intuition" and "intangibles." The able practitioner frequently insists that it is impossible to formulate simple, clear rules about how to reach a social objective. He insists that different actions have to be taken according to the various situations, that plans have to be highly flexible and sensitive to the changing scene.

If one tries to transform these sentiments into scientific language, they amount to the following statements. a) Social events depend on the social field as a whole, rather than on a few selected items. This is the basic insight behind the field theoretical method which has been successful in physics, which has steadily grown in psychology and, in my opinion, is bound to be equally fundamental for the study of social fields, simply because it expresses certain basic general characteristics of interdependence. b) The denial of "simple rules" is partly identical with the following important principle of scientific analysis. Science tries to link certain observable (phenotypical) data with other observable data. It is crucial for all problems of interdependence, however, that—for reasons which we do not need to discuss here—it is, as a rule, impracticable to link one set of phenotypical data *directly* to other phenotypical data. Instead, it is necessary to insert "intervening variables" (Tolman, 1938). To use a more common language: The practitioner as well as the scientist views the observable data as mere "symptoms." They are "surface" indications of some "deeper-lying" facts. He has learned to "read" the symptoms, like a physicist reads his instruments. The equations which express physical laws refer to such deeper-lying dynamic entities as pressure, energy, or temperature rather than to the directly observable symptoms such as the movements of the pointer of an instrument.

The underlying methodological principle is but one expression of the nature of the relation between concepts, scientific facts and scientific fact finding. In the words of Cassirer,

> Strictly speaking, the experiment never concerns the real case, as it lies before us here and now in all the wealth of its particular determinations, but the experiment rather concerns an ideal case, which we substitute for it. The real beginnings of scientific induction furnish the classical example of this. Galileo did not discover the law of falling bodies by collecting arbitrary observations of sensuously real bodies, but by defining hypothetically the concept of uniform acceleration and taking it as a conceptual measure of the facts. This concept provides for the given time-values a series of space-values, such as proceed according to a fixed rule, that can be grasped once for all. Henceforth we must attempt to advance to the actual process of reality by a progres-

sive consideration of the complex determinations, that were originally excluded: as, for example, the variation of acceleration according to the distance from the center of the earth, retardation by the resistance of the air, etc. (Cassirer, 1923, p. 354).

If we consider the factors involved in the measurement of motion, ... it is evident that the physical definition of motion cannot be established without substituting the geometrical body for the sensuous body, without substituting the "intelligible" continuous extension of the mathematician for sensuous extension. Before we can speak of motion and its exact measurement in the strict sense, we must go from the contents of perception to their conceptual limits. ... It is no less a pure conceptual construction, when we ascribe a determinate velocity to a non-uniformly moving body at each point of its path; such a construction presupposes for its explanation nothing less than the whole logical theory of infinitesimal analysis. But even where we seem to stand closer to direct sensation, where we seem guided by no other interest than to arrange its differences as presented us, into a fixed scale, even her theoretical elements are requisite and clearly appear. It is a long way from the immediate sensation of heat to the exact concept of temperature (Cassirer, 1923, p. 142).

The dynamics of social events provides no exception to this general characteristic of dynamics. If it were possible to link a directly observable group behavior, B, with another behavior, B^1, —B = F (B^1) where F means a simple function—then simple rules of procedure for the social practitioner would be possible. When the practitioner denies that such rules can be more than poor approximations he seems to imply that the function, F, is complicated. I am inclined to interpret his statement actually to mean that in group life, too, "appearance" should be distinguished from the "underlying facts," that similarity of appearance may go together with dissimilarity of the essential properties and *vice versa*, and that laws can be formulated only in regard to these underlying dynamic entities—k = F (n,m) where k,n,m refer not to behavioral symptoms but to intervening variables (Lewin, 1935).

For the social scientist this means that he should give up thinking about such items as group structure, group tension, or social forces as nothing more than a popular metaphor or analogy, which should be eliminated from science as much as possible. Although there is no need for social science to copy the specific concepts of the physical sciences, the social scientist should be clear that he, too, needs intervening variables and that these dynamic facts rather than the symptoms and appearances are the important points of reference for him and the social practitioner alike.

Mathematization and Integration of the Social Sciences

The relation between theory formation, fact finding and mathematization, which Cassirer has described in regard to the physical sciences, has come much to the fore in the psychology of the last decade. Different psychological trends have led from different sides and with partly different objectives to a strong emphasis on mathematization. This need springs partly from a desire of a more exact scientific representation of the results of tests or other fact findings and has led to an elaborate development of statistical procedures. In part the emphasis on mathematization springs from the desire of a deeper theoretical insight (Hull, 1943; Köhler, 1938; Lewin, 1938, 1944). Both geometrical and algebraic concepts are employed to this end.

Mathematical economics since Pareto (1909) is another example of the development of a social science which shows many of the characteristics by Cassirer.

One of the most striking illustrations of the function of theorems, concepts, and methods in the development of science is their role in the integration of the social sciences which is just beginning to take place. It may be appropriate to mention this problem and to refer briefly to considerations I have presented elsewhere (Lewin, 1947).

Many aspects of social life can be viewed as quasi-stationary processes. They can be regarded as states of quasi-stationary equilibrium in the precise meaning of a constellation of forces the structure of which can be well defined. The scientific treatment of social forces presupposes analytic devices which are adequate to the nature of social processes and which are technically fitted to serve as a bridge to a mathematical treatment. The basic means to this end is the representation of social situations as "social fields."

This technical analysis makes it possible to formulate in a more exact way problems of planned social changes and of resistance to change. It permits general statements concerning some aspects of the problem of selecting specific objectives in bringing about change, concerning different methods of bringing about the same amount of change, and concerning differences in the secondary effects of these methods. The analytic tools used are equally applicable to cultural, economic, sociological, and psychological aspects of group life. They fit a great variety of processes, such as production levels of a factory, a workteam and an individual worker; changes of abilities of an individual and of capacities of a country; group standards with and without cultural value; activities of one group and the interaction between groups, between individuals, and between individuals and groups. The analysis concedes equal reality to all aspects of group life and to social units of all sizes. The application depends upon the structural properties of the process and of the total situation in which it takes place.

How is it possible, one may ask, to bring together under one heading and procedure such diversified data? Does that not necessarily mean losing in concreteness what one might gain in scientific generality?

In the same way as the natural sciences, the social sciences have to face the problem of how to get hold conceptually of the disturbing qualitative richness of psychological and cultural events, how to find "general" laws without giving up reaching the individual case. Cassirer describes how the mathematical constructive procedure solves this problem by changing, as it were, the very meaning of equality and scientific abstraction. Speaking of equalities of mathematical sets he says, "This similarity, however, means nothing more than that they are connected by a definite rule, such as permits us to proceed from one manifold to another by continued identical application of the same fundamental relation"; (Cassirer, 1923, p. 31). "The genuine concept does not disregard the peculiarities and particularities which it holds under it, but seeks to show the *necessity* of the occurrence and connection of just these particularities" (p. 19).

> The individual case is not excluded from consideration, but is fixed and retained as a perfectly determinate step in a general process of change. It is evident anew that the characteristic feature of the concept is not the "universality" of a presentation, but the universal validity of a principle of serial order. We do not isolate any abstract part whatever from the manifold before us, but we create for its members a definite relation by thinking of them as bound together by an inclusive law. And the further we proceed in this and the more firmly this connection according to laws is established, so much the clearer does the unambiguous determination of the particular stand forth (p. 20).

The consideration of quasi-stationary equilibria is based on analytic concepts which, within the realm of the social sciences, have emerged first in psychology. The concepts of a psychological force, of tension, of conflicts as equilibria of forces, of force fields and of inducing fields, have slowly widened their range of application from the realm of individual psychology into the realm of processes and events which had been the domain of sociology and cultural anthropology. It seems that the treatment of economic equilibria by mathematical economics, although having a different origin, is fully compatible with this development.

The fusion of the social sciences will make accessible to economics the vast advantages which the experimental procedure offers for testing theories and for developing new insight. The combination of experimental and mathematical procedures which Cassirer describes has been the main vehicle for the integration of the study of light, of electricity, and of the other branches of physical science. The same combination seems to be destined to make the integration of the social sciences a reality.

References

Cassirer, E. (1923). *Substance and function, and Einstein's theory of relativity*. London: The Open Court Publishing Company.

Hull, C. L. (1943). *Principles of behavior*. New York: Appleton Century.

Köhler, W. (1938). *The place of value in a world of facts*. New York: Liveright.

Lewin, K. (1935). *A dynamic theory of personality*. (D. Adams & K. Zener, Trs.). New York: McGraw-Hill.

Lewin, K. (1938). The conceptual representation and the measurement of psychological forces. *Contributions to psychological theory* (Vol. 1, No. 4). Duke University Press.

Lewin, K. (1944). Constructs in psychology and psychological ecology. *Studies in Topological and Vector Psychology* (Vol. 3). University of Iowa.

Lewin, K. (1947). Problems of group dynamics and the integration of the social sciences: I. Social equilibria. *Human Relations, 1,* 2–38.

Pareto, V. (1909). *Manuel d'Economie politique* (A. Bonnet, Tr.). Paris: Brière.*

Tolman, E. C. (1938). The determiners of behavior at a choice point. *Psychological Review, 45,* 1–41.

Editor's Note. Actually Lewin provided no reference beyond the date, but this is almost certainly the work he had in mind.

2 _____

The Conflict Between Aristotelian and Galileian Modes of Thought in Contemporary Psychology

In the discussion of several urgent problems of current experimental and theoretical psychology I propose to review the development of the concepts of physics, and particularly the transition from the Aristotelian to the Galilean mode of thought. My purpose is not historical, rather do I believe that certain questions, of considerable importance in the reconstruction of concepts in present-day psychology, may be clarified and more precisely stated through such a comparison, which provides a view beyond the difficulties of the day.

I do not intend to infer by deduction from the history of physics what psychology "ought" to do. I am not of the opinion that there is only one empirical science, namely, physics; and the question whether psychology, as part of biology, is reducible to physics or is an independent science may here be left open.

Since we are starting from the point of view of the researcher, we shall, in our contrast of Aristotelian and Galileian concept formation, be less concerned with personal nuances of theory in Galileo and Aristotle than with certain rather ponderable differences in the modes of thought which determined the actual research of the medieval Aristotelians and of the post-Galilean physicists. Whether some particular investigator had previously shown the later sort of thinking in respect of some special point, or if some very modern speculations of the relativity theory should accord in some way with Aristotle's, is without relevance in the present connection.

In order to provide a setting especially for the theoretical treatment of the dynamic problems, I shall consider first the _general_ characteristics of Aristotelian and Galileian physics and of modern psychology.

From the _Journal of General Psychology_, 1931, _5_, 141–177. Translated by D. K. Adams.

I. General Character of the Two Modes of Thought

A. In Physics

If one asks what is the most characteristic difference between "modern" post-Galileian physics and Aristotelian, one receives, as a rule, the following reply, which has had an important influence upon the scientific ideals of the psychologist: The concepts of Aristotelian physics were *anthropomorphic* and *inexact*. Modern physics, on the contrary, is quantitatively exact, and pure mathematical; functional relations now occupy the place of the former anthropomorphic explanations. These have given to physics that abstract appearance in which modern physicists are accustomed to take special pride.

This view of the development of physics is, to be sure, pertinent. But if one fixes one's attention less upon the "style" of the concepts employed, and more upon their actual functions as instruments for understanding the world, these differences appear to be more of a secondary nature, consequences of a deeper lying difference in the conception of the relationship between the world and the task of research.

1. Aristotelian Concepts

a. Their valuative character. As in all science, the detachment of physics from the universal matrix of philosophy and practice was only gradually achieved. Aristotelian physics is full of concepts which today we consider not only as specifically biological, but preeminently *as valuative* concepts. It abounds in specifically normative concepts taken from ethics, which occupy a place between valuative and non-valuative concepts: The "highest" forms of motions are circular and rectilinear, and they occur only in "heavenly" movements, those of the stars. The "earthly" sublunar world is endowed with motion of inferior types. There are similar valuative differences between causes: On one side there are the good or, so to speak, authorized forces of a body which come from its tendency toward perfection (Τέλος), and on the other side the "disturbance" due to chance and to the opposing forces (βία) of other bodies.

This kind of classification in terms of values plays an extraordinarily important part in mediaeval physics. It classes many things with very slight or unimportant relationships together and separates things that objectively are closely and importantly related.

It seems obvious to me that this extremely "anthropomorphic" mode of thought plays a large role in psychology, even to the present day. Like the distinction between earthly and heavenly, the no less valuative distinction between "normal" and pathological" has for a long time sharply differentiated two fields of psychological fact, and thus separated phenomena which are fundamentally most nearly related.

No less important is the fact that value concepts completely dominate the conceptual setting of the special problems, or have until very recently done so. Thus, not till lately has psychology begun to investigate the structural (Gestalt) relations concerned in perception, thus replacing the concept of optical *illusion*, a concept derived not from psychological but from epistemological categories, which unwarrantedly lumps all these "illusions" together and sets them apart from the other phenomena of psychological optics. Psychology speaks of the "errors" of children, of "practice," of "forgetting," thus classifying whole groups of processes according to the value of their products, instead of according to the nature of the psychological processes involved. Psychology is, to be sure, beyond classifying events *only* on the basis of value when it speaks of "disturbances," of inferiority and superiority in development, or of the quality of performance on a test. On all sides there are tendencies to attack actual psychological processes. But there can hardly be any doubt that we stand now only at the beginning of this stage, that the same transitional concepts that we have seen in the Aristotelian physics to lie between the valuative and the non-valuative are characteristic of such antitheses as those of intelligence and feeblemindedness, or of drive and will. The detachment of the conceptual structure of psychology from the utilitarian concepts of pedagogy, medicine, and ethics is only partly achieved.

It is quite possible, indeed I hold it to be probable, that the utility or performance concepts such as, for example, a "true" cognition versus an "error," may later acquire a legitimate sense. If that is the case, however, an "illusion" will have to be characterized not epistemologically but biologically.

b. Abstract classification. When the Galileian and post-Galileian physics disposed of the distinction between heavenly and earthly, and thereby extended the field of natural law enormously, it was not due solely to the exclusion of value concepts, but also to a changed interpretation of *classification.* For Aristotelian physics the membership of an object in a given class was of critical importance, because for Aristotle the class defined the essence or essential nature of the object, and thus determined its behavior in both positive and negative respects.

This classification often took the form of paired opposites, such as cold and warm, dry and moist, and compared with present-day classification had a rigid, "absolute" character. In modern quantitative physics dichotomous classifications have been entirely replaced by *continuous gradations.* Substantial concepts have been replaced by functional concepts (Cassirer, 1910).

Here also it is not difficult to point out the analogous stage of development in contemporary psychology. The separation of intelligence, memory, and impulse bears throughout the characteristic stamp of Aristotelian classification; and in some fields, for example, in the analysis of feelings (pleasantness and unpleasantness), or of temperaments (Sommer, 1925), or of drives (Lewin, 1929, p. 28), such dichotomous classifications as Aristotle's are even today of great significance. Only gradually do these classifications lose their importance and yield to a conception which seeks to derive the same laws for all these fields, and to classify the *whole* field on the basis of other, essentially *functional*, differences.

c. *The concept of law*. Aristotle's classes are *abstractly* defined as the sum total of those characteristics which a group of objects have in common. This circumstance is not merely a characteristic of Aristotle's logic, but largely determines his conception of *lawfulness* and *chance*, which seems to me so important to the problems of contemporary psychology as to require closer examination.

For Aristotle those things are lawful, conceptually intelligible, which occur *without exception*. Also, and this he emphasizes particularly, those are lawful which occur *frequently*. Excluded from the class of the conceptually intelligible as "mere chance" are those things which occur only *once*, individual events as such. Actually since the behavior of a thing is determined by its essential nature, and this essential nature is exactly the abstractly defined class (that is, the sum total of the common characteristics of a whole group of objects), it follows that each event, as a particular event, is chance, undetermined. For in these Aristotelian classes individual differences disappear.

The real source of this conception may lie in the fact that for Aristotelian physics *not all* physical processes possess the lawful character ascribed to them by post-Galileian physics. To the young science of physics the universe it investigated appeared to contain as much that was chaotic as that which was lawful. The lawfulness, the intelligibility of physical processes was still narrowly limited. It was really present only in *some* processes, as, for example, the courses of the stars, but by no means in all the fleeting and transitory events of the earth. Just as for other young sciences, it was still a *question* for physics, whether and how far physical processes were subject to law. And this circumstance exercised its full effect on the formation of physical concepts, even though in philosophical "principle" the idea of general lawfulness already existed. In post-Galileian physics, with the elimination of the distinction between lawful and chance events, the necessity also disappeared of proving that the process under consideration was lawful. For Aristotelian physics, on the contrary, it was necessary to have criteria to decide *whether* or not a given event was of the lawful variety. Indeed the regularity with which similar events occurred in nature was used essentially as such a criterion. Only such events, as the celestial, which the course of history proves to be regular, or at least frequent, are subject to law; and only insofar as they are frequent, and hence "more" than individual events, are they conceptually intelligible. In other words, the ambition of science to understand the complex, chaotic, and unintelligible world, its faith in the ultimate decipherability of this world, was limited to such events as were *certified* by repetition in the course of history to possess a certain persistence and stability.

In this connection it must not be forgotten that Aristotle's emphasis on frequency (as a further basis for lawfulness, besides absolute regularity) represents, relative to his predecessors, a tendency toward the extension and concrete application of the principle of lawfulness. The "empiricist" Aristotle insists that not only the regular but the frequent is lawful. Of course, this only makes clearer his antithesis of individuality and law, for the individual event as such still lies outside the pale of the lawful and hence, in a certain sense, outside the task of science. Lawfulness remains limited to cases in which similar events recur, and classes (in Aristotle's abstract sense) reveal the essential nature of the events.

This attitude toward the problem of lawfulness in nature, which dominated mediaeval physics and from which even the opponents of Aristotelian physics, such as Bruno and Bacon, escaped only gradually, by small steps, had important consequences in several respects.

As will be clear from the preceding text, this concept of lawfulness had throughout a quasi-statistical character. Lawfulness was considered as equivalent to the highest degree of generality, as that which occurs very often in the same way, as the extreme case of regularity, and hence as the perfect antithesis of the infrequent or of the particular event. The statistical determination of the concept of lawfulness is still clearly marked in Bacon, as when he tries to decide through his *"tabula praesentia"* whether a given association of properties is real (essential) or fortuitous. Thus he ascertains, for example, the numerical frequency of the cases in which the properties "warm" and "dry" are associated in everyday life. Less mathematically exact, indeed, but no less clear is this statistical way of thinking in the whole body of Aristotelian physics.

At the same time—and this is one of the most important consequences of the Aristotelian conception—regularity or particularity was understood entirely in *historical* terms.

The complete freedom from exceptions, the "always" which is found also in the later conceptions of physical lawfulness, still has here its original connections with the frequency with which similar cases have occurred in the *actual, historical* course of events in the everyday world. A crude example will make this clearer: Light objects, under the conditions of everyday life, relatively frequently go up; heavy objects usually go down. The flame of the fire, at any rate under the conditions known to Aristotle, almost always goes upward. It is these frequency rules, within the limits of the climate, mode of life, etc., familiar to Aristotle, that determine the nature and tendency to be ascribed to each class of objects, and lead in the present instance to the conclusion that flames and light bodies have a tendency upward.

Aristotelian concept formation has yet another immediate relation to the geographically–historically given, in which it resembles, as do the valuative concepts mentioned above, the thinking of primitive man and of children.

When primitive man uses different words for "walking," depending upon its direction, north or south, or upon the sex of the walker, or upon whether the latter is going into or out of a house (Lévy-Bruhl, 1922), he is employing a reference to the historical situation that is quite similar to the putatively "absolute" descriptions ("upward" or "downward") of Aristotle, the real significance of which is a sort of *geographic* characterization, a place definition relative to the earth's surface.[1]

The original connection of the concepts with the "actuality," in the special sense of the given historic–geographic circumstances, is perhaps the most important feature of Aristotelian physics. It is from this almost more even than from its teleology that his physics gets its general anthropomorphic character. Even in the minute particulars of theorizing and in the actual conduct of research it is always evident, not only that physical and normative concepts are still undifferentiated, but that the formulation of problems and the concepts that we would today distinguish, on the one hand, as "historic"[2] and, on the other, as non-historic or "systematic" are inextricably interwoven. (Incidentally, an analogous confusion exists in the early stages of other sciences, for example in economics.)

From these conceptions also the attitude of Aristotelian physics toward lawfulness takes a new direction. So long as lawfulness remained limited to such processes as occurred repeatedly in the same way, it is evident, not only that the young physics still lacked the courage to extend the principle to all physical phenomena, but also that the concept of lawfulness still had a fundamentally historic, a temporally particular, significance. Stress was laid not upon the "general validity" which modern physics understands by lawfulness, but upon the events in the historically given world which displayed the required stability. The highest degree of lawfulness, beyond mere frequency ($\dot{\epsilon}\pi\grave{\iota}$ Yò $\pi o\lambda\grave{\upsilon}$), was characterized by the idea of always eternal ($\dot{\alpha}\epsilon\grave{\iota}$). That is, the stretch of historic time for which constancy was assumed was extended to eternity. General validity of *law* was not yet clearly distinguished from eternity of *process*. Only permanence, or at least frequent repetition, was proof of more than momentary validity. Even here in the idea of eternity, which seems to transcend the historical, the connection with immediate historic actuality is still obvious, and this close connection was characteristic of the "empiricist" Aristotle's method and concepts.

Not only in physics but in other sciences, for example, in economics and biology, it can be clearly seen how in certain early stages the tendency to empiricism, to the collection and ordering of "facts," carries with it at

---

[1]In the following pages we shall frequently have to use the term "historic–geographic." This is not in common usage, but it seems to me inaccurate to contrast historic and systematic questions. The real opposition is between "type" (of object, process, situation) and "occurrence." And for concepts that deal with "occurrences," the reference to "absolute" geographic space-coordinates is just as characteristic as that to "absolute" time-coordinates by means of dates.

At the same time, the concept of the "geographic" should be understood in such a general sense as to refer to juxtaposition, correlative to historical *succession*, that the concept is applicable, for example, to psychical events.

[2]There is no term at present in general use to designate non-historical problem formulations. I here employ the term "systematic," meaning thereby, not "ordered," but collectively non-historic problems and laws such as those which form the bulk of present-day physics. (See above.)

the same time a tendency to historical concept formation, to excessive valuation of the historical.

2. Galileian Physics

From the point of view of this sort of empiricism the concept formation of Galileian and post-Galileian physics must seem curious and even paradoxical.

As remarked above, the use of mathematical tools and the tendency to exactness, important as they are, cannot be considered the real substance of the difference between Aristotelian and Galileian physics. It is indeed quite possible to recast in mathematical form the essential content of, for example, the dynamic ideas of Aristotelian physics. (See below.) It is conceivable that the development of physics could have taken the form of a mathematical rendition of Aristotelian concepts such as is actually taking place in psychology today. In reality, however, there were only traces of such a tendency, such as Bacon's quasi-statistical methods mentioned above. The main development took another direction and proved to be a change of content rather than a mere change of form.

The same considerations apply to the "exactness" of the new physics. It must not be forgotten that in Galileo's time there were no clocks of the sort we have today, that these first became possible through the knowledge of dynamics founded upon Galileo's work (Mach, 1921). Even the methods of measurement used by Faraday in the early investigations of electricity show how little exactness, in the current sense of *precision* to such and such a decimal place, had to do with these critical stages in the development of physics.

The real sources of the tendency to quantification lie somewhat deeper, namely in a new conception by the physicist of the nature of the physical world, in an extension of the demands of physics upon itself in the task of understanding the world, and in an increased faith in the possibility of their fulfillment. These are radical and far-reaching changes in the fundamental ideas of physics, and the tendency to quantification is simply one of their expressions.

a. Homogenization. The outlook of a Bruno, a Kepler, or a Galileo is determined by the idea of a comprehensive, all-embracing unity of the physical world. The same law governs the courses of the stars, the falling of stones, and the flight of birds. This "homogenization" of the physical world with respect to the validity of law deprives the division of physical objects into rigid abstractly defined classes of the critical significance it had for Aristotelian physics, in which membership in a certain conceptual class was considered to determine the physical nature of an object.

Closely related to this is the loss in importance of logical dichotomies and conceptual antitheses. Their places are taken by more and more fluid transitions, by gradations which deprived the dichotomies of their antithetical character and represent in logical form a transition stage between the class concept and the serial concept (Cassirer, 1910).

b. Genetic concepts. This dissolution of the sharp antitheses of rigid classes was greatly accelerated by the coeval transition to an essentially functional way of thinking, to the use of *conditional-genetic* concepts. For Aristotle the immediate perceptible appearance, that which present-day biology terms the *phenotype*, was hardly distinguished from the properties that determine the object's dynamic relations. The fact, for example, that light objects relatively frequently go upward sufficed for him to ascribe to them an upward tendency. With the differentiation of phenotype from *genotype* or, more generally, of "descriptive" from "conditional-genetic" (Lewin, 1927) concepts, and the shifting of emphasis to the latter, many old class distinctions lost their significance. The orbits of the planets, the free falling of a stone, the movement of a body on an inclined plane, the oscillation of a pendulum, which if classified according to their phenotypes would fall into quite different, indeed into antithetical classes, prove to be simply various expressions of the same law.

c. Concreteness. The increased emphasis upon the quantitative which seems to lend to modern physics a formal and abstract character is not derived from any tendency to logical formality. At the same time as the development of the problem of classification, or rather, much earlier, the tendency to a full description of the concrete actuality, even that of the particular case, was influential, a circumstance which should be especially emphasized in connection with present-day psychology. The particular object in all departments of science is determined not only in kind and thereby qualitatively, but it possesses each of its properties in a special intensity or to a definite degree. So long as one rewards as important and conceptually intelligible only such properties of an object as are common to a whole group of objects, the individual differences of degree remain without scientific relevance, for in the abstractly defined classes these differences more or less disappear. With the mounting aspirations of research toward an understanding of actual events and particular cases, the task of describing the differences of degree that characterized individual cases had necessarily to increase in importance, and finally required actual quantitative determination.

It is the increased desire, and also the increased ability, to comprehend *concrete particular cases*, and to comprehend them fully, which, together with the idea of the *homogeneity* of the physical world and that of the continuity of the properties of its objects, constituted the main impulse to the increasing quantification of physics.

d. Paradoxes of the new empiricism. This tendency toward the closest possible contact with actuality, which today is usually regarded as characteristic and ascribed to an "anti-speculative" tendency, led to a mode of concept formation diametrically opposed to that of Aristotle, and, surprisingly enough, involved also the direct antithesis of his "empiricism."

The Aristotelian concepts show, as we have seen above, an immediate reference to the historically given reality and to the actual course of events. This reference, or at any rate *this immediate* reference to the historically given, is lacking in modern physics. The fact, so decisively important for Aristotelian concepts, that a certain process was only once, or very frequently, or invariably repeated in the course of history, is practically irrelevant to the most essential questions of modern physics.[3] This circumstance is considered fortuitous or "merely historical."

The law of falling bodies, for example, does *not* assert that bodies very frequently fall downward. It does *not* assert that the event to which the formula, $s = \frac{1}{2}gt^2$, applies, the "free and unimpeded fall" of a body, occurs regularly or even frequently in the actual history of the world. Whether the event described by the law occurs rarely or often has nothing to do with the law. Indeed, in a certain sense, the law refers only to cases that are *never* realized, or only approximately realized, in the actual course of events. Only in experiment, that is, under artificially constructed conditions, do cases occur which approximate the event with which the law is concerned. The propositions of modern physics, which are often considered to be "anti-speculative" and "empirical," unquestionably have in comparison with Aristotelian empiricism a much less empirical, a much more constructive character than the Aristotelian concepts based immediately upon historic actuality.

B. Psychology

Here we are confronted by questions which, as real problems of actual research and of theory, have strongly influenced the development of psychology and which constitute the most fundamental grounds of its present crisis.

The concepts of psychology, at least in certain decisive respects, are thoroughly Aristotelian in their actual content, even though in many respects their form of presentation has been somewhat "civilized," so to speak. The present struggle and theoretical difficulties of psychology resemble in many ways, even in their particulars, the difficulties which culminated in the conquest over Aristotelian ways of thinking in physics.

1. Aristotelian Concepts

a. Fortuitousness of the individual case. The concept formation of psychology is dominated, as was that of Aristotelian physics, by the question of regularity and indeed of regularity in the sense of frequency. This is obvious in its immediate attitude toward particular phenomena as well as in its attitude toward lawfulness. If, for example, one shows a film of a concrete incident in the behavior of a certain child, the first question of

---

[3]So far as it is not immediately concerned with an actual "History of the Heavens and the Earth" or a geography. (See below.)

the psychologist usually is: "Do all children do that, or is it at least common?" And if one must answer this question in the negative the behavior involved loses for that psychologist all or almost all claim to scientific interest. To pay attention to such an "exceptional case" seems to him a scientifically unimportant bit of folly.

The real attitude of the investigator toward particular events and the problem of individuality is perhaps more clearly expressed in this actual behavior than in many theories. The individual event seems to him fortuitous, unimportant, scientifically indifferent. It may, however, be some extraordinary event, some tremendous experience, something that has critically determined the destiny of the person involved, or the appearance of a historically significant personality. In such a case it is customary to emphasize the "mystical" character of all individuality and "originality," comprehensible only to "intuition," or at least not to science.

Both of these attitudes toward the particular event lead to the same conclusion: that that which does not occur repeatedly lies outside the realm of the comprehensible.

b. Lawfulness as frequency. The esteem in which frequency is held in present-day psychology is due to the fact that it is still considered a *question* whether and how far the psychical world is lawful, as in Aristotelian physics it was due to a similar uncertainty about lawfulness in the physical world. It is not necessary here to describe at length the vicissitudes of the thesis of the lawfulness of the psychic in philosophical discussion. It is sufficient to recall that even at present there are many tendencies to limit the operation of law to certain "lower" spheres of psychical events. For us it is more important to note that the field which is considered lawful, not in principle, but in the actual research of psychology—even of experimental psychology—has only been extended very gradually. If psychology has only very gradually and hesitantly pushed beyond the bounds of sensory psychology into the fields of will and affect, it is certainly not due only to technical difficulties, but mainly to the fact that in this field actual repetition, a recurrence of the same event, is not to be expected. And this repetition remains, as it did for Aristotle, to a large extent the basis for the assumption of the lawfulness or intelligibility of an event.

As a matter of fact, any psychology that does not recognize lawfulness as inherent in the nature of the psychic, and hence in *all* psychical processes, even those occurring only once, must have criteria to decide, like Aristotelian physics, whether or not it has in any given case to deal with lawful phenomena. And, again, as in Aristotelian physics, frequency of recurrence is taken as such a criterion. It is evidence of the depth and momentum of this connection (between repetition and lawfulness) that it is even used to define experiment; a scientific instrument which, if not directly opposed to the concepts of Aristotelian physics, is at least significant only in relatively modern times.[4] Even for Wundt repetition inhered in the concept of experiment. Only in recent years is psychology beginning

---

[4] The Greeks, of course, *knew* of experiment.

to give up this requirement, which withholds a large field of the psychic from experimental investigation.

But even more important perhaps than the restriction of experimental investigation is the fact that this extravagant valuation of repetition (i.e., considering frequency as the criterion and expression of lawfulness) dominates the formation of the concepts of psychology, particularly in its younger branches.

Just as in Aristotelian physics, contemporary child psychology regards as characteristic of a given age, and the psychology of emotion as characteristic of a given expression, that which a group of individual cases have in common. This abstract Aristotelian conception of the class determines the kind and dominates the procedure of classification.

c. Class and essence. Present-day child psychology and affect psychology also exemplify clearly the Aristotelian habit of considering the abstractly defined classes as the essential nature of the particular object and hence as an "explanation" of its behavior. Whatever is common to children of a given age is set up as the fundamental character of that age. The fact that three-year-old children are quite often negative is considered evidence that negativism is inherent in the nature of three-year-olds, and the concept of a negativistic age or stage is then regarded as an explanation (though perhaps not a complete one) for the appearance of negativism in a given particular case!

Quite analogously, the concept of drives, for example, the hunger drive or the maternal instinct, is nothing more than the abstract selection of the features common to a group of acts that are of relatively frequent occurrence. This abstraction is set up as the essential reality of the behavior and is then in turn used to explain the frequent occurrence of the instinctive behavior, for example, of the care of infant progeny. Most of the explanations of expression, of character, and of temperament are in a similar state. Here, as in a great many other fundamental concepts, such as that of ability, talent, and similar concepts employed by the intelligence testers, present-day psychology is really reduced to explanation in terms of Aristotelian "essences," a sort of explanation which has long been attacked as faculty psychology and as circular explanation, but for which no other way of thinking has been substituted.

d. Statistics. The classificatory character of its concepts and the emphasis on frequency are indicated methodologically by the commanding significance of statistics in contemporary psychology. The statistical procedure, at least in its commonest application in psychology, is the most striking expression of this Aristotelian mode of thinking. In order to exhibit the common features of a given group of facts, the *average* is calculated. This average acquires a representative value, and is used to characterize (as "mental age") the properties of "the" two-year-old child. Outwardly, there is a difference between contemporary psychology, which works so much with numbers and curves, and the Aristotelian physics. But this difference, characteristically enough, is much more a difference in the technique of execution than in the actual content of the concepts involved. Essentially, the statistical way of thinking, which is a necessary consequence of Aristotelian concepts, is also evident in Aristotelian physics, as we have already seen. The difference is that, owing to the extraordinary development of mathematics and of general scientific method, the statistical procedure of psychology is clearer and more articulate.

All the efforts of psychology in recent years toward exactness and precision have been in the direction of refinement and extension of its statistical methods. These efforts are quite justified insofar as they indicate a determination to achieve an adequate comprehension of the full reality of mental life. But they are really founded, at least in part, on the ambition to demonstrate the scientific status of psychology by using as much mathematics as possible and by pushing all calculations to the last possible decimal place.

This formal extension of the method has not changed the underlying concepts in the slightest: They are still thoroughly Aristotelian. Indeed, the mathematical formulation of the method only consolidates and extends the domination of the underlying concepts. It unquestionably makes it more difficult to see their real character and hence to supplant them with others; and this is a difficulty with which Galileian physics did not have to contend, inasmuch as the Aristotelian mode of thought was not then so entrenched and obscured in mathematics. (See above.)

e. Limits of knowledge. Exceptions. Lawfulness is believed to be related to regularity, and considered the antithesis of the individual case. (In terms of the current formula, lawfulness is conceived as a correlation approaching $r = \pm 1$.) So far as the psychologist agrees at all to the validity of psychological propositions, he regards them as only *regularly* valid, and his acceptance of them takes such a form that one remains aware of a certain distinction between mere regularity and full lawfulness; and he ascribes to biological, and above all to psychological propositions (in contrast to physical) only regularity. Or else lawfulness is believed to be only the *extreme* case of regularity,[5] in which case all differences (between lawfulness and regularity) disappear in principle while the necessity of determining the degree of regularity still remains.

The fact that lawfulness and individuality are considered antitheses has two sorts of effect on actual research. It signifies in the first place a limitation of research. It makes it appear hopeless to try to understand the real, unique, course of an emotion or the actual structure of a particular individual's personality. It thus reduces one to a treatment of these

---

[5]As is well known, the concept of possible exceptions and the merely statistical validity of laws has very recently been revived in physical discussion. Even if this view should finally be adopted, it would not in any way mean a return to Aristotelian concepts. It suffices here to point out that even in that event, it would not involve setting apart within the physical world a class of events on the basis of its "degree" of lawfulness, but the whole physical universe would be subject only to a statistical lawfulness. On the relation of this statistical view to the problem of precision of measurement, see Lewin (1927).

problems in terms of mere averages, as exemplified by tests and question-naires. Anyone to whom these methods appear inadequate usually en-counters a weary skepticism or else a maudlin appreciation of individu-ality and the doctrine that this field, from which the recurrence of similar cases in sufficient numbers is excluded, is inaccessible to scientific com-prehension and requires instead sympathetic intuition. In both cases the field is withdrawn from experimental investigation, for qualitative prop-erties are considered as the direct opposite of lawfulness. The manner in which this view is continually and repeatedly advanced in the discussion of experimental psychology resembles, even to its particulars, the argu-ments against which Galileian physics had to struggle. How, it was urged at that time, can one try to embrace in a single law of motion such qual-itatively different phenomena as the movements of the stars, the flying of leaves in the wind, the flight of birds, and the rolling of a stone downhill. But the opposition of law and individual corresponded so well with the Aristotelian conception and with the primitive mode of thinking which constituted the philosophy of everyday life, that it appears often enough in the writings of the physicists themselves, *not*, however, in their physics but in their philosophy.[6]

The conviction that it is impossible wholly to comprehend the individ-ual case as such implies, in addition to this limitation, a certain laxity of research: It is satisfied with setting forth mere regularities. The demands of psychology upon the *stringency* of its propositions go no farther than to require a validity "in general," or "on the average," or "as a rule." The "complexity" and "transitory nature" of life processes make it unreasona-ble, it is said, to require complete, exceptionless, validity. According to the old saw that "the exception proves the rule," *psychology does not regard exceptions as counter-arguments so long as their frequency is not too great.*

The attitude of psychology toward the concept of lawfulness also shows clearly and strikingly the Aristotelian character of its mode of thought. It is founded on a very meager confidence in the lawfulness of psychological events, and has for the investigator the added charm of not requiring too high a standard of validity in his propositions or in his proofs of them.

f. Historic–geographic concepts. For the view of the nature of lawful-ness and for the emphasis upon repetition which we have seen to be char-acteristic of Aristotelian physics, in addition to the motives which we have mentioned, the *immediate* reference to the concerned "actuality" in the historic–geographic sense was fundamental. Likewise, and this is evi-dence of the intimacy with which these modes of thought are related, present-day psychology is largely dominated by the same immediate ref-erence to the historic–geographic datum. The historical bent of psycholog-ical concepts is again not always immediately obvious as such, but is bound up with nonhistoric, systematic concepts and undifferentiated from

---

[6]To avoid misunderstanding, the following should be emphasized: When psychologists criticize the opposition of individual and law, as is customary in psychology, it does not mean that we are unaware of the complex problems of the concept of individuality.

them. This quasi-historical set forms, in my opinion, the central point for the understanding and criticism of this mode of concept formation.

Although we have criticized the "statistical" mode of thought, the particular formulae used are not ultimately important to the questions under discussion. It is not the fact that an arithmetic mean is taken, that one adds and divides, that is the object of the present critique. These operations will certainly continue to be used extensively in the future of psychology. The critical point is not that statistical methods are applied, but *how* they are applied, and especially, what cases are combined into groups.

In contemporary psychology the reference to the historic–geographic datum and the dependence of the conclusions upon frequency of actual occurrence are striking. Indeed, so far as immediate reference to the historic datum is concerned, the way in which the nature of the one-, two-, or three-year-old child is arrived at through the calculation of statistical averages corresponds exactly to Bacon's collection of the given eases of dryness in his *tabulae praesentiae*. To be sure, there is a certain very crude concession made in such averages, to the requirements of non-historic concepts: Patently pathological cases and sometimes even cases in which an "unusual" environment is concerned, are usually excluded. Apart from this consideration, the exclusion of the most extreme abnormalities, the determination of the cases to be placed in a statistical group is essentially on historic–geographic grounds. For a group defined in historic–geographic terms, perhaps the one-year-old children of Vienna or New York in the year 1928, averages are calculated which are doubtless of the greatest significance to the historian or to the practical school man, but which do not lose their dependence upon the "accidents" of the historic–geographic given even though one go on to an average of the children of Germany, of Europe, or of the whole world, or of a decade instead of a year. *Such an extension of the geographic and historic basis does not do away with the specific dependence of this concept upon the frequency with which the individual cases occur within historically–geographically defined fields.*

Mention should have been made earlier of that refinement of statistics which is founded upon a *restriction* of the historic–geographic basis, as, for example, a consideration of the one-year-old children of a proletarian quarter of Berlin in the first years after the War. For such groupings usually are based on the qualitative individuality of the concrete cases as well as upon historic–geographic definitions. But even such limitations really contradict the spirit of statistics founded on frequency; even they signify methodologically a certain shift to the concrete particulars. Incidentally, one must not forget that even in the extreme case of such refinement, perhaps in the statistical investigation of the "only child," the actual definition is in terms of historic–geographic or at best of sociological categories; that is, according to criteria which combine into a single group cases that psychologically are very different or even antithetical. Such statistical investigations are consequently unable as a rule to give an explanation of the dynamics of the processes involved.

The immediate reference to the historically given actuality which is characteristic of Aristotelian concept formation is evident also in the dis-

cussion of experiment and nearness to life conditions. Certainly one may
justly criticize the simple reaction experiments, the beginnings of the experimental psychology of the will or the experiments of reflexology on the
grounds of their wide divergence from the conditions of life. But this divergence is based in large part upon the tendency to investigate such processes
as do not present the individual peculiarities of the particular case but
which, as "simple elements" (perhaps the simplest movements), are common
to all behavior, or which occur, so to speak, in everything. In contrast, approximation of life conditions is required, say, of the psychology of will. By
this is usually meant that it should investigate those cases, impossible to
produce experimentally, in which the most important decisions of life are
made. And here also we are confronted by an orientation toward the historically significant. It is a requirement which, if transferred to physics,
would mean that it would be incorrect to study hydrodynamics in the laboratory; one must rather investigate the largest rivers in the world. Two
points then stand out in the field of theory and law: the high valuation of
the historically important and disdain of the "ordinary" in the field of experiment, the choice of processes which occur frequently (or are common to
many events). Both are indicative in like measure of that Aristotelian mix-
ing of historical and systematic questions which carries with it for the systematic the connection with the abstract classes and the neglect of the full
reality of the concrete case.

2. Galileian Concept Formation

Opposed to Aristotelian concept formation which I have sought briefly to
characterize, there is now evident in psychology a development which appears occasionally in radical or apparently radical tendencies, more usually in little halfsteps, sometimes falling into error (especially when it tries
most exactly to follow the example of physics), but which on the whole
seems clearly and irresistibly to be pushing on to modifications which may
ultimately mean nothing less than a transition from Aristotelian to Galileian concept formation.

   a. No value concepts. No dichotomies. Unification of fields. The most important general circumstances which paved the way for Galileian concepts
in physics are clearly and distinctly to be seen in present-day psychology.
   The conquest over *valuative*, "anthropomorphic" classifications of phenomena on bases other than the nature of the mental process itself is not
by any means complete, but in many fields, especially in sensory psychology, at least the chief difficulties are past.
   As in physics, the grouping of events and objects into paired opposites
and similar logical dichotomies is being replaced by groupings with the
aid of *serial* concepts which permit continuous variation, partly owing simply to wider experience and the recognition that transition stages are always present.
   This has gone farthest in sensory psychology, especially in psycholog-

ical optics and acoustics, and lately also in the domain of smell. But the tendency toward this change is also evident in other fields, for example, in that of feeling.

Freud's doctrine especially—and this is one of its greatest services—has contributed largely to the abolition of the boundary between the normal and the pathological, the ordinary and the unusual, and hereby furthered the *"homogenization"* of all the fields of psychology. This process is certainly still far from complete, but it is entirely comparable to that introduced in modern physics by which "heavenly" and "earthly" processes were united.

Also in child and animal psychology the necessity is gradually disappearing of choosing between the two alternatives of regarding the child as a little adult, the animal as an undeveloped inferior human, or else trying to establish an unbridgeable gap between the child and adult, animal and man. This homogenization is becoming continually clearer in all fields, and it is not a purely "philosophical" insistence upon some sort of abstract fundamental unity but influences concrete research in which differences are fully preserved.

b. Unconditional general validity of psychological laws. The clearest and most important expression of increasing homogeneity, besides the transition from class to serial concepts, is the fact that the validity of particular psychological laws is no longer limited to particular fields, as it was once limited to the "normal human adult" on the ground that anything might be expected of psychopathics or of geniuses, or that in such cases "the same laws do not hold." It is coming to be realized that every psychological law must hold without exception.

In actual content, this transition to the concept of strict exceptionless lawfulness signifies at once the same final and all-embracing homogenization and harmonization of the whole field that gave to Galileian physics its intoxicating feeling of infinite breadth, because it does not, like the abstract class concepts, level out the rich variety of the world and because a single law embraces the whole field.

Tendencies toward a homogeneity based upon the exceptionless validity of its laws have become evident in psychology only very recently, but they open up an extraordinarily wide perspective.[7]

The investigation of the laws of structure—particularly the experi-

---

[7]The association psychology contains an attempt at this sort of homogeneity and it has really been of essential service in this direction. Similarly, in our time reflexology and behaviorism have contributed to the homogenization of "man and animal" and of "bodily and mental." But the Aristotelian view of lawfulness as regularity (without which it would have been impossible to support the law of association) brought this attempt to nothing. Consequently, the experimental association psychology, in its attempt at the end of the nineteenth century to derive the whole mental life from a single law, displayed the circular and at the same time abstract character that is typical of the speculative early stages of a science, and of Aristotelian class concepts.

Indeed, it seems almost as if, because of the great importance of frequency and repetition for Aristotelian methodological concepts, the law of association had been designed to make use of these as the actual *content* of psychological principles, inasmuch as frequent repetition is regarded as the most important cause of mental phenomena.

mental investigation of wholes—has shown that the same laws hold not only within different fields of psychological optics but also in audition, and in sensory psychology in general. This in itself constitutes a large step in the progress toward homogeneity.

Further, the laws of optical figures and of intellectual insight have turned out to be closely related. Important and similar laws have been discovered in the experimental investigation of behavioral wholes, of will processes, and of psychological needs. In the fields of memory and expression, psychological development appears to be analogous. In short, the thesis of the general validity of psychological laws has very recently become so much more concrete, particular laws have shown such capacity for fruitful application to fields that at first were qualitatively completely separated, that the thesis of the homogeneity of psychic life in respect to its laws gains tremendously in vigor and is destroying the boundaries of the old separated fields.[8]

c. Mounting ambitions. Methodologically also the thesis of the exceptionless validity of psychological laws has a far-reaching significance. It leads to an extraordinary increase in the demands made upon *proof*. It is no longer possible to take exceptions lightly. They do not in any way "prove the run," but on the contrary are completely valid disproofs, even though they are rare, indeed, so long as one single exception is demonstrable. The thesis of general validity permits of no exceptions in the entire realm of the psychic, whether of child or adult, whether in normal or pathological psychology.

On the other hand, the thesis of exceptionless validity in psychological laws makes available to investigation, especially to experiment, such processes as do not frequently recur in the same form, as, for example, certain affective processes.

d. From the average to the "pure" case. A clear appreciation of this circumstance is still by no means habitual in psychology. Indeed, from the earlier, Aristotelian point of view the new procedure may even seem to conceal the fundamental contradiction we have mentioned above. One declares that one wants to comprehend the full concrete reality in a higher degree than is possible with Aristotelian concepts, and yet considers this reality in its actual historical course and its given geographical setting as really "accidental." The general validity, for example, of the law of movement on an inclined plane is not established by taking the average of as many cases as possible of real stones actually rolling down hills, and then considering this average as the most probable case.[9] It is based rather

---

[8]For this section compare especially Wertheimer (1923), Köhler (1929), Koffka (1924), and Lewin (1926). A review of the special researches is found in Köhler (1924).

[9]In psychology it is asserted, often with special emphasis, that one obtains perhaps from the construction of baby tests, a representation of the "general human," through the fact that those processes are selected which occur most frequently in the child's *daily life*. Then one may expect with sufficient probability that the child will spontaneously display similar behavior in the test.

upon the "frictionless" rolling of an "ideal" sphere down an "absolutely straight" and hard plane, that is, upon a process that even the laboratory can only approximate, and which is most extremely improbable in daily life. One declares that one is striving for general validity and concreteness, yet uses a method which, from the point of view of the preceding epoch, disregards the historically given facts and depends entirely upon individual accidents, indeed upon the most pronounced "exceptions."

How physics arrives at this procedure, which strikes the Aristotelian views of contemporary psychology as doubly paradoxical, begins to become intelligible when one envisages the necessary methodological consequences of the change in the ideas of the extent of lawfulness. When lawfulness is no longer limited to cases which occur regularly or frequently but is characteristic of *every* physical event, the necessity disappears of demonstrating the lawfulness of an event by some special criterion, such as its frequency of occurrence. Even a "particular case" is then *assumed*, without more ado, to be lawful. Historical rarity is no disproof, historical regularity no proof of lawfulness. For the concept of lawfulness has been quite detached from that of regularity; the concept of the complete absence of exceptions to laws is strictly separated from that of historical constancy (the "forever" of Aristotle).[10]

Further, the content of a law cannot then be determined by the calculation of averages of historically given cases. For Aristotle the nature of a thing was expressed by the characteristics common to the historically given cases. Galileian concepts, on the contrary, which regard historical frequency as "accident," must also consider it a matter of chance which properties one arrives at by taking averages of historical cases. If the concrete event is to be comprehended and the thesis of lawfulness without exception is to be not merely a philosophical maxim but determinative of the mode of actual research, there must be another possibility of penetrating the nature of an event, some other way than that of ignoring all individual peculiarities of concrete cases. The solution of this problem may only be obtained by the elucidation of the paradoxical procedures of Galileian method through a consideration of the problems of dynamics.

---

[10]The contrast between Aristotelian and Galileian views of lawfulness and the difference in their methods may be briefly tabulated as follows:

		For Aristotle	For Galileo
1.	The regular is	Lawful	Lawful
	The frequent is	Lawful	Lawful
	The individual is	Chance	Lawful
2.	Criteria of lawfulness are	Regularity Frequency	Not required
3.	That which is common to the historically occurring cases is	An expression of the nature of the thing	An accident, only "historically" conditioned

II. Dynamics

A. Changes in the Fundamental Dynamic Concepts of Physics

The dynamic problems of physics were really foreign to the Aristotelian mode of thought. The fact that dynamic problems had throughout such great significance for Galileian physics permits us to regard it as a characteristic consequence of the Galileian mode of thought (Mach, 1921). As always, it involved not merely a superficial shift of interest, but a change in the content of the theories. Even Aristotle emphasized "becoming," as compared with his predecessors.

It is perhaps more correct to say that in the Aristotelian concepts statics and dynamics are not yet differentiated. This is due especially to certain fundamental assumptions.

1. Teleology and Physical Vectors

A leading characteristic of Aristotelian dynamics is the fact that it explained events by means of concepts which we today perceive to be specifically biological or psychological: *Every object tends, so far as not prevented by other objects, toward perfection*, toward the realization of its own nature. This nature is for Aristotle, as we have already seen, that which is common to the "class" of the object. So it comes about that the class for him is at the same time the concept and the goal (Τέλος) of an object.

This teleological theory of physical events does not show only that biology and physics are not yet separated. It indicates also that the dynamics of Aristotelian physics resembles in essential points the animistic and artificial mode of thought of primitive man, which views all movement as life and makes artificial "manufacture" the prototype of existence. For, in the case of manufactured things, the maker's idea of the object is, in one sense, both the cause and goal of the event.

Further, for Aristotelian concepts the cause of a physical event was very closely related to psychological "drives": The object strives toward a certain goal; so far as movement is concerned, it tends toward the place appropriate to its nature. Thus heavy objects strive downward, and, indeed, the heavier the more strongly, while light objects strive upward.

It is customary to dismiss these Aristotelian physical concepts by calling them "anthropomorphic." But perhaps it would be better, when we consider that the same fundamental dynamic ideas are today completely dominant in psychology and biology, to examine the actual content of the Aristotelian theses as far as possible independently of the "style" of their presentation.

It is customary to say that teleology assumes a *direction of events toward a goal*, which causal explanation does not recognize, and to see in this the most essential difference between "teleological" and "causal" explanation. But this sort of view is inadequate, for the causal explanation of modern physics uses directed quantities, mathematically described vectors. Physical "force," which is defined as "the cause of a physical change," is considered a directed, vectorial factor. In the employment of vectorial factors as the foundation of dynamics there is thus no difference between the modern and the Aristotelian view.

The real *difference* lies rather in the fact that *the kind and direction of the physical vectors in Aristotelian dynamics are completely determined in advance by the nature of the object concerned.* In modern physics, on the contrary, the existence of a physical vector always depends upon the *mutual relations of several physical facts*, especially upon the relation of the object to its environment.[11]

2. Significance of the Whole Situation in Aristotelian and Galilean Dynamics

For Aristotelian concepts, the *environment* plays a part only insofar as it may give rise to *"disturbances,"* "forced" modifications of the processes which follow from the nature of the object concerned. The vectors which determine an object's movements are completely determined by the object. That is, they do not depend upon the relation of the object to the environment, and they belong to that object once for all, *irrespective of its surroundings at any given time.* The tendency of light bodies to go up resided in the bodies themselves; the downward tendency of heavy objects was seated in those objects. In modern physics, on the contrary, not only is the "upward tendency" of a lighter body derived from the relation of this body to its environment, but the "weight" itself of the body depends upon such a relation.

This decisive revolution comes to clear expression in Galileo's classic investigations of the law of falling bodies. The mere fact that he did not investigate the heavy body itself, but the process of "free falling or movement on an inclined plane" signifies a transition to concepts which can be defined only by reference to a certain sort of *situation* (namely, the presence of a plane with a certain inclination or of an unimpeded vertical extent of space through which to fall). The idea of investigating free falling, which is too rapid for satisfactory observation, by resorting to the slower movement upon an inclined plane presupposes that the dynamics of the event is no longer related to the isolated object as such, but is seen to be dependent upon the whole situation in which the event occurs.

Galileo's procedure, in fact, includes a penetrating investigation of precisely the situation factors. The slope of the inclined plane, i.e., the proportion of height to length, is defined. The list of situations involved (free falling, movement on an inclined plane, and horizontal movement) is exhausted and, by varying the inclination, classified. The dependence of the essential features of the event (for example, its velocity) upon the essential properties of the situation (the slope of the plane) becomes the conceptual and methodological center of importance.

---

[11]Naturally this applies to "internal causes" which involve the mutual relation of the parts of a physical system.

This view of dynamics does not mean that the nature of the object becomes insignificant. The properties and structure of the object involved remain important also for the Galileian theory of dynamics. But the situation assumes as much importance as the object. Only by the concrete *whole which comprises the object and the situation are the vectors which determine the dynamics of the event defined.*

In carrying out this view, Galileian physics tried to characterize the individuality of the concerned total situation as concretely and accurately as possible. This is an exact reversal of Aristotelian principles. The dependence of an event upon the situation in which it occurs means for the Aristotelian mode of thought, which wants to ascertain the "general" by seeking out the like features of many cases, nothing more than a disturbing force. The changing situations appear as something fortuitous that disturbs and obscures the essential nature. It was therefore valid and customary to *exclude the "influence of the situation" as far as possible*, to "abstract" from the situation, in order to understand the essential nature of the object and the direction of its goal.

3. Getting Rid of the Historical Bent

The actual investigation of that sort of vectors obviously presupposes that the processes involved occur with a certain *regularity* or frequency. For otherwise an exclusion of the differences of the situation would leave no similarities. If one starts from the fundamental concepts of Aristotelian dynamics, the investigation of the dynamics of a process must be more difficult—one might think here of emotion in psychology—the more it depends upon the nature of the situation concerned. The single event becomes thereby unlawful in principle because there is no way of investigating its dynamics.

The *Galileian* method of determining the dynamics of a process is directly opposed to this procedure. Since the dynamics of the process depend not only upon the object but also and primarily upon the situation, it would be nonsensical to try to obtain general laws of processes by excluding the influence of the situations as far as possible. It becomes silly to bring in as many as possible different situations and regard only those factors as generally valid that are observed "under all circumstances," in any and every situation. It must, on the contrary, become important to comprehend *the whole situation involved, with all its characteristics, as precisely as possible.*

The step from particular case to law, from "this" event to "such" an event, no longer requires the confirmation by historical regularity that is characteristic of the Aristotelian mode of thought. *This* step to the general is automatically and immediately given by the principle of the exceptionless lawfulness of physical events.[12] What is now important to the investigation of dynamics is not to abstract from the situation, but to hunt out

---

[12]It is impossible here to go more fully into the problem of induction (Lewin, 1927).

those situations in which the determinative factors of the total dynamic structure are most clearly, distinctly, and purely to be discerned. *Instead of a reference to the abstract average of as many historically given cases as possible, there is a reference to the full concreteness of the particular situations.*

We cannot here examine in great detail the question, why not all situations are equally useful for the investigation of dynamics, why certain situations possess a methodological advantage and why as far as possible these are experimentally set up. Only one circumstance requires elucidation, which seems to me very seldom to be correctly viewed, and which has given rise to misunderstandings that have had serious consequences for psychology.

We have seen above how Galileian concepts separated the previously undifferentiated questions of the historical course of events, on one side, and of the laws of events on the other. They renounced in systematic problems the immediate reference to the historic–geographic datum. That the procedure instituted does not, as might at first appear, contradict the "empirical" tendency toward the comprehension of the full reality may already be clear from our last consideration: The Aristotelian immediate relation to the historically regular and its average really means giving up the attempt to understand the particular, always situation-conditioned event. Only when this *immediate* relation is completely abandoned, when the place of historic–geographic constancy is taken by the position of the particular in the whole situation, and when (as in experimental method) it is the same whether the situation is frequent and permanent or rare and transitory, only then does it become possible to undertake the task of understanding the real, always ultimately unique, event.

4. The Meaning of the Process Differential

Methodologically there may seem to result here another theoretical difficulty which can perhaps be better elucidated by a simple example than by general discussion. In order that the essentials may be more easily seen, I choose an example not from familiar physics but from problematical psychology. If one attempt to trace the behavior of a child to psychical *field forces* among other things—the justification for this thesis is not here under discussion—the following objection might easily be raised: A child stands before two attractive objects (say a toy, T, and a piece of chocolate, C) which are in different places (see Figure 1). According to this hypothesis, then, there exist field forces in these directions (a and b). The proportional strength of the forces is indifferent, and it does not matter whether the physical law of the parallelogram of forces is applicable to psychical field forces or not. So far, then, as a resultant of these two forces is formed, it must take a direction (r) which leads neither to T nor to C. The child would then, so one might easily conclude according to this theory, reach neither T nor C.[13]

---

[13] I am neglecting here the possibility that one of the field forces entirely disappears.

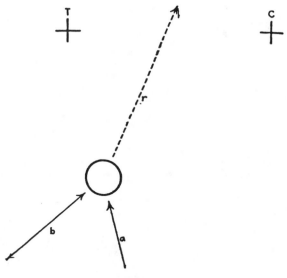

Figure 1

In reality such a conclusion would be too hasty, for even if the vector should have the direction r at the moment of starting, that does not mean that the actual process permanently retains this direction. Instead, the *whole situation changes with the process*, thus changing also the vectors that at each moment determine the dynamics, in both their strength and direction. Even if one assumes the parallelogram of forces and in addition a constant internal situation in the child, the actual process, because of this changing in the situation, will always finally bring the child to one or the other of the attractive objects (Figure 2).[14]

What I would like to exhibit by this example is this: If one tries to deduce the dynamics of a process, particularly the vectors which direct it, from the actual event, one is compelled to resort to process differentials. In our example, one can regard only the process of the first moment, not the whole course, as the immediate expression of the vector present in the beginning situation.

The well-known fact that all, or at least most, physical laws are differential laws (Poincare, 1917) does not seem to me, as is often supposed, to prove that physics endeavors to analyze everything into the smallest "elements" and to consider these elements in the most perfect possible isolation. It proceeds rather from the circumstance that physics since Galileo no longer regards the *historic course of a process* as the immediate expression of the vectors determinative of its dynamics. For Aristotle, the fact that the movement showed a certain total course was proof of the existence of a tendency to that course, for example, toward a perfect cir-

---

[14]Even if the distances of the attractive objects and the strength of their attractions were equal the resulting conflict situation would lead to the same result, owing to the liability of the equilibrium.

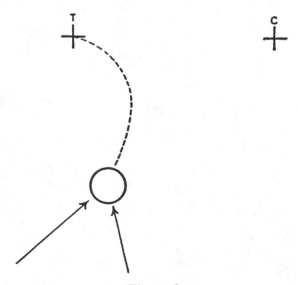

Figure 2

cular movement. Galileian concepts, on the contrary, even in the course of a particular process, separate the quasi-historical from the factors determining the dynamics. They refer to the whole situation in its full concrete individuality, to the state of the situation at every moment of time.

Further, for Galileian concepts, the forces, the physical vectors which control the situation, are proved by the resulting process. However, it is valid to exclude the quasi-historical in order to get the "pure" process, and hence necessary to comprehend the type of process by recourse to the process differential, because only in the latter, and hence unmixed, is it expressed. This recourse to the process differential thus arises not, as is usually supposed, from a tendency to reduce all events to their "ultimate elements," but as a not immediately obvious complementary expression of the tendency to derive the dynamics from the relation of the concrete particular to the concrete whole situation and to ascertain the type of event with which this total situation is dynamically related as "purely" and as unmixed with historic factors as possible.

Experimentally also it is important to construct such situations as will actually yield this "pure" event, or at least permit of its conceptual reconstruction.

5. Methodological

It remains to examine more closely the logical and methodological consequences of this mode of thought. Since law and individual are no longer antitheses, nothing prevents relying for proof upon historically unusual, rare, and transitory events, such as most physical experiments are. It becomes clear why it is very illuminating, for systematic concepts, to produce such cases, even if not exactly for the sake of their rarity itself.

The tendency to comprehend the actual situation as fully and concretely as possible, even in its individual peculiarities, makes the most precise possible *qualitative* and *quantitative* determination necessary and profitable. But it must not be forgotten that only this task, and not numerical precision for its own sake, gives any point or meaning to "exactness."

Some of the most essential services to knowledge of the quantitative, and in general of the mathematical, mode of representation are (1) the possibility of using *continuous* transitions instead of dichotomies in characterization, thereby greatly refining description, and (2) the fact that with such "functional concepts" it is possible to go from the particular to the general *without losing the particular in the general* and thereby making impossible the return from the general to the particular.

Finally, reference should be made to the method of "approximation" in the description of objects and situations, in which the "continuous," functional mode of thought is manifest.

B. Fundamental Dynamic Concepts in Psychology

The dynamic concepts of psychology today are still thoroughly Aristotelian,[15] and indeed the same internal relations and motives seem to me here displayed, even to the details.

1. Aristotelian Ideas: Independence of the Situation. Instinct

In content, which is easiest to exhibit and indeed hardly requires exposition, psychological dynamics agrees most completely with Aristotelian concepts: It is "teleology" in the Aristotelian sense. The traditional mistake of regarding "causal" explanation as an explanation without the use of directed forces has notably retarded the progress of dynamics, since psychological dynamics, like physical, cannot be understood without the use of vector concepts. It is not the fact that directed quantities are employed in psychological dynamics that gives it its Aristotelian character, but the fact that the process is ascribed to vectors connected with the object of investigation, for example, with the particular person and *relatively independent of the situation*.

The concept of instinct in its classical form is perhaps the most striking example of this. The instincts are the sum of those vectors conditioned by "predispositions" which it is thought must be ascribed to an individual. The instincts are determined essentially by finding out what actions occur most frequently or regularly in the *actual life* of the individual or of a group of like individuals. That which is *common* to these frequent acts (e.g., food-getting, fighting, mutual aid) is regarded as the *essence* or essential nature of the processes. Again, completely in the Aristotelian sense,

---

[15]The same holds, incidentally, for biology, which I cannot here especially examine, although I regard psychology in general as a field of biology.

these abstract class concepts are set up as *at once the goal and the cause* of the process. And indeed the instincts obtained in this way, as averages of historical actuality, are regarded as more fundamental the more *abstract* the class concept is, and the more various the cases of which the average is taken. It is thought that in this way, and *only* in this way, those "accidents" which inhere in the particular case and the concrete situation can be overcome. For the aim which still completely dominates the procedure of psychology in large fields is founded upon the effort to *free itself of the connection to specific situations.*

2. Intrinsic Difficulties and Unlawfulness

The whole difference between the Aristotelian and Galileian modes of thought becomes clear as soon as one sees what consequences, for a strict Galileian view of the concept of law, follow from this close and fixed connection of the instinct to the individual "in itself." In that case the instinct (e.g., the maternal) must operate *continually* without interruption; as the explanation of negativism by the "nature" of the three-year-old child entails for Galileian concepts the consequence that *all* three-year-old children must be negative *the whole day long*, twenty-four hours out of the twenty-four.

The general Aristotelian set of psychology is able to dodge these consequences. It is satisfied, even for proof of the existence of the vectors which should explain the behavior, to depend upon the concept of "regularity." In this way it avoids the necessity of supposing the vector to be existent in every situation. On the basis of the strict concept of law it is possible to disprove the hypothesis, for example, of the existence of a certain instinct by demonstrating its non-existence in given concrete cases. Aristotelian concepts do not have to fear such disproofs, inasmuch as they can answer all references to concrete particular cases by falling back on mere statistical validity.

Of course these concepts are thereby also unable to explain the occurrence of a *particular case*, and by this is meant not the behavior of an abstractly defined "average child," but, for example, the behavior of a certain child at a certain moment.

The Aristotelian bent of psychological dynamics thus implies not only a limitation of explanation to such cases as occur frequently enough to provide a basis for abstracting from the situation, but it leaves literally *any* possibility open in any particular case, even of frequent events.

3. Attempts at Self-Correction: The "Average" Situation

The intrinsic difficulties for dynamics which the Aristotelian mode of thought brings with it, viz., the danger of destroying the explanatory value of the theory by the exclusion of the situation, are constantly to be observed in contemporary psychology, and lead to the most singular *hybrid* methods and to attempts to include the concept of the situation *somehow*.

This becomes especially clear in the attempts at quantitative determination. When, for example, the question is raised and an attempt made to decide experimentally how the strengths of various drives in rats (perhaps hunger, thirst, sex, and mother love) compare with each other, such a question (which corresponds to asking in physics which is stronger, gravitation or electromotive force) has meaning only if these vectors are ascribed entirely to the rat and regarded as practically independent of the concrete whole situation, independent of the condition of the rat and its environment at the moment. Such a fixed connection is, of course, ultimately untenable, and one is compelled at least in part to abandon this way of thinking. Thus the first step in this direction consists in taking account of the *momentary condition of the drive* with regard to its state of satiation: The various possible degrees of strength of the several drives are ascertained, and their *maximal* strengths are compared.

It is true, of course, that the Aristotelian attitude is really only slightly ameliorated thereby. The curve expresses the statistical average of a large number of cases, which is not binding for an individual case; and, above all, this mode of thought applies the vector independently of the structure of the situation.

To be sure, it is not denied that the situation essentially determines the instinctive behavior in the actual particular case, but in these problems, as in the question of the child's spontaneous behavior in the baby tests, it is evident that no more is demanded of a law than a behavioral average. The law thus applies to an "average" situation. It is forgotten that there is no such thing as an "average situation" any more than an average child.

Practically, if not in principle, the reference to the concept of an "*optimal*" situation goes somewhat further. But even here the concrete structure of the situation remains indeterminate: Only a maximum of results in a certain direction is required.

In none of these concepts however are the two fundamental faults of the Aristotelian mode of thought eliminated: The vectors determining the dynamics of the process are still attributed to the *isolated object, independently* of *the concrete whole situation*; and only very slight demands are made upon the *validity* of *psychological principles* and the comprehension of the concrete actuality of the individual single process.

This holds true even for the concepts immediately concerned with the significance of the situation. As mentioned before, the question at the center of the discussion of the situation is, quite in the Aristotelian sense, how far the situation can "hinder" (or "facilitate"). The situation is even considered as a constant object and the question is discussed: Which is more important, heredity or environment? Thus again, on the basis of a concept of situation gotten by abstraction, a dynamic problem is treated in a form which has none but a statistical historical meaning. The heredity or environment discussion also shows, even in its particulars, how completely these concepts separate object and situation and derive the dynamics from the isolated object itself.

The role of the situation in all these concepts may perhaps be best exhibited by reference to certain changes in painting. In mediaeval paint-ing at first there was, in general, no environment, but only an empty (often a golden) background. Even when gradually an "environment" did appear it usually consisted in nothing more than presenting, beside the one per-son, other persons and objects. Thus the picture was at best an assembling of separate persons in which each had really a separate existence.

Only later did the space itself exist in the painting: It became a whole situation. At the same time this situation as a whole became dominant, and each separate part, so far indeed as separate parts still remain, is what it is, for example, in such an extreme as Rembrandt, only in and through the whole situation.

4. Beginnings of a Galileian Mode of Thought

Opposed to these Aristotelian fundamental ideas of dynamics there are now signs in psychology of the *beginnings of a Galileian mode of thought*. In this respect the concepts of sensory psychology are farthest advanced.

At first, even in sensory psychology, explanations referred to isolated single perceptions, even to single isolated elements of these perceptions. The developments of recent years have brought about, first slowly but then more radically, a revolution in the fundamental dynamic ideas by showing that the dynamics of the processes are to be deduced, not from the single elements of the perception, but from its *whole structure*. For it is impos-sible by a consideration of the elements to define what is meant by "figure" in the broader sense of the word. Rather, the whole dynamics of sensory psychological processes depend upon the "ground" (Rubin, 1921) and be-yond it upon the structure of the whole surrounding field. The dynamics of perception are not to be understood by the abstract Aristotelian method of excluding all fortuitous situations, but—this principle is penetrating today all the fields of sensory psychology—only by *the establishment of a form of definite structure in a definite sort of environment*.

Recently the same fundamental ideas of dynamics have been extended beyond the special field of perception and applied in the fields of higher mental processes, in the psychology of instinct, will, emotion, expression, and in genetic psychology. The sterility, for example, of the always circular discussion of heredity or environment and the impossibility of carrying through the division, based upon this discussion, of the characteristics of the individual, begin to show that there is something radically wrong with their fundamental assumptions. A mode of thought is becoming evident, even though only gradually, which, corresponding somewhat to the biolog-ical concept of phenotype and genotype, tries to determine the predispo-sition, not by excluding so far as possible the influence of the environment, but by accepting in the concept of disposition its necessary reference to a group of concretely defined situations.

Thus in the psychological fields most fundamental to the whole be-havior of living things the transition seems inevitable to a Galileian view of dynamics, which does not derive all its vectors from single isolated objects, but from the mutual relations of the factors in the concrete whole situation, that is, essentially, from the momentary condition of the individual and the structure of the psychological situation. *The dynamics of the processes is always to be derived from the relation of the concrete individual to the concrete situation,* and, so far as internal forces are concerned, from the mutual relations of the various functional systems that make up the individual.

The carrying out of this principle requires, to be sure, the completion of a task that at present is only begun: namely, the providing of a workable representation of a *concrete psychological situation* according to its individual characteristics and its associated functional properties, and of the concrete structure of the psychological *person* and its "internal" dynamic facts. Perhaps the circumstance that a technique for such a *concrete representation*, not simply of the physical but of the psychological situation, cannot be accomplished without the help of topology, the youngest branch of mathematics, has contributed to keeping psychological dynamics, in the most important fields of psychology, in the Aristotelian mode of thought. But more important than these "technical" questions may be the general substantial and "philosophical" presuppositions: too meager scientific courage in the question of the *lawfulness* of the psychical, too slight demands upon the validity of psychological laws, and the tendency, which goes hand in hand with this leaning toward mere regularity, to specifically *historic–geographic concepts*.

The accidents of historical processes are not overcome by excluding the changing situations from systematic consideration, but only by taking the fullest account of the individual nature of the concrete case. *It depends upon keeping in mind that general validity of the law and concreteness of the individual case are not antitheses, and that reference to the totality of the concrete whole situation must take the place of reference to the largest possible historical collection of frequent repetitions.* This means methodologically that the importance of a case, and its validity as proof, cannot be evaluated by the frequency of its occurrence. Finally, it means for psychology, as it did for physics, a transition from an abstract classificatory procedure to an essentially concrete constructive method.

That psychology at present is not far from the time when the dominance of Aristotelian concepts will be replaced by that of the Galileian mode of thought seems to me indicated also by a more external question of psychological investigation.

It is one of the characteristic signs of the "speculative" early stage of all sciences that "schools," representative of different "systems," oppose each other in a way and to an extent that is unknown, for example, in contemporary physics. When a difference of hypotheses occurs in contemporary physics there still remains a common basis that is foreign to the schools of the speculative stage. This is only an external sign of the fact that the concepts of that field have introduced a method that permits step-by-step approximation to understanding. Thereby results a continuous progress of the science which is constantly more narrowly limiting the consequences for the whole structure of differences between various physical theories.

There seems to me much to indicate that even the development of the schools in contemporary psychology is bringing about a transition to a similar sort of constant development, not only in sensory psychology but throughout the entire field.

References

Cassirer, E. (1910). *Substanzbegriff und Funktionsbegriff, Untersuchungen über die Grundfragen der Erkenntniskritik.* Berlin: B. Cassirer.

Koffka, K. (1924). *The growth of the mind: An introduction to child psychology.* (R. M. Ogden, Trans.). New York: Harcourt, Brace; London: Kegan, Paul.

Köhler, W. (1924). *Gestaltprobleme und Angänge einer Gestalttheorie.* Berlin.

Köhler, W. (1929). *Gestalt psychology.* New York: Liveright.

Lévy-Bruhl, L. (1922). *La mentalité primitive.* Paris: Alcan.

Lewin, K. (1926). *Vorsatz, Wille und Bedürfnis, mit Vorbemerkunge über die psychischen Kräfte und Energien und die Struktur der Seele.* Berlin: Springer.

Lewin, K. (1927) *Gesetz und Experiment in der Psychologie.* Berlin-Schlachtensee: Benary.

Lewin, K. (1929). *Die Entwicklung der experimentellen Willinspsychologie und die Psychotherapie.* Leipzig: S. Hirzel.

Mach, E. (1921). *Die Mechanik in ihrer Entwicklung.* Leipzig: Brockhaus.

Poincare, H. (1917). *La science et hypothese.* Paris: E. Flammarion.

Rubin, E. (1921). *Visuellwahrgenommene Figuren.* Copenhagen: Gyidenalske.

Sommer, R. (1925). Über Persönlichkeitstypen. *Berliner Kongress für experimentelle Psychologie.*

Wertheimer, M. (1923). Untersuchungen zur Lehre von der Gestalt. II. *Psychologische Forschung, 4,* 301–350.

3

Psychoanalysis and Topological Psychology

The attempt to use topological and vector concepts in psychology originated in connection with studies concerning need, will, and personality; in other words, in a field closely related to the interests of psychoanalysis. Moreover, the topological psychologists have tried for a number of years to investigate experimentally some of the basic psychoanalytical phenomena such as substitution.

Indeed there are more than superficial similarities between these approaches: (1) For both, the center of interest lies in the problems of emotions, personality structure, and personality development. (2) Both try to break down the barriers separating the different parts of psychology. (3) Both emphasize the psychological meaning of actions and objects instead of merely their physical appearance and their "superficial" properties. (4) Both are unsatisfied with descriptions and try to deal with the conditions and causal interrelations of psychological phenomena.

Still there are, I think, important differences between the two approaches which might roughly be classified as follows:

1. Concerning the methodology used: (a) Psychoanalytical ideas are based mainly on case study and a very special exploratory and therapeutic technique. Topological psychology uses all scientific methods but relies mainly on experiments. (b) Topological psychology is not satisfied with the way theories are proven in psychoanalysis. It insists upon the much more rigid and higher standards of experimental psychology as have been developed in perception psychology.

2. Concerning the form of the theories: Psychoanalysis has more or less consciously preferred richness of content to logical strictness of theory. This attitude of Freud was, I think, timely and probably more fruitful than the opposite position would have been especially in view of the therapeutic aim of psychoanalysis. Today a growing number of psychoanalysts would probably agree that the psychoanalytical theories are rather anthropomorphic and not suf-

From *Bulletin of the Menninger Clinic*, 1937, *1*, 202–211.

ficiently conceptual in character. Psychoanalysis retains too much the properties of a speculative "school," and uses derivations which are more instinctive than logical. In other words, psychoanalysis is a *body of ideas* rather than a *system of theories and concepts*.

3. Concerning the content of the theory: (a) Psychoanalysis tends to give *historical* answers to *systematic* problems. Topological psychology emphasizes the necessity of distinguishing these types of problems strictly, and has been mainly concerned with systematic problems. (b) Topological psychology emphasizes the necessity of developing concepts concerning the psychological environment just as much as those concerning the person. It derives all psychological events from the life space as a whole, which includes both person and environment, whereas psychoanalysis deals mainly with the person. Brown (1934) has touched upon some of these agreements and differences in a recent paper.

It may be well to elaborate on a few of these problems. Let me start by considering some points upon which psychoanalysis is superior to any kind of theory based on an experimental procedure. The psychoanalysts have had the opportunity to acquire a much more thorough and detailed knowledge of the intimate history of the person. The system of ideas is rich and elaborated in detail and touches the deep layers of personality. When Freud developed his ideas, it was commonly believed, even by the experimentalists themselves, that experimental psychology would be unable to reach deep layers of the person. Today it has been shown by a variety of experiments that this is possible, but the knowledge the psychoanalyst gains about the broader life situation and the deeper goals of the patient far surpasses the results reached in experimental research.

Psychoanalysis is especially superior in what one can call the *historical aspect of psychological events*. However the modern experimental procedure is likely to become more and more "historical." This means (1) it will take into account the historical situation of the person as a whole; (2) it will often have to create experimentally a special history by letting the subject go through a series of situations in order to build up the situation one wants to study.

Unfortunately the efficiency of psychoanalysis in the field of "historical" problems is not only an asset but a liability. It is typical for the period of "schools" (Lewin, 1931) that historical problems (concerning origins) and systematic problems (concerning general laws) are not distinguished clearly enough. Historical and systematic problems are both important, and cannot in the long run be treated independently of each other. But it is time for psychology to realize that these groups of problems are sufficiently different to have definite logical properties and methodological requirements of their own. The shortcomings of psychoanalysis, in not distinguishing sufficiently historical and systematic questions, might be considered one of the weakest points in its methodology and its content.

As far as methodology is concerned one has to emphasize that laws can be established in psychology only by an experimental procedure. It is often claimed that the procedure of the psychoanalyst is something like an experiment, in which the recovery of the patient proves that the theory was correct. I fully recognize the value of these "natural experiments" for making certain ideas more probable. Yet they cannot fulfill sufficiently the function of systematic experimentation.

The superiority of the experimental method is based mainly on two facts: (1) If one studies a certain phenomenon by analyzing given cases one is but poorly protected against the danger of overlooking one of the many important factors which always operate together in creating a certain phenomenon. The first task of an experimental process is to create the phenomenon that one wants to study. The experimenter is therefore forced to discard a view which is too narrow because the phenomenon simply will not appear if any important factor has been overlooked by the theory. The experimental procedure is, by its very nature, an all-around procedure that has to take into account both the situation and the person as a whole. One of the main virtues of the experimental method is, therefore, that it is a good way to disprove theories and that it is highly self-correcting. (2) The experimental method may permit quantitative statements concerning the dynamic factors involved.

The insufficient separation of historical and systematic problems greatly influences the content of the psychoanalytical theory. In this respect psychoanalysis has much in common with the older associationism. Both theories often answer the question, "Why does a person behave in a certain way?" by pointing to a similar behavior in his ontogenetic or phylogenetic past. For instance a trauma, a fixation, or other experience in childhood may be given as the cause of behavior or attitude of the adult. Topological psychology, on the other hand, strictly adheres to the "Principle of Concreteness" (Lewin, 1936). According to this principle only existing facts can influence behavior. This means that the psychological processes of today cannot be influenced by psychological facts of yesterday which today have as little existence as the psychological facts of tomorrow.[1]

The psychoanalyst is likely to react to this criticism in the same way as the associationists did a decade ago, and answer: "By pointing to the past in explaining present behavior we refer, of course, to those present facts in the person which have originated, or been influenced in his history. We don't need to state this obvious truth. Our historical language is to be understood merely as shorthand."

I wish to recognize fully the importance of historical factors for the origin of the present state of the person and the situation. Still I do not believe that the historical language of psychoanalysis is merely a matter of shorthand. This is not easy to prove because the vagueness of the conceptual side of psychoanalysis, together with the legitimate aspects of the historical approach, generally makes it possible to give a number of jus-

---

[1] Of course the content of the psychological facts of today may deal with the past or the future.

tifications and to leave back doors open in nearly every case, if one separates it from the whole psychoanalytical system and procedure.

The shortcomings might be revealed by discussing the way in which psychoanalysis makes use of the similarity between two occurrences as a criterion of their historical dependence. For instance, it has been stated that certain emotional expressions of the adult have their particular properties *because* as a child he behaved similarly under similar conditions; also the similarity of emotional expression among men has been derived from their common origin and more specifically from similar experiences of their ancestors. But such a derivation is as wrong as if one would derive the emotional expression of a child from similar behavior which might, under similar conditions, occur in him as an adult. Topological psychology accepts the sentence: "The same conditions lead to the same effect," because this sentence expresses merely what is meant by lawfulness, namely, independence from absolute time and space indices. If, therefore, under the same conditions the same behavior occurs, this is not to be regarded as something which needs any explanation; it is merely an expression of the lawfulness of the field concerned. It is scientifically inadequate to give any "historical explanation" of this similarity.

On the contrary one can assume historical influences only if a repetition of a situation leads to *different* behavior. Not similarity, but a dissimilarity of effects of similar situations (or similarity of effects in dissimilar situations) has historical significance; it shows that some change of the person or the environment has occurred and that the similar situation has become, out of historical reasons, in fact dissimilar. If one were to find the structure of the life space in a certain emotional state, for instance in despair, to be essentially the same at different age levels no historical explanation would be needed or even permissible. Instead, the specific character of the behavior would be "explained" by (derived from) the specific dynamical properties of the contemporary life space.

In my opinion, the problem of systematic versus historic explanation is basic for nearly every important question of psychoanalysis. If only the present state of the person influences his behavior today, as topological psychology claims, and if at the same time certain experiences and structures of the child have a direct influence upon the adult, as psychoanalysis claims, one would have to assume an immense rigidity of acquired structures within a living being. The problem of the extent to which the dynamic structure of the person remains unchanged during development, and in what way changes do occur is one of the basic problems of psychology. But it will not be possible to attack it in any satisfactory manner unless the differences between historical and systematic problems are better understood and each is treated according to its nature. (We will return to this point when discussing regression.)

The last point I would like to mention concerns the *conceptual* side of psychoanalysis.

Any attempt to deal scientifically with causal problems involves the necessity of leaving the field of directly observable phenomena and of introducing "intervening concepts" (Tolman; i.e., constructs like force, libido, drive, which can be observed only indirectly). In this regard both psycho-analysis and topological psychology are opposed to a certain primitive empiricism, the idea of which seems to be the limitation of science to collecting directly observable facts. The necessary corollaries to the constructive method are: (1) clearly defined, logical properties of the construct and (2) coordinating definitions between the constructs and directly observable phenomena. Without sharp coordinating definitions, and without a most rigid procedure in their actual application, the constructive method is bound to become merely speculation. The standards of topological psychology in this respect are well above those of psychoanalysis.

As with most psychological theories concerning needs, personality, fantasy, etc., psychoanalysis is unsatisfactory from a logical point of view. The concepts used are far from showing the strict properties of mathematical concepts; in other words, the derivations and conclusions are made more by feeling than by logic in the strict sense. If one asks a psychoanalyst whether the libido is an energy or a force, he generally answers in line with the definitions given in the psychoanalytical literature that libido is a directed energy.

It would probably not be fair to take such language entirely seriously and to ask in what field the libido changed its locomotion; how the direction, and the amount of change in direction can be determined; how the momentum of the libido is measured, etc. Still, psychology will never reach the state of a logical and empirically sound science if it does not first raise its level of aspiration in regard to its conceptual requirements. Moreover, topological and vector psychology seems to be able to offer a variety of concepts which are mathematically strict, yet fully adequate to the nature of psychological processes, and which are not restricted to any particular school. As an example of the mathematization of a psychoanalytical problem by topological and vector concepts, I might refer briefly to the problem of regression.

Regression in psychoanalysis means the turning back of the libido from a progressive development to the position, or the direction of a more primitive state. Some psychoanalysts distinguish "topical, temporal, and formal" regression, besides the regression of the libido.

The content expressed in the terms *regression* and *primitivation* seems to be far removed from the possibility of mathematization. Yet as soon as one is able to represent in a mathematical way the main differences between the child and an adult, such a possibility offers itself readily. One of the differences between an adult and a child is that the adult is a more differentiated system. The degree of differentiation is to be defined as the number of sub-parts within the person which are functionally separated to a certain degree. There is not space here to indicate the meaning of functional separation and how it can be determined (Lewin, 1936, p. 185). It must suffice to emphasize that the functional separation between neighboring systems is a relative one. Therefore the degree of differentiation, or in other words the number of sub-parts within a person, is to be considered different for different types of processes and for different strengths of the forces involved. Relative to greater forces, for instance in a situation of high pressure, a person is a less differentiated system than under normal conditions. In other words: A person under pressure should "regress" to a more "primitive" level at least as far as his degree of differentiation is concerned.

This very schematic presentation of the treatment of regression by means of topological and vector concepts may suffice to show what I have in mind. It is characteristic of such a procedure that the concept of differentiation is taken seriously with respect to its mathematical properties and as a representation of a set of concrete systems. A functional criterion is taken for differentiation, namely the functional interdependence. From these concepts as premises the relative character of the degree of differentiation of a person follows purely logically; it follows also that the degree of differentiation of a given system will diminish under circumstances which can be characterized with some specificity. So far, the procedure consists in the development of a system of concepts, statements, and conclusions within the realm of logical dynamics. The coordinating definitions (Reichenbach), in other words the empirical aspects of the procedure, enter when the younger person is coordinated to a less differentiated system than the older one. This coordination, of course, has to be made plausible by empirical data. So far as the problem of regression is concerned, the procedure succeeds not only in representing regression in mathematically well defined terms; it implies at the same time a variety of statements about the conditions and the effect of regression, in other words it involves a deductive theory of regression which can be tested experimentally.

Experiments by Barker, Dembo, and Lewin (1941) seem to show that these conclusions are, in fact, correct. They permit quantitative measurements of regression. As regression is defined by mathematical concepts within a framework of other well determined concepts and statements, it is possible to deduce in advance certain types of regression and to link them, for instance, with the question of attention, brain injuries, and other conditions in which the number of systems of the person involved in a given activity are reduced permanently or temporarily. In this way a number of apparently unrelated facts are linked. New experimental investigations are suggested, and a variety of independent possibilities for proving or disproving the theory are opened.

The theory of regression indicated so far is entirely unhistorical. According to it, the regressive behavior would occur under the described circumstances even if the person in question were created as an adult Golem. In other words: Even a person without childhood who never had experienced child-like behavior should regress to child-like behavior. This implies the possibility that regression might lead to behavior very different from what has actually happened in the history of the individual. The close relation psychoanalysis finds in regression between the present behavior of the adult and certain experiences in childhood may be, to a great extent, merely the result of the psychoanalytical method of revealing the person's history, i.e., by free associations, dream analysis and other procedures, which according to topological psychology themselves depend upon the *present* state of the person. It is at least conceivable that the history "behind" a psychoneurosis as revealed by psychoanalytical methods differs greatly from the actual history. Such a discrepancy would probably not interfere with the therapeutic effect of the treatment, because the sickness, the associations, and the cure all depend upon the present state of the person and all three might be consistent with each other in spite of important differences between the actual history of the person and that revealed psychoanalytically. One will be able to study the historical side of the problem of regression in a satisfactory way only if one can establish the actual historical data independently.[2]

It might be well to conclude with a few words about an experimental attack on the fundamental psychoanalytical problem of substitution. This term is linked with cultural problems, psychopathological problems, problems of dreams and others. Here again we find that the degree of perfection of the concept is entirely out of line with its elaborate and manifold application.

It is, of course, difficult to develop a concept of substitution so long as the underlying idea of need or drive is not conceptually clear. Topological and vector psychology provide means for a conceptually more determined and empirically testable concept of need by coordinating a need (in the state of hunger) to a system in tension. This coordination makes it possible, among other things, (1) to define the "substitute value" and to give empirical criteria for it; (2) to deduce the conditions under which activities should and should not have a substitute value. Starting with these definite working hypotheses, it was possible to investigate experimentally the way in which substitute value depends upon the similarity of the two activities, upon the degree of difficulty of the substitute action, upon the flexibility of the material involved, and upon the degree of reality and fluidity of the situations. Here again, experiment provides the advantage of quantitative statements. The greater conceptual exactness permits definite conclusions in different psychological fields, for instance, for personality problems and for feeblemindedness. At the same time, it opens a variety of possibilities for testing the empirical value of the theory in a much more precise way than that offered by psychoanalytical procedure.

In summary, the psychoanalytical theory has developed a system of ideas unequaled in richness and detailed elaboration in the fields of needs, dreams, and personality. Its method of case study has the advantage of revealing the intimate history of the individual and the deeper personality layers in a way unreached by other methods. The psychoanalytical method does not give those opportunities for testing laws which the experimental procedure provides. It is necessary to bring the problems involved to a decidedly higher level, conceptually. Topological and vector psychology, which in themselves are neutral to psychological schools, seem to be of decided help in this respect. Above all, it is necessary to distinguish historical and systematic problems and to eliminate historical answers to systematic questions. As the systematic and historical problems in psy-

---

[2] Psychoanalysis itself has made important steps in this direction.

chology can finally be solved only by dealing with both together, cooperation of the two approaches might prove to be fruitful.[3]

References

Barker, R., Dembo, T., & Lewin, K. (1941). Frustration and aggression: An experiment with young children. *University of Iowa Studies in Child Welfare, 18*, no. 1.
Brown, J. F. (1934). Freud and the scientific method. *Philosophy of Science, 1*, 323–338.
Lewin, K. (1931). The conflict between Aristotelian and Galileian modes of thought in contemporary psychology. *Journal of General Psychology, 15*, 141–177.
Lewin, K. (1936). *Principles of topological psychology*. New York: McGraw-Hill Book Co.

---

[3]The work of Dr. H. Murray and his co-workers at the Harvard Psychological Clinic and of Dr. J. F. Brown at the Menninger Clinic seem to be important steps in this direction.

Part II

Research Psychologist

Introduction

These selections are some of Lewin's reports of his research that have since been recognized as "classic." Each introduces a psychological principle that has withstood the tests of time and later research.

The first three articles report programs of studies of motivation. Lewin's review of research on intentions (Selection 4) introduces the idea that perceptions are influenced by motivation, anticipating the "new look" in the psychology of perception of the 1950s. Lewin's rejoinder to Charlotte Bühler's critique of Gestalt theory (Selection 5) introduces the idea that psychological development essentially consists of the organization of increasing complexity—particularly here, the complexity of motives and the means for satisfying them. The research on levels of aspiration (Selection 6) introduces the multiplicative relationship between goals and the means to reach them, now known as the value X expectancy principle that governs the probability that a motive will prompt action.

The last two selections in this collection of research reports present specific experiments on the effects of changes in situations. The experiments in which small children were systematically frustrated from playing with attractive toys (Selection 7) further advanced the idea of psychological development as increasingly organized complexity. Lewin proposed a critical distinction between regression and retrogression, regression being a reversion to a less complex, more disorganized psychological state and retrogression being a reversion to an earlier psychological state in the individual's life history. These experiments demonstrated that a high level of tension generated by frustration causes regression. The situational changes made systematically in the research reported in the last article (Selection 8) in this section were in the styles of adult leadership of boys' clubs. The new and enduring idea in this research was methodological: It showed how small groups can be used to conduct controlled experiments on social conditions, such as democratic, autocratic, and laissez faire governance, that were not thought to be accessible to experimental methods.

It is worth noting that the articles span the years from 1926 to 1941; perhaps more significant, they begin in Germany and end in the United States, and their styles reflect their cultures. The first two articles (Selections 4 and 5) were written originally in Germany. Lewin is the sole author, and these reports have a strong theoretical emphasis. The later American reports (Selections 6, 7, and 8) are strong on details of methods and data; theoretical discussion comes later. They are coauthored. These differences almost certainly reflect a change in the academic cultures in which the works were written.

Intention, Will, and Need (Selection 4)

In the article entitled "Intention, Will, and Need," Lewin challenged the capacity of associationist theories to explain much of human behavior. He chose as his exemplar the act of intending, not because it is a common act—Lewin pointed out that intending is actually fairly rare—but because it is especially revealing: Intentions demonstrate the significance of the person in the situation; one does not merely respond to stimuli but decides to do something about them and, in deciding, changes the situation for oneself. Drawing from research findings and common observation, Lewin first laid out "some facts" about intentional acts that he argued associationist theories cannot explain. Then he invoked field theory to explain these acts, casting intentions into the field theoretical rubric of needs, albeit of a special kind.

"Two Fundamental Types of Life Processes" (Selection 5)

Lewin continued to promote the idea that people's needs matter in this critique of an article by Charlotte Bühler. In this instance, however, he did not challenge the diminution of the significance of the active human mind, such as he found in associationist theory; rather, he answered the charge that his and his colleagues' Gestalt theory did likewise. In addition, Lewin offered a field-theoretical explanation of certain behavior as scientifically more respectable than Bühler's.

In arguing the case for the importance of the acting person in Gestalt theory, Lewin had to distinguish his own work and thought somewhat from that of his then better-known colleagues. Actually, Gestalt explanations of perceptual phenomena treated the person's contribution as automatic; the neural system interpreted incoming sensations more or less accurately and gave rise to immediate perceptual experience. Lewin, however, was extending Gestalt theory beyond perception to action, which required invoking other attributes of a "working mind." This article begins with Lewin's placing himself in relation to these ideas, citing his own recent research with his students.

In the second section of this article, Lewin illustrated his belief that people, particularly their motives, matter by using his kind of Gestalt theory to criticize certain of Bühler's ideas, which were not scientifically tenable for Lewin.[1]

---

[1] I think Bühler's approach appeared to Lewin to be of the vague kind of holism that prevailed at the time among German humanists; indeed, Bühler later championed humanistic psychology and became a prominent leader of the school; see Bühler and Allen, 1972.

Level of Aspiration (Selection 6)

The subject of this selection is essentially motivation, inasmuch as it concerns the reasons people set certain goals for themselves and then act intentionally to achieve them. By the time this article was written, psychological field theorists had developed many concepts and propositions, with motivation at the core (Lewin's *Principles of Topological Psychology* was published in 1936), and so were already capable of organizing the numerous findings about level of aspiration. Indeed, field theory had explicitly guided the program of studies that began in Germany and developed in response to the studies' findings. Thus, almost half of this article was devoted to field-theoretical interpretation.

This article, in many respects, recalls the style of presentation and a prevailing interest in theory that predate Lewin's emigration to the United States in 1933, even though it was written 5 or 6 years later. It is an invited chapter in which Lewin and his colleagues summarize and interpret a large body of research on the subject. At the same time, the style is partly American in its five tables of data and in its coauthorship.

"Level of Aspiration" contains many features that express Lewin's philosophy of science and its actualization in psychological research. The program of research was theory driven. The theory was holistic, and it assumed purposive human beings. The authors expressed many of their findings in terms of mathematical logic, giving them the advantages of concisely relating their findings to one another and, by mathematical manipulation, of generating hypotheses for future research. Many and varied psychological phenomena were shown to be derivable from a few fundamental propositions. In many ways, "Level of Aspiration" is the image of Lewin's aspirations for psychological research.

Frustration and Regression (Selection 7)

Lewin was, among many other things, an active developmental psychologist through most of his career. Considering the implications of field theory for developmental psychology, he early advanced the fundamental proposition that development was a process of increasing differentiation (Lewin, 1927). According to this view, to say that organisms develop means that their component parts become more numerous and specialized in structure and function. In human psychology, motives and goals proliferate and become more specific; and the capacities for attaining goals become more specialized and skills more finely honed.

Any theory of psychological development, and especially one applied to children, invites comparison with psychoanalytic theory, and this monograph on "Frustration and Regression" does so explicitly. The substantive comparison is apparent. In this article, Barker, Dembo, and Lewin proposed that the "regression" of psychoanalytic theory is actually two separate processes: (a) retrogression, a return to psychological conditions of an earlier period in the individual's life history, which may or may not be significantly less differentiated, and (b) regression, a return to an earlier, "primitive," less differentiated psychological state common to all people earlier in their development. Field theory holds that the conditions for retrogression and regression are overlapping but quite different in some respects. Most relevant here, a high level of psychological tension tends to bring about regression; it will not necessarily have this tendency toward retrogression.

Another clear comparison involves the consequences of frustration. Two years before the publication of this article, Dollard et al. (1939) published a book that made much of the frustration–aggression hypothesis. The hypothesis was the linchpin for a coordination of psychoanalytic and Hullian learning theory. Lewin believed that both psychoanalytic theory and learning theory attended excessively to the person—the individual's personality, in psychoanalytic terms, or to the individual's well-learned habits, in the terms of learning theory—and insufficiently to the person's more or less accurate construal of the immediate situation. He argued that both aggression and regression were consequences of high tension, and which one would occur depended on the situation at the time.

Two other comparisons between field theory and psychoanalytic theory are only implied in this monograph. Lewin had already made these comparisons explicit (see Selection 3). He asserted that field theory differs from psychoanalytic theory in the rigor of its theory, epitomized in its use of mathemathical logic, and in its openness to experimental test. Both of these features are prominent in this work.

Patterns of Aggressive Behavior in Experimentally Created "Social Climates" (Selection 8)

Selection 8 is an early report of findings from Lewin's best known experiment: the study on the effects of different modes of adult leadership of boys' clubs. I think it is fair to say that "group dynamics" started here.

This study made innovative use of the experimental method in three ways:

1. It is an experiment with "real" groups—"real" in the sense that, as far as their members were concerned, their groups existed for reasons other than the experiment. Two or more interdependent participants had been observed before for the purpose of research, but their participation was as witting participants and nothing else.
2. The conditions of participants' interdependence were systematically manipulated for research purposes.
3. The scientists dared to operationalize and manipulate such lofty phenomena as "democratic," "autocratic," and "laissez faire" modes of governance in a laboratory.

For what purpose was this innovative, elaborate, time-consuming, and enormously labor-intensive experiment done? Primarily, I think, to show that such critical "real world" social phenomena as modes of governance could be studied scientifically, even experimentally, and also to demonstrate in a scientifically respectable way that democracy was superior, even worth dying for (note the time of the study). Rigorous experiment though it is, of the kind of design capable of testing causal hypotheses deduced from theory, the study did not spring from a theoretical base. As this presentation of it shows, the study's design and methods and its "concrete" subject matter were its main objects; theory came after. The rest, as it is said, is history.

References

Bühler, C. M., & Allen, M. (1972). *Humanistic psychology*. Monterey, CA: Brooks/Cole.

Lewin, K. (1927). Kindlicher ausdruck [Children's expression]. *Zeitschrift für Pädagogische Psychologie, 28,* 510–526.

Dollard, J., Miller, N. E., Doob, L. W., Mowrer, O. H., Sears, R. R., Ford, C. S., Hovland, C. I., & Sollenberger, R. T. (1939). *Frustration and aggression*. New Haven, CT: Yale University Press.

4

Intention, Will, and Need*

I. A Few Facts[1]

1. The Influence of Time on the Effect of the Intention; The Immediate Cessation of the Effect After Consummatory Action

Intentional actions are usually considered the prototype of all acts of will. Theoretically, a complete intentional action is conceived of as follows: Its first phase is a *motivation process*, either a brief or a protracted vigorous struggle of motives; the second phase is an act of choice, decision, or intention, terminating this struggle; the third phase is the consummatory intentional action itself, following either immediately or after an interval, short or long. The second phase, the act of intending, is considered the central phenomenon of the psychology of will. The problem is: How does the act of intending bring about the subsequent action, particularly in those cases in which the consummatory action does not follow immediately the act of intending? It has been demonstrated that in such cases, the act of intending need not be repeated before the action.

Indeed, Ach's (1905) experiments have shown that an instruction given in hypnosis is carried out upon a post-hypnotic signal without the subject's knowledge of the instruction. When the occasion (Ach's "referent-presentation") implied in the act of intending occurs, it suffices to initiate the intended consummatory action (Ach's "goal-presentation"). For instance, an optic signal will initiate the pressing of a lever. The question is: What are the further characteristics of this after-effect of the act of intending?

According to prevailing theory, the act of intending creates such a relationship between the "referent-presentation" and "goal-presentation"

From *Psychological Forschung*, 1926, 7, 330–385. The translation is by D. Rapaport, which appeared originally in 1951, in his edited volume, *Organization and Pathology of Thought*. New York: Columbia University Press, pp. 95–153.

*Editor's Note. Rapaport omitted some of the original text in his translation; these omissions are indicated by . . . . in this reprint. I have also omitted Rapaport's commentaries on the text, although I found them informative for my own commentary.

[1]For a detailed survey and discussion of the available experimental investigations into the psychology of will, see Lindworsky (1919).

that the appearance of the former results in an action consistent with the latter. According to the association theory (Mueller, 1911, 1913, 1917), an association of the referent- and goal-presentations is the cause of this process. Even the theory of the determining tendency (Ach, 1905, Chaps. I, II), which denies the associative character of this relationship, assumes that a coupling created by the act of intending between the referent- and goal-presentations is the cause of the intentional action.

The origin of such theories becomes clear if it is remembered that the experimental analysis started with so-called reaction experiments, in which the intention was to carry out certain actions upon arbitrarily chosen signals, which had nothing or very little to do with the actions themselves.

Let us open up the problem by raising an apparently extraneous question: What role is played by the length of time elapsing between the act of intending, and the consummatory action? Does the after-effect of the intention decrease progressively as associations do, according to the so-called curve of forgetting? It must be said right away that this after-effect persists over astonishingly long time-spans, even for relatively unimportant and outright nonsensical intentions.

Students were instructed: "Coming to the next laboratory hour (8 days hence), you will twice go up and down the stairs leading to the Psychological Institute." An astonishingly high percentage of the students carried out the instruction, even though they did not renew the intention in the intervening period.

Following certain processes, however, this after-effect ceases in a typical and abrupt fashion. For instance, someone intends to drop a letter into a mailbox. The first mailbox he passes serves as a signal and reminds him of the action. He drops the letter. The mailboxes he passes thereafter leave him altogether cold. In general, the *occurrence of the occasion* (referent-presentation) as a rule has no effect once the intentional action has been "consummated."

The apparent obviousness of this statement makes it especially necessary that its theoretical implications be made explicit. According to the laws of association, dropping the letter into the first mailbox should create an association between the mailbox and the dropping of the letter; the forces, whether associative or any other kind, which lead to dropping the letter, should also be reinforced by it. This is a stumbling block for association psychology; moreover, it casts doubt on whether the coupling between occasion and consummation (referent- and goal-presentations) plays really the essential role here. If the effect of the act of intending is that a tendency toward consummation arises when the occasion implied in the act of intending occurs, then it is hard to see why on a second occasion this tendency should not appear to the same and even to a greater degree. (The actual absence of the letter, after it was mailed, would prevent full consummation; yet the inhibitory effect of this failure would be expected only at the third mailbox, unless very complex auxiliary hypotheses were employed.) To explain the phenomenon we cannot fall back on a time-decrement of the intention-effect, since when repetitive action is intended (for example, to paste an announcement on each mailbox), the intention becomes effective on each occasion. In the case of the intention to mail a letter, however, the forces directed toward action seem suddenly exhausted once the letter is mailed. Thus, the cause of the process does not seem to be simply that the coupling between the referent- and goal-presentations drives toward action when the occasion arises.

A mailbox may elicit the tendency to drop the letter—or at least to check whether or not it has been dropped—even after it has been mailed. This happens mainly with important letters. Such cases are amenable to experimental study.

In studies using reaction experiments for this purpose, the following considerations must be kept in mind. If the subject is instructed, "You will press the lever when you see this signal," the signal will not play the role which a meaningful occasion, objectively connected with the action, would. It will play the role of a "signal," which may acquire the meaning of "command," and may therefore have repeated effects. The repetition of the signal then amounts to the verbal instruction: "Repeat the task again." (For instance, the policeman's raised hand amounts to a direct command.) We shall discuss such cases again. If the subject is given the task to nail together a frame, and the occasion for this is so chosen that it fits meaningfully into the process-whole—that is, it becomes an occasion and not a command—typically no tendency to repeat the completed task appears. For instance, if the occasion for this frame to be nailed together is when Mr. X. brings in a nail box, there will be no tendency to repeat nailing the frame if Mr. X. brings in the nail box again.

2. The Effect of Intentions When Occasion and Consummatory Action Are Not Predetermined, or When the Occasion Fails to Appear

It is usually assumed that, in the prototype of intentional action, the act of intending defines a *quite specific* occasion and a *specific* consummatory action. The reaction experiments, which were the point of departure for the experimental investigation of will, may serve as a useful paradigm. The referent-presentation may, for instance, be an optimal signal and the goal-presentation the pressing of a lever.

Not in every act of intending are occasion and consummatory action so specifically defined.

First of all, *the consummatory action may remain quite indeterminate.* For instance, a person may intend to talk someone into doing a certain thing; the act of intending may leave it entirely open what words and arguments he will use, whether he will first go for a walk with him to make friends without even mentioning the matter, and so forth. The intention to avoid a ball *may* contain the provision that one will veer left; but it may leave it entirely open whether one will veer right or left, jump, or duck.

Such general intentions are more the rule than the exception, and they are not less effective than specific intentions. On the contrary, it is usually more purposeful to let the mode of consummation grow from the focal *concrete consummatory situation* than to define it beforehand un-equivocally . . . .

The same holds for the precise definition of the occasion in the act of intending. Actually, vitally important and far-reaching intentions, like the decision to pursue an occupational goal or to be a well-behaved child, are extraordinarily indefinite on this point. The actions to be executed and the occasions therefore are left wide open. Indeed, *the very same intention* may give rise, according to the conditions, to *quite contrary actions*. "Good be-havior" requires now action, now foregoing of action.

But even where the act of intending predetermines definite occasion and consummatory action, we often encounter the astounding phenome-non that the intention takes effect all of a sudden *in response to quite other occasions and by different consummatory actions.*[2] This, however, is rare where there is no meaningful objective relationship between occasion and consummatory action, as in the so-called reaction-experiments. But it is frequent where, as in everyday life, there is an *objective* connection between the occasion and the consummatory action implied.

Somebody resolves to write a postal card to an acquaintance soon after returning home in the evening. In the afternoon he gets to a telephone. It reminds him to communicate with the acquaintance, and he does. Or: I resolve to drop a letter in the mailbox when I leave. A friend comes to see me, and I ask him to take care of the letter.

Two points in these examples seem important. In the first case an experience (seeing the telephone) very different from the occasion implied by the act of intending (the return home) actualizes the forces emanating from or connected with the intention. This experience assumes the role of the intended occasion: It initiates a consummatory action, though another than that implied in the act of intending. It is an action which from the vantage point of the act of intending is a *substitute* action or, more cor-rectly, an equivalent action "appropriate to the situation."

In order to maintain the view that the forces striving toward the in-tentional action derive from a coupling between the occasion and the con-summation created by the act of intending, and that these forces are re-leased by the occurrence of the occasion, one might attempt to explain the effectiveness of the "substitute occasion" and the occurrence of the substi-tute action by assuming that they are special cases of the same "general idea" to which both the intended occasion and consummatory action be-long. It has been demonstrated, however, by the psychology of thinking that such a theory of general ideas is in contradiction to concrete psycho-logical facts (Selz, 1913).

The main objection to the concept of coupling is that it leaves unex-plained why after such *substitute actions*, the later actual occurrence of the intended occasion generally *no longer arouses a tendency* to consum-mate the intended action. Why is it that once the letter is entrusted to a

---

[2]Concerning the range and displacement of such actualizing-stimuli, see Lewin, 1917.

friend the mailbox no longer challenges one, though a hundred different interpolated actions will not destroy the effects of the intention? There is no doubt that it is a salient characteristic of intention-effects that they usually cease, once the intended action or its equivalent is consummated. This, however, is not understandable once the forces driving toward the intentional action are conceived of as arising from couplings either of an associative or a non-associative sort.

The following example demonstrates the difficulties of this conception even more clearly. Somebody resolves to tell something to an acquaintance who is about to visit; but the visit is canceled. When *the occasion* fails to occur, the intention-effect is not simply canceled, instead new occasions are sought. This shows directly that *here a state of tension is pressing toward discharge by means of a specifically directed action.*

The objection does not hold that in such cases the original intention is general (to communicate something to the acquaintance) and not specific (to communicate on a certain occasion). There are such general intentions, but certainly there are specific ones also. Occasionally, the intentional action will not take place after the intended occasion has failed to occur: In such cases the intended action is "forgotten." Such exceptions will be discussed later on.

The internal tensions may initiate the consummatory action when the expected occasion is delayed too long. For instance, in a race there is a strong tendency *to start prematurely.* Reaction experiments show similar phenomena. In political life also we observe *premature* acting before the intended occasion had occurred.

The effect of intentions in which both occasion and consummatory action are left indeterminate; the effect of occasions different from those implied by the act of intending (substitute occasions appropriate to the situation); the occurrence of objectively equivalent actions; the search for new occasions and the premature actions when the expected occasion fails to occur; the cessation of the intention-effect once the intended action or its substitute has been consummated—all indicate that it is unsatisfactory to describe the causes of intentional actions as forces which on definite occasions drive to definite actions connected with them by a *coupling.*

3. The Resumption of Interrupted Activities

Another group of related phenomena should be discussed in greater detail.[3]

The consummation of an intended action is interrupted. Were the coupling between occasion and consummation decisive, nothing would happen without a repeated occurrence of the occasion, provided that the initiation of the consummatory action creates no new forces. The experimental setting used makes it possible to compare the results with those cases in which the effect of the intention is exhausted by the response to the first

---

[3]These phenomena have been studied by Miss Ovsiankina (1928) at the Berlin Psychological Institute.

occasion. I shall mention only a few of Ovsiankina's results which are relevant to our present subject.

The activities used in the experiment were in general *not* particularly *interesting*: for example, reproduction of a figure by colored building-stones, copying a rank–order correlation table, threading beads, making an animal from plasticine.

In the moment the activity is interrupted, a strong, *acute* effect is observed: Subjects *resist* interruption even of not particularly agreeable activities. This assumes occasionally quite stubborn forms. The forces opposing interruption appear to be closely connected with, among other things, the course, structure, and whole-quality of the activity.

In our present context it is of particular interest what happens when the subject, following instructions, interrupts one activity to start and *complete another*. In brief, a *strong tendency to resume the first activity is observed*.

The experiments used two kinds of interruption. First, *incidental interruptions*: The lights go out, presumably due to power failure; the experimenter drops a box of small objects and the polite subject helps to pick them up, and so on. Second, interruptions by direct instruction to start *another activity*.

Though often the incidental interruptions took as much as twenty minutes, the original activity was resumed without exception. After the interruptions by other tasks, resumption was frequent, at times even after a full hour. The subjects knew that the experimenter did not expect resumption; indeed, in some cases the experimenter actually *prohibited it*.

The *act of resumption* is of particular interest to us. The resumption tendency is reinforced when the subject catches sight of the material of the interrupted first activity, for instance, of the piece of paper on which he began to draw. *But even when there is no such external stimulus, the tendency to resumption is present.* The behavior observations and the subjects' self-observations indicate that a few seconds after the interrupting activity is finished, there appears an urge to resume the first activity, even if the subject did not think of it while engaged in the other. This urge appears first in an indefinite form, "There is still something to be done," without the subject's knowing what it actually is.

This is usually not a *persistence* of activity, such as occurs in continuous rhyming of nonsense syllables, but rather a typical tendency toward the consummation of an action, that is, toward the equilibration of an inner tension. Accordingly, the resumption tendency is more often absent if the interrupted activity is a continuous, rather than an end-activity.

. . . The intensity of the resumption tendency does not depend directly upon the intensity of the intention which preceded the activity (Boumann, 1919; Lewin, 1917; Lindworsky, 1919; Sigmar, 1925) but rather upon *the subject's internal attitude toward that activity*. "Pure experimental subjects"—that is, subjects who "do everything the experimenter wants," subordinating their will to his—show little or no resumption tendency. The subject must actually have the will to carry out the specific activity.

The *central goals of will* which prompt the subject to accept the instructions of the experimenter are also important here. If the subject is asked to do some work because the experimenter needs it in other experiments, then the subject accepts this work not as a "subject" but as a person who wants to do a favor for the experimenter—that is, as a professional colleague or a social being. This is then a "serious activity," and the resumption tendency is much stronger in it than in a mere "experimental activity."

We are faced with the following facts: A force is demonstrated which drives, even after relatively long intervals, toward the completion of interrupted activity. The manifestation of the force does not require an external stimulus to prompt resumption of the task; frequently, the resumption occurs spontaneously.

Further examples: Questions discussed but not settled in a meeting, usually continue to preoccupy us and may lead to long soliloquies, particularly if the questions are personally important. If we are interrupted in helping a schoolchild with a mathematical problem, it may recur to us for a long while even if quite uninteresting. If we slip into reading some stupid fiction but do not finish it, it may pursue us for years. The important experimental finding is that "interest" is not the decisive factor in such cases.

Finally, a few words about those theoretically important cases in which, because of a specific objective relationship between the original activity and the interrupting activity, no resumption tendency appears. A child telling a story is interrupted and told to draw the content of the story. No resumption tendency appears, obviously because the drawing somehow completed the interrupted storytelling. This is a substitute consummation. Such cases seem to be particularly revealing of the forces active in the execution of intentions. Even in real resumption, the completing activity need not be the missing part of the original activity. It may be a quite differently structured activity directed "toward" the goal, or only playful handling of the material of the original activity.

4. The Forgetting of Intentions

An obvious, and in one sense, direct approach to the study of intention-effects is the investigation of the forgetting of intentions.

Two concepts of forgetting must be carefully distinguished. The first pertains to the usual conception of *memory*: the ability to reproduce knowledge once possessed. The ability to repeat an action once performed we will also consider reproduction, though in some respects it is an essentially different process (Lewin, 1922, Part II, pp. 125ff).

The second concept of forgetting pertains to *intentions which are not carried out*. In everyday life, we call it "forgetfulness." It is obvious that we usually remember the content of the intention, even though we have forgotten to carry it out. In such cases the memory-knowledge of the act of intending is extant. A good memory, ability to reproduce knowledge and actions, need not be accompanied by the virtue of not being "forgetful" in carrying out intentions—though some connections between the two may exist. . . .

Our concern here is the second concept of forgetting, the *failing to carry out an intention*.

We will disregard those cases where forgetting of intentions is due to momentary strong preoccupation with other matters. The remaining cases promise immediate insight into the conditions under which intentions fail.

As mentioned, intention effects do not seem to show a time-decrement. *The passage of time can no more be considered to be cause of real happening in psychology than it is in physics*. Progressive time-decrements are usually referable to normal life processes. But even then the question remains: What in the whole life process is the *concrete cause*, for instance, of the forgetting of a given intention.

In an experimental investigation of the forgetting of intentions (Birenbaum, 1930), the subject was to do a number of tasks and, at the end (or at another definite point) of each, sign and date the paper used. After the completion of each task, the sheet was handed over to the experimenter.

The following results were obtained:

a. Generally, an intention is not an isolated fact in the psyche, *but belongs*, rather, *to a definite action-whole*, to a definite *region of the personality*. Thus, for instance, the signature is usually not embedded in the "objective work" of the task, but rather in that "personal" region which is involved in "handing the work over" to the experimenter.

Thus the transition from the action-region in which the intention is *embedded* to another may bring about the forgetting of the intention. An example from these experiments: The signature is often forgotten when six *similar* activities are followed by a seventh which is different.

A region of intention-effects may be sealed off simply by a pause of a few minutes. After the pause, the signature is often forgotten. It is clear that we are not dealing here with a time-decrement of the intention since, even without renewal of the intention, the signing is usually not forgotten when the subject works on ever-new tasks without pauses, and, since the signature is usually still affixed, even when the "pause" lasts not five minutes but a whole day.

The apparent reason for this paradox is that, in a continuous series of experiments, a pause of five minutes is a very considerable interruption; after it, the subject enters a new region, as it were, in which the previous intentions hold little or not at all. If, however, a second group of the experiments takes place the next day, then for the subject it is a "resumption of yesterday's experiment" and not, as in the first case, a "proceeding to new experiments." Therefore, the subject reenters the situation of the preceding day without difficulty. In fact, it is not necessary to repeat the experimental instructions on the second day in other experiments either: In preparing himself subjectively for the experiment, the subject again accepts the previous instructions.

Such embedded intentions are not forgotten if—but only if—the action region to which they belong is alive. This is true for everyday life also. Forgetting of an intention, or rather unresponsiveness of an intention to the intended occasion or another proper one, is observed when the occasion presents itself at a time or in a situation where those psychic complexes in which the intention is embedded are not alive. The most frequent cases of forgetting, which we usually attribute to being preoccupied with something else, are probably not solely due to the *intensity of the other experience*. If these intensive experiences belong to the *same* psychic complex, they may even reinforce the intention. Furthermore, forgetting may occur without intensive preoccupation if the momentarily prevailing psychological region is sufficiently distant from the intention. Yet pure intensity-relationships do seem to play some role.

b. The *occasion*, also, is of significance for the problem of forgetting. For instance, the subject will forget to sign his name, quite regularly, if he must change to signing on a larger paper or on one of a different color. Obviously, the paper reminds the subject of the intention, as does the mailbox of the letter to be mailed, or the knot in the handkerchief of something not to be forgotten; they have what I would like to call a *valence*. We have discussed cases in which, though the intentions were quite specific, a whole varied series of events and objects had valences (mailbox—friend). The valence may be fixated, however, as in the example of the paper, to a very specific object. . . .

c. One of the tasks in the experiments mentioned was the drawing of the subject's own monogram. In this task, the subjects regularly forgot to sign their names. Association theory would have us expect the opposite: Due to the strong coupling between the monogram and the signature, forgetting of the intention to sign should be particularly rare on this task.

Detailed analysis indicates, however, that this is a kind of *substitute consummation*. In view of the whole situation, the subject could hardly have assumed that the monogram would sufficiently identify his work for the experimenter. Actually, the signature is "forgotten" without further consideration. The need to sign, established by the act of intending, is apparently somehow satisfied by this monogram signature (though other factors are also at play here). It is significant that monogram writing done as "craft work," and not as "writing one's own monogram," does not have the effect of substitute consummation.

Such substitute- or even part-consummations are frequent causes of forgetting in everyday life also. I shall mention two examples that actually occurred. A man wishes to buy collar buttons. He forgets it repeatedly. Now he makes a detour, to go by a street in which there certainly are men's stores. He is satisfied and happy that he did "not forget his shopping." He arrives at the library and notices that he did not buy the buttons.

A teacher resolves to ask her pupil about a certain matter. About the middle of the study hour she remembers it and is glad that "she remembered it just in time." She ends up without having carried out the intention. (In these cases, as in those of everyday life in general, there is naturally no unequivocal proof that going through the street or the mere remembering of the intention, as substitute consummations, were really the causes of forgetting.)

It is often observed that even making a written note of an intention is conducive to forgetting it, though according to the association theory it should reinforce the coupling between the referent- and the goal-presentation. Making a note is somehow a consummation, a discharge. We rely on the note to remind us in due time and weaken thereby the inner need not to forget. This case is similar to the one where remembering the intention to ask something acts as a fulfillment, so that the question is never actually asked.

There are, however, cases where taking notes, even if they are never seen again, facilitates remembering. In these cases the note-taking may, for instance, connect the intended action with a certain personality region (such as the region of occupation) or a certain style of living (such as orderliness), so that the total energy of this region partakes in carrying out the intention.

d. When not a result of substitute consummation, forgetting can often be traced to natural *counter-needs*. The intention to write an unpleasant letter often remains ineffective even if repeated: We forget it whenever we have leisure for it. Freud has called attention to these hidden resistances. Even though not all forgetting can be traced to such natural—and certainly not always to sexual—needs, nevertheless it is of central significance for our problem that *the after-effect of an intention proves to be a force, which may clash with and be made ineffective by needs*.

We have already discussed the positive relation of intention effects to the needs from which the intention itself arose. (See, for instance, the resumption of "serious" activities.) The ease of forgetting depends upon the intensity of the genuine-need underlying the intention. Signatures were much less frequently forgotten in mass experiments than in experiments with individual subjects. The need to distinguish one's work (other factors being equal) is much greater in a mass experiment.

Whether or not an intention is carried out in the face of obstacles *depends not on the intensity of the act of intending, but rather on the broader goals of will, or natural needs, on which the intention rests*. The study of forgetting has also shown that calm, affect-free acts of intending are usually more effective than those of particularly great or vehement intensity. This may be related to the fact that affective and vehement actions—in general, but with certain exceptions—have less achievement-effect than calm actions.

Under what conditions does an act of intending, and particularly an intensive act of intending, occur? An instructive though exaggerated adage says: "What one intends, one forgets." This means that only *when there is no natural need for an action*, or when there is a natural counter-need, is *it necessary to form an intention*. If the act of intending is not based on a genuine-need, it promises little success. It is precisely when there is no genuine-need that we attempt to substitute for it an "intensive act of intending." (To put it paradoxically: Either there is no need to make a certain intention, or it promises little success.)

Wilde (*Dorian Gray*) is acute when he says, "Good intentions are useless attempts to meddle with the laws of nature. Their origin is mere vanity and their results are absolute zero."

II. The Theory of Intentional Action

1. The Effect of the Act of Intending Is a Quasi-Need

The experiments on forgetting of intentions, and even more those on resumption of interrupted activities, prove that the intention is a force. To take effect, this force does not require the actual occurrence of the occasion anticipated in the act of intending in order to elicit the intentional action as its consequence.

There exists rather an internal pressure of a definite direction, an internal tension-state which presses to carry out the intention even if no predetermined occasion invites the action.

The clearest subjective experience of this state of affairs occurs in the resumption of interrupted tasks, when after completion of the interrupting activity a general pressure—that "there is still something I want to do"—appears. In this case, which is frequent in everyday life also, the content of the intention is not yet clear and only the internal tension as such is perceived. Only later does the goal, that is, what one wants to do, become conscious. Indeed, it happens in everyday life that, in spite of searching for it, one cannot remember what he really wanted. (Such indeterminate tensions occur sometimes even where a predetermined occasion by itself reminds one of the intentional activity.) (Compare Ach, 1910.) But in such cases, consummatory activities often occur under internal pressure without the stimulation of specific occasions.

It could be argued that in the experiments mentioned, the fact that there is nothing definite to do at the completion of the interrupting activity serves as the "proper occasion." . . . Indeed, the "completion of a certain activity" may actually acquire the genuine valence of an occasion, for instance, if the intention is to do a certain thing at the completion of an activity. As a rule, however, "not having anything to do" cannot be considered as an occasion with a definite valence, as is the mailbox for mailing a letter. The effect of momentarily "not being particularly occupied" is only that certain inner tensions pressing toward the motor region penetrate more easily the motor region when it is not otherwise heavily taxed. (The conditions are naturally quite different in the case of real boredom.)

The state of tension arising from the act of intending need not be consciously expressed in conscious tension-experiences. As a rule, it exists over long periods of time, only in latent form, as during the interrupting activity, but that does not make it less real. These facts are related to the psychic function of the motor-region and of consciousness, as well as to the structuring of the psyche into relatively segregated complexes. These latent tension-states may break through momentarily into consciousness even during the interrupting activity, as an experience of pressure toward the original activity.

(A) Missing and Unforeseen Occasions

The recognition that the driving-force of intentional activity is not an associative coupling but an internal tension-state—that is, a directed internal pressure—makes it possible to explain the various phenomena we described.

Now it becomes understandable why, when the occasion fails to occur, another is sought out, and why, when one keeps waiting too long for the occasion and the internal pressure is too great, premature action results.

We also understand now why the intention is responsive not only to the intended occasions, but also to entirely different objects and events (mailbox and friend). The internal state of tension breaks through as soon as there is a possibility to eliminate or at least decrease the tension, that is to say, as soon as a situation appears to permit activity in the direction of the goal.

(B) The Cessation of Psychological Forces Following Consummation or Substitute Consummation

As soon as the presence of internal tension, and not an associative coupling, is considered the decisive cause of the consummatory action, the disappearance of the valence of the intended occasion after consummation can also be deduced. In the extreme case, the effect of the intended occasion fails to occur altogether, because the internal tension is discharged in a "substitute consummation."

Clearly, the forces arising from acts of intending are closely related in type to those psychological forces which we usually called *needs*, and these in turn derive either from drives or from central goals of will, such as the will to pursue a vocation.

(C) Parallel Phenomena in Genuine- and in Quasi-Needs

(1) Genuine-needs and natural valences. Drive-needs, such as hunger, are internal tensions, directed pressures, driving toward so-called "satisfying actions." For drive-needs, also, certain "occasions" play an essential role; they too respond to certain alluring objects and events which have a *valence* for them.

Our psychologically given environment does not consist of a sum of optical, acoustic, and tactile sensations, but of objects and events. (For a detailed discussion of this issue, see Katz, 1911). The recognition of this has slowly established itself in psychology. It is traditional to attribute certain feeling-tones to these objects and events; they are pleasant or unpleasant, pleasurable or painful.

Furthermore, it is common knowledge that the objects and events of the environment are not neutral toward us in our role of *acting* beings. Not only does their very nature facilitate or obstruct our actions to varying degrees, but we also encounter many objects and events which face us with a will of their own: *They challenge us to certain activities.* Good weather and certain landscapes entice one to a walk. A stairway stimulates the two-year-old child to climb it and jump down; doors, to open and to close them; small crumbs, to pick them up; dogs, to pet them; building stones, to play with them; the chocolate and a piece of cake want to be eaten. This is not the place to discuss in detail the nature, kinds, and functions of these "objects and events" which have valences. We will refer here only to a few of their basic characteristics, and will avoid discussing the role which experience and habit play in establishing them.

The intensity with which objects and events challenge us varies greatly. The shadings of such challenge range from "irresistible temptations," to which child as well as adult yields unthinkingly and against which self-control helps little if at all, to those which have the character of "command," to the weaker "urgings" and "attractions," which can be easily resisted and become noticeable only when the person tries to find something to do. The term "valence" comprises all these shadings.

We distinguish positive and negative valences, according to whether we are attracted by something (a good concert, an interesting man, a beautiful woman) or repelled by it (a discomfort, a danger). This dichotomy is correct in that the valences of the first group all press us to *approach* the objects and events in question, while those of the second press us to *retreat* from them. It would be, however, a mistake to assume that this is the crucial feature of valences. It is much more characteristic for valences that they press toward definite *actions*, the range of which may be narrow or broad, and that these actions may be a great variety even within the group of positive valences. The book entices reading, the cake to eating, the ocean to swimming, the mirror to looking, confused situation to decisive action.

The valence of a structure is usually not constant, but depends greatly—in its kind and degree—on the internal and external situation of the person. The study of the vicissitudes of valences reveals their nature.

The meaning of a structure having a valence is transparent enough in certain basic cases: In these, the objects which have the valence are *direct means of need satisfaction* (the cake, the concert if one goes to listen and not to be seen, etc.). In such cases we speak of *independent valences.*

There are, besides, objects and events which have valences due to their relation to the direct means of need satisfaction in the given situation; for instance, they can facilitate satisfaction. They are means to an end and have only a momentary significance. Other such *derivative valences* arise from a space or time extension of structures which have original valences. The house, the street, and even the city in which the beloved lives, may each acquire a valence. The transition between these two kinds of valences is naturally fluid, and the concept of independent valence is also relative.

A valence may undergo great changes, depending on the action-whole in which the object or event in question appears: The mirror which has just enticed the subject to take a look at her hair-do and dress becomes a neutral "instrument" as soon as she is given a task involving the use of the mirror. Similar changes of a most extreme sort occur with the objects of a landscape in war at the time of battle (Giese, 1925; Lewin, 1917). Besides their dependence upon the momentarily prevailing action, valences have other vicissitudes: Greatly tempting delicacies become uninteresting as soon as one is *satiated*. In fact, *oversatiation* typically changes the sign of the valence: What was attractive prior to it, repels after it. Oversatiation may even lead to a lasting fixation of a negative valence. (Now and then, it happens that for years one will avoid a favorite dish after once getting sick on it.) In general, however, a rhythmic rise and fall, following the periodicity of the corresponding needs, is typical for valences.

The vicissitudes of certain valences may be followed over long periods of time, for instance, those which accompany the development of the individual from infancy, through childhood and adolescence into adulthood, and old age. Their course corresponds to the changes in needs and interests, and plays a fundamental role in development. The development of the achievement–abilities of an individual does not depend only on the potentialities of "endowment." For instance, the development of speech or of intellectual achievement, is basically influenced by the degree and direction of such "inclinations," which are the motors of psychic processes.

These vicissitudes, the exploration of which has only begun (C. Buehler, 1922; Lau, 1924; Spranger, 1924) seem to be similar to the vicissitudes of valences which accompany changes in the general goals of will that govern the individual. The will to follow an occupation is an example of such general goals of will. Once a choice of an occupation is made, certain things which have until then been neutral obtain a positive or a negative valence (Lau, 1924). Much that at first would seem "natural" inborn inclination or disinclination—preference for a certain kind of work, tendency to cleanliness and meticulousness—can be derived from the occupational goal of the individual.

A man's world changes fundamentally when his fundamental goals of will change. This holds not only for the great upheavals which follow a decision to take one's life or change one's occupation, but even for those temporary suspensions of the usual goals of will which occur when one is on vacation. Familiar things may then suddenly acquire a new look; those which went unnoticed a hundred times become interesting, and important occupational matters turn indifferent.

This change of strong positive or negative valences to complete indifference is often astonishing even to the person concerned, and has frequently been described in poetry, particularly in relation to the erotic sphere. Such change of valence is often the first indication of a change in one's internal situation and may even precede awareness of change in inclinations. The occurrence or absence of a change of valence is frequently the actual criterion of whether a decision—for instance, "to begin a new life in some way"—is apparent or *real*; that is, whether the decision occurred only in subjective experience or is a psychologically effective dynamic change. Conversions are particularly far-reaching and abrupt changes of this sort: "persecute what you have worshipped and worship what you have persecuted."

The structure of the relation between valences and these general goals of will is thus basically the same as that between valences and the goals of single activities.

These brief considerations show that the natural valences are most closely related to certain inclinations and needs, some of which derive from the so-called "drives," and others from central goals of will of varying degrees of generality. Indeed, since a change of valence corresponds to every change of need, the proposition that *"such-and-such a need exists"* is to a certain extent equivalent to the proposition that *"such-and-such a region of structures has a valence for such-and-such actions."*

(2) The effects of quasi-needs and genuine-needs. The relation of genuine needs and natural valences, however, is not such that to each need there always belongs a definite structure with a corresponding valence. It is typical for new needs which have not yet been frequently satisfied, and thus particularly for needs previous to their first real gratification, that they have a broad range of possible valences. For instance, for the purpose of systematic study, the prototype of sexual and erotic inclinations is not that stage at which a firm fixation on one or more definite people and a specialization of satisfying action has already taken place, but one at which the inclination is diffuse and the region of valences is broad and indefinite (von Allesch, 1921). Yet development does not always proceed from a diffuse to a differentiated and specialized stage. There are processes in which an inclination, at first specific, diversifies. For instance, a child of a year and a half likes at first to "open and close" only a certain clock-case, and only gradually takes to opening and closing of doors, closets and chests of drawers. A diffuse phase followed by gradual specialization and consolidation may also be the course of needs related to general goals of will—for instance, occupational will. (Yet a highly specialized goal may be present from the beginning.)

In the case of such diffuse drive- or central-needs, the *situation* to a great extent determines the valence which will have an effect and the actions which will be carried out. The need to "get ahead in an occupation" implies little or nothing, for or against any specific kind of consummatory action. It remains quite indefinite whether one should write or telephone, do activity A or a quite different activity B. Even jobs considered typically "beneath the dignity of one's occupation" and therefore usually avoided (for instance, letter-filing by a bookkeeper), may be considered an honor and done with delight in certain situations (for instance, when a bookkeeper is entrusted to file particularly confidential documents). Thus activities of identical achievement may appear now highly desirable and now taboo, depending on their occupational significance. Even for quite specialized and fixated needs there usually exists a certain, and mostly not even a narrow, range of valences, the actual evocation of which depends only on the concrete situation.

The situation is quite similar to that which obtains for intentions, where occasion and consummatory action are often quite indeterminate. There, too, exists a certain latitude of valences eliciting the intention effects, even when the act of intending has established definite occasions.

This parallel between the effect of a genuine-need and the effect of an intention extends also to many other essential points which will be discussed below. Because of this parallel, whenever an intention is extant, we will assume that a quasi-need is present.

Both for genuine-needs and intention-effects there exist certain objects or events of valence, which when encountered arouse a tendency to definite actions. In neither case is valence and action so related that an associative coupling between the two is the cause of the action. The action-energy of drive-needs also originates essentially in certain *internal tensions*, the significance of external drive-stimuli notwithstanding. Where occasions and means of drive satisfaction do not appear from the outside they are *actively sought out*, just as in the case of intention effects.

As an argument against this conception, the so-called *habits* could be marshaled. In fact, popular psychology, and until recently scientific psychology also, considered habits as couplings between certain occasions and actions, and these couplings as the energy source of habit actions. The examples marshaled to support the theory were of this sort: We are not always hungry when we take our meal at set hours. According to recent experimental results (Lewin, 1922; Sigmar, 1925), such cases can be understood if we assume that the action in question is embedded, as a dependent part, in a broader action-complex—for instance, in the "daily routine" or "style of life"—so that its energy, the motor of the action, derives from other need sources. It seems to me that even in such habit actions and special fixations, the structure of the driving forces is still rather clearly discernible: *The significance of external drive-stimuli notwithstanding, needs imply states of tension which press toward satisfaction.* Satisfaction eliminates the tension-state and may, therefore, be described as psychological "satiation."

The valences which a region of structures and events has before satisfaction (in the "hunger state") are eliminated by satiation. The region becomes neutral. Needs and intentions are analogous in this respect also; we have described the sudden neutralization of the valence of a structure by the "consummation" of the intentional action. This basic phenomenon of the intention-effect, which a theory of associative couplings can hardly explain without complex auxiliary hypotheses, becomes understandable if the intention-effect is considered to be the arising of a quasi-need and *the consummation of the intention to be its "satisfaction," that is, satiation.*

In fact, *satisfaction experiences occur very frequently at the end of consummatory actions, even in experimental investigations.*

Over and above the phenomenal relationship of consummation and satisfaction experience, the thesis concerning quasi-needs gains support by affording a dynamic explanation and derivation of the characteristics of intention-effects.

If a latent tension-state pressing toward equilibration (satisfaction) plays the primary role here, then the intention effect should be elicited *by every objectively relevant occasion* and not only by that implied in the act of intending—provided that these occasions exist psychologically and are not paralyzed by counter-forces. If the occasion fails to occur, it is—as a result of the latent state of tension—*actively sought out*, just as in the case of drive-needs and other genuine-needs. If the tension-state is too intensive, then here also inexpedient actions akin to "premature start" come about.

Genuine-needs and quasi-needs show a great deal of agreement also in their special relations to valences. (Since the following data derive only from observations of everyday life, they are in urgent need of experimental exploration, for which they should be considered only as points of departure.)

Increase in the intensity of the genuine-need usually broadens the region of valences also. In states of extraordinary hunger, objects which are otherwise unpalatable and disgust-arousing may attain positive valence. In extremes, earth is eaten and cannibalism becomes frequent. (In such cases, people partly obey the need with inner disgust, but partly the phenomenal valences are changed.) Even in less extreme instances, increasing need-intensity results in a noticeable spread of valences (Katz & Toll, 1923). The same holds for the so-called intellectual needs. . . . There are similar observations concerning quasi-needs also. The region of occasions other than the intended one to which the intention also responds, usually spreads as the tension resulting from the intention increases. For dispatching an important letter urgently, the visit of a friend or any other occasion is more likely to be utilized than when the letter is an indifferent one. (Later on, I shall discuss exceptions related to the nature of vehement activity.)

(3) Fixation in genuine-needs and quasi-needs. Fixation is one of the crucial phenomena pertaining to the relation between valences and genuine-needs. It denotes the occasional narrowness of the region of valences in comparison to the region of objects or events which "per se" would seem relevant.

For instance, a child who has several dolls will play always with one and the same doll, or give it disproportionate preference. The child will maintain that the doll "is always well behaved," or "she never lies." Even when the child is out of sorts and pays little attention to the other dolls, she will still love this one. . . .

The fixation on *certain* valences and on *certain* modes of satisfaction plays a great and significant role in psychic life. It is known how extraordinarily intense the fixation of any genuine-need can be, to a human being, or an occupation, or a certain work, and how exclusive a role that fixation may play, and how difficult it often is to resolve.

Such fixations result apparently in an unusually strong valence of the structure in question and have a certain *exclusive function*: Other structures lose their valence, entirely or partly. Similarly with the fixation to certain modifications of the satisfying *activity*.

Something quite analogous may be observed in quasi-needs also. An occasion implied by the act of intending may have a fixating effect, narrowing the range of the objectively relevant occasions to which less specific intentions might have been responsive. This holds for consummatory actions too: For instance, without the specific intention to bring up certain arguments, one would argue in a discussion appropriately to the situation and therefore purposively; but specific fixation of the arguments by a preceding act of intending often results in statements inappropriate to the situation. But, as a rule, fixation does not have an entirely exclusive effect, either for genuine- or for quasi-needs. In spite of the fixation, a certain range of other valences usually persists, particularly if the pressure of the genuine- or quasi-need is strong.

With genuine-needs, the occasion and kind of the *first satisfaction* has a particularly fixating effect (first love). This is also true for those intentions which press toward repetitive action. If several occasions are possible before the first consummation, then later this first occasion will stand out from the others. This holds for the first satisfying consummatory action too[4] and plays therefore a considerable role in the so-called training process. In this, which is by no means a uniform process psychologically, valences and their vicissitudes are of great significance (Blumenfeld, 1925; Lewin, 1922, Part II, p. 124). In learning any activity (for example, turning a lathe), many things lose their natural valences: Large wheels or sudden events which are at first frightening become neutral. In turn, other structures and events, at first unnoticed, obtain definite and clear valences when embedded in the new total context. . . .

In repeating intentional actions, usually certain modes of consummation crystallize. In this crystallization process, frequently called "automatization," the course of activity becomes rigid and lifeless. The quasi-need in early repetitions compares to that in later ones, as a young organism does to an old one. All the potentialities which together provide the conditional-genetic definition of the quasi-need actually exist in the beginning: The need is responsive to a variety of occasions and its form of consummation readily *adapts to the situations*. In later repetitions, however, the *form of consummation* becomes *relatively rigid*: Historical factors limit the range of possible modes of behavior. (In some cases, as mentioned, fixation seems to exist from the beginning on.)

As a rule, a *growing independence* of the need- or quasi-need action accompanies, and may even be the prerequisite of, this ossification. A relatively independent specific organism comes about, which acts without requiring the control of the total personality and whose communication with other needs and quasi-needs is limited.

The experiments on the measurement of will may serve as an example

---

[4]This may be the origin of "latent attitudes" and "activity-readinesses." See Koffka, 1912.

(Ach, 1905; Lewin, 1922). In these experiments, the process—for instance, the occurrence of intended errors (habit-errors)—depends only indirectly on the underlying needs, but directly on the specific form of consummation: A definite "activity-readiness" (Lewin, 1922)—implying a definite form of consummation—and not the presence of a definite quasi-need, decides whether or not a habit-error will occur.

But even in such ossified quasi-needs, the energy-source remains the quasi-need itself, that is, in final analysis, the genuine-need underlying it.

Whether it is the act of intending or the course of the first consummations which *establishes* the valences and consummatory actions, the process establishing them is closely related to that of fixation of genuine-needs. It differs in essential points from *associations* as encountered in learning syllables by rote or in any other "change of the stock of knowledge" (Lewin, 1922; Selz, 1913, 1922).

It makes no difference whether the association is conceived as one between occasion and consummation, or one between the occasion and its valence accrued from the intention. The valence of an object, just like its figural Gestalt (though the former varies more than the latter), is not independent of it as a second psychic structure. The valence of an object is as much a part of its essence as its figural Gestalt. In order to avoid misunderstandings, it would be better to speak not of changes in the valence of the object, but of *different* structures which are only figurally and externally identical. A structure whose valence has changed with the change in situation—for example, the mailbox before and after mailing the letter—is psychologically a different structure. . . .

The following consideration appears at first contrary to our conception. We saw that consummation of the intended action—satiation of the quasi-need—as a rule eliminates the valence, since it leaves no real tension driving toward consummation. Everyday observations, however, seem to indicate that such valences can persist for a while even after consummation. It does happen that though the letter has been mailed, a mailbox subsequently passed again reminds us to mail it.

It is conceivable that this is the inverse of those cases discussed below, in which a *substitute satisfaction* causes the forgetting of the intended action. Here, mailing the letter, while objectively achieving the desired result, did not have the *psychic* effect of satisfaction; at any rate, it did not completely eliminate the tension of the quasi-need. Our concern is not with the external activity as such, but with the elimination of tensions.

The same question arises for valences related to genuine-needs:

When a small child refuses some food, bringing the spoon to his mouth is often enough to make him start eating. The older child displays greater control over the direct valence to which the younger yields as to a drive: He shuts his mouth tight, turns his head, and so on. Yet the same result can be attained by distracting the older child's attention. (Above a certain age, not even distraction avails.)

Two factors are essential to this phenomenon. First, the valence has a *stronger effect* if it is not "attended to." Increased "attention" prevents the direct effect of this "stimulus" (valence). We explain this seemingly paradoxical state of affairs by assuming that the field-forces exert their effect more directly when distraction weakens the controls.

The case of distraction is complicated by the negative valence of the food.

Secondly, the full spoon near the mouth has a valence for the child even if he dislikes the food. Popular psychology would explain this as a "habit," a frequent label, anyway, for fixation effects. Since there is no need present for the food in question, the valence must be that of the spoon or that of the spoon's being brought near the mouth in this situation. It appears that the valence has an effect here, even in the absence of a momentary need. Similarly, in everyday life, we often do with reluctance things which on other occasions we have done with pleasure.

It is justifiable to ask: Is there some genuine- or quasi-need for the activity in these cases even if the major need is absent? It is possible that here we have tensions which are intermediary forms between genuine- and quasi-needs and are related to those general goals of will which shape our everyday life: arising, dressing, taking meals, going to sleep. This assumption is supported by the observation that such valences will persist as a rule only for a short while in the face of contrary needs, which in the long run will change the "style of life."

Only experimental analysis can answer the question whether these explanations hold for all cases, or whether under certain conditions—as in fixation—valences persist in spite of the satiation of the quasi-need.

Fixations play an important role in psychic life, and our discussion of them in genuine- and quasi-needs is not meant to be a systematic theory. Nor do we assert here that genuine associative couplings have no role in fixation.

We advance only a few fundamental propositions: The restriction of a valence to a definite occasion and the fixation of a specific mode of consummation are extremes in a continuum in which broad regions of events and structures have valences. The theory of quasi-needs, in contrast to the customary conception, considers that the pure and fundamental form of intention processes is found in those cases which are free of specializing fixations limiting the effect of other objectively feasible occasions. The energy sources of these processes are the genuine- or quasi-needs underlying them, and the fixated valences are also mainly related to these. The fixation is not itself the source of the action, but only the determiner of its form or occasion. Even if the relation of occasion and consummatory action were actually an associative coupling, this relation would not be analogous to the association of syllables or other kinds of knowledge, but rather to the fixation of a valence to a definite occasion. . . .

(4) Substitute consummation. If a quasi-need and not an associative coupling between occasion and consummation is the source of intentional action, then some basic problems of *substitute consummation* are also easily clarified.

Genuine-needs too have substitute satisfactions. Genuine-needs and quasi-needs both have a whole variety of substitute consummations. The differences between these varieties are in part fundamental, but it is not easy to define them conceptually because of the transitions between them, and the mixed types among them. We will use the term *substitute consummation* for all of them, and will refer only to a few main variants, without discussing the important questions they raise.

(a) Consummation appropriate to the situation. This is objectively equivalent to the intended consummation and is adapted to the situation. Example: Instead of mailing the letter as originally intended, we ask a friend to take care of it. This is not really a substitute consummation; the course of the consummatory action alone is different from that which was anticipated. We know that this is actually the common form of intentional acts, since genuine- as well as quasi-needs usually leave the mode of consummation wide open. The theory of quasi-needs (in contrast to that of associative couplings) has no difficulties with this kind of substitute consummation, in which the goal of the original need is actually reached. The consummatory action eliminates the tension (satiates the quasi-need) and causes the valences to disappear. This holds, we repeat, for genuine needs also.

(b) "Pars pro toto" consummation. Example: Instead of buying an object, we go through the street where we can buy it; instead of actually carrying out an intention, we record it in a notebook. The consummatory action goes "in the direction of" the original goal, but apparently halts somewhere along the line. Yet the typical dynamic effects of incomplete consummation do not appear and the need-tensions are rather well equilibrated, though the consummation proper did not take place and may, for instance, have been forgotten. Specific satisfaction experiences following partial consummation seem to contribute to the failure of the consummation proper to occur. . . .

(c) Unreal consummation, apparent consummation, shadow consummation, and the closely related surrogate consummation. Example (from Dembo, 1931): Failing to throw a ring over a certain bottle, one throws over another more easily reached, or over any near-by hook. There is no action toward the real goal here. The goal itself is not brought nearer, but the consummatory action resembles somehow that of the genuine consummation. Usually a certain momentary satisfaction results, which however soon yields to the original need. It is relatively easy to produce such cases experimentally—for instance, as "avoidance actions" in difficult tasks.

How can need-tensions press to actions which are not even in the direction of eliminating the need? This important question will not be discussed here in detail. The assumption that we have here a tendency "just to do something" (as in affective restless-activity) would be an insufficient explanation. Various assumptions are possible, such as "spread" of the original need to actions of an identical type, or actual satisfaction of the original need by the substitute action (based on the identity of the consummatory action). In the latter case, the occasional perseverance of the need would be explained as its revival due to recurring stimulation (valence). (This does not exhaust the possible theories: For example, there is a clear relation here to the easily misunderstood Freudian "symbol" concept).

Surrogate satisfactions occur even with drive-needs or central goals of will when the satisfying-action proper encounters obstacles: We are "satisfied with less" and reduce our aspirations. There exist all degrees of such surrogates, from satisfactions which are not quite complete to those which are mere sham or shadow. Someone who likes to give commands but has no authority will often want to "have his say" at least or even just "be in on it." The youngster who cannot signal the train will shout "Ready, go" after the station-master. A child who would like to escape from an orphanage has instead a burning desire for a suitcase. A student who cannot afford to buy a piano collects piano catalogs instead.

In cases like the last, the action may attain independence, giving rise to "substitute needs." (The concept of sublimation is relevant to this point.)

(d) Hidden apparent consummations. The second bottle mentioned in (c) may be replaced by a teddy-bear or something similar, and the type of action itself may "change" until it is hardly recognizable. This may occur when the situation demands that the substitute consummation be concealed, for instance, when it is embarrassing.

Besides the intensity of the tension underlying the need in question, *the general level of satisfaction or frustration of the subject* is also crucial in evoking substitute consummations. The experiments on forgetting already mentioned have demonstrated this. The signature is more readily forgotten when the subject is particularly satisfied with his other achievements. . . .

(D) The Real Relations Between Quasi-Needs and Genuine-Needs

(1) Quasi-needs and counter-needs. To consider the intention-effect, a quasi-need amounts to more than a formal analogue to genuine-needs: *It makes a real relationship between intention-effect and genuine-need demonstrable.*

The various natural needs may conflict with each other: Their tension-systems are not completely isolated. In part, they are subordinate factors of a general tension-state, and in part, there is some real communication between them, corresponding to the connections of the spheres and complexes in question within the psyche as a whole. (This has often been disregarded in the treatment of drives.)

Similar considerations hold for the real relations of quasi-needs to each other and to genuine-needs. This explains the ready "forgetting of intentions" when pitted against a strong genuine *counter-need*.

The relation and the clashing of quasi-needs and genuine-needs lead us to the problem of *freedom of intentions*. The extraordinary liberty which man has to intend any, even nonsensical actions—that is, his freedom to create in himself quasi-needs—is amazing. This is characteristic of civilized man. Children, and probably also preliterates, have it to an incomparably lesser degree. It is likely that this freedom distinguishes man from kindred animals more than does his higher intelligence. (This distinction is obviously related to the problem of "control.")

Yet, one cannot arbitrarily intend "just anything" if the criterion of intending is the formation of an actual quasi-need. Without a real need one cannot resolve to kill oneself or an acquaintance, or even to do something serious against one's true interests. Not even under the pressure of hypnosis are such intentions carried out. These examples make the real relations between quasi-needs and genuine-needs particularly clear.

In children, the range of the apparent arbitrariness of intentions is even narrower. Often they cannot endow even relatively neutral objects or events with positive valence by means of quasi-need. The actions they want to intend must arise in part at least from natural valences. (These issues play a great role in the education of the small child.)

(2) Quasi-needs and genuine-needs of identical direction. The real relation between quasi-needs and genuine-needs explains the unanimous result, at first paradoxical of various experimental investigations, *that the intensity of the act of intending does not decide the effectiveness of the intention.*

The fact that particularly intensive acts of intending are often less effective than weaker ones is, as said before, in part due to the general ineffectiveness of *vehement* as compared to controlled activity. Here, the act of intending itself is considered as an action.

More important is the following consideration. The tensions and valences to which the act of intending gives rise are not primary. They derive from some genuine-needs, which in turn arise from drives or general goals of will. After a quasi-need arises from a genuine-need, it still remains *in communication with the complex of tensions implicit in the genuine-need.* Even if the intentions to drop a letter in the mailbox, to visit an acquaintance, yes, even to learn a series of nonsense syllables as an experimental subject, are relatively closed and segregated activities, the forces underlying them are not isolated, but arise from general needs, such as the will to do one's occupational work, to get ahead in one's studies, or to help a friend. The effectiveness of the intention does not depend on the intensity of the act of intending but, other factors being equal, rather on the *intensity* (vital nature) and *depth* of the genuine-need, in which the quasi-need is embedded.

The *genuine-needs* in question are those which give rise to the intention, that is, those which lead one to decide for the action. In the intention to mail a letter, the decisive need is to inform somebody, and this in turn arises from a more general goal of will.

In the course of the consummatory action, however, tensions and forces become frequently manifest which had little or no role in forming the intention. Once an intention is set up or an action is initiated, often the "whole person" becomes immediately engaged in it; thus communication is established with tensions related to "self-esteem" and "fear of insufficiency." There are great individual differences in the ease with which such auxiliary forces connect with intentional actions, and become at times their sole driving force: For instance, to persist as far as possible with a decision once made, is the corollary of a certain life-ideal. The *situation* too has a significant influence in determining the role of these auxiliary forces. For instance, Mrs. Birenbaum's finding, that the signature is less easily forgotten in *mass experiments* than in individual ones, probably to be explained as the effect of such forces.

The communication with various genuine-needs may be extant from the beginning on, as in the case of the mass experiments. Frequently, however, it is not yet present at the act of intending, and arises only subsequently. This relation of needs is not merely theoretical, like that which obtains between different yet conceptually comparable types of needs. It is a *real communication* between concrete tension-systems. One can establish only from case to case, but not in general, when communication between systems is extant or absent. Such communication of systems comes about at a definite time, by a real process, which may progress slowly or break through suddenly.

Whether or not, besides these genuine-needs, there is an individually variable *reservoir of active energy*, used by intentional action not based on genuine-needs, is an open question awaiting experimental exploration. Some observations on encephalitics (their quick transition to micrography, their "getting stuck" after a brief spurt) are conducive to such explanation.

The idea that the effectiveness of intentions depends not on their intensity, but rather on the depths of the underlying genuine-need, is in agreement with Lindworsky's (1919, p. 142) repeatedly quoted studies. He too rejects the idea that the repetition of an act necessarily strengthens its driving force. To him, the decisive factor is the relation of the intention to certain values of the individual. . . .

An individual's valuation of an object or event undoubtedly exerts crucial influence on his motivation processes and total behavior. But we will have to keep in mind that it is not an objective scale of values which is relevant to our problem, but rather the subjective momentary valuations like those which a child has for a pet dog or a piece of chocolate. These valuations always vary with the changing situation and with the person's "degree of satiation" at the moment. Two facts, however, must be stressed: a) The value of an object is not simply identical with its valence. (A sum of gold somewhere may represent a great value for one person without tempting him to steal it, while for another person it may have a strong valence prompting to steal.) Naturally, valuations and valences can be related; at times, however, they are independent. b) Not values, *but definite, real psychic tensions, psychic systems, are energy-sources of processes*. These energy systems are the *dynamic* facts which determine the course of processes. . . .

The experimental subject's "acceptance of an instruction" implies dynamically an intention which is hardly distinguishable phenomenally from mere understanding. Often the mere "thought," that "this could be done in such a way" or "it would be nice if this would happen," fulfills the function of an intention.

Dostoevski (1931) describes an extreme case of this kind in which, though there is no act of intending and a decision is impossible, suddenly the *dynamically real* psychic factors lie exactly as they would subsequent to a decision: "He felt it distinctly and suddenly, he knew it with full clarity, that he would flee, yes that he really would flee, but he knew also that he was now completely unable to answer the question whether he should flee *before* or *after* [murdering] Shatoff. And he felt that he would surely not flee '*before* Shatoff,' but rather absolutely only '*after* Shatoff,' and that it was so decided, signed and sealed." . . .

In other cases, which are—at least phenotypically—very similar, no such effect occurs. It seems to make a great deal of difference whether a need remains at the stage of mere *wish* or crystallizes into a definite quasi-need. The crucial difference seems to be that crystallization of a quasi-need creates, in principle, an avenue to the motor-region which did not exist before. But not even here is the clear experience of "I really want it" crucial, but rather whether or not a real avenue to the motor-region is created.

(3) The dynamic independence (segregation) of quasi-needs. The degree to which other needs influence a quasi-need in the course of the consummatory action varies greatly.

A subject is instructed to touch two copper cords with two fingers of one hand and to press with the other a lever which closes the circuit. The subject suffers a strong electric shock. There are subjects who, having once decided to do this task, give one a particularly "factual" impression. The course of action becomes very direct (some observers say it becomes "soldierly"). The subjects' introspections corroborate these observations. For example, one subject's experience was that she acted "as in a dream," and had strikingly little more to report.

Other subjects' behavior follows a much less direct course. The internal vacillation and contradictory tensions preceding the decision continue even *after* the decision to accept the instructions. Here the decision does not set a sharp dividing line after the preceding processes, as in the subjects of the "factual" type. Paradoxically, however, it is not the subjects of the "factual" type who have little anxiety about the electrical shock; their fear of pain is considerably greater than that of the more "subjective" type.

The difference illustrated by this example always plays an important role in the consummation of intentions, and is related to general and fundamental problems of psychic structure which can be merely touched upon here. The psyche of an individual is not a homogeneous unity in which every structure and event is equally related to every other; nor does the mutual influence of these psychic structures and processes depend solely on their intensity, power, or significance. There are psychic regions and complexes which are most closely related to each other, while they are segregated in various degrees from other psychic complexes. The extent to which a psychic event or force influences other psychic structures depends on whether they are embedded in the same or in different complexes.

The independence and segregation of a complex varies from case to case. An example from the motor sphere: A beginner in moving-picture photography stops involuntarily on any sudden and unexpected happening in the field of the picture, and is influenced even by events outside of it, such as every movement of his own head and other hand, all of which prevent his turning the handle of his machine evenly. The experienced operator is undisturbed by all these influences. He has segregated the movement of his arm, the procedure of turning the handle, from his other hand movements and impressions, and has developed it into a *relatively independent action organism. . . .*

Such cases are usually described as "mechanical" action. In the present context, however, it is not the *reflex character* or *stereotypy* of the action which is essential. Even in activities of irregular course, for instance, in catching irregularly thrown balls, or in turning a handle the friction of which is changing, a correction may "quite mechanically" take place by changes in the catching movement or in muscle tension. The mechanism often works like a real organism in which "perceptual basis" and "motor sphere" are turned together. (Naturally, as with any other organism under given conditions, a mechanism too may change from a natural flexibility to rigid automatism.)

The crucial fact here is that an *independent "action-organism"* came about, not that it is mechanical. With a beginner, the turning of the handle is a subordinate part of the motor-region as a whole (which is tuned to the perception-basis as a whole); with the experienced moving-picture photographer, the turning of the handle is an independent partial motor-region, which is segregated from the rest of the motor-region and tuned together with a previously subordinate part of the perception-basis into an independent action-organism. The kind and intensity of Gestalt-ties, of system-relations, undergoes a dynamic change: Old bonds are dissolved and a new, relatively closed structure is formed.

The previous example of the decision-effect implies an analogous process. In the subject to whom the task was especially painful, and whose consummatory activity was nevertheless particularly factual and direct, the tensions of the quasi-need arising from the act of decision are far more strongly *segregated from the rest of the ego* than in the other subjects. The boundary created between this quasi-need and the other psychic complexes has a double effect. It renders the consummatory action more independent from the other psychic tensions (therefore its directness), and it also affords the individual greater protection against the painfulness of the process (therefore, its dream-character). Thus it becomes understandable that the objectification and isolation of this specific psychic complex occurred precisely in those subjects who were particularly afraid of the pain.

In war, in the course of battle, there often is opportunity to make such observations on the so-called "plucky" soldier.

The degree of independence of the quasi-need from other need tensions thus shows great situational and individual variability.

(E) Remembering Finished and Unfinished Activities

The effects of tension-states may be observed not only in the intentional actions to which they give rise, but also indirectly in facts of memory-psychology. We may ask, for instance, which is remembered better—an intentional action that is completed, or one that is not completed. At first one would assume that the completed ones will be remembered better, because the subject was longer at them.

The experiment (Zeigarnik, 1927) shows something quite different. The subject is given twenty tasks to do in an experimental hour. The experimenter interrupts part of these before their completion. Shortly after the subject has done the last of the tasks, he is tested to see which of them he remembers.

The results show that *the interrupted tasks are remembered, on an average 50 percent better than the completed ones*. There are characteristic differences for various kinds of activities (end-activity versus continuous activity, interesting activity versus indifferent activity), and for various types of subjects. In the present context we must remain quite general, and state only that the *tension-state* which persists after the interruption of the intentional action expresses itself not only in a tendency to resume the action, but also memory.

These tensions do not always, or for all subjects, cause better remembering; they may also result in *repression phenomena*. However, particularly in subjects of a certain childish type, these tensions favor remembering.

2. The Conditions of Intention-Formation; Intentional Action, "Will Action" (Controlled Action), and "Drive-" (Field-) Action

If we make a gross estimate of the frequency of intentions in everyday life, considering at first only those intentions which are attended by an experience of a specific act of intending, we find to our surprise that *acts of intending are not very frequent*. True, the day often begins with an act of intending. Usually about 50 percent of students state that their rising that morning was preceded by the specific intention to get up. But throughout the rest of the day, while dressing, breakfasting, going to work, acts of intending are rare.

This scarcity of intending is not explained alone by the assumption that habits or generalized intentions determine the daily routine. Children at play in new situations do not give the impression of frequent acts of intending, not even when they play roughly or fight. Not even the changes which occur when something new attracts them, or when they want something the other child has are mediated by acts of intending; instead we observe immediate responses, usually described as "drive-like" or "involuntary." *In cases where genuine-needs are directly in play, it is typical that no acts of intending preceded the action.* (Under such conditions, in terms of the theory of quasi-needs, an act of intending would make no sense.)

But not all actions which are not preceded by an act of intending are drive-like. In a conversation, for instance, the answers and the exchanges in general are rarely preceded by specific acts of intending, which occur mainly when one is about to lie or to conceal something. Yet we must realize that such talk—questions and answers without preceding acts of intending—is not all drive-like, but mostly of a volitional character. There are many other everyday actions—for instance, occupational—which, though not preceded by specific acts of intending, are neither automatized nor uncontrolled and drive-like. These and other facts, a discussion of which would lead us too far afield, contradict the view that intentional action is the prototype of will action. To establish the action-type to which a psychological event belongs, we will have to regard the character of its course, rather than whether it has been preceded by another act.

Accordingly, the following cases are typically not "drive-actions" but "will-actions": When one does not shun menacing danger or pain, but faces or even goes forth to meet it; when one takes an insult calmly; when one is cool and unfriendly toward a friendly person. This type of action, on which our attention now centers, is *controlled action* (Klages, 1932).

If we disregard the *automatized* and—in the strict sense of the term —*reflex-like* actions, the use of the term "drive" proves equivocal. By *drive-action*, we mean first of all an "involuntary action, directed by forces *not under the control* of the individual."

Such action is not always an instant effect of a stimulus-constellation and may be preceded by delay, yet sudden response to a stimulus-constellation is indeed often the sign of an uncontrolled reaction. Thus the second meaning of the concepts "drive-like, involuntary, impulsive" is that the action they qualify is the *opposite of those preceded by a specific act of intending.*

It must be stressed that genuine intentional action, preceded by a specific act of intending, is not always of that controlled character which would be the opposite of drive-action in the first sense. Naturally, an intentional action may take the form of controlled action. When a child decides to go past a dog of which he is afraid, the walking past is occasionally a controlled action; then the child passes the dog with a controlled and calm, though cautious, bearing. *The intentional action is, however, often not a controlled action,* or may show only little control. For instance, in the example given, the intention is often carried out in the form of entirely uncontrolled running past the dog.

In this case, the course of events is as though the intention were a force simply added to the others of the situation (the psychological field), and as though the action ensued in accordance with the force-distribution so created in an altogether drive-like, uncontrolled fashion.

Such uncontrolled or little controlled consummatory action is frequent in intentional actions, and is—in some respects—more characteristic of them than is controlled consummation. The common, simple reaction experiment—certainly a genuine intentional action, based solely on the preceding intention of the subject—is usually, to judge by the consummation and the events following the signal, the pure type of an uncontrolled activity. (Only failures tend to change it into controlled action.) We find it particularly in successful intentions that the action following the appearance of the occasion (dropping the letter into the mailbox) is involuntary, that is, closer to uncontrolled than to controlled actions. Like the term "drive action," its opposite term "voluntary action" has two meanings. It may refer to intentional as well as to controlled action. Thus it will be desirable, for the sake of conceptual clarity, to avoid using the terms "will" and "drive" wherever there is the slightest chance for misunderstanding. Instead of these terms one might use: (a) *controlled action*, and its counterpart "uncontrolled" or "field action," as I prefer to call it (action directly determined by the field forces);[5] (b) *intentional action*, which does not imply any definite type of consummatory action, but only a preceding act of intending, that is, its origin in a quasi-need.

We can be certain of the following. The character of the consummatory action is not determined by the fact that it originated in an intention. The consummation *may* take the form of controlled action, but it is the relatively uncontrolled forms which are characteristic and theoretically essential, since in many respects the intention-effects become particularly clear in these. Objects and events, to which otherwise the person would have remained indifferent, attain a valence due to the intention, and directly initiate uncontrolled pure field-actions. (The theory of determining tendencies, also, emphasizes particularly these cases.)

Now it is clear the essential achievement of the intention is one of preparation.[6] Due to the act of intending, at some subsequent time a psychological field appears which otherwise would not have existed, or at least not in the same form. *Forming an intention creates conditions which allow us later simply to abandon ourselves to the effects of the field* (letter and mailbox), or permit a field to be so transformed, or so supplied with additional forces, that a controlled action becomes feasible or easier.

Now we can state the conditions under which intentions arise. The intention is not characteristic of will-action in its sense of controlled action. An intention, in the narrower sense, arises only where there is a certain *foresight* (which need not imply a precise picture of the future), and the situation as foreseen does not include those valences which by themselves would bring about the desired actions in the form of pure field-actions. An intention also arises when the foreseen situation by itself would lead to field-actions contrary to the desired action.

A typical example, from experiments Miss Dembo undertook for an-

---

[5]Naturally, controlled activity, too, is subject to the forces of the total field. However, it is characteristic of controlled activity that the whole person does not enter the field; he maintains a certain degree of reserve and perspective and therefore has the activity in hand. In other words, the demarcation of the psychic systems differs here from that in uncontrolled activity: The "ego systems" have either a greater independence, or their dominance is firmer.

[6]This is also G. E. Mueller's (1911, 1913, 1917) view of intentions, though his theory is fundamentally different from that presented here.

other purpose, follows. The subject was forbidden to leave a certain place, yet would like to; she does not dare to, that is, cannot carry out her leaving in the form of a controlled action. Her way out is to form the intention: "I will go as soon as the clock gets into this or that position." (Similar occurrences are frequent in everyday life.) Thus she creates valences for the future, which will then directly press her to leave, and bring about or facilitate the intended action. (It is an interesting question why, when it is impossible to leave immediately, it is possible to form such an intention. We cannot enter this problem here.)

The following cases are also related to the fact that intentions aim at influencing future situations. It does happen that, in fear of certain anticipated events and situations, we "armor ourselves with firm intentions." If the actual situation proves harmless, we then get the feeling of having hammered at an open door. The relation between intention and foresight becomes particularly clear in such cases, where the *knowledge* of the future was erroneous, and the actual situation does not have the counterforces expected. . . .

Concomitant to the intention is usually another process, which is called *decision*. The main functional effect of this process is that it opens or facilitates for the internal tension an access to activity, to motility, either momentarily or in principle (that is, for a future situation). Thus, decision does not create new psychic tensions (if they accompany it, they are not its essence); rather, it creates for an already existing tension a new *access*, in a form previously not extant, *to the* motor-region. The pure phenomenological expression of this dynamic fact of decision is the experience, "I really want it," (Ach, 1905; Michotte & Pruem, 1910), "fiat!" (James, 1892) meaning "this is how I will do it." When in a person there are several simultaneous tension-systems of opposing directions, a decision often amounts to the effecting of some kind of equilibrium among them, or to isolating some of them. (Claparède, 1925; Koffka, 1925). At any rate, the internal situation created is one in which a more or less unitary tension-system controls the action. Occasionally in such cases, an internal vacillation is observed before the decision (the so-called struggle of motives).

In this connection it is customary to speak of choice, the implication of which is that in the interest of clear-cut action it is often necessary to suppress some of the tension-systems competing for the access to the motor region. This is not always completely successful, however; then, in spite of the choice, the tensions originating from the suppressed systems will make themselves mildly noticeable in the action. Thus unpurposeful mixed actions may come about, resulting in an inhibition or weakening of the activity.

Decisions as here functionally defined, like intentions, have no unequivocal indicators in experience. The firmness of a decision and the intensity of the act of decision are not directly related, and even functionally essential decisions may occur without clear-cut decision-experiences.

Intentions in the functional sense (formation of quasi-needs), and decisions in the functional sense (the suppression or equilibration of simultaneous internal tensions in their claims for control of action), appear at times as closely related, and only conceptually separable, functional components of a process; at other times they appear separately in relatively pure forms. The internal decision, the choice of a certain direction, may result in a specific intention for a certain form of consummation. But the intention, the arising quasi-need, usually implies in principle an access of its own to the motor-region, and unless there are internal counter-tensions, requires no specific act of decision for this purpose. . . .

In contrast to the usual procedure, we want to stress that similar concepts will have to be applied to drives and other genuine-needs also. The pressure of needs always leaves open a certain region of concrete consummatory activities and possible occasions (excepting the cases of pronounced fixation), and *only need and situation* (where the latter is not considered as momentary in time) *together determine unequivocally the phenotypical aspect of the concrete process.*

III. Summary

Intentional action is not the prototype of will-action. It occurs in all forms of transition, from controlled action to uncontrolled, drive-like, field-action. . . . All in all, intentional actions belong more to the field-actions than to the controlled actions.

Accordingly, the majority of controlled (will) actions are not preceded by an act of intending. Intentional actions are relatively rare. They are prepared actions, where the act of intending, which is as a rule controlled, prepares an *uncontrolled field-action.*

The effects of intentions are twofold. One of these effects is the *creation* or transformation of certain *future psychic fields*; the other, the creation of immediate or future access to the motor-region for certain psychic tensions. These effects appear frequently together, but at times also separately.

The first of these effects, as a functional factor, may be designated as "intention" in the strict sense, the second as "decision" in the strict sense.

The *decision* equalizes tensions of differing directions which already exist in the total person, or at least changes the internal situation so that the action will be controlled by relatively homogeneous tensions.

Another effect of the intention is that occasions which would have remained neutral without the act of intending acquire valence and issue in certain consummatory actions. In individual cases, the *occasions* as well as the *consummatory actions* may be unequivocally established and limited by the act of intending. But these cases are not the prototype of intention; and even in them, the forces underlying the intentional action cannot be considered associative couplings, established by the act of intending, between the idea of the occasion and the idea of consummation.

The act of intending often leaves the consummatory action, as well as the occasions to which it is to respond, indeterminate. In these cases, and as a rule even where the act of intending implies a definite occasion, the intention may respond to various occasions not foreseen, which have certain objective relations to the intention, or rather to the need underlying it. The same holds for consummatory actions.

Dynamically, the intention is defined as the formation of a quasi-need, of a tension-state, which is very similar to and has real relationships with genuine needs.

(a) To each quasi-need (just as to each genuine-need) there corresponds a certain region of objects and events which have a valence that entices to actions (satisfying actions of the need, which satiate the quasi-need, that is, discharge the tension).

The consummatory actions of a quasi-need vary with the concrete consummatory situation. The quasi-need may press to a single or to repetitive action.

(b) The extent of the region of structures which have a valence depends, among other things, on the strength of the quasi-need. Where this region is unnaturally narrow, the situation is similar to that where genuine-needs are fixated on certain occasions and satisfactions. Fixation may come about by the act of intending or by the (first) consummation, but is not always reinforced by repetition.

(c) The *need-tension* is the primary fact: If sufficiently intensive, and the occasion is delayed, it leads to premature beginning of the consummatory action; when the occasion fails to appear, to actively seeking it out; and when the action is interrupted, to resume it or better retain it in memory.

(d) When the quasi-need is satiated, the valences in general disappear, even in cases of fixation. The valences of the occasion implied by the act of intending usually disappear, even if the consummation occurs in a form or on an occasion not foreseen in the act.

(e) Genuine consummation may be replaced by various forms of substitute consummation. To some extent these have the same effects as consummation proper, and thus may lead to forgetting an intention and failure to resume an interrupted activity.

(f) The quasi-need, created by the act of intending, is not an isolated structure in the whole psyche, but is usually embedded in a *certain* psychic complex or region of the personality. It is in communication with other quasi-needs and genuine-needs derived from certain general goals of will, or drives. The intensity of the intention-effect depends on the intensity and centrality of these needs. The needs to which the quasi-need has real relationships are not necessarily those which have led to the act of intending. The effect of a quasi-need may be inhibited by contrary genuine-needs.

(g) The phenomenal intensity of the act of intending and its other phenomenal characteristics have no decisive significance.

References

Ach, N. (1905). *Ueber die Willenstaetigkeit und das Denken*. Goettingen: Vandenhoeck und Ruprecht.

Ach, N. (1910). *Ueber den Willensakt und das Temperament*. Leipzig: Quelle and Meyer.

Allesch, G. von. (1921). *Bericht ueber die drei ersten Lebensmonate eines Schimpansen*. Sitzungsberichte: Preussische Akademie der Wissenschaften.

Birenbaum, G. (1930). Das Vergessen einer Vornahme. Isolierte seelische Systeme und dynamische Gesamtbereiche. *Psychologische Forschung, 13*, 218–284.

Blumenfeld, W. (1925). Das Suchen von Zahlen im begrenzten ebenen Felde und das Problem der Abstraktion. *Zeitschrift für angewandte Psychologie, 26*, 58–107.

Boumann, L. (1919). Experimentelle Untersuchungen ueber den Willen bei Normalen und Psychopathen. *Psychiatrie Neurologie Bladen, 23*, 237–319.

Buehler, C. (1922). *Das Seelenleben des Jugendlichen*. Jena: Fischer.

Claparède, E. (1925). Does the will express the entire personality? In C. McF. Campbell (Ed.), *Problems of personality* (pp. 37–43). London: Kegan Paul.

Dembo, T. (1931). Der Aerger als dynamisches Problem. *Psychologische Forschung, 15*, 1–144.

Dostoevski, F. (1931). *The possessed*. New York: Dutton.

Giese, F. (1925). *Handbuch psychotechnischer Eignungspruefungen* (2d ed.). Halle, Germany: Marhold.

James, W. (1892). *Psychology*. New York: Holt.

Katz, D. (1911). Die Erscheinungsweisen der Farben und ihre Beeinflussung durch die individuelle Erfahrung. *Zeitschrift für Psychologie*, (Suppl. 7). Leipzig: Barth.

Katz, D., & Toll, A. (1923). Die Messung von Charakter und Begabungsunterschieden bei Tieren. *Zeitschrift für Psychologie, 93*, 287–311.

Klages, L. (1932). *The science of character*. Cambridge, MA: Sci-Art.

Koffka, K. (1912). *Zur Analyse der Vostellungen und ihrer Gesetze*. Leipzig: Quelle & Meyer.

Koffka, K. (1925). Psychologie. In M. Dessoir (Ed.), *Lehrbuch der Philosophie: Die Philosophie in ihren Einzelgebieten* (pp. 497–602). Berlin: Ullstein.

Lau, E. (1924). *Beitraege zur Psychologie der Jugendlichen in Pubertaetszeit* (2d ed.). Langensalza: Belz.

Lewin, K. (1917). Die Psychische Tatigkeit bei der Hemmung von Willensvorgangen und das Grundgesetz der Assoziation. *Zeitschrift fur Psychologie, 77*, 212–247.

Lewin, K. (1922). Das problem der Willensmessung und der Assoziation. *Psychologische Forschung, 1*, 191–302; *2*, 65–140.

Lindworsky, J. (1919). *J. Der Wille*. Leipzig: Barth.

Michotte, A., & Pruem, E. (1910). Étude expérimentale sur le choix volontaire et ses antécédents immédiats. *Archives de Psychologie, 10*, 117–299.

Mueller, G. (1911, 1913, 1917). Zur Analyse der Gadaechtnistaetigkeit und des Vorstellungsverlaufes. *Zeitschrift für Psychologie*, (Suppl. 5, 8, 9).

Ovsiankina, M. (1928). Die Wiederaufnahme unterbrochener handlungen. *Psychologische Forschung, 2*, 302–379.

Selz, O. (1913). *Ueber die gesetze des geordneten denkverlaufs*. Bonn: Cohen.

Selz, O. (1922). *Zur Psychologie des produktiven Denkens: eine experimentelle Untersuchung*. Bonn: Cohen.

Sigmar, J. (1925). Ueber die Hemmungen bei der Realisation eines Willensaktes. *Archiv für Psychologie, 52*, 91–176.

Spranger, E. (1924). *Psychologie des Jugendalters*. Leipzig: Quelle and Meyer.

Zeigarnik, B. (1927). Ueber das Bahalten von erledigten und unerledigten Handlungen. *Psychologische Forschung, 9*, 1–85.

5

"Two Fundamental Types of Life Processes"

1. The General Theses

In a basic discussion, Charlotte Bühler (1928) develops several theses on the meaning of environmental effects and of the mind that appear important primarily because the concept of need becomes the focus of this comparison. Since this presents a question fundamental and critical for research and concept formation, one may elaborate on the substantive problems in the form of a discussion of these theses.

Charlotte Bühler contrasts two types of processes with reference to several experimental findings, to whose disparities she attributes a fundamental significance for the theory of psychological processes.

"The first type we know well from its use: A stimulus occurs and a 'response' ensues. A stimulus occurs, which means that some event in the external world impinges on the system and then causes movement in it" Bühler, 1928, p. 229). This "stimulus–response" process is contrasted to the second type, the "task engagement and completion process" (p. 235). Such tasks may not be viewed as themselves brought about by the stimulus, "an internal resolve remains critical." "Only when the stimulus becomes the motive does the behavior ensue; the stimulus is not the origin at all, if it were not intended as a motive; and this intention must of course come from a source other than the stimulus. *It comes from the subject*" (p. 229, emphasis added). Even internal stimuli are not at issue here, for it is true of them just as it is of external stimuli: "They are in an *objective* structure and induce, by changing it, *secondarily* behavior, namely action. On the other hand, the motivated act is different from the response that is caused by the stimulus, particularly in that its origin evidently lies in a completely different sphere or let us say in a different reality of the individual. For the present we know about it only that it manifests itself in the intention. Hence, we will provisionally say that it is, in contrast with the *objective structure*, the *subjective reference*" (p. 229, emphasis added). Crucial for the second process is therefore that it is a "*process*

From *Zeitschrift für Psychologie*, 1929, *113*, 209–238; translated for this volume by Dr. Anja Spindler.

guided primarily by the mind" (p. 231, emphasis added). It represents "situated acts" in the sense of Brentano, Stumpf and Husserl (p. 231).

Following Karl Bühler, Ch. Bühler draws the far-reaching conclusion that one has to begin with psychological theory that is basically *dualistic* in approach. "A duality of starting points regarding regulation and *an independent status of both principles of regulation* is said to be necessary. The organism is . . . quite certainly not just a stimulus-encountering, but also a goal-pursuing system" (p. 235). This is said to become particularly obvious in the child's pleasure-in-acting.*

As positions opposed to the requisite theoretical approach of basic *duality*, besides Freud's views, Köhler's and my theories are mentioned prominently. The holistic consideration of the individual is said to make our views on this point particularly misguided. Köhler's organism is said to be a machine to an even higher degree than the creature of his predecessors, since "even as a unit and as a whole it is inevitably controlled by the stimulus, exactly like an obedient car, whose complicated mechanism in all its parts is centrally directed from few vantage points" (p. 233). With the former as with the latter, a diversity of the structure between motivation and consummation has been rendered uniform in operation. Neither view posits a working mind however. With reference to my own expositions, Ch. Bühler says: "Herewith the individual is as much as ever 'field', arena, and object of influences, to which he or she responds, the only difference with the previous psychology being that he or she now reacts as a whole and as a unit and not out of separate single impulses. The regulation of the system flows from the stimulus side, not from the side of the person" (p. 232). "Here is a particular instance in which the stimulus is not adequate, but the *second, superior guiding principle* is left out of consideration" (p. 233, emphasis added).

Ch. Bühler emphasizes that there is no inevitable and unequivocal regulation by the stimulus. The psychologist who works with the stimulus is said always to insert the response-willing individual silently into his or her calculation. After presupposing the highest entity, namely the will, the person's consent, one can then, according to Ch. Bühler, easily demonstrate the unequivocality of the response. In contrast, she thinks it necessary to emphasize that "living beings, when food appears before them, depending on their need, can devour or leave it."

The difference between the event types, which should be considered primary in the scientific assessment of mental life, is hence absolutely *fundamental* in nature. They represent two completely different "spheres" or even "realities" of the individual. It is the difference between the dead physical "mechanism" and the person endowed with a will, who owns "a working mind" (p. 233).

Elsewhere among other things, this distinction appears in a much less definitive fashion; e.g., when it is remarked that the "living system is reg-

---

Editor's Note. Funktionlust appears as "pleasure function" in C. Bühler's and M. Allen's *Introduction to Humanistic Psychology*, 1972. This does not seem to Dr. Spindler and me to convey its meaning very well, however.

ulated on the one hand by the objective stimulus, on the other hand however by its subjective needs," or when it is pointed out that both principles
in a more or less pronounced way control the child from the first day on,
when surely the superior mental principle is still at zero and attains a
greater significance only over the course of development.

To deal with the duality theory in this weakened form is hardly necessary. That the organism's behavior depends, aside from external stimuli,
also on its subjective state is a proposition that is disputed by nobody, has
received a particular application for developmental theory in Stern's "theory of convergence," and is certainly not in any way new.

Furthermore, with respect to this double dependency of actual events
(first on the current inner state of the system, second on environmental
influences), a living creature certainly does not differ from physical systems.[1] Remaining with such general statements, one may merely state
that in the organism we are dealing with a system whose internal state
can change relatively quickly and in part relatively independently from
the nature of the current environment. To repeat, this also applies to many
physical systems.

However, one should emphasize that in psychology this inner alteration of the organism—occurring partly in rapid, partly in slow rhythm—
has not been taken sufficiently into consideration. Referring to the theory
of instincts (see, e.g., Ch. Bühler's summary[2]), I have pointed out that it
does not take this changeability adequately into account and that the *drive*
concept as a rule must be replaced by the concept of "'need.'" In this connection, it must be recognized as one of the need's characteristic dynamic
features that the state of the need system from which a behavior results
changes fundamentally due to the consequent behavior (Lewin, 1926b,
1928). (I am referring to the state of hunger, of satiation and over-satiation.) Hence, this inner constancy of tendencies, which is usually ascribed
to the drive and the instincts, does not exist here even for relatively short
periods of time.

That Ch. Bühler currently emphasizes the concept of need appears to
me a happy accommodation of our views. However, Ch. Bühler believes
herself to be in opposition to the view of Köhler and myself, since she
assumes our view to be: The behavior of the organism is controlled only
by the stimuli of the external world. It were [subjunctive mood] our view
that the "individual is "'field'"[3] and object of influences" (Köhler, 1928, p.
232), to which he or she merely responds. Ch. Bühler states in contrast:
"As is well known, the individual whose eye is met by a beam of light can
turn this eye toward or away from the stimulus. This does *not at all depend on the ray of light* but on the individual's condition or will" (p. 232,
emphasis added).

---

[1]The behavior of a physical system also depends not only on the kind of external influence but no less on the nature of the respective system, and changes with the alteration of
the internal state.

[2]See the *Report on the 10th Congress of Experimental Psychology*, Bonn, 1927 (1928,
pp. 2–23).

[3]This usage is not a mistake but appears twice in Bühler's essay.

Here, however, we are in fact of a different opinion: The behavior of the individual certainly varies, e.g., according to his or her current interests, but certainly varies just as much depending on the nature of the stimulus. One therefore has to stress here in contrast to Ch. Bühler—and elsewhere even she herself supports this view—that the organism's behavior *also* depends on the nature of the stimulus.

On the other hand, as stated, it is quite far from our intention to ignore or somehow minimize the fundamental significance of the "subjective" condition, namely, the organism's current state.

In my exposition on psychological forces and energies, upon which B.'s polemics rest, I explicitly stated my position on the question raised here, of the individual's regulation by the environment:

> The presence or absence of reservoirs of such (i.e., mental) energy, such as particular needs or need-like tensions, becomes significant throughout the field of will and drive psychology in manifold ways again and again. It matters if the interest or the striving toward a goal ends with the *satiation* of the mental need in question; if an intended act after its consummation or substitute consummation does not happen again when a second analogous opportunity arises; if the routine habitual act fails to appear even after occurrence of the accustomed stimulus, in the case of particular energies not prompting the act; this fact is after all of fundamental significance to the questions of *affective* events.
>
> The close connection that links the field of perception and the sequence of events, according to the point of view presented above (concerning the regulation by the environment), should therefore not let us forget that *the forces that control the course of events remain ineffective or do not even appear if there are no mental energies present, if there is no link to the mental systems under tension that sustain the events* (Lewin, 1926b, p. 27. Emphasis in the original).

Following this, I deal more closely with specific questions that belong here.

Going beyond theoretical discussions, our experimental studies on the psychology of behavior and affect have since investigated empirically especially the field of mental factors, in particular of needs, and have progressed to a substantially more detailed formulation of concepts.

Zeigarnik's work (1927), for example, focused in its investigation deliberately on needs or quasi-needs as systems of the mind. (This would seem to be the first experimental investigation of this kind.) She has provided quite essential explanations of the dynamic nature of such need systems, on the different kinds of their release (*real, substitute gratification, diffuse release*) and has shown among other things how such a system can also be altered by certain processes in 'mentally adjacent areas' or by effective events within the total person. Ovsiankina (1928) has variously explored further the question of *the causal conditions* and of the effect of such mental need systems, e.g., the question of the relation between quasi-needs and real needs. Karsten (1928) examined the significance of psychological needs and the alteration of their stages of hunger, satiation and over-satiation, for instance, the effect of greater or lesser ego-proximity and the particular kind of association among the mental domains, especially the significance of adjacent domains on the speed of *satiation* and co-satiation.

These experimental findings have led to certain fundamental conceptions of the nature of needs, which in this early period of this entire field are of course still in the beginning stages, although they have already established certain dynamic conditions. Ch. Bühler's thesis on behavior that originates in a task, in an internal need, "For the present we know about it only that it manifests itself in the intention," seems to me presently surely far too pessimistic.

It is in any case hard to understand how one can say about a research approach which subjects the dynamics of mental systems, particularly the need systems, to a deliberate, systematic investigation, that it overlooks the needs, that it makes the individual the field of stimuli. On the other hand, in contrast to any dualistic attempt 'fundamentally' to separate the *events originating internally from needs* from environmentally caused events, it should be emphasized that *concrete behavior may be understood in terms of these events*[4] only if, beyond the knowledge of the need system's state, the topology of the respective psychological environment is sufficiently known.

Here the conceptual formulation of our theory is fundamentally different from Ch. Bühler's duality theory. We are not 'monistic' in the sense that we make the individual the "arena of stimuli." However we do not think it justified to postulate immediately, because of the dissimilarity of mental event types, this basic 'logical division' (characteristic in the early stages of all sciences), which explains the disparity between two processes by declaring *this very difference a principle not further derivable*. One then is soon given to drawing at will on one, then on the other "principle"; and the shift from one to the other goes on uncontrolled and without basis.

I have repeatedly emphasized that the task at hand is as little in psychology as in any other science to construct a monistic system in the sense that one falls back on a *single concept*, such as the concept of Gestalt or structure. One will rather, from the outset on, have to employ a certain abundance of associated dynamic concepts.

The question of 'monism' in the usual sense, namely the question of the association between physical and psychological processes, is anyway not unequivocally related to the problem of monism discussed here. One may reject Ch. Bühler's duality thesis and yet—regarding the questions of the relation between psychology's and biology's propositions on the one hand and physics' propositions on the other (which, it seems to me, should be posed from the perspective of theory of science)—be of the opinion that psychology's propositions have indeed a derivative relation with biology's propositions; but that biology's propositions in their whole structure can be derived just as little from physics' propositions as for instance the laws of economics (Lewin, 1922b).

Perhaps it is better, instead of general discussion, to pursue in detail

---

[4]In any case, the energy source of mental behavior lies, in a certain sense, *within* the organism.

the consequences of these different fundamental attitudes by means of a concrete example.

2. Theoretical Consequences

a) Environmental and Internal Factors and the Comparison of Stimulus- and Need-Processes

Our views correspond in so far as what Ch. Bühler calls the *stimulus–response process* should be fundamentally distinguished from the consequence of *needs*. When one starts at a loud bang, or for example turns around when one's name is called, this is a process of a substantially different type than when one looks for food because of hunger or visits the opera out of desire for music.

Ch. Bühler rightly stresses that even the concept of the *"internal stimulus"* does not suffice for explaining this difference. The reason for this, however, does not lie, in my opinion, in the concept of the internal and external stimulus not doing the principle of "the active mind" justice, but rather in a very much less fundamental cause: The psychological processes concerned display certain differences, or proceed according to different laws. In the field of habits—e.g., in cases of need habits, the addictions, the "stimulus" has in reality the function of a means to gratification; it is actively sought out. In the case of the response habit, on the other hand (if one has for instance "learned" to carry out a particular movement in response to a particular word), the stimulus indeed induces the response, yet it does not have the function of a means to need gratification: Its absence does not result in a state of hunger and an active search.

I used this difference quite a while ago (Lewin, 1922a, p. 117ff.) for the comparison of *response habits* and *need habits*, with their substantially different laws and, as mentioned, made it the starting point for further distinctions.

Ch. Bühler sees here the consequences of two different "principles," the "objective structure" and the "subjective reference," which require a duality theory that makes impossible any more detailed formulation of concepts regarding this point. Furthermore, concerning the approach of theories, in my opinion one must not forget (1) that both processes take place within the same person, within the same total organism, (2) that both kinds of processes influence each other and can occur in manifold combinations within a totality of comprehensive events, (3) that although indeed very profound differences exist, there are nevertheless certain similarities and there are probably events whose type lies in-between the two types (Lewin, 1922a).

Above all, however, the distinction between such event types can never be other than the starting point for the examination of the more profound dynamic associations: One does justice to the difference between these two event types, just as among all other event types, only with a theory of psychological *laws* and of the *dynamic construction of the total person* that allows the *derivation* of the actual differences between psychological events, but *also does not exaggerate* the existing differences. Each conceptual differentiation, however, has a strong tendency to *strain* existing differences and to *simplify* the actual circumstances.

In the duality theory, this tendency to simplify has an effect in several respects. Ch. Bühler views the contrast between stimulus–response process and task engagement–completion process as in the one case motivation coming *from inside*, in the other case *from outside*. Therein lies, as mentioned, certainly some truth. But this difference is instantly exaggerated. One should on no account expect effects from outside only for stimulus–response processes; rather, external characteristics play an important role also in need processes, which I call *demand characteristics*. Each need, whether it is of a diffuse or a fixed nature, corresponds to a smaller or larger and more or less fixed range of possible objects and events which are potential means of gratification for the respective need. The range and the quality of these demand characteristics change accordingly with the state of needs. *Demand characteristics and need are correlative concepts.*[5]

It is therefore necessary to distinguish sufficiently from other "stimuli" the environmental influence on the organism of those incentives that result in particular need gratifications. It was for this very purpose that the concept of demand characteristic was introduced. It is intended to express as much the status of the direct or indirect gratification as an *environmental* structure as its immediate relationship with the *need*. In other words, one must not conceive of the environment as the mere embodiment of "stimuli" and discount the effect from the outside in instances where this effect rests on the status of the respective environmental characteristic as a means of gratification. *The strongest effect from the outside occurs precisely because of the fact that environmental objects can have particular relationships with needs, owing to their positive or negative demand characteristics.*[6]

The comparison of need processes and stimulus–response processes hence does not simply run parallel with the contrast 'outside—inside.'

b) The Insulation of the Ego

Coming up against that "fundamental" differentiation between the forces within the individual and the influences that impinge upon the individual from the environment, any psychology that strives to comprehend concrete behavior has to adhere to two basic insights:

---

[5]See Lewin, 1922a. The experimental findings have thus far, in part in a rather surprising manner, confirmed this very far-reaching thesis. See also Ovsiankina, 1928.

[6]As mentioned, there are likely to exist transitions between demand characteristics and stimuli, and it really should not be argued here that only the force of an object's demand characteristics is significant to the individual, which would coincide with Rignano's theory (1928). See also Köhler, 1928.

1. The individual exists within an environment in relation to which he or she displays a relative insulation. This thesis means on the one hand that actual behavior depends on the vectors of the current psychological environment; on the other hand that there exists, nevertheless, a certain dynamic separateness of the psychological organism in relation to the environment. The degree of this separateness varies substantially among different individuals and among developmental stages; for example, it is lower in impulsive and superficially affective individuals than in controlled (Lewin, 1926a). (These individual differences themselves show that this is not a case of a "fundamental" contrast.)

2. This environment should be defined as essentially *psychological* with regard to the respective individual (as long as it has an effect on the organism, not as an immediate physically coerced change but rather by means of perception in the broadest sense of the word). Thus it should *not* be defined as the embodiment of those objects that, according to the concepts of physics, of technical science, or of sociology, "objectively" constitute the current environment of the individual; but rather as fundamentally psychologically correlative with experiences, attitudes, needs—in short, correlative with the current state of the respective individual. (Child psychology's requirement to view the world as a child— more precisely, from the current state of the respective child—is only one of the manifold applications of this proposition.[7] The existence of demand characteristics and their alteration according to the stages of need represents only one basic example of this correlative relationship between environment and the state of the ego.

Therefore, in line with our previous exposition, we consistently represent the individual for the explication of each concrete behavior:

---

[7]In her study of the child's interests, which she reported on at the 11th Congress of Experimental Psychology, Hetzer arrives at the conclusion that the child comes to consider objects not as "objects" according to their "objectively" physical content, but, as she expresses herself somewhat ambiguously, as "stimulus material," as facts of the child's world and interests, which may be very different for "similar" objects. The consequent proposition (this fact of course applies to the adult as well and plays a large role in all of our experimental work) means essentially not much more than that we are dealing with psychology. Every study that—like most statistical investigations and calculations—is based on "objects" in Hetzer's sense—that is, objects in adults' sense or as meant in the scientific techniques of categorization and summarization—[every such study] seems, in our opinion, to start a priori with false or only very narrowly valid approaches. As indispensable as statistical investigations of this kind are in child psychology for a general orientation to what kinds of behavior on average occur, one must be cautious about drawing conclusions regarding laws in the strict sense from statistical investigations, which do not assess the actual psychological environment of the single case.

There is probably no need to emphasize again that this thesis has nothing to do with the assertion that the "objective" Gestalt factors of objects are a matter of indifference to the individual so that, for example, the unities of perceived objects are based merely on their significance for needs and affects. See Wertheimer (1922, 1923).

1. as a *total person* with a *certain structure*. Consequently, the state of the particular mental system deserves special attention as perhaps the energy source of contemporary actions (e.g., the location of this system in certain peripheral or ego-proximal psychological areas, the degree of its connection with or separation from other psychological systems, etc.);

2. as a relative unity within a psychological *environment* of particular topology and particular field forces. Given the direct relationship between the role that precisely this unity in fact plays (or does not play) as a particular environmental vector for this individual and the current dynamic structure of this individual, then the psychological environment upon which the representation should be based is in no way—as a fundamental distinction between internal and environmental structures would have it—a simple function of the geographic–physical environment. If and to what extent the psychological environment corresponds with the individual's physical–geographic environment is a question for each unique case.[8]

These field representations are meant to be substantially different from the schematic illustrations of abstract, conceptual relations, as they are now frequently being proffered—namely, a real mathematical representation of the concrete psychological situation. How, given the topology of the situation, field forces have an effect on expression and bodily posture as well, I have attempted to pursue elsewhere (Lewin, 1927a).

It should be noted in any case that the environment in our context is to be defined primarily in psychological terms, moreover specifically according to its topology and direction. It may, for example, very well be possible that an event that presents itself physically–geographically as a reversal of direction, psychologically represents a progression in the original direction. The conception of the seemingly "aimless" action occasioned by the "pleasure-in-acting" (compare below p. 127ff.) will also frequently have to be largely corrected if one shifts from the primitive physical–geographical definition of the environment and its directions to the psychological determination of direction and topology of the environment.

Finally, it should be especially emphasized that, even for actions that doubtlessly originate in "inner needs," the manifest psychological behavior in its concreteness may be derived only if, aside from the type of *internal* state, the topology and the field forces of the currently prevailing psychological *environment* are also known. Even a specific internal state still allows a more or less extensive range of variation in actual behavior. One arrives at an unequivocally determined behavior only if, aside from the

---

[8]See Karsten, 1928; Ovsiankina, 1928. I pointed out elsewhere that because of a relatively large, although by no means complete conjunction of the geo-physical and the psychological topology of certain situations for the child, film recordings have a heightened psychological significance.

general laws of psychological events, not only the individual's current dynamic structure but also the psychological environment is known.

This holds true, in my opinion, even for those extreme cases of internally contingent events, for which one might perhaps most easily assume an independence from the specific environmental constellation: in diffuse discharge of excessive internal tensions in the form of *restless behavior*. In this case too, the topology of the field is in reality not irrelevant. If such restlessness is, for example, dependent on the one hand on the presence of a positive demand characteristic, and on the other hand on a "barrier" between it and the individual, the proposition holds: The restless behavior occurs such that an increase of the distance to the demand characteristic is avoided; that is, the movement occurs, insofar as the barrier permits, as perpendicular as possible to the direction of the field forces.[9]

c) The "Need for Activity"

Ch. Bühler regards those mental processes that originate in the "pleasure-in-acting" as particularly characteristic for the second type of life processes. While in stimulus–response processes, the organism is said to respond merely to an environmental influence, in those processes which are induced by pleasure-in-acting, the original spontaneity comes from the individual. The individual and not the environment is said to be the source of events.

This pleasure-in-acting is essentially defined as the urge to do "anything at all." The child "roams about in boredom, pokes about here and there, handles this and that, until his or her need for activity finally encounters an object that becomes the stimulus that appeals to him or her, material that he or she now will get busy with and work on" (Bühler, 1928, p. 228).

For this "primarily internally" generated type of action, the first phase is above all characteristically, "that which one rightly denotes by talking of '*aimless functioning*,' which prompts discontentment, until an object, material for activity has been found" (p. 228. Emphasis added.). Readiness for action may be observed in the child at all developmental levels, e.g., in the adolescent as well as in the adult, for instance, when he or she "suddenly lets the material drop" and then "stands currently at a loss and with a kind of desperation or dissatisfaction because he or she lacks at this moment any material for his or her activity."

Ch. Bühler believes it possible to prove that "this readiness for action which seeks an object for activity, . . . formally represents the same attitude . . . in the actively behaving living being at all developmental stages . . . , that can be fulfilled with different contents" (p. 229).

Thus the following is claimed:

---

[9]See the film demonstration in the *Report on the Ninth International Congress of Psychology*.

1. The need to act prompts any aimless action, independent of the stimulus.
2. It represents *one* particular need (namely, the need to act) which can from a certain age on be recognized at all stages of life.
3. This uniform need to act is the source of genuine mental processes of the type which has to do, not with a mechanistic "objective" system, but with an "active mind."

The concept of pleasure-in-acting is used by Karl Bühler to denote those phenomena in the child when volitional behavior occurs not as a means to an end but for its own sake. When children charge about at the end of winter as if set free, the determining wish in this is certainly not to reach a certain place but the tendency to charge about.

Ch. Bühler has now extended the concept of pleasure-in-acting to all activities when an act flows not from external pressure but out of some internal need.[10] The evidence for this idea of *one* comprehensive need to act, which is manifested in the most diverse forms and directions, Ch. Bühler believes to find in similarity of behavior, indeed in the similarity with which a restless striving, due to an unsatisfied need to act, becomes manifest at the most diverse stages of life.

An extensive formal similarity in fact exists in these cases, and indeed the similarity resides, in my opinion:

1. in that they are always cases where a *state of tension* exists that manifests itself in the form of *restless behavior*, typical for states of tension;
2. in that they involve needs which currently are not yet (or no longer) focused and limited to a highly specific means of gratification, but rather are *relatively diffuse*.

There exists therefore a "state of hunger" of a psychological need and undoubtedly of a relatively diffuse need, of a need whose means of gratification are not clearly defined or might not even be known to the individual.

Moreover, a very extensive formal similarity of behavior appears also

---

[10]One might employ the term *"pleasure-in-acting"* as an allusion to a series of pursuits and actions which do not have the character of behavior instrumental to the achievement of certain purposes but rather themselves constitute the gratifying behavior, especially for those cases where an urge for *movement* is the focus of the need. The danger of undue expansion to any need gratification suggests itself so easily, as Ch. Bühler's expositions in particular show, that this term had perhaps better be avoided completely; instead the respective need should be characterized by *the respectively appropriate degree of generality* with respect to its content, e.g., the need to dance, the need for bodily movement, etc.

It should be noted that the problems which are raised by the term "pleasure-in-acting" belong, in my opinion, in two fairly different realms of problems. In one instance, it is a special case of the problem of *"enjoyment"* for which the contrast between purposeful instrumental action and the actual gratifying acts (acts that are ends in themselves) is essential. Second is the contrast between occupation with a *task* that stands outside of one's own ego and action at whose center one's *own* being, the *ego* stands.

in *needs* that are narrowly defined or even *fixed* to a particular object, as long as the need's state of hunger is *sufficiently strong*: Out of longing for a particular person or out of the need for a particular activity, a restless urge for "any activity at all" can typically arise. What is to Ch. Bühler the characteristic feature of the readiness to act, namely *"aimless* activity," is very pronounced in such cases of strong states of hunger too.[11] Moreover, in these cases, frequently after a phase of restless, so to speak, "seeking," a certain "discovery" ensues. Here lie important relations to the problem of substitute gratification.

Needs in the state of hunger, and especially diffuse, unsatisfied needs, lead without doubt to modes of behavior that show certain *commonalities*. The existence of *one* identical need, namely, the "need to act," as a cause of these common aspects is, however, by no means proven by this.

If the concept of a need is to denote more than a summary of certain superficially similar events—if, beyond classification according to superficial phenomenological peculiarities, which is certainly not uncommon in motivational psychology, one wants to employ the need concept to characterize particular *dynamic* facts, specifically particular sources of mental energy,—one may not simply regard the similarity of behavior as proof of the identicality of the energy source. Otherwise, one could, for example, simply postulate a "restlessness need" to be a special need because of the strong similarity across restless behavior, which surely originates in the individual. (Although particular motives, e.g., the death motive and the power motive, have been postulated in a similarly unavailing manner in the theory of motives.) If one wants to trace back a series of actions to one need, one will have to examine whether the *real gratification* of the need (the conversion of the respective need's state of hunger into the state of satiation) ensues in all relevant cases in fact through the *same* process and means of gratification. If this is not the case, one will have to speak of two relatively separate needs. This requirement for determining the identity of the need source is perhaps not even sufficient, but in any case necessary.

Of course, matters are complicated by several further factors that make substantially more difficult the determination of identity or non-identity of needs and their differentiations.

1. As already mentioned, there are *diffuse* needs, which means that the range of objects which possess demand characteristics and the kinds of satisfying behavior can display considerable variation.
2. Owing to the only relative isolation of the need system, the hunger state of a particular need remains not without influence on *the total person's state of tension*, and conversely, as a not-yet-published study has shown experimentally, one's need state can also be substantially changed through the alteration of the organism's total state of tension. Especially the similar effects of differ-

---

[11]This is already indicated by the circumstance that with increasing hunger the range of demand characteristics usually grows.

ent needs, e.g., the restless behavior accompanying somatic hunger and longing for a person, would seem to depend essentially on this effect of the one system on the state of the total personal system.

3. Finally, *different* needs can more or less *communicate* with each other, hence form "weak dynamic Gestalten" (Köhler, 1921) within a stronger dynamic total unit. (This is important particularly for the differentiation between needs across development.)

Despite all these facts which substantially complicate the concrete determination of the identity or non-identity of sources of needs, it can however be established *negatively*, that one *cannot speak of an identity of needs as long as in each case profoundly different processes are necessary to convert the state of hunger into a state of satiation.*

If, after these fundamental considerations, we ask for justification to assume a special need to act, it seems to me the evidence supporting this justification has by no means been produced.

Since the mental structure of need systems is by no means the same for *different individuals*, it would of course be conceivable that there are *particular individuals* in whom something like a "need to act" exists as a special mental energy source in the structure of their total person. Perhaps there are human beings in whom the need to do *"anything at all"* marks not only an experiential state (see below p. 130) but actually a dynamic fact. One may think of the "squirrely person," of people who have to "poke their noses" into everything, constantly stir things up, talk as pompously as possible about things which they do not know anything about, thus of people who so to speak *suffer from pleasure-in-acting*.

However, it seems questionable whether even in these cases a special need to act should be assumed as an independent source of mental energy, or whether we are dealing with the consequence of certain general peculiarities of the person's total structure, one in which a sufficiently harmonized hierarchy of goals has not been achieved or in which an especially large tension exists between ego and environment.

These people's need to do anything at all usually follows, in reality, a particular direction, namely, a direction which "looks good" socially.

Aside from individuals who suffer from the need to act, it appears to me that in the cases to which Ch. Bühler refers, the postulation of a special need to act that exists *apart* from the other needs and is *not* identical with the individual's *total state of tension*, is not feasible. Do all those processes of "restless seeking"—which we can observe in the adolescent as much as in the adult who lost his or her job, or in the child who charges outside at the end of winter—really originate in the *same* need? One can, in my opinion, unequivocally contradict this. Certainly there exists in every one of these cases a certain range of variations in behavior that actually satisfies the underlying need. For this reason one cannot define the particular underlying need as a tendency for *one* highly specific behavior. That, aside from the range of variation existing for each need, in very many cases altogether different needs prevail, becomes obvious through the following circumstances. Offer to the adult who has lost his or her job those activities that the child with a need to act responds to with delight and that grant him or her satisfaction. The adult will reject them and, should he or she be forced to engage in these activities, satisfaction of his or her hunger for employment will certainly not result; no more will the activity that represents a fulfillment to the child or the adult satisfy the longing of the adolescent.

I therefore do not think it correct that, dynamically speaking, there exists a need to function "in any way." Certainly the state is experientially frequent so that the person initially feels only the urge for just any activity. However, as experimental findings have established (Ach, 1910; Ovsiankina, 1928), this *vague indefiniteness of experience* is found also for needs which have a *highly specific* content, cases in which one therefore can definitely not speak of a general pleasure-in-acting as the cause of events; for example, when dynamically the tendency exists to complete a highly specific interrupted task.[12] On the contrary, dynamically it would certainly be false to propose a general readiness function for any activity as a cause of the acts. One should therefore not let oneself be lured, either by the typical experience of "being vaguely driven" (which, by the way, exists usually only in the initial stages) or by the fact that there exists at any given time a certain domain of possible consummatory acts, into assuming the tendency for just "any activity at all" to be a mental source of behavior.

This applies to the child as much as to the adult. Even when the child restlessly searches around out of "readiness function" until he or she finds what satisfies, this searching around certainly shows that there are very many activities that the child currently *rejects*, thus that this is by no means a tendency for just *any* activity at all. Even for the small child, for whom the actual sequence of events most easily suggests the assumption of a need for any activity at all, a closer observation shows that there are still very many activities which currently hold no gratification value for the child. In very many cases there exists in the ready one- or two-year old child even the inclination for highly specific behavior: He or she does not want to romp around in any way, but rather at this moment, for example, to play in the sand and specifically not to play in the sand just in any way but to play in the sand in a very particular way. By itself, it is very possible, with a certain degree of probability, that the variation in gratifying behavior is generally larger in the child, corresponding to the diffuse nature of many of his or her needs. All in all, this question is not at all particularly clarified yet in relation to the cases one thinks of first when speaking about a readiness function. The mere impression of adults that the child asks for anything and not for something particular signifies very little in itself. *Rather, experimental proof should first be established that in these cases all activities indeed have equal status as gratifying acts*

---

[12]In this case, too, there is a certain variable range of behavior that can take on the function of a substitute behavior for the actual interrupted task. The range of these substitute acts is, however, limited and by no means will "any" effort do.

*in relation to the need to act before one can use the concept of need to act
in the dynamic sense.* As mentioned, our knowledge altogether contradicts
such a thesis.

The concept of the need to act shows a striking parallel with the concept of *deflation drive* that is used by several national economists. In an
attempt to place certain processes outside the realm of economic laws,
Oppenheimer states the contrast: "Acting according to the law of the
smallest amount of energy (acting economically)" and "acting out of an
overflowing urge for activity (deflation drive)." In the latter case work
would not be "the application of effort." It does not involve a "cost expense,"
and therefore these acts stand outside the laws of economics (Oppenheimer, 1910, pp. 15, 23).

It cannot be our task to discuss the value or non-value of such a conceptual formulation in economics. However, from a psychological point of
view one will have to state that a great number of activities that are no
doubt included in economics (such as steps taken in the management of a
business, a venture, and other clearly economic actions), in many concrete
cases originate doubtlessly in the deflation drive (if one wants to use this
concept for instance).

The similarity between "deflation drive" and "pleasure-in-acting" is
striking, apart from content, in the sense that in establishing the concepts,
the purpose in both instances is to rescue a certain "higher" domain from
the lower, so to speak, "common reality." In the field of psychology, certain
processes are to be removed from the domain of "mechanistic systems"
and assigned to the "active mind."

Ch. Bühler's inclination to make the need to act more and more the
embodiment of all true mental needs, of all forces that originate within
the individual, is apparently most closely related to her espoused duality
principle and to the linkage between the dualistic idea and the contrast
of "inside" and "outside." For the more fundamentally one conceptualizes
such a differentiation, the stronger is the tendency, seen very commonly
in young scientists, to attribute to each of the resulting parts a particularly
pronounced uniformity. One is inclined in such cases toward an over-
emphasis on the wholeness and the primitivization of each part.[13]

---

[13]A simple psychological law of Gestalt formation probably comes into effect here, which
reveals itself as much in the field of perceptual psychology as in the child's contrast of angel
and devil, heaven and hell. This psychologically natural tendency appears to play a certain
role in the concept of pleasure-in-action, inasmuch as in establishing the comprehensive
need to act, the integration of the working mind, which is the more encompassing principle,
becomes manifest. One has often felt compelled to point out, particularly in relation to
Gestalt theory, that the integration of the person is not sufficiently considered by the position of Gestalt theory, that Gestalt theorists are so to speak not Gestalt-theoretical enough.
I have emphasized elsewhere that such tendencies for Super-Gestalt virtually nullify the
scientific meaning of Gestalt theory. As consequential as such theses sound initially, so they
necessarily in the end lead back to merely summative work. Granted, the total person
displays indeed a relative *integration*, certainly often inadequately taken into account. However, within this personal totality there are even so *relatively separate* systems; and a psychology that does not take this separation seriously to its real extent but everywhere wants
to see nothing but totalities is inevitably bound to fail.

This psychological tendency to overstate the contrast is closely associated with the tendency to base as much as possible on this differentiation. Ch. Bühler believes it possible to relate her distinction directly to the
concept of intentionality that plays a fundamental role in Husserl's system. Herewith she unintentionally blurs the supposed meaning of intention and *motivation* (compare Pfänders' exposition, 1900) with the conceptually altogether heterogeneous meaning of *causal effect*.

d) Familiarity and Attraction

Ch. Bühler seeks to support the role she ascribes to the need to act as a
mental principle by referring to certain investigations in child psychology.
She closely relates the awakening of the "intention" and the parallel formation of the need to act with the alteration of *attraction* and *aversion
effects* of *familiar* and *unfamiliar* events. As long as the neonate is essentially a system responding to stimuli, the effect of unfamiliar events is
said to be emphatically aversive. The mental principle of intentionality
corresponds, however, primarily to a marked attraction to the unfamiliar
and a marked aversion to the familiar. Ch. Bühler provides a graphical,
schematic representation of how this ruling principle is thought to super-
cede the first primitive principle and gradually take over control.[14]
    Although this thesis is not necessarily connected with the previous
discussion, it is perhaps useful to deal briefly with this specific question.
It is doubtlessly correct that the initially marked attractive familiarity of
an event may, with repeated experience, initially fall into indifference and
later direct rejection, and that in its place the tendency toward something
new (hence pleasure in the unfamiliar) becomes noticeable. A principle of
perception psychology seems to be working here, which I denote "psychological satiation" (Lewin, 1928), and on whose dynamics we have in hand
a thorough experimental study (Karsten, 1928). In the field of behavior,
e.g., the playful or serious activity of the child, very often an increase in
interest in the new task initially manifests itself (the first phase). However, further repetitions lead, because of psychological satiation, to indifference, even rejection (over-satiation) with a strong need for different behavior, which appears initially in "variations," later perhaps in a "Gestalt
disintegration." Karsten has already indicated that there are analogous
phenomena in the field of sensory psychology,[15] and I have pointed out
corresponding phenomena of psychological satiation in the field of perception, e.g., in advertisement and fashion (Lewin, 1928). Even in the cases
of altered interest with respect to perceptual objects to which Ch. Bühler
refers, the force to produce effects of marked attraction or aversion appears not to be inherent in familiarity or unfamiliarity; rather, there ap-

---

[14]Ch. Bühler believes it possible ultimately to establish a general law of attraction and
aversion, which appears to me extraordinarily questionable, but which I do not want to
discuss here in greater detail.

[15]She relies here on extensive, unfortunately as yet unpublished work by Köhler; also
see Gottschaldt, 1929.

pears as a rule a close relation between attraction and aversion effects of a repetitive experience and the state of certain *needs* or overlapping goals (that in many respects play an equivalent role).

Ch. Bühler believes that she must draw on two completely different principles for the explanation of attraction and aversion effects of the familiar, of which *one* (the principle of the "objective structure") must explain the reduction in marked attraction down to the zero point, while the mental principle will explain the further change to aversion and the increasing interest in the unfamiliar. Once recognizing that the association with the alteration of needs—their phases of hunger, satiation and over-satiation —applies just as much to psychological needs as to the strictly speaking somatic ones, the necessity and possibility of such splitting of a total process dissolves.

The independent empirical findings also contradict altogether the splitting of the satiation process into two fundamentally opposite event types. Even in adults it very frequently happens that the first repetitions show an increase in interest, a positive accentuation of familiarity. When continuing repetition results in gradual satiation and shifts into over-satiation, this zero point does by no means indicate, according to the experimental findings, a fundamental differentiation. Rather, according to Karsten, one can actually typically observe in this period a strong backward and forward vacillation of the "attraction accentuation" between relative comfort and a pronounced aversive emphasis.[16]

Furthermore, based on other empirical facts, the thesis of the attractive or aversive effect of familiarity does not at all merit elevation to law, which Ch. Bühler holds possible, and indeed not even when we momentarily disregard the particularly "fundamental" interpretation of this difference. It can by no means be maintained that just any stimulus becomes initially pleasant to the small child through repetition. There are, for example, stimuli which always remain unpleasant. On the other hand, the fact that a familiar stimulus can become unpleasant with repetition becomes noticeable not only in the older child—hence, when the principle of intentionality has reached a sufficient strength—but already in the first days, as soon as one bases the investigation on *biologically meaningful* stimuli. The neonate who, in the state of hunger responds positively to the touch of the nipple, reacts altogether negatively a few minutes later, in a state of satiation. It is, furthermore, commonly known that the familiar can indeed be markedly attractive for the adult.

One therefore will not only have to reject any attribution of such alterations to such disparate principles but also take the greatest caution when attempting to establish general laws from statistical determinations

---

[16]Once having recognized the relative integration of the satiation process, it makes good sense, all things considered, to question whether the law of satiation already constitutes an elementary psychological law or whether one is not merely dealing with a regularly occurring interaction of various factors. I am inclined like Karsten, who already provides essential clues to this problem, toward the second assumption for particular reasons (which concern the nature of repetition and the questions of gratification and of the demand level); however, this has nothing to do with Ch. Bühler's "fundamental" distinction.

that more or less disregard the genuine biological meaning, the meaning of the respective stimulus for the respective individual in his or her particular situation. How repetition works is, as Karsten's investigations have incisively shown, by no means a simple function of repetition as such (or familiarity or unfamiliarity) but depends on one hand on the *specific nature of the respective event,* on the other hand, *on the meaning which the repetition holds for the respective individual in the concrete situation.*[17]

I need hardly mention that I am well aware of the tremendous change from the neonate to the adult. In my opinion too, the particular alteration of the environmental structure of the infant, which Ch. Bühler seeks to characterize by means of the concept of intention, plays a very important role. (The thought occurs here of the alteration of a relatively broad set of conditions, from "sensation" to "perception" in Werner's sense.[18] However, it is not very fruitful to the conceptual penetration of these problems, if, when explaining them, one retreats to contrasts of principles. As frequently happens, so here too a crude quantitative procedure comes into play, so to speak, as a complementary phenomenon to this seemingly so fundamental and qualitative approach: In a similar way as in association psychology, the *repetition* as such is thought to produce a fundamental alteration. But the "objectively" same stimulus as well as the fact of repetition can for the newborn and for the older child mean biologically something very different in each case. Especially in the first period of life, such fundamental alterations of the child's experienced world doubtlessly take place: Stimuli that are psychologically fairly similar to the adult, even when repeated have at this stage—for example, as a result of dissociation from a "base" of psychological existence that has in the meantime completely changed—become so different that one must initially ask whether the circumstances are similar enough for a common statistical summary. Furthermore, the fact of repetition may signify in no way a mere shifting of the particular stimulus in the direction of greater familiarity. That one lives in a world in which a particular event occurs for the second time or even repeatedly may under certain circumstances profoundly change the meaning of this event, even of the entire world view. This certainly applies to a higher degree, particularly to the small child.

In the specific questions raised here, the issue at hand is not the contrasting of disparate *principles*, probably not even the contrast between different psychological *laws*; rather, that the adult and the child in different developmental stages, because of psychologically substantially different environments, behave differently toward superficially identical events.

In child psychology no less than in general psychology, one will presently have to acknowledge that extensive gathering together, describing, and statistical ordering of independent facts is a scientifically absolutely necessary and valuable task. However, if one wants to approach the dy-

---

[17]Karsten has shown experimentally, for example, that repetitions which are externally and also motorically identical can have psychologically and somatically entirely different effects, depending on the meaning of these repetitions for that person.

[18]See his expositions at the 11th Congress for Psychology.

namics that lie under the surface and a theory of psychological processes, one will have to beware the disposition characteristic of partly speculative systems that, incapable of really bridging the tension between independent individual fact and generally valid law, are inclined toward establishing principles that are as over-arching as possible, seemingly philosophical, but in concrete application not very compelling. In the "higher" fields of psychology as well, one has to accept the obligation to burden psychological theory with the full weight of the requirement that it should not only fit a particular group of cases but remain intact, with all its implications, when facing the totality of possible examples; and moreover, that, despite its general validity, it provides a clear way to derive the dynamic individuality of every unique concrete case. One will, however, then have to abandon concept formulation by classification, which seeks to rise to generality by "abstractly" omitting individual differences,[19] thus necessarily replacing general validity with vagueness.

References

Ach, N. (1910). *Über den Willensakt und das Temperament*. Leipzig: Quelle und Meyer.

Bühler, C. (1928). Two fundamental types of life processes. *Zeitschrift für Psychologie, 108,* 222–239.

Bühler, C., & Allen, M. (1972). *Introduction to humanistic psychology*. Monterey, CA: Brooks/Cole.

Gottschaldt, K. (1929). Über den Einfluss der Erfahrung auf die Wahrnemung von Figuren. II. *Vergleichende Untersuchungen ueber die Wirkung figuraler Einpraegung und den Einfluss spezifischer Geschehensverlaeufe auf die Auffassung optischer Komplexe. Psychologische Forschung, 12,* 1–87.

Karsten, A. (1928). Psychishe Sättigung. *Psychologische Forschung, 10,* 142–254.

Köhler, W. (1921). *Die physischen Gestalten im Ruhe und in stationärer Bewegung*. Berlin: Schlachtensee.

Köhler, W. (1928). Bemerkung zur Gestalttheorie. *Psychologische Forschung, 11,* 188–234.

Lewin, K. (1922a). Das Problem der Willenmessung and das Grundsetz der Association. *Psychologische Forschung, 2,* 65–140.

Lewin, K. (1922b). *Der Begriff der Genese in Physik, Biologie und Entwicklungsgeschichte. Eine Unterschung zur vergleichenden Wissenschaftslehrer*. Berlin: Gebruder Borutraeger.

Lewin, K. (1926a). Trieb- und Affektäusserungen psychopathischer Kinder (vergleichen mit Normalen und Schwachsinnigen). *Zeitschrift für Kinderforschung, 32,* 414–448.

Lewin, K. (1926b). *Vorsatz, Wille und Bedürfnis*. Berlin: Springer.

Lewin, K. (1927). *Gesetz und Experiment in der Psychologie*. Berlin-Schlachtensee: Weltkris-Verlag.

Lewin, K. (1928). Die Bedeutung der "psychische Sättigung" für einige Problems der Psychotecknik. *Psychotechnische Zeitschrift, 3,* 182–188.

Oppenheimer, F. (1910). *Theorie der reinen und politischen Öconomie*. Berlin: W. de Gruyter.

Ovsiankina, M. (1928). Die Wiederaufnahme unterbrochener Handlungen. *Psychologische Forschung, 11,* 302–379.

Pfänder, A. (1900). *Phänomenologie des Wollens*. Leipzig: J. B. Barth.*

---

[19]These present questions of theory of knowledge I addressed in detail in Lewin, 1927a.
*Editor's Note. Actually Lewin did not provide a reference here, but this seems to be the work he had in mind.

Rignano, E. (1928). Die Gestalttheorie. *Psychologische Forschung, 11*, 172–187.*

Wertheimer, M. (1922). Untersuchen sur Lehrer von der Gestalt I. *Psychologische Forschung, 1*, 47–58.

Wertheimer, M. (1923). Untersuchen sur Lehrer von der Gestalt II. *Psychologische Forschung, 4*, 301–350.

Zeigarnik, B. (1927). Das Behalten beendeter und unbeendeter Handlungen. *Psychologische Forschung, 9*, 1–85.

6

Level of Aspiration

Almost any set of psychological problems, especially those in the fields of motivation and personality, inevitably involves goals and goal-directed behavior. The importance of setting up goals for behavior is especially accentuated in a culture with as strong a competitive emphasis as ours. Until recently, however, little formal attempt has been made to study goals as phenomena in themselves and the effects of attainment or nonattainment of goals on the behavior of the individual.

The concept of "level of aspiration," introduced by Dembo (1931), made explicit the possibility of observing goal levels occurring in the course of a relatively specific activity, designating some of the factors associated with fluctuation of such goals and linking the experimentally observed manifestations of goal-striving to the individual's behavior in other situations. The experimental results stemming from her observations and those of Hoppe (1930), who performed the first experiment directed toward analysis of the aspiration phenomena, have mounted until at the present time there is a considerable body of data bearing on the problems of that goal-striving behavior which occurs within a range of difficulty, i.e., *level of aspiration*. Gradually also seem to be emerging the common factors which establish the level of aspiration phenomena with reference to other fields and problems of psychology, notably to social standards and forces, conflict and decision, personality characteristics, value phenomena, success and failure, and developmental aspects of personality. This is, then, an appropriate time to look backward at the trends of the last decade and forward to the future directions in which research may profitably be directed. A review of the relevant literature up to 1941 may be found in Frank (1941), and Rotter (1942a, 1942b) has examined critically the material which seeks to evaluate the methodological aspects of level of aspiration.

Kurt Lewin, PhD, Tamara Dembo, PhD, Leon Festinger, PhD, and Pauline Snedden Sears, PhD

From J. McV. Hunt, Ed., 1944. *Personality and the behavior disorders*, New York: The Ronald Press, pp. 333–378.

What Is the Level of Aspiration?

A Typical Sequence of Events

In discussing the many problems and aspects of the level of aspiration, it may be helpful to consider a sequence of events which is typical for the situations concerned. A person has scored 6 in shooting at a target with ring 10 at the center. He decides the next time to try for 8. He attains 5, is much disappointed, and decides to try the next time to reach 6 once more.

Within such a sequence we can distinguish the following main points (Figure 1):

1. The (last) past performance (in our example: "has scored 6").
2. The setting of the level of aspiration, e.g., deciding how high to set the goal for the next performance ("try for 8").
3. The execution of action, e.g., the new performance ("attains 5").
4. The reaction to the level of attainment, such as feeling of success or failure ("disappointment"), leaving the activity altogether, or continuing with the new level of aspiration ("try again for 6").

Each of these four points can be discussed in relation to one another. In case an individual begins a new activity, no past performance would appear within the sequence, although he might have had experience with similar activities.

Each point within the time sequence represents a situation that has characteristic problems. For the dynamics of the level of aspiration, point 2 (setting of the level of aspiration) and point 4 (reaction to achievement) are particularly significant. Two problems arise immediately, then, out of consideration of this sequence: (a) What determines a level of aspiration?

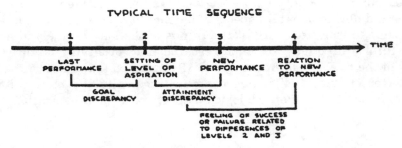

Figure 1. Four main points are distinguished in a typical sequence of events in a level of aspiration situation: last performance, setting of level of aspiration for the next performance, new performance, and the psychological reaction to the new performance. The difference between the level of the last performance and the level of the new goal is called goal discrepancy; the difference between the goal level and that of the new performance is called attainment discrepancy. This difference is one of the bases of the reaction at the point 4.

(b) What are the reactions to achieving or not achieving the level of aspiration?

Description of Terms Involved in the Sequence

Some of the terms and factors involved may well be identified before proceeding to discussion of the experimental data.

Action goal–ideal goal; inner-discrepancy; confidence level. We have mentioned before that the level of aspiration presupposes a goal which has an inner structure. In our example the individual will not merely shoot, but tries to hit the target and even a certain area of the target. What he would really like to do is hit center. This is his "ideal goal." Knowing that this is "too difficult" for him, at least at the present, he sets his goal at 8 for the next action. This we will call his "action goal." It is the level of the action goal which is usually taken as the criterion for the level of aspiration for an individual at a given time. Frank, one of the early investigators in this field, defines the level of aspiration as "the level of future performance in a familiar task which an individual, knowing his level of past performance in that task, explicitly undertakes to reach" (1935a).

Setting the action goal at point 2 of the time sequence (Figure 1) does not mean that the individual has given up his ideal goal. In order to understand this behavior, we must consider the action goal as within the whole goal structure of the individual. This may include quite a number of more or less realistic goal levels. Goal levels within one goal structure may include a high dream goal, a somewhat more realistic wish goal, the level which the person expects to reach when he tries to judge the situation objectively, and a low level he might hit if luck were against him. Somewhere on that scale will be what can be described as the action goal, e.g., what the person "tries for" at that time; somewhere his ideal goal will be located. Sometimes the individual comes closer to his ideal goal, sometimes the distance between the ideal goal and the action goal becomes wider. This is called "inner discrepancy."

Another characteristic of the goal structure is the discrepancy between the level of the action goal and the level of the expected performance. This difference might be characterized directly as the "goal–expectation discrepancy." This discrepancy will depend in part on the "subjective degree of probability" which the individual holds with reference to his chances of reaching his action goal. One expression of the subjective probability is the confidence level.

Past performance–goal; goal discrepancy. One can compare the level of aspiration, e.g., the level of the action goal at point 2 in our time sequence (Figure 1) with the level of the past performance (point 1 of our time sequence). The difference between the two levels has been called the "discrepancy score." Since there are other discrepancies important for the level of aspiration, we will call this one "goal discrepancy." The goal discrepancy is said to be positive if the level of the goal lies above that of the past performance; otherwise, it is called a negative goal discrepancy.

Level of aspiration and attainment; attainment score; success; failure. The individual has set his level of aspiration and then has acted with this goal in mind (point 3 of the time sequence, Figure 1). The level of this performance can be called "attainment or performance score." The difference between the level of aspiration and the attainment score may be called "attainment discrepancy." It is said to be positive if the attainment is higher than the level of aspiration. It is called negative if the attainment falls short of the level of aspiration.

The direction and size of the attainment discrepancy are two of the major factors for the feeling of success or failure. The term "success" or "failure" will be used to indicate the psychological factor of feeling success or failure and not as indicating the difference between the level of aspiration and the achievement. Everyday language speaks of success and failure in both meanings, sometimes referring to the difference between points 2 (level of aspiration) and 3 (new performance) of our time sequence, sometimes referring to point 4. The difference between points 2 and 3 is called "attainment discrepancy." The success and failure indicate a reaction to this discrepancy (point 4 of the time sequence).

Operational definitions: Verbal goal and true goal. How the different goal levels and performance levels can be measured or defined operationally is a technical question which frequently has to be answered differently in different experimental settings. To observe or measure the level of performances (points 1 and 3 of the time sequence) is frequently not difficult if one uses proper activities.

More difficult is a direct measurement of the level of aspiration or other points of the psychological goal structure, such as the ideal goal or the level of expectation. Once the laws of the level of aspiration are known it will be possible to use a number of reactions for an indirect determination. Today one of the best methods of determining the level of aspiration, the ideal goal or the level of expectation is, as a rule, the direct expression of the subject. Of course, there is the danger that the verbal or written statement of the individual may actually not reveal his "true" action goal, his "true" ideal goal, or "true" expectation. It would not be a safe procedure to ask an individual after the performance, e.g., at point 4 of our time sequence, what his level of aspiration had been at point 2, because after failure his verbal expression might easily be a rationalization. It is important to have the verbal expression given during that situation to which it refers. In case the social atmosphere is sufficiently free, the direct expression of the individual is at present for many settings the best approximation and, therefore, the best operational definition of the various goal levels. For the action goal, the actual behavior of the individual in a choice among tasks on various levels of difficulties can be used as a behavioral measure.

The problem of the determination of true and/or verbal level of aspiration has proved a difficult one for many of the earlier investigators in this field. Hoppe (1930) employed various lines of evidence in inferring a given subject's momentary level. Since later investigators have preferred to use more definite behavior for the inference of aspiration level, the breadth of the operations studied has been to a certain extent restricted in the interests of methodological precision. Gardner (1940b) has clarified the theoretical situation resulting from the attempts to improve on Hoppe's methods of measurement without making entirely specific the consequences of the methodological changes.

Size of goal units. An individual may throw a ring over a stake. He may or may not reach his goal. In another case his goal might be to throw a series of five rings over a stake. How good his achievement is (nothing missed, three missed) can be stated in this case only after all five rings are thrown. His reaction to this achievement with the feeling of success or failure will be related to the achievement as a whole rather than to each ring separately.

The size of the units of activity to which the goal refers is an important point to be considered in the discussion of the level of aspiration. The maximum size and the complication of units to which a goal might refer are important characteristics of certain maturity levels in children. To avoid misunderstandings one will always have to keep in mind the size and character of the activity unit to which the goal refers.

What Determines the Level of Aspiration?

Reference Scales

Experimental work on the level of aspiration has brought out the variety of influences which are present for a single decision as to action goal. Some of these influences are probably rather stable and permanent in their effects; i.e., their value will be much the same for all individuals of a given culture in a variety of competitive situations. It has been found, for example, that nearly all individuals of Western culture, when first exposed to a level of aspiration situation, give initially a level of aspiration which is above the previous performance score, and under most conditions tend to keep the goal discrepancy positive. The effects of cultural pressures toward improvement in performance, and the value which positive discrepancies have for many individuals in stimulating them to greater endeavor, have been brought out by a number of investigators in this field (e.g., Gould, 1939). Such influences may be conceived of as frames, involving a scale of values, within which the individual makes his decision as to a goal. The relative dominance or potency of each scale of reference is a function (a) of more temporary situational factors and (b) of general cultural factors. For either of these the momentary level of aspiration can be regarded as determined (a) by the individual's perception of his position on each reference scale which is relevant to his present situation, and (b) by the forces which act upon him in these positions. This point of view will be developed more extensively in the summary. Here will be considered the experimental data relevant to understanding the various phenomena.

Temporary Situational Factors

Success and Failure Within a Series

The statement can be made that generally the level of aspiration will be raised and lowered respectively as the performance (attainment) reaches or does not reach the level of aspiration. In speaking of shifts in the level of aspiration which rigidly adhere to the above principle, Jucknat (1937) has introduced the term "typical" cases. The existence of "atypical" cases will be discussed later. This experimenter used two series of ten mazes in a range of difficulty, one series in which the mazes were solvable and one in which they were not. With thirty children as subjects, the following results were obtained: In the solvable series the level of aspiration rose from a beginning level of 5.6 to an end level of 7.5. Of the observed shifts in level of aspiration, 76% were upward and 24% downward. In the nonsolvable series the level of aspiration fell from a beginning level of 6.5 to an end level of 3.6. Of the observed shifts, 84% were downward and 16% upward. Thus, under one condition 76% and under the other 84% of the shifts were "typical" ones, and the general trend followed the "typical" pattern.

Festinger (1942a), analyzing data specifically for this purpose, obtained the following results. After attainment of the level of aspiration there were 51% raisings, 41% staying on the same level, and 8% lowerings of the level of aspiration. After nonattainment of the level of aspiration these figures are 7%, 29%, and 64%, respectively. There were 219 shifts after attainment and 156 shifts after nonattainment.

Jucknat has carried this type of analysis one step further with a rating of the *reaction* to the attainment or nonattainment, i.e., the strength of success or failure judged to be experienced by the subject. Table I gives these results.

From this it appears that the stronger the success the greater will be the percentage of raising the level of aspiration, and the stronger the failure the greater the per cent of lowering the level of aspiration.

Thus we find that there is a high degree of agreement not only as to the direction which the shift in level of aspiration will take after success and failure, but even as to the percentage of such changes which will occur.

Transfer

Jucknat (1937) continued her work by investigating the effects of success or failure in one task on the level of aspiration for a subsequent task.

Table I.   Frequency of Raising or Lowering of the Level of Aspiration After Different Intensities of Success and Failure

	Shifts after success				Shifts after failure		
	S!!	S!	S	DS	F	F!	F!!
Number of cases	24	45	29	34	36	41	17
Percentage raising	96	80	55	56	22	19.5	12
Percentage lowering	4	20	45	44	78	80.5	88

Note.   Taken from Tables 3a and 3b, Jucknat, 1937, p. 99. S!! = very good success; S! = good success; S = just successful solution without evidence of distinct success; DS = solution with considerable effort; F = weak failure without evidence of serious feelings; F! = strong failure; F!! = very strong failure.

Using the same two series of pencil and paper mazes, on one of which the subjects always get success and the other on which they always get failure, she finds that the reactions to the series given first affect the level of aspiration behavior in the other series of tasks, the extent of the effect depending upon the extent to which the second series is regarded as a continuation of the first series. When the success series follows the failure series, the beginning level of aspiration for the second is lower than it was for the first series. When the failure series follows the success series, the reverse is true. If the success and failure series are made to look more different than previously, the effects are less marked although in the same direction as described above.

This indicates that less transfer of reactions to attainment of the level of aspiration occurs when the two series do not appear to constitute a single task. Thus the beginning level of aspiration for the second series is always put somewhere between the beginning and end levels of the first series. When the two series appear contiguous, the beginning level of the second series is nearer the end level, but when the two series appear different, the beginning level of aspiration for the second is nearer to the beginning level of aspiration of the first. The effect of one series on the other is then a partial one, the amount depending upon the similarity between the tasks.

Frank (1935b) finds that the level of aspiration on a "normal" task differs according to whether it followed an easy activity or a hard one. The average height of the beginning level of aspiration is higher when the normal task follows the easy activity than when it follows a hard one.

Range of Level of Aspiration

It is important to answer various further questions: Within what absolute levels of difficulty will the person set his goal level; within what ranges of performance will feelings of success and failure be experienced; and when will the person cease setting up aspiration levels for a given task?

There are some indications. An adult usually does not set any level of aspiration in connection with buttoning his overcoat nor does he set one in connection with physically impossible accomplishments. When faced with a difficulty continuum, the individual will set up goals near the boundaries of his ability. Experimental verification of this may be found in Hoppe (1930). Using a task which was ordinarily performed in about 88 seconds by the subjects, Hoppe found it impossible to produce feelings of success by setting a goal of 120 seconds or more nor could he produce failure by imposing a goal of 60 seconds or less. Under these circumstances the individual set up his own goals. Success and failure were experienced only when the goals ranged from 65 to 110 seconds.[1]

This tendency against setting up levels of aspiration in regions of activity which are either "too" easy or "too" difficult is also reflected on those occasions of stopping activity after a series of trials. Data on such cessation of activity is reported by Hoppe (1930) and Jucknat (1937). Hoppe reports that out of 42 cases of spontaneous stopping, ten stopped after a complete success "when raising the level of aspiration seems impossible either because the limits of personal ability have been reached or because the nature of the task or the instructions hinders such raising." Twenty-three cases stopped after complete failure "when the last possibility of getting a success is exhausted." Eight cases stopped after a single success following a series of failures when the previous failures had demonstrated the unlikeliness of a success with a higher level of aspiration. One case stopped after a single failure. Jucknat reports that of those subjects stopping after successes, 42% stopped on reaching the maximum possible achievement, 50% stopped after insufficient success, and 8% stopped before the maximum in spite of good successes.

From the above reported data it seems that in general there is a tendency to stop when the possibilities of achieving further success are not good. R. R. Sears (1942) found, furthermore, that subjects under failure conditions needed significantly more reminding than did subjects working under a success condition in order to have them state the level of aspiration. Here no stopping was permitted, but the failure subjects were able to a certain extent to withdraw themselves from the situation by not making the verbal statement of their goals.

General Cultural Factors

Standards of One's Own Group

The level of aspiration situation may involve certain clearly defined reference scales, i.e., the individual's performance is judged on a reference

---

[1]There are two cases out of 124 which did feel success when a goal of 150 seconds was imposed. The rest fall within the limits mentioned.

scale of another individual or the group to which he belongs. Anderson and Brandt's (1939) experiment illustrates the effects of this procedure. Their subjects (fifth-grade children) were given a series of six cancellation tests spaced a half-week apart. The relative performance scores of the subjects were posted on a graph so that each subject could see how he stood in relation to the group but could not identify the position of any other child. Before each succeeding test the subjects were asked to write down privately the score they thought they could make on the succeeding trial. The graphs showing the relative standing were kept up to date throughout the experiment. Grouping the subjects according to performance quartiles gives clear-cut trends showing the effectiveness of the knowledge of group standing. For the upper quartile (those scoring highest in the group) the level of aspiration was, on the average, 5.8 points below the performance level. For the second quartile the level of aspiration was, on the average, 1.9 points above the performance level. For the third quartile the level of aspiration was 2.1 points above the performance level. For the fourth, or lowest, quartile the level of aspiration was 13.6 points above the performance level. In short, we find a consistent trend in which those subjects who find themselves above the average of the group tend to have a negative discrepancy score, those finding themselves close to the average of the group tend to have a slightly positive discrepancy score, while those finding themselves below the mean of the group tend to have a very large positive discrepancy score. The correlation between discrepancy score and position of performance with respect to the group mean, taking positive and negative discrepancies into account, was $-.46$, i.e., the lower the performance relative to that of the group, the larger the discrepancy. The same result was found for college students, working in small groups, by Hilgard, Sait, and Margaret (1940). Here public announcement of the performance scores was made, while the levels of aspiration were recorded privately. These workers also performed a second experiment (1940) in which the ranking of the subjects in the group was experimentally controlled by giving some of the subjects hard problems, others problems of medium difficulty, and others easy problems. These three groups form the low, medium, and high performance groups. In this experiment the effect of the position in the group on the level of aspiration is more marked than when the natural performance was allowed to have its effect. Whereas all three groups start off with approximately the same amount of positive discrepancy score, by the last four trials the group that had easy materials has a discrepancy score of -3.4; the group that had medium materials has a discrepancy score of $+1.0$; and the group that had the difficult problems has a discrepancy score of $+4.2$. These experiments give reason to assume the existence of a frame of reference in which the individual's performance is placed on the scale formed *by the performances of his group*. Gardner's (1939) technique of reporting performance scores in terms of prearranged percentile values has the effect, similarly, of placing the subject's score with reference to that of others, and his finding that the goal discrepancies were higher at the lower portions of the performance curve than vice versa is consistent with the other findings.

Standards of Other Groups

The fact that the level of aspiration is subject to regular and consistent influence by the subject's knowledge of his own standing relative to that of his group suggests the possibility that knowledge of performances of other groups, identifiable as more or less prestigeful or superior than the subject's own, may have a similar effect. The scale of values defined by the "own group" may, in effect, be extended upward and downward with knowledge about other groups. Chapman and Volkmann (1939) made the first attack on this problem. By giving groups of college students comparison scores of (a) literary critics, (b) students, (c) WPA workers, for a test of "literary ability," they were able to manipulate the level of aspiration in a clear-cut way. The comparison scores were actually all equal but this fact was not known to the subjects. The heights of the aspiration levels for the various groups followed this order, from lowest to highest: (a) comparison with experts (critics), (b) no comparison, (c) comparison with own group (students), and (d) comparison with inferiors (WPA). The subjects giving these results had not taken the test and they were therefore ignorant of their own performance scores, although they knew the maximum possible score and the score obtainable by chance. Gould and Lewis (1940) and Festinger (1942a) followed this experiment with others which offer corroborative evidence for the influence of group standards of varying prestigefulness. The latter investigator used as the chief experimental measure the *change* in goal discrepancy score from a condition in which the subject had no scores but his own previous ones with which to compare his present performance, to an experimental condition in which his score was made to appear either above or below one of three groups: (a) high school, (b) college, and (c) graduate students. The subjects, themselves, were college students. The trends which the results show are illustrated in Figure 2, which gives the change in size and direction of goal discrepancy scores

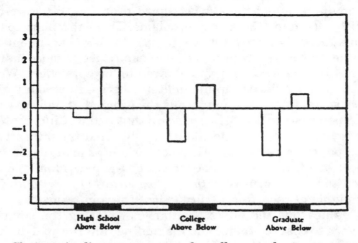

Figure 2. Changes in discrepancy score for college students compared to groups of low, medium, or high prestige.

when the subjects believed that their performances were either inferior to (below) or superior to (above) those of one of the comparison groups. Here we have a reference scale with a gradient of positive valence related to the prestige of the comparison group. This scale of values is analogous to that reported in the previous section in which the individual was placed with reference to his own group, but in the present case the individual is placed with reference to other groups which are conceptualized in a definitely valuative way. This frame of reference will be identified as that embodying comparisons with *other groups* of varying prestige.

Aspirations of Group

The individual may orient himself with respect to others' aspirations as well as to their performances. Hertzman and Festinger (1940) have explored this problem. After the average discrepancy scores for the subjects in a first experimental session had been determined, the subjects were given a second experimental session a week later at which they were told the average score and average level of aspiration of a group of other people of their own scholastic standing. The scores attributed to the group were arranged so that the individual's performance was equal, on the average, to the performance of the group. The positive or negative sign of the group goal discrepancy, however, was reported as opposite to that of the subject. The results showed that the level of aspiration changed significantly from the first to the second session in the direction of conforming to the group, i.e, the changes observed in level of aspiration were changes in the direction of the group level of aspiration. Changes from the first to the second session were statistically significant. Interviews with the subjects indicated that the conscious effect of such conforming to the group was very slight, or even nonexistent. The subjects' main conscious set was toward the scores (performances) of the group rather than toward the levels of aspiration. This would make one tend to suspect that although such conforming to group atmospheres exists, its effect in most cases is weak as compared to the effect of the performance of the group. It is, however, a frame of reference which may exert considerable influence under some conditions.

Psychological Effects of Socio-economic Background

A study by Gould (1941) gives evidence that goal discrepancies are related to various factors in the background of the subjects. Those individuals giving relatively low (negative or low positive) discrepancy scores, when compared to those giving predominantly high positive scores, are found to be also in a relatively more favorable social and economic position. Indices as more college training and income of the subjects' fathers, extent to which the students are not required to work their way through school, birth of the parents in this country, and expectancy of larger salaries in the future are found on the side of those subjects showing lower discrepancy scores. This reference scale and the one to be discussed in the next section represent attitudes toward endeavor and aspiration which have been determined before the subject comes to the experiment. Their effects are apparently similar to those in which an external standard is set by the experimenter on the foundation of internalized attitudes and values.

Habitual Success and Failure

Jucknat (1937) has evidence of the effect of another background factor on level of aspiration. When her experimental group of 500 children is divided into those who have been consistently good, medium, or poor students in their school work, differences in the height of the first level of aspiration are found between the groups. Faced with mazes placed in an ascending order of difficulty from 1 to 10, the group of good students set an initial level of aspiration rather high in the scale, between 7 and 10. The medium students' average was in the middle ranges, between 5 and 6. The poor students tended to set the aspiration level either low or high, between 1 and 4 on the one hand or between 7 and 10 on the other.

P. S. Sears (1940) selected small groups of children who had had clearly different school experience over a period of time with respect to success and failure. Those of the past failure group showed a higher goal discrepancy on the average than those of the past success group. More pronounced, however, was the wide variability among subjects of the failure group, such that the range of discrepancies was from very high positive to negative scores. The variability among subjects of the success group was much less, with discrepancies almost entirely within the small positive range.

Reality Levels

When a subject is asked to state his goal verbally, he may interpret this question in many different ways and the stated goal will differ according to the particular interpretation made. Gould (1939) showed this to be the case when she asked her subjects the question "What will you do next time?" Some subjects took the question to mean what they thought they really would get. Others interpreted the question as meaning what they hoped to get and responded accordingly. Gould distinguished three general groups in regard to interpretation of the experimental question: (a) those who set their level of aspiration at a minimum which the individual undertakes to overreach; (b) those who set it at a maximum which represents a mark they hope to come close to (actually being prepared not to reach it); (c) those who set their stated level of aspiration at about the average of their performance.

Thus a variety of attitudes on the part of the subjects will influence the nature of the results obtained through statements of aspiration levels. The stated action goal may represent, as Gould says, an incentive in one case and in another a protection against possible failure. The desire to come as close as possible to the level of aspiration, or to "guess accurately," may be a factor in some cases. Frank (1936) used comparison questions for eliciting the level of aspiration and finds that subjects who were asked "What do you think you will do?" were more likely to adopt a goal of trying to come close to their "guesses" than subjects who were asked "What do you intend to do?"

Festinger (1942a) found that subjects who were asked "What score would you like to get next time?" had a significantly higher discrepancy score (2.19) than subjects who were asked "What score do you expect to get next time?" (−.10). The former group was also significantly more variable than the latter in its goal discrepancy score. This result is completely corroborated in a study by Irwin and Mintzer (1942). Different attitudes, such as those occasioned by the two questions used by Festinger, may be interpreted as possessing different degrees of reality. The subject who tells what he expects to get seems to be realistic and keeps his level of aspiration close to his performance. The subject who tells what he hopes or what he likes, seems to become wishful and unrealistic and raises his goal far above his performance level.

There is some evidence favoring this type of interpretation. Frank (1935c), reasoning that a play situation is less bound to reality than a serious situation, finds that the discrepancy scores for a task like quoit-throwing which has a playful character are greater than for tasks of a more serious nature such as printing. Sears (1940) finds that the subjects with a low positive discrepancy score (realistic subjects) show more flexibility in the level of aspiration than those with a high positive discrepancy score (irrealistic subjects), i.e., they are more sensitive to changes in the performance. Corroborating this is the finding by Irwin and Mintzer (1942) that their "realistic" group showed a significantly greater number of changes of the level of aspiration than did the other group. Festinger (1942a) found that when compared to the performance of other groups, the unrealistic subjects behaved so as to avoid failure to a greater extent than did the realistic subjects by refusing to be influenced by an unpleasant external standard.

We may summarize these experimental findings as follows: The realistic attitude will produce a small discrepancy score with a level of aspiration that is flexible and responsive to changes in performance. The unrealistic attitude will produce a large discrepancy score with a level of aspiration; which is unresponsive to reality influence, and may reflect a wishful attitude toward the attainment of the action or stated goal.

In an attempt to control more adequately the attitude of the subject, Preston and Bayton (1941) asked their subjects to state three levels of aspiration; namely, the least they expected to do, the most they hoped to do, and what they actually thought they would do. Their results show that while the least estimates are unrelated to either of the other two estimates, there is a high correlation between the actual and maximum estimates. In addition, the actual estimates are always closer to the maximum than to the least estimates. This suggests that even a statement involving a supposedly objective ("actual") estimate will, in the absence of external factors designed to control the subjects' attitudes, tend in the upward rather than the downward direction. The actual as well as the maximum estimate thus appears to be more influenced by wishful considerations than does the least estimate. The latter may be regarded by the subject as a performance which he *might* (but hopes he will not) sink to if conditions are especially adverse.

Individual Differences

Previous sections have shown that numerous factors tend to influence the level of aspiration in certain rather consistent ways. Application of the principles resulting from the previous discussion to the prediction of a specific individual's behavior involves an additional problem, viz., to what extent are the experimentally observed behavior patterns samples of behavior which may occur in more than one goal-striving situation? This is the problem of generality of the behavior pattern, whether the generality be that involved in setting levels of aspiration for two motor tasks or that involved in estimating one's score on a golf game and on an important examination. The generality is measured by the correlation of the behavior in two different situations. Whether the operations measured in these situations are the subject's own verbal statements involving explicit goals or are nonverbal behaviors interpreted by another person, the relations obtained are representative of the extent to which the same reference scales and other dynamic factors are involved in both. Viewed in this way, the problem of generality is one determining within what limits the same factors will be found playing a significant role in different situations.

Closely allied to the study of generality by correlation of specific aspiration level scores is the analysis of the relation between experimentally obtained scores and other personality variables. Not all of these variables are conceptually relevant to goal-setting, but because most of them have been first observed clinically in the goal-setting situation, the majority are closely related to that aspect of behavior. Both generality and the establishment of relationships with other variables involve comparison of individuals in two or more situations.

A third problem is that of the variability of behavior within a single situation. Instead of asking whether one individual maintains, in different situations and on various measures, the same relative position with respect to other members of the group, we may inquire as to the extent of difference between individuals on a single measure under specified conditions. For example, one might ask whether there is a greater variability in a highly structured situation than in one in which various individual interpretations are possible, and if so, what the conditions are for structuralization of goal situations. This problem has so far received little attention in the literature, but there is evidence that, in a gross way, the heterogeneity of behavior is important for understanding the behavior in such situations. Once the factors determining the individual's behavior in one experimental situation have been established, the analysis may be continued, as described above, in terms of the generality of his position on various tasks and operations which may be significant for generalizing about his behavior.

The literature in this field falls naturally into several groups. First, the most experimental work has been directed toward ascertaining the extent of generality of the *goal discrepancy score* in various tasks, and this will be first discussed. Second, many workers have felt the inadequacy of thus depending on a single measure culled from the wealth of material which the level of aspiration situation yields, and have attempted to utilize measures other than the total discrepancy. Two types of study have appeared so far: (a) those of the statistical generality of the secondary measures, and (b) those attempting an analysis of the "course of events" or patterning of the level of aspiration behavior. Third, the relationship of aspiration responses to factors beyond the confines of the experimental level of aspiration situation has been investigated. Although this problem is commonly referred to as that of correlated "personality traits," it is as has been shown, that of more broadly conceived generality of goal behavior combined with exploration of relations to other, possibly independent, variables. Fourth, there is the examination of variability within a group of persons put under various experimental conditions.

Generality of the Goal Discrepancy Score

Hoppe (1930) was aware of the broad problem of generality and devoted some time to demonstrating the consistency of the behavior of different individuals. The first specific study of generality of the discrepancy was performed by Frank (1935a). Correlating the discrepancy scores for two different sessions on the same task he finds correlations ranging from .57 to .75 for two of his tasks. For the third task the correlations are .26 and .63. From these data he concludes that the level of aspiration behavior is consistent and explains the low correlation for the third task (quoits) by the fact that it was more of a play (irreal) situation, and therefore the individual's reactions to it are less bound by realistic factors which tend to stabilize the behavior in the other situation. Correlations within the same session of the discrepancy scores between his first two tasks, printing and spatial relations, also yield fairly large coefficients, ranging from .50 to .65. Correlations involving the quoits were mostly either zero or slightly positive. Gould (1939), using six different tasks, three given in one session and three in another, finds intercorrelations among the tasks on the discrepancy score ranging from .44 to .04 with a median intercorrelation of .29. When the correlations were calculated separately for those tasks given in the same session and for those given in different sessions, the median intercorrelation for the discrepancy score on tasks given in the same session goes up to .46 while the median intercorrelation for discrepancy score on tasks given in different sessions stays at .30. Gould's correlations, although lower than those obtained by Frank, still indicate some tendency toward consistency. The fact that the correlations were higher for tasks in the same session leads Gould to make the interpretation that the individuals respond more to the situation than to the task itself.

The difference between the results of Gould and Frank is perhaps due to the greater diversity of tasks used by Gould and the lesser amount of control over the subjects' attitudes in the Gould experiment.[2] Gardner (1939), more adequately controlling the latter factor, obtains generality correlations close to Frank's. Gardner's technique involves arranging the situation so that all subjects have the same scores. The series of scores present in one place a rising curve of performance (successful experience), in another place a falling curve (failure experience), with occasional reversals in order. Four tasks were used and generality correlation coefficients were calculated for the discrepancy scores at different places along the performance curve. The mean correlation for the beginning level of aspiration was .37. A mean correlation of .37 was also obtained for the average of three consecutive discrepancy scores in that part of the curve where the performance remained on the same level. In the middle portion of the curve, the performance rapidly increases for three trials and then after a single reversal increases for another two trials. The mean correlation coefficient for the average of the discrepancy scores for the five increasing performances was .55. After this rising portion, the performance curve slowly but regularly falls for five performances. The mean intercorrelation for the average discrepancy scores of these five trials was .61. The intercorrelations of the average discrepancy scores over the whole series of performances with the exception of the first two and last two trials yields a mean of .57.

Conflicting results on the question of generality are to a large extent reconciled in the results obtained by Heathers (1942). With the idea that the amount of generality observed will depend to a large extent on the similarities of the different situations, Heathers varied three factors of the objective situation to determine their influence on the degree of generality: the scale or units in which the performance scores were presented to the subject, the shape of the curve which the series of performance scores followed, and the motivation of the subjects. Prearranged performance scores were used and the subject was asked to tell what score he was "going to try to make on the next trial," or what his goal was.

When the scale of units in which the scores were reported to the subjects and the shape of the performance curve are both the same in two tasks, the correlation of the discrepancy scores for these tasks is .87. When the curves are the same but the scale in which the scores are reported is different for the two tasks, this correlation drops to .67. The difference between these two correlations is statistically significant, indicating that the difference in scale is enough of a difference in similarity between the

---

[2] The two tasks for which Frank obtained relatively high correlations were rather similar in nature, and it will be remembered, for the quoits, which were quite different from his other tasks, the correlations were lower. In addition, the question used by Gould, "What will you do next time?" probably allows more fluctuation of attitude than the question of "What do you intend to do?" used by Frank. Gardner asked the subject where he "expected to stand" in relation to a group of students.

two situations to reduce significantly the degree of generality. No significant differences were found between correlations for the group having both scale and curve constant and the group for which the scale was constant but the curve was varied. Generality in both instances is very high, with correlations ranging from .74 to .86. There is evidence that variation in shape of curve will produce differences in generality if, as the author concludes, "the contours of the curve are different enough to provide the subject with different interpretations concerning the amount and rate of his improvement." In the present case the average amount of increase for all the curves was about the same from beginning to end, and therefore the total success and failure experience is presumably roughly equivalent. Reliable differences in generality are obtained when the curves are split so that amounts of improvement, with consequent changes in amount of success stimulation, are varied. These results indicate how important it is to distinguish in detail the specific success and failure conditions for any measure of generality.

When both the shape of the curve and the scale are varied, the results are significantly different from the case where they were both held constant. For the latter group the correlations range from .93 to .79 while for the former group they vary from .35 to .74.

In another group of subjects the motivation to perform well on the tasks was varied by making the task an intelligence test and offering prizes for good performances for one group. The generality correlation coefficient for the group that was highly motivated to do well was .93 for the two tasks in the first experimental session. The comparable correlation for the group which was not highly motivated to do well was .84. This difference is significant statistically. Significant differences do not appear, however, in the correlations obtained from a second session at which it appeared that the high level of motivation arranged for the experimental group had considerably declined.

It is interesting to note that the average intercorrelation for tasks during the same experimental session is .81 while the average intercorrelation for tasks in different experimental sessions is .62. This latter value of .62 agrees rather well with the average intercorrelation of .57 reported by Gardner (1940a). The relatively greater constancy of the subjects' attitudes and moods within the same experimental session undoubtedly makes for a greater similarity between tasks on the same day as compared with tasks on different days.

One can also look at the question of generality by investigating the extent to which experience of success or failure in one situation will affect the level of aspiration in another situation. This might be called a "transfer effect." Jucknat's and Frank's findings on this problem have been reported already. The transfer effect of success and failure is greatest when the subject finds the two tasks to be similar or two parts of one larger activity.

Generality of Other Measures Related to the Level of Aspiration

Rotter (1942b), calculating test–retest generality after a period of one month, found the following correlations on a motor performance task in a situation where the subject was rewarded for correct estimates and penalized for incorrect. For the number of times the subject reached or exceeded his estimate, the coefficient is .46; for the shifts up and down respectively, following such "success" or "failure" to reach the estimate .56; frequency of shifts, .70. All the coefficients are statistically significant and indicate a certain stability of measures of aspiration behavior other than discrepancy.

Patterning of discrepancy scores and other measures related to level of aspiration has been observed by many investigators and rough attempts at formulation of such patterns are described by Sears (1940), working with school children, and Rotter (unpublished) for adults.

In the case of neither investigation is it found that patterns are rigidly marked off from one another; rather, these combinations of factors are described as rough approximations of constellations which may prove to have psychological significance.

Both workers find that there is a pattern represented by (a) the "low positive discrepancy score," utilized in a realistic way with adequate adjustment to both success and failure. Responsiveness of the level of aspiration up or down following changes of similar direction in performance score is rather high; flexibility (shifts) of the level of aspiration is average, (b) the "low negative discrepancy score" pattern is chiefly characterized by a protectively low action goal, which is ordinarily kept below the level of performance. Slightly less responsiveness and flexibility are found to be associated with this kind of response than with the preceding.

Sears gives data on two more patterns, the "high positive discrepancy" pattern, with very low flexibility and responsiveness, and the "mixed" pattern in which responses are irregular and highly variable throughout the successive trials of one task. Rotter distinguishes seven more types of pattern: the "medium high positive discrepancy" associated with responsiveness to success and failure and a realistic attitude; the pattern of "achievement following" in which the level of aspiration is constantly changed to conform as exactly as possible to the level of the previous performance; the "step" pattern, characterized by shifts in an upward direction only; the "very high positive" pattern, with responses largely of a phantasy nature; the "high negative" pattern; the "rigid" pattern, showing an absence of shifts regardless of achievement, and the "confused" or "breakdown" pattern.

Hilgard and Sait (1941) asked subjects to estimate their past as well as their future performance, and thus obtained two discrepancies in addition to the usual goal discrepancy: (a) estimate of past performance minus (true) past performance, and (b) estimate of future performance minus (true) future performance. The third difference used was the familiar goal discrepancy. Odd–even reliabilities for all three discrepancies are satisfactory, and generality coefficients between two motor tasks fairly high. The authors conclude that subjective distortion enters into estimates made of both past and future performance, i.e., goal strivings are not only oriented toward the future, but also influence an individual's perception of his past. These influences are not consistent in direction for different individuals, but do show considerable generality, i.e., for the same individual, the direction of the distortion appears rather consistent from task to task.

Preston and Bayton (1941) further vary the standard technique in asking subjects (a) what they actually expect to get, (b) the least they would be likely to get, and (c) the most they would hope to get. Generality of these estimates from task to task is rather high. In a second paper (1942), correlations between the various estimates are presented. Those between the least and the actual estimates and between least and maximum are all negligible, while correlations between the actual and the maximum estimates are appreciable (range from .45 to .84).

Personality Characteristics

All workers in this field are agreed that the level of aspiration situation is a favorable milieu in which to observe individual traits relating to the competitive and goal behavior of the subject. So far, however, objective demonstration of relationships has proceeded but slowly.

The problem basic for personality characteristics as determinants of the level of aspiration behavior is the evaluation of relative weights which different reference scales have for a given individual. For example, social standards may play a relatively greater role for one subject than for another in the same objective situation; failure may be more decisive than success and a wishful attitude may be more characteristic of a given subject in a certain situation than is a more realistic attitude.

Hoppe (1930), Jucknat (1937), and Frank (1935c) describe types of personality traits which are deduced from the level of aspiration situation and which are regarded as influential in determining the behavior in that situation, e.g., ambition, prudence, courage to face reality. Independent measures of the personality factors were not obtained by these investigators.

Gould and Kaplan (1940) and Gardner (1940a) have made correlational studies relating certain broad personality variables to goal discrepancy scores. The former investigators found only insignificant relationships between discrepancy scores and scores (a) for dominance–feeling (Maslow inventory) and (b) extroversion–introversion (Guilford). Gardner obtained ratings for his subjects on a number of broad traits culled from the observations of Hoppe, Jucknat, and Frank. These also show low correlations with discrepancy scores, although in each case the findings were in the same direction as the hypotheses of the previous investigators would suggest.

Frank (1938) reports correlations obtained in connection with Murray's personality studies. Size of goal discrepancy is positively correlated (.20 or higher) with personality variables involving, according to Frank's analysis, the following factors: "(1) the wish to do well (often unaccompanied by the will to do well), (2) a subjective attitude, and (3) the ability to dismiss failures." Evidently some slight relationships make their appearance through such correlational techniques, but the evidence is far too slim to provide a solid basis for future thinking in this area. The variables so far investigated are probably too broad and generalized to be usefully isolated as correlatives or determinants of specific level of aspiration scores such as the goal discrepancy.

More fruitful than correlational studies has been analysis of factors associated with "high," "medium," and "low," or "negative" discrepancy scores. Results showing differences in security of socio-economic and academic status between groups of subjects which show chiefly one of these types of scores have been discussed in a previous section. Gardner's "high" and "low" discrepancy groups give results which are confirmatory though based on small numbers of subjects and statistically not highly significant. In his experiment, the ten subjects having the highest average (positive) discrepancy scores were also rated highest on (a) *dissatisfaction with status* and (b) *importance attached to intellectual achievement*. The ten subjects having the lowest discrepancy scores were rated lowest on (a) *subjective achievement level*, (b) *general sense of security*, (c) *tendency to face failure frankly*, (d) *realism*, and (e) *motivation*, and were rated highest on *fear of failure*. These ratings were made outside of the experimental situation by raters who were thoroughly acquainted with the subjects.

Sears (1941) has made clinical studies of selected small groups of children who were highly motivated for good school work and had been either (a) highly successful or (b) unsuccessful at obtaining good school status over a period of several years. When these subjects were divided according to size of discrepancy scores for experimental school type tasks, certain related factors emerged as also differentiating these groups. Children using predominantly a "high" discrepancy pattern are poorer in school achievement than the other groups and are rated as showing an attitude of low self-confidence accompanied by rather free admission of their incompetence. Here is an example of a specific relationship between goal setting for success and self-confidence. The correlation holds between behavior in the experimental level of aspiration (for school tasks) area and the aspirations (also for school tasks) observed in the schoolroom and clinical situations. Those children showing characteristically the "low positive" discrepancy ("realistic") reaction are, on the other hand, rated as highly confident, successful and comfortable in their achievement. Behavior problems and unfavorable personality traits (rated by the teacher) appear less frequently in them than in the other groups. A third group, called in this study the "negative discrepancy" group, is equivalent to Gould's and Gardner's "low" groups. These children fall in between the other two in confidence and academic success, but are differentiated from both others in terms of high ratings for self-consciousness, socially- rather than self-oriented motivation, defensiveness and self-protection in their attitudes toward failure. It is of some interest with respect to generality of aspiration that when in this study the subjects rated themselves on a paper and pencil questionnaire with reference to a number of diverse life activities, their averages for the ratings "how good I am at" and "how good I wish I were at" followed the course to be predicted on the basis of the aspiration level classification if the "how good I am at" rating is conceived as analogous to a performance score and the "how good I wish I were at" rating analogous to a level of aspiration score. The high positive discrepancy group showed the greatest difference between perceived and wished-for skills, the low positive group the next difference, and the negative discrepancy group the least difference.

Similar findings are reported by Rotter (unpublished) who has amplified and elaborated the discrepancy patterns as previously described. Three patterns of response, the low positive, low (slightly) negative, and medium high discrepancy score patterns are designated arbitrarily as "socially acceptable" methods of solution for the self-evaluation problem presented in the level of aspiration situation.[3] Six other patterns, including the very high positive and high negative discrepancies, step, rigid, confused, and achievement-following patterns, are designated as "socially unacceptable." Prison inmates were classified, in terms of past history and present behavior in situations involving self-evaluation, into (a) a "normal" group, in which goals had in actual behavior been held fairly close to the experiences of achievement, (b) a "defeated" group, whose behavior was characterized by lack of confidence, strong fear of failure, and protection against failure by setting very low explicit goals, (c) a "conflict–tension" group characterized by inability to reach a decision in problem situations. The "normal" group of prisoners showed in the level of aspiration situation a preponderance of the "socially acceptable" patterns over the "unacceptable," while acceptable and unacceptable were approximately evenly balanced in the "defeated" and "conflict–tension" groups. Of the other subjects employed, college cripples as compared to college normals had a relatively high percentage in the protective high negative discrepancy score pattern. College students showed higher percentages of "achievement-following" and "step patterns" than did the hospital employees, but were not up to them or to the "normal" prison group in terms of percentage of acceptable patterns used.

Yacorzynski (1942) has studied the relation between degree of effort expended on a task and the direction of the aspiration level. An inverse relation appears between these two variables; i.e., an increasing degree of effort is associated with a decreasing number of predictions that the scores will improve. *Confidence* in one's own ability, he feels, may increase predictions of improved scores on successive trials and also decrease the amount of effort shown.

Variability Within a Group

A given attitude permits according to its nature greater or smaller individual differences. Thus as we have seen before, the realistic attitude binding the subject to his performance will not permit so much deviation from this point as appears in the wide range of irreality or wishful thinking.

---

[3]In this case a premium was put on exact estimation of performance by specially designed instructions similar to those of Hausmann (1933).

The distribution of individual scores according to these attitudes can be measured by the variability of the group.

Festinger (1942a) finds that a group forced to a realistic attitude is less variable than one for which the instructions permitted various degrees of realism. McGehee (1940) devised an experiment in which the future of performance was estimated by an observer while the person performing set a level of aspiration. The levels of aspiration were regularly more variable than the estimates of the other person, though in this case the differences do not reach complete reliability.

Sears (1940) found reliable differences in spread of scores (group variability) between groups whose past school experience of the task had been either successful or unsuccessful. The success subjects showed on the average lower discrepancies than did the failure subjects and appeared more realistically oriented to their levels of aspiration, but the most marked differences between groups were those of the variability of the scores. The failure group showed a spread of discrepancies varying from negative to high positive, while the success group scores were concentrated within the low positive range. Further, those subjects of the failure group who utilize the high positive discrepancy maintain their discrepancies rigidly, without the responsiveness to performance and attention to the performance scores which seem to be related to a realistic attitude.

Another kind of variability is that shown by the individual subject in the generality of his behavior on different tasks. Gould (1939) finds a correlation of .33 between variability of this kind and height of discrepancy. That is, there is a tendency for those having low or negative discrepancies to respond more to the situation as a whole than to the specific task, while those with high discrepancy scores on some tasks tend to vary more in their responses from task to task.

The Development of the Level of Aspiration

The age level at which a level of aspiration can be said to exist depends upon a number of considerations. Observational evidence suggests the existence of a "rudimentary" level of aspiration in very young children. Repeated efforts toward a difficult accomplishment are observed in the very young child, e.g., in his attempts to walk independently, to pull off an article of clothing, or to sit down upon a chair. However, before these behaviors can be regarded as precursors of the level of aspiration phenomena previously discussed, it is necessary to postulate the development of the child's thought processes to a level which permits cognition, comparison, and choice of psychological values in general and specifically of that value continuum or scale called "overcoming of difficulties."

Steps Preceding the Fully Developed Level of Aspiration

Fales (1937) considered the child's wanting to do something by himself rather than with someone's help as a stage preceding the full development of the level of aspiration. This type of behavior may be called "rudimentary aspiration." The level of aspiration differs from "rudimentary aspiration" by being the stage at which achievement *levels* can be distinguished.

The strivings for "independence" as a rule occur only in a situation where moderate difficulties exist. Thus the child tries to become independent in his marginal areas of ability.

Fales studied two- and three-year-old children in a nursery school performing the activity of putting on and taking off wraps. The percentage of refusal of help was taken as a measure of "rudimentary aspiration." This was found to exist already at the two-year-old level.

Fales next trained one group of children in taking off their wraps and compared this group before and after training with a group which was not trained. The comparison observations were made in putting on the wraps. The group which received the training, that is, the group which became more skillful and more secure in its performance, increased considerably in percents of refusal of help as compared with the group which did not receive training.

In another experiment Fales praised one group of children for their endeavors. They were compared with a group which was not praised. The praised group increased in "independence" considerably more than the control group and even exceeded the trained group mentioned above. It may be concluded that training the child to become more skillful and rewarding the independent behavior by praise promotes "rudimentary aspiration."

Anderson (1940) used a ring-throwing task with three groups of children averaging about three years, five and a half years, and eight years of age, respectively. This investigator distinguishes four aspects of behavior, each of which shows different developmental steps. They are:

(1) *Manner of throwing*, i.e., the child can get the rings on by actually placing them, by dropping them, or by throwing the rings from a distance. The developmental steps follow this order.

(2) *Rethrowing of rings*: Rings which were missed may or may not be rethrown by the child. The latter indicates a higher developmental stage. When rings are rethrown they may be rethrown immediately or after a whole series has been thrown. The latter is again a higher developmental step.

(3) *Size of unit*: Of those subjects who threw the rings, some regarded each ring as a unit while others regarded the series of five rings as a unit. The latter is considered a higher developmental step.

(4) *Amount of failure*: The willingness of the subject to risk missing rings was also taken as an indication of a higher development of level of aspiration behavior.

Taking the above described factors into consideration, Anderson attempted to determine the "maturity" of the level of aspiration. The highest possible maturity score is 9. The mean maturity scores for the oldest, middle, and youngest groups are 8.54, 6.34, and 2.13, respectively. The differences among all these groups are statistically significant. The maturity scores for the groups on each of the separate factors making up the total score follow the same pattern. Thus we find the maturity of the level of aspiration, in terms of adult standards, increased with age.

Anderson's experiments show that in his experimental set-up all components of the level of aspiration observed in adults in a similar situation can be found in the eight-year-olds. Jucknat's (1937) findings are consistent with these results. She finds no differences in the level of aspiration behavior in regard to beginning and end levels in a group of children between the ages of 11 and 12 and a group of adults. The tasks she used were solvable and unsolvable mazes.

There are conditions under which the level of aspirator behavior of the child can appear less mature than it actually is under optimal conditions. Such a condition exists when the "means to a goal" character of the task is emphasized. Anderson reduced the emphasis on performance *per se* by giving a reward for getting many rings on the stick. The mean maturity scores for the oldest, middle, and youngest groups were reduced to 7.34, 5.03, and 1.03, respectively. The differences between the reward and nonreward situations are significant for each group, the maturity score being uniformly lower in the reward situation.

A regression to a lower developmental level with respect to the maturity of the level of aspiration probably could be produced in children in a frustration situation. This can be expected because frustration experiments in adults (Dembo) showed that subjects, performing the ringthrowing task, would start to rethrow rings and, instead of throwing them from the distance, place them on the stick when severely frustrated.

For further research it would be important to investigate the development in respect to different reference scales (see pp. 141–157 and pp. 172–174) of the level of aspiration.

Summary and Theoretical Considerations

The studies of the level of aspiration have grown from empirical findings and have been influenced by various considerations. Some studies have tried to determine the factors which influence the raising and lowering of the level of aspiration and to understand the conditions of success and failure; others concern themselves with the question of the degree to which personality traits play a role. A theoretical survey and summary may help to clarify a situation which is at present a bit chaotic, and to give orientation to further experimentation. No attempt will be made in this summary to take in all the results. Essentially we will follow the "resultant valence theory" which has been presented by Escalona (1940) and elaborated by Festinger (1942b). Gould and Lewin (unpublished manuscript) have brought this theory into a wider setting by linking it to various "frames of reference."

Level of Aspiration as a Choice Situation; Valences and Probability

A basic problem of the level of aspiration can be formulated as an apparent discrepancy between the tendency to set up higher and higher goals (that is, a willingness to enter difficult undertakings) and the customary notion that life is governed by the tendency to avoid unnecessary effort (parsimony). Have we to assume an innate tendency to "strive for higher things" to explain the fact that the individual prefers the difficult task or prefers doing certain activities himself rather than using the easy way of being helped by someone else?

According to Escalona, this problem can be solved if one considers the psychological situation as it exists at the time when the individual makes up his mind about the next goal; that is, the point 2 of our sequence.

The psychological situation at the moment can be characterized as a choice situation (Figure 3). The person has to decide whether he will choose a more difficult, an equally difficult, or an easier level; for instance, whether he will try to finish the job on hand in 10 minutes or only in 12 or 15 minutes. (Actually, he could also "stop" entirely, which means a change to a different activity. We will consider this aspect of the choice later.)

One can state analytically for this as for any other choice situation that that action is chosen as a goal for which the sum of attractiveness (position valence) minus the sum of disagreeableness (negative valence) is a maximum. To determine this maximum, one should know the factors which bring about the positive or negative valences of these different actions. We will discuss some of these factors in a step-by-step order, going from the general to the specific.

The choice in the case of the level of aspiration involves the relative valences of variations in the *same* activity; in dealing with a choice between different tasks, e.g., target shooting, multiplying two-place numbers, and solving puzzles, a great many factors enter into the valences or attractiveness. Prediction is more difficult in this case since wide individual differences result. In level of aspiration situations, analysis of the choice is somewhat simplified by the fact that the general character of the activity is constant. The choice is determined by the different valences which different degrees of difficulties within the same activity have for the person.

The individual faces the possibility of succeeding or failing, and the positive or negative valence of such a future success or failure on the various levels is one of the basic elements for the decision. To determine the valence (Va) of each level (n) of activity $[Va(A^n)]$, we have to consider the negative valence that future failure has on that level $[Va(Fai^{A^n})]$ and the positive valence of success on that level $[Va(Suc^{A^n})]$.

$$Va(A^n) = Va(Suc^{A^n}) + Va(Fai^{A^n}).[4]$$
(1)

---

[4] As the valence of failure is usually negative (neg Va) and the valence of success is

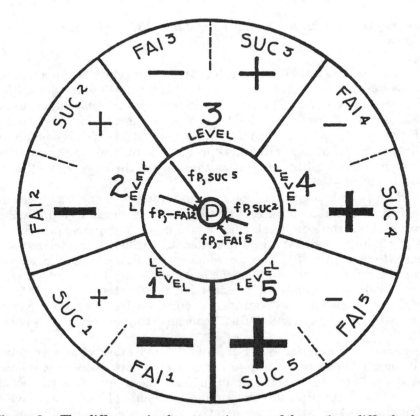

Figure 3. The difference in the attractiveness of the various difficulty levels 1 to 5 of the activity is determined by the valence of success increases, that of failure decreases with increasing difficulty level. Correspondingly, the force toward success, for instance, f_{P,Suc^5} is greater than the force f_{P,Suc^2} on level 2. The force away from failure $f_{P,-Fai^5}$ is smaller than $f_{P,-Fai^2}$. Therefore, the total valence of the more difficult level is higher than the easier level.

The valences of future success and failure on various levels may be illustrated by the example of doing twenty simple additions in a given time. To the adult subject, achievement on a very easy level, such as finishing the twenty simple additions in one hour, would not bring any appreciable feeling of success. This is "child's play." The valence of success on this level 1 (Table II, columns 2 and 3) is approximately zero. The valence of success on levels of greater difficulty, such as finishing these additions in 50 minutes, 40 minutes, and so on, continues to be zero until the tasks cease to be altogether "too easy." Then the valence of achievement starts to be perceptibly positive although at first very small. In our example (Table II), we assume that at the difficulty level 4, the valence of success will equal 1.

With increased difficulty, the valence of success also increases. Finally,

---

usually positive (pos Va) formula (1) means that usually the former is subtracted from the latter: $Va(A^n) = \text{pos } Va(Suc^{A^n}) - \text{neg. } Va(Fai^{A^n})$.

we reach the level of difficulty that taxes the person's ability to capacity. There the valence is likely to be at a maximum (arbitrarily indicated by 10). Still more difficult levels beyond the boundary zone of ability will probably have the same high positive valence.

Higher on the scale there are degrees of difficulty which seem "entirely out of reach of the individual," for instance, solving the twenty additions in 20 seconds (level 14), and levels above this which are "humanly impossible," for instance, finishing the task in 5 seconds. Such levels are usually not even considered, and one might leave these values blank on the scales. The greater the degree of difficulty, therefore, the higher the valence of success within the boundary zone of ability.

The absolute value of the negative valence of failure usually changes in the opposite direction. On levels of extreme difficulty, the negative valence of failure would be negative. Even on the level of very difficult performance, failure might have no negative valence. The negative valence increases until it reaches a maximum in the area of relatively easy tasks. There it remains close to a maximum and finally drops out of consideration somewhere in the area of too easy tasks.

Within the crucial range of difficulty we can say that:

$$\text{pos } Va(Suc^{A^{high}}) > \text{pos } Va(Suc^{A^{low}}) \tag{2}$$

$$\text{neg } Va(Fai^{A^{high}}) < \text{neg } Va(Fai^{A^{low}}) \tag{3}$$

The total valence of the level according to formula 1 is the algebraic sum of these valences. As the positive valence of success increases with difficulty and the negative valence of failure decreases we can conclude, from formulae 2 and 3, that the total valence on the high level should always be greater than the total valence on the lower level because

$$Va(^{A^{high}}) = Va(Suc^{A^{high}}) + Va(Fai^{A^{high}})$$

$$> Va(Suc^{A^{low}}) + Va(Fai^{A^{low}}) = Va(^{A^{low}}). \tag{4}$$

The analytical considerations lead therefore to the conclusion that, given the valence of success and failure which is predominant in our culture, there is nothing paradoxical in the fact that people reach out for difficult tasks. We rather have now to explain why it is not always the most difficult task which is chosen.

Probability of Future Success; the Basic Theoretical Assumption

The answer is that we have to deal here with a *future* success and failure. The individual is, therefore, not only influenced by the attractiveness of such an event but also by the probability of its occurrence as this is seen by him (Figure 4).

Table II.   Examples of Reference Scales Underlying a Level of Aspiration / **Table IIa**

1 Levels of possible objective	2 Valences of Fut. Suc.	3 Valences of Fut. Fai.	4 Subjective probability Succeeding	5 Subjective probability Failing	6 Weighted valence of Fut. Suc.	7 Weighted valence of Fut. Fai.	8 Resultant weighted valence	Resultant weighted valence when group standard has potency = .3
15	10	0	0	100	0	0	0	0
14	10	0	0	100	0	0	0	0
13	10	0	0	100	0	0	0	0
12	10	0	0	100	0	0	0	0
11	10	0	5	95	50	0	50	47
10	9	0	10	90	90	0	90	63 Level of aspiration
9	7	−1	25	75	175	−75	100	−35
8	6	−2	40	60	240	−120	120	−24
7	5	−3	50	50	250	−150	100	−50
6	3	−5	60	40	180	−200	−20	−98
5	2	−7	75	25	150	−175	−25	−93
4	1	−9	90	10	90	−90	0	−30
3	0	−10	95	5	0	−50	−50	−50
2	0	−10	100	0	0	0	0	0
1	0	−10	100	0	0	0	0	0

Too difficult ← (rows 15–10)

Too easy → (rows 2–1)

Level of aspiration   ↑ $g\ ds = 1$ (at level 7)

$g\ ds = 3$ ← Level of aspiration (Table IIa)

Level of past performance and of expectation

Note. Column 1 indicates the possible objectives. The "too difficult" and "too easy" levels correspond to the areas where the subjective probability of failing (column 5) and of succeeding (column 4) are 100% or close to 100%. Columns 2 and 3 give valences of future success and failure on each level; they vary between 0 and 100. Columns 6 and 7 represent the weighted valences, e.g., valence times probability, according to formulae 5a and 5b. Column 8 gives the resultant valence according to formula 6 (see p. 168).

In this schematic example, the level of past performance is assumed to have been on the level 7. The individual expects his next performance to lie on the same level, perhaps because he has found it difficult to reach that level. This "level of expectation" corresponds to the 50–50 level of subjective probability. The level of aspiration according to formula 6 is determined by the maximum value of the resultant weighted valence, that is, in our example the value of 120 corresponding to difficulty level 8. The goal discrepancy score (*g ds*), that is, the level of aspiration minus the level of past performance, equals 1.

Table IIa represents the resultant weighted valence in a case where the valences of future success and failure are based on two reference scales: The one is the scale related to group standards as expressed in column 2 and 3 of Table V; the other scale of reference might have the same distribution of values as that in columns 2 and 3 of Table II. This distribution of values might be an expression, for instance, of the valences based on one's own past performance.

The relative weight or "potency," of these two frames of references might be 3 (group standard) to 7. In such cases the valence of future success or failure would be determined by the sum of the corresponding values on the two frames of reference multiplied by that fraction which represents the relative potency of that scale. For instance, the valence of future success on the level 7 would be $5 \times .7 + 2 \times .3$; that of future failure would be $-3 \times .7 - 10 \times .3$. These values would have to be weighted by the subjective probability of success and failure as usual.

Our example shows that the poor student in our case would set his level of aspiration less high if he is not exclusively influenced by the reference scale of the group standard: the goal discrepancy equals 3 instead of 4 as in Table V.

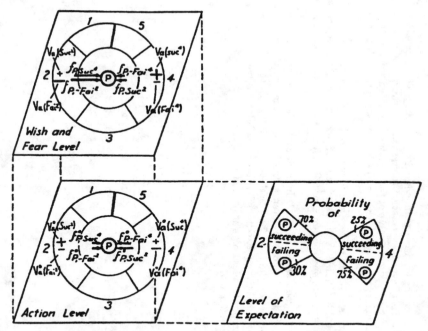

Figure 4. Figure 3 takes into account the valences of success and failure but not the probability of the succeeding or failing at the various degrees of difficulty. Such a situation corresponds psychologically to a constellation which may exist on the "wish and fear level." The constellation of forces on the "action level" depends, in addition, on the individual's perception of the future, that is, the structure of the "level of expectation." Notice the difference in the direction of the resultant forces on the wish and on the action level.

1, 2, . . . , 5 tasks of increasing degrees of difficulty;
$Va(Suc^2)$ valence of success in task 2 on wish and fear level
$Va(Fai^2)$ valence of failure in task 2 on wish and fear level
$Va(Suc^2)$ weighted valence of success in task 2 on action level
$Va(Fai^2)$ weighted valence of success in task 2 on action level
f_{P,Suc^2} force toward success in task 2
$f_{P,-Fai^2}$ force away from failure in task 2
f^o_{P,Suc^2} weighted force toward success in task 2.

Columns 4 and 5 (Tables II and III) give values for subjective probability of succeeding or failing. The probability of success increases from zero to 100% with decreasing difficulty and the probability of failure changes in the opposite direction.

Escalona sets forth the "resultant valence theory" according to which the choice is determined, not by the valence of future success or failure as such, but rather by these valences modified by the probability of the occurrence of these events. The most simple assumption is that this "weighted" valence of success [$^oVa(Suc^{A^n})$] is the product of the valence and of the probability of success.

Table III. Example of Reference Scales Underlying a Level of Aspiration

1 Possible objective	2 Valences of	3	4 Subjective probability	5	6 Weighted valence of	7	8 Resultant weighted valence
	Fut. Suc.	Fut. Fai.	Succeeding	Failing	Fut. Suc.	Fut. Fai.	
15	10	0	0	100	0	0	0
14	10	0	0	100	0	0	0
13	10	0	0	100	0	0	0
12	10	0	5	95	50	0	50
11	10	0	10	90	100	0	100
10	9	0	25	75	225	0	225
9	7	−1	40	60	280	−60	220
8	6	−2	50	50	300	−100	200
7	5	−3	60	40	300	−120	150
6	3	5	75	25	300	−125	175
5	2	−7	90	10	180	−70	110
4	1	−9	95	5	95	−45	50
3	0	−10	100	0	0	0	0
2	0	−10	100	0	0	0	0
1	0	−10	100	0	0	0	0

Level of aspiration

$att\ ds = -2$

$g\ ds = 3$

→ Level of new performance

Level of past performance

⌐ "Post-factum goal line"

Note. Table III shows the same level of past performance and the same distribution of valences of success and failure as Table II. However, the 50–50 level of subjective probability, corresponding to the expectation for the next performance, lies one level higher. As a result, the maximum resultant weighted valence is raised so that the goal discrepancy score ($g\ ds$) is now 3.

The level of new performance is 8. The attainment discrepancy ($att\ ds$) is, therefore, −2 and would usually lead to the feeling of failure. In our case, the individual consoles himself by setting up a "post-factum" goal line on the level of his past performance, in this way creating a "satisfactory" post-factum attainment score of +1.

$$^\circ Va(Suc^{A^n}) = Va(\text{Suc}^{A^n}) * \text{Prob. } (Suc^{A^n}) \qquad (5a)$$

The corresponding formula for failure is:

$$^\circ Va(Fai^{A^n}) = Va(Fai^{A^n}) * \text{Prob. } (Fai^{A^n}) \qquad (5b)$$

Columns 6 and 7 in Tables II and III give the values of the weighted valences of future success and failure. The sum of these valences will be called "resultant weighted valence" $[^\circ Va(A^n)]$.

$$\text{Level of aspiration} = n \text{ if } ^\circ Va(A^n) = \text{maximum} \qquad (6)$$

Column 8 gives the values for these "resultant weighted valences." In Table II, the maximum of the resultant weighted valence lies on level 8 of the scale of possible objectives. It means that under the given conditions the individual will choose the objective 8 as his goal. We can represent that by indicating a "goal line" across the diagram. The curve of resultant weighted valence shows a decrease from the level of maximum toward both the levels of greater and of smaller difficulties.

Mathematically the 50–50 level of probability of failure and success is identical with the "most probable achievement." That level of achievement which is subjectively the most probable is usually meant when one speaks of one's expectation. In other words, the level of expectation is identical with the subjective 50–50 probability of failure and success.

Table III shows the same distribution of valences of success and failure, but in this example we assume that the individual expects to show a better performance next time. This rise of his expectation from level 7 to level 8 raises the position of the maximum resultant valence from level 8 to level 10.

In case of realistic judgment, the individual will place his expectation somewhere within the boundary zone of his ability. Given a distribution of valences like that in Table II or III, the goal line will tend to lie relatively close to the subjective 50–50 level of probability. It can be concluded, therefore, that the level of aspiration should tend to lie close to the boundary zone of ability of the person at that time. Indeed, the experiments show that, on the whole, the probability scale has sufficient weight to keep the level of aspiration close to that zone. A young child will not generally try to lift a weight as heavy as his father can, although he might try to reach the level of aspiration of his older sibling. The factors which tend to move the goal line outside the boundary zone of ability will be discussed presently.

The theory thus far explains several groups of experimentally established facts: (a) the tendency to seek a relatively high level of aspiration; (b) the tendency of the level of aspiration to go up only to certain limits; and (c) the tendency of the level of aspiration to stay out of an area too difficult and too easy.

It is probably safe to assume that the subjective *probability* of success is, for the same person, more or less inverse to the probability of failure, that is, probability of success plus the probability of failure equals 100.

However, it would be incorrect to assume that the *valence* of success and the valence of failure are always inverse. Great differences exist among people in regard to the degree to which they are ruled by the tendency to avoid failure or by the tendency to seek success. Some people appear very much afraid of failure and to them, the possibility of failure is uppermost in their minds. These people would show high negative valences on column 3 (see Table IV). In general, this lowers the level on which the maximum weighted valence lies. That this derivation is well in line with the experimental findings relative to the effect of fear of failure on the discrepancy score will become clearer if we consider in more detail the factors which determine the distribution of values on the scales of valences and on the scales of subjective probability.

We are now going to discuss factors underlying the distribution of values in columns 2, 3, 4, and 5, Tables II to IV.

Scales of Reference

Factors Determining the Values on the Scale of Probability

Past experience. A main factor which determines the subjective probability of future success and failure is the past experience of the individual in regard to his ability to reach certain objectives.

In case an individual has had *much experience* in this particular activity, he will know pretty well what level he can expect to reach or not to reach. That means that his 50–50 level of probability of succeeding or failing will be well defined and the gradient of values on the probability scale will be steep; the steepness will be the greater the less the performance of the individual in this particular task fluctuates. Thus, the experiments about transfer show that success or failure in one area influences the level of aspiration in a second area less if the person is well at home in the second area than if this area is new to him.

At the other extreme are cases where the subjective probability is practically undetermined. Hence the observations are also in line with the theory. In fields of activity which a person *tries* for the first time in his life and where he is unable to judge his probable performance, the individual frequently does not spontaneously set himself a definite level of aspiration. Instead, he goes into the action without definite goal level; in popular terms he merely "tries it out."

It is not only the average past performance which determines the subjective probability. If, for instance, the *sequence* of achievements follows an order such that the later trial is better than the previous one, the individual will feel that he "is steadily improving." He is then likely to expect that he has not yet reached the end of the learning process and will place the 50–50 level of probability higher than his last achievement. This will tend to lead to a rise in the level of aspiration (Table III).

One would expect that the *last* success and failure will have a particularly great influence on the subject's expectation of the future achieve-

Table IV. Example of Reference Scales Underlying a Level of Aspiration

1	2	3	4	5	6	7	8
Possible objective	Valences of		Subjective probability		Weighted valence of		Resultant weighted valence
	Fut. Suc.	Fut. Fai.	Succeeding	Failing	Fut. Suc.	Fut. Fai.	
15	10	0	0	100	0	0	0
14	10	0	0	100	0	0	0
13	10	0	0	100	0	0	0
12	10	0	0	100	0	0	0
11	10	0	5	95	50	0	50
10	9	0	10	90	90	0	90
9	7	-2	25	75	175	-150	25
8	6	-4	40	60	240	-240	0
7	5	-6	50	50	250	-300	-50
6	3	-10	60	40	180	-400	-220
5	2	-14	75	25	150	-350	-200
4	1	-18	90	10	90	-180	-90
3	0	-20	95	5	0	-100	-100
2	0	-20	100	0	0	0	0
1	0	-20	100	0	0	0	0

$g\,ds = 3$

Note. The values on the scale of valence of future success and on the scales of subjective probability are the same as in Table II. The negative valences on the failure scale are doubled, expressing the great weight which failure has for the individual. It is obvious that, as a rule, the greater negative values on column 3 would tend to lower the position of the resultant weighted valence. In our example, the greater fear of failure actually raises the level of the resultant valence in an atypical way from the level 8 to the level 10. Such atypical cases where fear of failure leads to a high level of aspiration and a high goal discrepancy score (equals 3) are frequently observed. They are one of the reasons why a group of individuals who fail show a great scattering of discrepancy scores.

ment level because of the greater psychological weight of the more recent experience. The fact that all the experiments find that much of lowering and raising is dependent upon the quality of the last performance proves in general the correctness of this statement.

However, it would be erroneous to treat the effect of past experiences only as a result of their recency. A given sequence of achievements will set up certain "*subjective* hypotheses" which the subject uses to predict his achievement. In the case of a nonachievement which is linked, for instance, to outside disturbances, the subject is not likely to lower his level of aspiration in the way he would if he believed that the nonachievement represented a genuine decrement in his performance ability. Each trial may be regarded by the subject as an additional datum to be added to what he already knows about the activity and may change his ideas about probability of achievement. Therefore, if the previous performance has been accompanied by feelings of success, the level of aspiration should tend to rise in most cases; if the previous performance has by its less good quality engendered failure reactions, the level of aspiration should tend to go down. It is well in line with this derivation that after "barely reached successes" as well as after "weak failures" the level of aspiration tends to remain unchanged.

In studying individual differences, we have become more and more aware that individual constancies (for instance, in regard to the discrepancy score) are much less if the sequence pattern is not kept constant. Future investigations will do well to be still more careful on this point.

Goal structure of activity. Aside from past experience, certain cognitive settings influence the expectation of future success and failure. If, for instance, the series of levels to be chosen from has a definite upper and lower limit, the probability of reaching what is in that setting "top performance" may appear less probable. The tendency to make higher and higher records in some sports seems to be related to a goal structure which appears to have no upper limit. The effect of using large or small numbers when the experimenter indicates success or failure seems to be based on similar factors.

Wish, fear, and expectation. The judgment of the probability of success or failure on a given level is not only determined by past experience and "realistic" considerations but also by wishes and fears, i.e., by the valence of future success and failure. This is proved by the fact, for instance, that knowledge of group standards influences our level of expectation. In other words, the various parts of the life space are an interdependent field: The realistic expectancy is based mainly on past experiences. The structure of the psychological past affects the structure of the psychological future. However, the expectancy of reality level of the psychological future is also affected by the wish and fear (irreality) level of the psychological future.

*Scales of Reference Underlying the Valences of Future Success
and Failure*

The numerical values for the valences along the scale of future success or
failure follow the general observation that the valence of success, within
limits, is an increasing function of the difficulty of the objective, and the
valence of failure a decreasing function of difficulty. This is usually correct
in our culture, but only as a first approximation. It is the result of a com-
posite picture, some of the constituents of which we will discuss briefly.

Group standards. Individuals belonging to a certain group are usually
deeply affected by the "standards" of this group. In matters of level of
aspiration, such a standard means that a frame of reference exists on
which the standard level is particularly significant.

In some cases, for instance, in case of the ideology underlying the
college term "Gentleman *C*," the group standard is equivalent to the maximum valence on the scale of success: To be either above or below this
standard is considered less desirable than the standard (Table V). The
fashion, particularly in democratic countries, frequently follows a similar
pattern of optimum rather than a maximum of elegance as the most desirable level.

In other cases, the group standard merely indicates a level at which
the valence gradient is particularly steep: There is little success valence
and much negative valence of failure immediately below the group standard, and much success and little failure valence directly above group
standard.

For Table V, which is an example of the first type, the resultant valences are figured for an individual who has his achievement score (50–
50 probability) definitely below the group standard, for one whose achievement lies at the group level, and for one individual above that level. One
can see that, independent of the level of probable achievement, the maximum resultant valence (and therefore the goal line) should lie close to
the group standard. The experimental results show that this is true. They
also show, as one would expect, that these phenomena are the more striking the greater the relative weight of such a frame of reference. (Compare
Table V and Table IIa.)

In extreme cases of regard for such standards, the most able person
should tend to keep his level of aspiration low and may even show a negative discrepancy score; the least able person should keep up a high level
of aspiration even at the price of a great positive discrepancy score. It is
obvious that such a constellation might lead to a level of aspiration well
above or below the "boundary zone of ability." This is illustrated by experimental data previously cited.

Standards set from outside do not need to come from a definitely structured group, such as the school class or an age group. Frequently they are
related to another individual, for instance, the father, the friends, the wife,
or they are based on certain requirements of law or society. As a rule,

Table V. Example of the Effect of a Group Standard. Comparison of an Individual With Low, Medium, and High Performance Level

Possible objective	Valence		Subj. prob. of success for a person with			Resultant weighted valence for a person with		
	Suc.	Fai.	Low perf.	Medium perf.	High perf.	Low perf.	Medium perf.	High perf.
15	6	0	0	0	10	0	0	60
14	6	0	0	0	25	0	0	150
13	6	0	0	5	40	0	30	240
12	6	0	0	10	50 Last performance	0	60	300
Group standard 11	8	0	5	25	60 Last performance	40	200	400
10	9	-1	10	40	75	0	300	650
9	10	-8	25	50	90	-350	100	820
8	6	-10	40	60	95 Last performance	-360	-40	520
7	2	-10	50	75	100	-400	-100	200
6	0	-10	60	90	100	-400	-100	0
5	0	-10	75	95	100	-250	-50	0
4	0	-10	90	100	100	-100	0	0
3	0	-10	95	100	100	-50	0	0
2	0	-10	100	100	100	0	0	0
1	0	-10	100	100	100	0	0	0

$g\ ds = 4$　　$g\ ds = 1$　　$g\ ds = -3$

Note. In this example, the group standard lies on the position of the maximum valence of success and on a steep gradient of the valence scale of failure. Columns 3, 4, and 5 indicate the subjective probability of success for three individuals whose performance is below the group standard, on the group standard and above the group standards, for instance, a poor, medium, and good student in a class. To condense the table, we are not presenting the scale of probable failure which is the converse of that of success. It is assumed in our example that our three individuals are rather realistic and that their level of expectation, that is, the 50–50 level of probable success, lies on the level of their past performance.

If the group standards were the only scale determining the valence of success and failure, the level of aspiration of all three individuals would lie on or above the group standard; this would mean that the poor student would have a high positive goal discrepancy score ($g\ ds = 4$); the best students, a negative discrepancy score ($g\ ds = -3$). In our example, the level of aspiration of the poor students would be even higher than that of the good one.

This example illustrates why the level of aspiration might be kept above or below one's own ability. As a rule, of course, the scale related to the group standards is only one of several reference scales underlying the valence of future success and failure. Table IIa gives the result of a combination with another reference scale.

there are, coexisting, quite a number of such scales of reference which include certain standards.

Past Achievements; the Space of Free Movement

Certain standards may result from the fact that the individual "competes with himself." In this case his "past achievements" not only determine the probability of future achievements; they also provide certain standards for future goals (Table IIa).

One factor which seems to be important for the striving toward the more difficult is the desire to reach beyond the area which has been accessible until then to the person. The totality of accessible areas of activities is called "space of free movement." A person's space of free movement is limited partly by the rules of society and the power of other persons, partly by his own ability or what is called the nature of things. The growth of the space of free movement is a fundamental factor of development, and the reaching out for the yet unreached is a powerful desire of the child and of many adults in many fields of activity. One can view the tendency to raise the level of aspiration as due partly to these desires.

In summing up we might state: A multitude of coexistent frames of reference may underlie the probability scale and the scale of valences of future success and failure. They can technically be recombined to these main scales if one attributes to each of the underlying frame of reference scales (uRS) the relative weight or potency with which it influences the individual; for instance, we would have three reference scales indicated by uRS^1, uRS^2, and uRS^3, underlying the valence of success. If uRS^1 were twice as influential as a motive for this individual as the reference scales uRS^2 and uRS^3, the value of the valence of success and failure on a given level would be calculated by referring to the corresponding levels on the underlying reference scale according to the formula $uRS^1 \times .5 - uRS^2 \times .25 - uRS^3 \times .25$. Table IIa presents an example. *Differences of "culture" as well as differences of "personality" might then be represented as a number of frames of reference and a pattern of relative weight.*

The Discrepancy Score and the Relative Potency of the Various Frames of Reference

The recent studies of the level of aspiration have expressed their results frequently in terms of goal discrepancy score, that is, of the difference between level of aspiration and past achievement. Although the discrepancy score in itself is an important aspect of the problems of the level of aspiration, most workers in the field agree that it has been somewhat overstressed. It is recognized that the discrepancy score is a resultant of many factors and that it is important to find out what are the particular factors behind a certain discrepancy score in a given case.

Discrepancy score, level of expectation, and the discrepancy between expectation and past performance. If a person were entirely realistic, his expectation would, on the average, coincide roughly with his future performance. That means that the discrepancy score between past performance and expectation should be the same as the difference between his past and his new performance. As a rule, it would be zero or slightly positive.

Actually our "expectation" is not entirely independent of our wishes and fears. However, this dependency is less close than that between these wishes and fears and the level of aspiration. From this follows that the discrepancy between the level of expectation and past performance should be less than the discrepancy between level of aspiration and past performance (discrepancy score). Experiments show the correctness of this conclusion.

They also show that the variability of the discrepancy is less in regard to expectation than in regard to the level of aspiration. This follows theoretically from the fact that the variability of the level of aspiration depends not only on the variability of the values on the probability scale but in addition on the variability of values on the valence scales.

The effect of the structure of the reference scales and of their relative potency. The example of discrepancy scores in Table II to V may suffice to show that the size and direction of the discrepancy score depend upon the level of the last achievement, upon the distribution of values along each of the reference scales, and upon the relative potency of each reference scale. It is, therefore, impossible to predict a discrepancy score accurately without knowing these data for the particular case. It is, however, possible to make certain general statements about the effect on the discrepancy score of a change in the relative potency of various reference scales, if the numerical values along these scales are kept constant and if we refer to situations where the learning improvement is not important.

Realism

Realism in matters of the level of aspiration refers to one or both of two factors:

(1) it refers to the probability scale and means closeness of expectation and "reality"; that is, closeness of the 50–50 level of "subjective" and of the "objective" probability. Such a correctness of judgment about one's own future action may be measured by the discrepancy between expectation and new performance.

(2) Realism refers to a tendency to keep the maximum resultant weighted valence close to the 50–50 level of subjective probability. This implies that the individual chooses a distribution of values on the valence scales in such a way that this closeness of expectation and action goal results. We have previously spoken

about the fact that the subjective probability scale is not entirely independent of the valence scale. Realism implies that, inversely, the distribution of the valence scale is not entirely independent of the probability scale.

It follows from this consideration that the absolute size of the goal discrepancy score would be the smaller the more realistic the person is. This is borne out by a number of findings:

(a)   Realism is obviously greater in case the subject is asked what he "expects" than what he would "like to get." Indeed, the discrepancy score is smaller in the first case (page 149).
(b)   The "realistic" attitude is greater in work than in play situations or activities. Correspondingly, the discrepancy score is smaller in the former (page 149).
(c)   Realism should be greater for "realistic" than for "irrealistic" persons. The experiments bear out the derivations (page 156).
(d)   Success, if not given in too strong doses, should make for a less tense emotional situation than failure, particularly in cases of repeated failure. Emotionality makes for an irrealistic attitude. We should expect, therefore, the absolute size of the discrepancy score to be greater in case of a chronic failure situation than in continued success. This derivation is again borne out by several experiments (page 156).

The Values on the Success Valence Scale Relative to the Values on the Failure Valence Scale

The discrepancy score should be the more positive the higher the values on the success scales are, relative to the absolute values of the failure scale on the same level, provided that the gradient on each scale is not changed. This is borne out by a number of findings.

The Readiness to Take Risks

Lowering the values of the failure scale means psychologically being less afraid of failure. This would tend to move the resultant valence and therefore the goal line up relative to the achievement, resulting in high positive discrepancy scores. In other words, the relative weight of the success and failure scale determines what is usually called the readiness of the individual "to take risks" or to be cautious.

The findings about individual differences are in line with this conclusion.

Being Inside or Outside the Failure Region

The tendency to avoid future failure, or the force on the person away from failure ($f_{p,-Fai}$) is a function of the present position of the person, particularly whether he sees himself at present in the region of "being successful" or "failing." It seems that the force $(f_{p,-Fai})$ is usually greater and, therefore, the values on the failure scale higher if the person is at present in the region of failing (Fai) than if he is in a region of not failing $(Nfai)$. This holds at least as long as the person does not "accept" being a failure. Accepting failure frequently creates a "don't care" attitude which is equivalent to the diminishing of the valence of failure. Usually, however, it holds:

$$f_{Fai,-Fai} > f_{NFai,-Fai} \qquad (7)$$

From this assumption, we can derive a number of conclusions which are all borne out by experiments.

1. A recent failure should tend to lower the level of aspiration. This is one of the major findings in the field. The "atypical" cases of raising the level of aspiration after failure (occurring in from 10% to 20% of the cases) would follow from a decrease in the realism of the situation or from acceptance of "being a failure."
2. The level of aspiration should decrease more after strong failure than after a weak failure. It should, of course, increase after success (page 142).
3. Due to the cumulative effects of the above mentioned factors the person who fails habitually should have a lower discrepancy score than the person who usually succeeds. Atypical cases of high positive discrepancy score after habitual failure would again be understandable as a result of the factors mentioned in paragraph 1 (page 148).
4. There should be a tendency to avoid finishing a series of trials with a failure since this means letting oneself remain relatively permanently in the area of failure (page 144).

The Variability of Discrepancy Score and the Ease of Changing the Level of Aspiration

The ease with which the level of aspiration can be changed, that is, the width of change by a small additional force, depends on the flatness of the curve of the resultant weighted valence near its maximum. Obviously, the same factor would determine the variability of the discrepancy score.

The gradient toward the more easy task in Table III, column 8, for instance, is less steep than in Table II, column 8. The steepness of the resultant valence curve depends on the steepness of the gradient on the various reference scales, their relative position to each other, and their potency.

For instance, if group standards play a great role and if the distribution of values along that scale shows as steep a gradient as in columns 2 and 3, Table V, a lowering of the potency of that scale and an increase of the potency of other reference scales (which have the distribution, for instance, of columns 2 and 3, Table II), would flatten out the curve of the resultant valences and make the individual more ready to change. Table IIa is an example of such a combination resulting in a small gradient on the resultant valence curve.

In cases where the probable achievement is quite precisely known and where the individual is realistic the gradient should be relatively steep.

Reaction to Achieving or Not Achieving the Level of Aspiration

After the person has set his level of aspiration and then acted, he reacts to his achieving or not achieving his goals. The main types of reactions are the following:

Feeling of Success and Failure

The experiments show that the feeling of success and failure does not depend on an absolute level of achievement. What for one person means success means failure for another person, and even for the same person the same achievement will lead sometimes to the feeling of failure and sometimes to the feeling of success.

What counts is the level of achievement relative to certain standards, in particular to the level of aspiration (goal line): If the achievement lies on or above the goal line, the subject will probably have a feeling of success; if it lies below the goal line he will probably feel failure, depending on the size of this difference and the ease with which the achievement has been reached.

Rationalization, Avoidance of Feeling of Failure

The forces $f_{P,Suc}$ and $f_{P,-Fai}$ that is, tendencies to seek success and avoid failure are one of the bases for the level of aspiration. They also influence strongly the events at the point 4 of our sequence. The tendency to stay out of the failure region can lead to what is called rationalization.

There are two ways in which an individual after failing to achieve his level of aspiration still may avoid the feeling of failure.

1. He might change his goal line *post factum*, for instance, after a person has tried for level 10 (Table III) but reached only 8 he might then say, "Well, that is still better than any previous achievement" (or better than the average of previous achievement, or better than another person). In other words, he might switch his standard in a way which amounts to a sufficient lowering of his goal line afterwards.
2. Severing the relation between achievement and the individual himself as a "responsible" person is another means of avoiding failure. Only if the result of the action is "attributed" to the person as actor and not attributed to other persons or to "nature" can we

speak psychologically of an "achievement" of this person. There is a tendency after failure to link the poor result to a faulty instrument, to sickness, or to any event "outside the power" of the individual involved. The fact that such severing of the link between the result and the individual is more frequent after poor than after good achievement shows that it can be due to the force of avoiding failure.

Continuing the Activity With a New Trial or Stopping

As a result of his achievement, the individual might decide to attempt a new trial in the same activity or to stop.

Whether a person will continue or stop depends on a great number of factors, such as the hope of doing better, his being on the whole successful or unsuccessful, his involvement in the particular activity, the alternative he would have in regard to other activities, and so on. Finally, however, the stopping or not stopping depends upon whether the force $f_{P,A}$ is smaller or greater than zero (where A means the activity on hand).

$$\text{Stopping occurs if } f_{P,A} < 0 \qquad (8)$$

In case no outside pressure is exerted on the individual to continue, the individual will stop if the maximum value on the resultant valence curve is still negative, or more correctly if this value is smaller than the valences of an alternative activity. In line with this theory, Escalona (1940) found that patients in a mental hospital who disliked going back to the ward were less ready to stop than those who wanted mainly to be left alone.

One factor which tends to lower the values of the resultant weighted valence curves is a general decrease of the probability of success. This explains why and when after a series of failures the person will stop.

The values for the person with low, medium, and high performance in Table V are an example of how the decrease in the probability of success leads to a higher negative resultant valence. Whereas for the successful person all values on the scale of resultant valences are positive, indicating an attractiveness of the activity as a whole, most of the values for the unsuccessful person are strongly negative. This indicates a negative valence for the task as a whole and the individual should stop if the only remaining positive value on the level should disappear.

In case of pressure, the individual will continue as long as the force away from the activity $f_{P,-A}$ is smaller than the pressure exerted.

In case the individual chooses to continue with the same activity, his level of aspiration will be determined by the factors we have discussed.

General Conclusion

These theoretical considerations show that most of the qualitative and quantitative results related to the level of aspiration can be linked with three factors, namely, the seeking of success ($f_{P,Suc}$), the avoiding of failure ($f_{P,-Fai}$), and the cognitive factor of a probability judgment. These forces operate in a setting which has to be characterized as a choice for a future objective. The strength of these forces and the values corresponding to the subjective probability depend on many aspects of the life space of the individual at that time, particularly on the way he sees his past experience and on the scales of reference which are characteristic for his culture and his personality.

On the whole, the study of the level of aspiration has reached a point where the nature of the problems and their relations to other fields is sufficiently clear to be useful as a guide for future research. Within the field of "goal behavior" one can distinguish problems of "goal striving" and problems of "goal setting." Goal striving is a "directed" behavior toward existing goals and is closely related to problems of locomotion toward a goal, of frustration reaching a goal and consummatory behavior. Goal setting is related to the question of what goal will emerge or become dominant after another goal has been reached or not reached. Within this field lie, for instance, the problems of psychological satiation and a major part of the problems of level of aspiration. The latter, however, are closely interwoven with all aspects of goal behavior.

Future research can, it appears, be conducted along two general lines.

1. One can try to understand more fully the general laws of the level of aspiration. The analysis is far enough along at present to encourage an attempt to determine quantitatively the values on the various scales of reference. Such an attempt would give insight, for instance, into the factors which determine our probability judgment about our future, and would be of considerable value for the general theory of cognitive processes and perception. It would permit a quantitative approach to such divergent questions as a theory of choice and compromise; the effect of past experience and group belonging to certain aspects of cultural values, e.g., their distribution, interdependence, and rigidity; the factors determining the "ability to take it"; and problems of development and regression in regard to complying to rules.
2. It is possible to use level of aspiration techniques as an instrument to compare different cultures and to characterize their systems of value in a quantitative way. Similarly, these techniques may become progressively more useful for measuring individual differences of value systems and of other major characteristics of the normal and abnormal personality.

References

Anderson, C. (1940). *The development of a level of aspiration in young children*. Iowa City: Dissertation, University, IA.

Anderson, H. H., & Brandt, H. F. (1939). Study of motivation involving self-announced goals of fifth grade children and the concept of level of aspiration. *Journal of Social Psychology*, *10*, 209–232.

Chapman, D. W., & Volkmann, J. (1939). A social determinant of the level of aspiration. *Journal of Abnormal Psychology*, *34*, 255–238.

Dembo, T. (1931). Der Arger als dynamisches Problem. (Untersuchungen zur Handlungs- und Affektpsychologie. X. Ed. by Kurt Lewin.) *Psychologische Forschung*, *15*, 1–144.

Escalona, S. K. (1940). The effect of success and failure upon the level of aspiration and behavior in manic-depressive psychoses. *University of Iowa Study of Child Welfare*, *16*(3), 199–302.

Fales, E. (1937). Genesis of level of aspiration in children from one and one-half to three years of age. (Reported in C. Anderson, 1940)

Festinger, L. (1942a). Wish, expectation, and group standards as factors influencing level of aspiration. *Journal of Abnormal Social Psychology*, *37*, 184–200.

Festinger, L. (1942b). A theoretical interpretation of shifts in level of aspiration. *Psychological Review*, *49*, 235–250.

Frank, J. D. (1935a). Individual differences in certain aspects of the level of aspiration. *American Journal of Psychology*, 119–128.

Frank, J. D. (1935b). The influence of the level of performance in one task on the level of aspiration in another. *Journal of Experimental Psychology*, *18*, 159–171.

Frank, J. D. (1935c). Some psychological determinants of the level of aspiration. *American Journal of Psychology*, *47*, 285–293.

Frank, J. D. (1936). A comparison between certain properties of the level of aspiration and random guessing. *Journal of Psychology*, *3*, 43–62.

Frank, J. D. (1938). Level of aspiration test. In H. A. Murray, et al. (Eds.), *Explorations in personality* (pp. 461–471). New York: Oxford University Press.

Frank, J. D. (1941). Recent studies of the level of aspiration. *Psychological Bulletin*, *38*, 218–225.

Gardner, J. W. (1939). Level of aspiration in response to a prearranged sequence of scores. *Journal of Experimental Psychology*, *25*, 601–621.

Gardner, J. W. (1940a). The relation of certain personality variables to level of aspiration. *Journal of Psychology*, *9*, 191–206.

Gardner, J. W. (1940b). The use of the term "level of aspiration." *Psychological Review*, *47*, 59–68.

Gould, R. (1939). An experimental analysis of "level of aspiration." *Genetic Psychology Monographs*, *21*, 1–116.

Gould, R. (1941). Some sociological determinants of goal strivings. *Journal of Social Psychology*, *13*, 461–473.

Gould, R., & Kaplan, N. (1940). The relationship of "level of aspiration" to academic and personality factors. *Journal of Social Psychology*, *11*, 31–40.

Gould, R., & Lewis, H. B. (1940). An experimental investigation of changes in the meaning of level of aspiration. *Journal of Experimental Psychology*, *27*, 422–438.

Hausmann, M. F. (1933). A test to evaluate some personality traits. *Journal of Genetic Psychology*, *9*, 179–189.

Heathers, L. B. (1942). Factors producing generality in the level of aspiration. *Journal of Experimental Psychology*, *30*, 392–406.

Hertzman, M., & Festinger, L. (1940). Shifts in explicit goals in a level of aspiration experiment. *Journal of Experimental Psychology*, *27*, 439–452.

Hilgard, E. R., & Sait, E. M. (1941). Estimates of past and future performance as measures of aspiration. *American Journal of Psychology*, *54*, 102–108.

Hilgard, E. R., Sait, E. M., & Margaret, G. A. (1940). Level of aspiration as affected by relative standing in an experimental social group. *Journal of Experimental Psychology*, *27*, 411–421.

Hoppe, F. (1930). Erfolg und Misserfolg. (Untersuchungen zur Handlungs- und Affectpsychologie: IX. Ed. by Kurt Lewin.) *Psychologische Forschung*, *14*, 1–62.

Irwin, F. W., & Mintzer, M. G. (1942). Effect of differences in instructions and motivation upon measures of the level of aspiration. *American Journal of Psychology*, *55*, 400–406.

Jucknat, M. (1937). Leistung, Anschpruchsniveau und Selbstbewusstsein. (Untersuchungen zur Handlungs- und Affectpsychologie: XX. Ed. by Kurt Lewin.) *Psychologische Forschung, 22,* 89–179.

McGehee, W. (1940). Judgment and level of aspiration. *Journal of Genetic Psychology, 22,* 3–15.

Preston, M. G. (1942). Use of the coefficient of correlation in the study of the D-score for the level of aspiration. *American Journal of Psychology, 55,* 442–446.

Preston, M. G., & Bayton, J. A. (1941). Differential effect of a social variable upon three levels of aspiration. *Journal of Experimental Psychology, 29,* 351–369.

Preston, M. G., & Bayton, J. A. (1942). Correlations between levels of aspiration. *Journal of Psychology, 13,* 369–373.

Rotter, J. B. (1942a). Level of aspiration as a method of studying personality: I. A critical review of methodology. *Psychological Review, 49,* 463–474.

Rotter, J. B. (1942b). Level of aspiration as a method of studying personality: II. Development and evaluation of a controlled method. *Journal of Experimental Psychology, 31,* 410–422.

Rotter, J. B. (unpublished). *Level of aspiration as a controlled method of personality study using selected groups.*

Sears, P. S. (1940). Levels of aspiration in academically successful and unsuccessful children. *Journal of Abnormal Social Psychology, 35,* 498–536.

Sears, P. S. (1941). Level of aspiration in relation to some variables of personality: Clinical studies. *Journal of Social Psychology, 14,* 311–336.

Sears, R. R. (1942). Success and failure: A study of motility. In Q. McNemar & M. A. Merrill (Eds.), *Studies in personality* (pp. 235–258). New York: McGraw-Hill.

Yacorzynski, G. K. (1942). Degree of effort: III. Relationship to the level of aspiration. *Journal of Experimental Psychology, 30,* 407–413.

7

Frustration and Regression: An Experiment With Young Children

II
Experimental Regression Through Frustration

The Problem Under Investigation

This study reports an attempt to create regression in children by frustration. It can be viewed from two angles. First, it tries to clarify the nature of regression and the conditions leading to it by testing certain theoretical assumptions about regression. Second, it can be viewed as a contribution to the study of frustration.

Some Situational Conditions for Regression

It is possible to derive from the conceptual representation of developmental levels certain conditions which should lead to regression.

We have seen that the developmental levels differ in a variety of aspects, such as degree of differentiation, organization, etc. In regard to each of these aspects it should be possible to set up theoretical predictions as to the conditions under which regression should occur, i.e., what conditions should result in dedifferentiation, in disorganization, etc. There exists, obviously, a great variety of possibilities in regard to each of these aspects and their combinations. We have been aware of some of these aspects from the beginning; others became apparent during the study. We will first discuss a few considerations which have led us to investigate regression and which have determined the experiments. A number of other factors which have been relevant will be dealt with when we discuss the experimental results.

One of the conditions which may lend to regression is a situation in which the person is under unusually high pressure or where he is in a state of particularly high tension. Indeed, from the conceptual represen-

With R. Barker and T. Dembo. Excerpted from *University of Iowa Studies in Child Welfare*, 1941, *18*. Whole no. 386, including only chapters II, V, and IX.

tation of developmental stages it follows that a state of high tension should lead to a regression in at least two respects. If the state of tension in some cells is kept high, the variety of patterns which can be realized is greatly diminished. In other words, in the case of very strong forces, or high tensions, the degree of differentiation of a given individual is reduced. Secondly, the organizational unity is likely to be affected because the high tension level makes the executive regions a less efficient medium. In other words, frustration processes of the type of spreading of tension, increase in importance relatively to organizational processes. In addition, dedifferentiation is likely to affect directly the degree of hierarchical organization.

The Effect of Frustration Activities Not Related to the Inaccessible Goal

A frustrating situation, i.e., a situation where an individual is prevented from reaching a desirable goal is one way of creating tension. There are a great number of experimental facts concerning animals, children, and adults which indicate this. The representation of the relation between frustration and tension is relatively simple, and has proved fruitful in a wide variety of conflict situations (reward and punishment [Lewin, 1935], physical or social obstacles to a goal [Fajans, 1933], anger situation [Dembo, 1931], substitution [Sliosberg, 1934]).

The experiments on animals and human beings have given us a fair knowledge of the main factors determining the strength of frustration, such as the relation to needs and to the distance between an individual and his goal. We know the usual development of such frustration situations, e.g., a tendency to take round-about routes, alternation between temporarily leaving the field and coming back, and the final giving up. The theory of these processes is relatively well developed (Dembo, 1931). We know some of the conditions which facilitate and hinder round-about routes in such a situation and some of the factors which determine the particular form of restless movements (Lewin, 1935).

If the tension in frustrating situations is too high, the actions in the direction of the goal are likely to become emotional and more "primitive." In other words, instead of trying to find round-about routes in an organized systematic way, direct actions occur which are frequently vague and primitive in character. We suppose most psychologists would agree that one can speak here quite correctly of regression of behavior. Indeed, the way an older person tries to reach a goal in the case of high tension shows certain similarities to the actions typical for a younger person (Dembo, 1931).

The experiments which we are going to report are not intended to provide additional proof of the fact that in a state of high tension, the action toward an obstructed goal regresses to a primitive level. They are an attempt to go one step further. If it is correct that a sufficiently high tension leads to a regressed state of the individual, this regression should show itself not only in the action toward the inaccessible goal but also in behavior which is not related to this goal.

Case studies indicate that the frustration of an individual in one area may affect his mood and his behavior in other areas of activity. The situation in the personal life of the individual may readily affect his occupational life. Popular opinion about the way frustration in one field affects a person's activity in another field is full of contradictions. Frequently it is held that much hardship and frustration have a favorable effect on the productivity of the artist. On the other hand, it is held that such situations hamper productivity.

From our theoretical consideration, it should follow that if the tension level is increased too greatly, the individual should regress. The following experiments test this hypothesis.

Degree of Constructiveness of Play as a Symptom of Regression

In experiments with young children it is not advisable to use extremely frustrating situations. It is necessary to restrict the intensity of frustration to degrees which are well within the limit of the everyday experience of most children. This makes it necessary to find a symptom of regression that is sufficiently sensitive to indicate small changes in the state of the person. We have chosen for this purpose the free play activity of the child. We did so mainly for three reasons.

First, we expected that certain properties of play which we will call the "constructiveness of play" were closely related to the developmental stage of the person. The term *constructiveness* should not be understood here as opposite to destructiveness. We have in mind such qualities as the degree of differentiation and organization of play activities quite independent of their content: for instance, independent of whether or not they involve building up or tearing down. (It is possible, of course, that destructive actions are usually more primitive than ones involving construction.)

Second, we have seen that the developmental level of behavior is not necessarily a reliable symptom for the developmental state of the individual. If the child is told to carry out a definite task, such as folding a piece of paper in a specific manner or any other minutely prescribed task, relatively little is left to the individual and the extent to which the activity will mirror the character of the individual is rather limited. In a situation of free play, little is enforced from outside, particularly if sufficient play material is provided and if this material is sufficiently flexible (Sliosberg, 1934). One would expect, therefore, that free play would indicate particularly well the state of the individual. The so-called "play technique" assumes that the play of a person reveals his needs and problems. From similar considerations we have assumed that the character of the play should be a useful symptom of the developmental state of a child and of any shifts in this state.

Third, the level of constructiveness of an individual's activity seems to be particularly closely related to his whole life space. Constructiveness is intimately linked with both the reality and irreality levels of the life space; fantasy and realistic judgment are closely interwoven in any constructive action. The extension of the life space and its degree of differentiation play an important role also. We have assumed, therefore, that constructiveness is a sensitive indicator for regression.

Experimental Procedures

General Arrangements

Technically, it has been the aim of this investigation to compare the behavior of children in a nonfrustrating or free play situation with their behavior in a frustrating situation. We have been especially concerned with productivity, or creativity of behavior.

Every child was observed on two occasions: first, in a free play situation during which the subject was placed in a standardized playroom and allowed to play without restriction, and second, in a frustrating situation during which the subject was placed in the same room with the same toys as on the first occasion, but to which a number of much more attractive, but inaccessible, toys had been added. The latter arrangement was provided by replacing one of the walls of the original room with a wire net partition through which the subject could easily see the fine toys, but through which locomotion was impossible.

The Subjects

The subjects in the experiment were children taken from three age groups of the preschool laboratories of the Iowa Child Welfare Research Station during the academic year 1935–1936. The number of children from each group is as follows: 10 children from the first group (2 to 3 years), 12 children from the second group (3 to 4 years), and 8 children from the third group (4 to 5 years). The chronological ages, mental ages, and IQs are given on the next page; these ranged from 28 to 61 months, 30 to 82 months, and 100 to 157 months, respectively. The Kuhlmann-Binet was used with the 10 youngest subjects, the Stanford-Binet with the older subjects.

Establishing a Free Atmosphere for the Child

In a free play situation, every effort was made to establish optimal conditions for constructive play. For this reason, insecurity on the part of the child was very undesirable and attempts were made to eliminate it.

To help give the children a feeling of security in order that they might behave freely and spontaneously, and also to allow the experimenter to become acquainted with them, several precautions were taken:

Subject	Chronological age (months)	Mental age (months)	IQ
1	28	37	133
2	28	30	107
3	29	41	141
4	29	32	110
5	30	30	100
6	33	39	117
7	34	35	103
8	35	39	112
9	37	42	114
10	40	44	111
11	42	49	117
12	43	62	145
13	45	51	111
14	46	72	157
15	47	56	119
16	48	58	121
17	49	55	113
18	49	66	135
19	51	59	116
20	51	65	128
21	52	62	120
22	53	65	122
23	53	80	151
24	55	82	150
25	55	73	133
26	58	64	110
27	58	64	111
28	59	67	113
29	59	70	119
30	61	72	118
M (10 youngest children)	32.3	36.9	114.8
M (20 oldest children)	51.7	64.6	125.5
M (total group)	45.2	55.4	121.9

1. Before starting experimentation, the experimenter took part in the activities of the preschool for 10 days.
2. A child was used as a subject only if his initial attitude toward the experimenter and toward coming to the experimental room was positive.

Each child was asked to take part in the experiment in the following way: "Do you want to come and play with me?" (This is a general procedure used by experimenters and testers in the preschool laboratories.)

Although the children in the school are accustomed to being tested and to participating in experiments with different people, willingness to participate varies from child to child and from situation to situation. Some children, upon hearing the experimenter invite another child to "come and play," spontaneously ask to go too; others go only after being requested, but comply willingly and without hesitation; still others are reluctant to go. These latter children were not used as subjects.

3. The children were familiar with the building in which the experiments were conducted, having to stop in it every day for routine medical inspection, and going to it frequently for tests and examinations.

4. Upon going to the experiment the child had to put on his wraps, and was helped by the experimenter. The experimenter tried to keep the child in a good mood, and to make the situation an open and free one while putting on and taking off the child's wraps and walking across the street with him. At the same time, these situations gave an opportunity to observe the child and his attitude toward the experimenter.

5. In all cases, where the above mentioned precautions did not seem sufficient to develop free and spontaneous behavior, we introduced a special preliminary play period. In this preliminary period the child was taken to the experimental room for fifteen or twenty minutes to play with blocks and balls during which the experimenter tried gradually to gain his confidence by playing with him. This precaution was required at the beginning of the school year, since at that time many children were newcomers to the preschool, and the general situation was strange to them. Later, when the children felt more secure and free, both in the school and with the experimenters, it was not thought necessary to use a preliminary play period.

The Free Play Situation

The arrangement of the experimental room in the free play situation is shown in Figures 1 and 2. It was 14 by 8½ feet, had two doors, and a window. The wall (see 9, Figure 1) consisted of two wooden frames, 12 by 3 feet, covered with wire mesh netting. These frames could be moved up and down in a vertical slot along the walls adjacent to them like window frames. In the free play experiment, the frames were in such a position that one of them rested on the floor, while the other extending from the top of this lower one, nearly reached the ceiling. On the back of each frame, that is, behind the wire mesh netting, an opaque canvas covering was stretched. The canvas was the same color as the room, making the partition appear to be the fourth wall.

One door (see 7, Figure 1) was used as the entrance door; the other (see 6) into which a one-way observation screen was built, was locked. Behind this one-way vision screen one of the experimenters was seated to act as an observer. The second experimenter, who conducted the experiment, sat in a child's chair (see 4) at a small table (see 5) near the window (see 8).

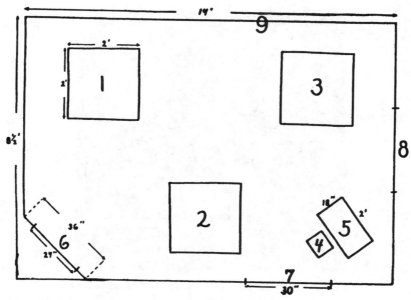

Figure 1. Diagram of the free play situation. 1. Square of paper on which the following toys are placed: a child's chair, teddy bear, doll, cup, small truck and trailer, saucer, teapot, ironing board and iron, and telephone receiver. 2. Square of paper on which the following toys are placed: box of crayons, two pieces of writing paper. 3. Square of paper on which the following toys are placed: motorboat, sailboat, duck, frog, fishing pole. 4. Experimenter's chair. 5. Experimenter's table. 6. Observation screen. 7. Entrance door. 8. Window. 9. Opaque partition (now functioning as a wall).

On the floor of the room were three squares of paper each 24 by 24 inches. A set of standardized play materials was placed on each. On the square designated as 1 (Figure 1), were a child's chair on which a small teddy bear and a doll were seated, a cup, a small truck and trailer, a saucer, a teapot without a lid, an ironing board and an iron (but nothing to iron), and a telephone receiver which squeaked when shaken. On square 2 were placed a box of crayons and two pieces of writing paper, 8½ by 11 inches.[1] On square 3, there was a small wooden motorboat, a sailboat, a celluloid duck, a frog, and a fishing pole and line on the end of which was a magnet.

After entering the experimental room with the child, the experimenter approached square 1, and picking up each toy said "Look, here are some things to play with. Here is a teddy bear and a doll. Here is an iron to iron with, etc." In proceeding this way, the experimenter named and demonstrated every toy on all three squares. Then he said, "You can play with everything. You can do whatever you like with the toys, and I'll sit down

---

[1]In the early experiments a peg-board, beads, a rolling wagon, and plasticine were also placed here.

Figure 2.   The setup in the free play situation.

here and do my lesson." The experimenter then sat on the chair at the table.[2]

The child was left to play alone for a 30-minute period. During this time the experimenter, as if occupied with his own work, sat at his table in the corner and took notes. If the child made a social approach, the experimenter responded, but attempts were made to keep this at a minimum without, however, becoming abrupt or curt. The experimenter entered the play situation of the child as little as possible, at the same time behaving naturally. The objective was to minimize the social factors in the situation and to provide an atmosphere of security and freedom for the child.

After a half hour, the experimenter made the first "leaving suggestion" to the child. He said, "I'm about through. Will you be ready to go pretty soon?" If the child said "No" or did not answer, the experimenter waited for about a minute and then said, "Shall we go to the preschool now?" If this suggestion was not accepted, the experimenter made a third leaving suggestion after a minute or two. If the child did not want to leave at the third suggestion, the experimenter started to leave the room, saying, "I have to go now." In every case this was sufficient to make the child want to leave the experimental room.

---

[2]This procedure was modified slightly in later experiments in order to make the child more curious about the toys. When the child was brought into the room, the toys were not yet distributed on the squares. A basket with the play materials stood in the corner and the experimenter took the basket and in the presence of the child distributed the toys on the squares. The experimenter named the single objects as he put them down.

The Frustration Situation

Three parts of the frustration experiment can be distinguished in the temporal order of their occurrence: (a) the prefrustration, (b) the frustration, and (c) the postfrustration periods.

Prefrustration period. The arrangement of the room in the prefrustration period is shown in Figures 3 and 4. The partition dividing the room was lifted so the room was twice the size it had been in the free play situation.

The squares, 1, 2, and 3 were in their usual places, but all toys except those on square 2 had been removed and incorporated in the much more elaborate and attractive new set of toys in the new part of the room.

In the added part of the room was a big doll house (3 by 3 feet), brightly painted and decorated. The child could enter the house through a doorway. Inside there was a bed upon which the doll was lying, and a chair in which the teddy bear sat. The ironing board with the iron on it stood against one wall and the telephone, this time on its base with a dial and bell, was in the corner. There was a stove with cooking utensils, and a cupboard. The house had electric lights, curtains, and a carpet.

Outside the house was a laundry line on which the doll's clothes hung. A rubber bunny sat near the entrance to the house. A large delivery truck (23 inches long) stood near the house, and behind it was the small truck and trailer used in the preceding experiment. Nearby was a child's table prepared for a luncheon party. On the table were cups, saucers, dishes, spoons, forks, knives, a small empty teapot, and a large teapot with water in it.

In the other corner of the new part of the room was a toy lake (3 by 3 feet) filled with real water. It contained an island with a lighthouse, a wharf, a ferry boat, small boats, fishes, ducks, and frogs. The lake had sand beaches.

In all cases the children showed evidences of great interest in the new toys, and at once started to investigate them. Each child was left entirely free to explore and play as he wished. During this time, the experimenter "did his lessons."

If, after several minutes, the child had played with only a limited number of objects, the experimenter approached and demonstrated the other toys, e.g., he dialed the telephone or showed the child how to get the water from the spout of the teapot. In general, the experimenter called to the child's attention every toy he had overlooked. Following this the experimenter returned to his place, and waited until the child had become thoroughly involved in play; this varied from 5 to 15 minutes.

The transition from prefrustration to frustration was made the following way: The experimenter collected in a basket all the play materials which had been used in the free play experiment and distributed them, as before, on the squares. He then approached the child and said, "And now let's play at the other end," pointing to the "old" part of the room. The child went or was led to the other end of the room and the experimenter

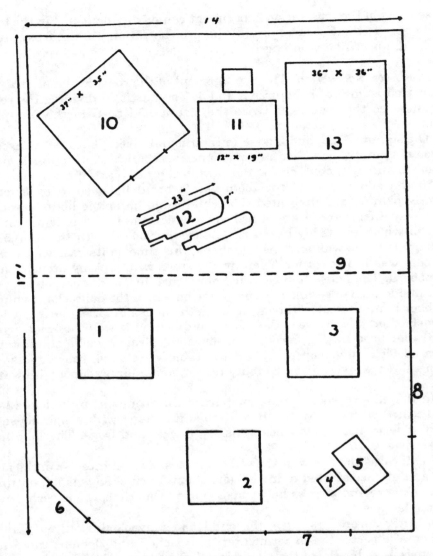

Figure 3. Diagram of the pre-frustration period of the frustration experiment. 1. Square of paper (without toys). 2. Square of paper on which are placed crayons and paper. 3. Square of paper (without toys). 4, 5, 6, 7, 8 as explained in caption of Figure 1. 9. Lifted partition. 10. Toy house containing the following toys: doll, chair, teddy bear, bed, ironing board, iron, telephone, stove with cooking utensils, cupboard, electric lights, curtain, and carpet. 11. Tea table with tea set. In front of it a child's chair. 12. Large truck and trailer. Nearby a small truck and trailer. 13. A lake with real water containing: island with light house, wharf, ferry boat, small boats, fishes, ducks, and frogs.

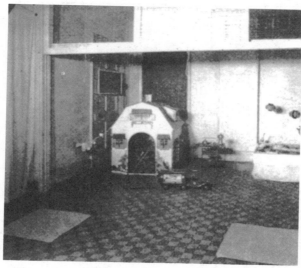

Figure 4.   The setup in the prefrustration period of the frustration experiment.

lowered the wire partition and fastened it by means of a large padlock. The part of the room containing the new toys was now physically inaccessible but visible through the wire mesh netting.

Frustration period. The arrangement of the room in this part of the experiment is shown in Figures 5 and 6. With the lowering of the partition, the frustration period began. This part of the experiment was conducted exactly as the free play experiment. The experimenter wrote at his table, leaving the child completely free to play or not, as he desired. Here again the child's questions were answered, but the experimenter remained aloof from the situation in as natural a manner as possible.

Thirty minutes after the lowering of the partition, the experimenter made the first leaving suggestion. Contrary to the behavior in the free play experiment, the child was usually willing to leave at the first suggestion.

After the experimenter had made sure that the child wanted to leave, the partition was lifted. Usually the child was pleasantly surprised and, forgetting his desire to leave, joyfully hurried over to the fine toys. If the child did not return spontaneously, the experimenter suggested his doing so, and a second suggestion was never necessary.

Postfrustration period. The lifting of the partition at the end of the frustration period was not done with an experimental purpose, but to satisfy the desire of the child to play with the toys and to obviate any undesirable after effects. The child was allowed to play with the house, lake, etc., until he was ready to leave.

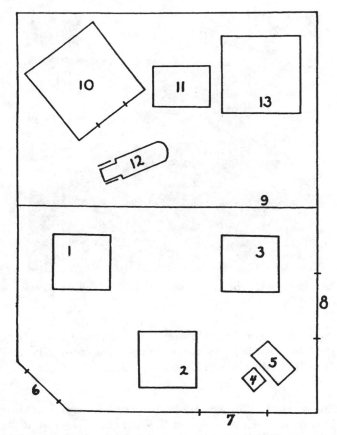

Figure 5. Diagram of the frustration period of the frustration experiment. 1, 2, 3: squares of paper on which the same toys are placed as in the free play situation (see Figure 1). 4, 5, 6, 7, 8: same as Figure 1. 9: transparent partition through which the house with toys (10), tea table with tea set (11), big truck and trailer (12), lake with lake toys (13) are visible.

Additional Remarks About the Technical Arrangements

Toys. Several requirements had to be fulfilled to make the toys adequate for the experiment:

1.   They had to be sufficiently attractive to interest the child on two occasions for at least half an hour.
2.   They had to be sufficiently interesting to children of the ages participating in the experiment.
3.   Toys had to be such as to allow for enjoyable play on different levels of constructiveness.
4.   Toys behind the barrier had to be much more attractive than the accessible toys.

Figure 6. The setup in the frustration period of the frustration experiment.

On the basis of our experience in eight preliminary experiments, the toys which have been described were selected as adequately fulfilling these requirements.

Involvement of the child. It was for the purpose of strengthening the child's desire for the inaccessible toys that he was first given an opportunity to play with them in the prefrustration period. The experimenter lowered the partition initiating the frustration period when he believed the subject had become thoroughly interested in the play. It was thought that the attraction of the toys would be approximately maximal at this time. Typically the children spent considerable time exploring the fine new toys before starting real play. The preliminary experiments had indicated that without giving the child time to become involved in the play with these toys, the later frustration was not very effective.

The Barrier and the Visual Accessibility of the Inaccessible

Toys. The barrier was chosen with a view to creating strong frustration. Two principles were followed here: A partition was selected which would provide (1) maximum visual accessibility to the toys behind it and yet one which (2) was very clearly physically impassable.

The first point is related to a question which is of prime importance for frustration both theoretically and practically. An individual is in a state of frustration only if, and as long as, the inaccessible goal is a part of his life space. Obviously if the individual is in no way aware of the inaccessible objects, for instance, of the toys in the other room he cannot be frustrated in regard to them because they do not exist for him psychologically. Even if the individual has known of the inaccessible objects, and has tried to get them, he may give up these attempts in a way which seems to be nearly equivalent to omitting them from the life space. This is particularly true if the matter is not of great importance to the individual. These considerations indicate that the amount of frustration depends upon the degree to which the nonaccessible goal is kept alive or present within the life space of the individual. This is well in line with the following experience.

In the preliminary experiments, a half-inch mesh netting was used, reducing the visibility of the toys. Since this was clearly unfavorable for setting up strong frustration, a larger mesh, i.e., chicken wire on the lower panel and hog fencing on the upper, was substituted. In addition to carefully arranging the barrier, the area behind it was more brightly illuminated than the other part of the room. The netting was attached to strong frames which were securely fastened with a big padlock in the presence of the child. This was to impress the child with the fact that there was no way of gaining access to the goal.

Minimizing the social factors in the situation. As mentioned before, the experimenter minimized the social aspects of the experiment as much as possible; he pretended that he had his own work to do and refrained from approaching the child. However, in order that the child should feel free and be at ease in the situation, the experimenter did not ignore the approaches of the child. If the child questioned him about the name or nature of the toys, he answered briefly, but not abruptly. If the child started to play with him, e.g., put the telephone to his ear and ask him to talk, the experimenter said a word or two and returned to his work.

Lowering the partition. To initiate the frustration period, the experimenter first asked the child in a matter-of-fact way to return to the "old" part of the room. Some children followed this request without protest, often seeming a little baffled as to what was happening. Other children ignored the request, or answered quietly in the negative and continued playing. Occasionally a child would protest the interruption and resist the experimenter's attempts to remove the toys. Such a child might even retrieve the toys and bring them back to the lake or the house. In such a case, the experimenter allowed the child to continue with his play for a short time, but soon repeated the request and began collecting the toys again.

The experimenter succeeded every time in getting the child to leave the fine toys without forcing him physically. The barrier was immediately lowered and locked with the big padlock. If the child wanted to know why the partition was lowered, the experimenter gave no explanation, but simply answered "you can play on this side now." This answer was deliberately vague and acquired any meaning that the child might give it. In this way the child was left free to look upon the lowering of the partition as an inexplicable occurrence, to ascribe it to the ill will of the experimenter, or to assume a general rule to which the experimenter, as well as he, had to comply. The attempt was made to make the situation as impersonal as possible.

Observation and Analysis

Observation techniques. The observations were made by two persons: an observer behind a one-way vision screen (see 6, Figure 1) and the experimenter (see 4, Figure 1). The observer made a running account of the child's behavior on an especially constructed, constant-speed polygraph, carrying paper one inch every thirty seconds.

To synchronize the record of the experimenter and the observer, a pen, fixed to a signal marker, was set close to a guide bar on the polygraph. By means of a switch hidden beneath his table, the experimenter could indicate, by using a code, the beginning or the end of any event he was observing. To measure the time spent in any event, a celluloid stencil was used with crosslines spaced to indicate five-second intervals.

The presence of two observers during the experiment had these advantages:

1. During periods when the experimenter was occupied with experimental procedures, the observer's record was available.
2. The behavior of the experimenter was recorded by the observer.
3. The presence of two observers made it possible for them to concentrate on different aspects of the behavior and thus to obtain more and better observations. The observer emphasized the activities of the child, the experimenter the conversation and the general meaning of what was happening.
4. The use of two observers permitted the role of experimenter and observer to be shifted between two persons and thus the influence of a single experimenter upon the result was avoided.

Preparation of the records. The raw data consisted of two synchronized running accounts of the course of events of the experimental session. These separate records were combined into a single more complete account. This was valuable since, as mentioned before, the observers concentrated their attention upon different aspects of the behavior. Furthermore, an observer behind a screen necessarily misses much; the verbalizations of the child are often incomprehensible, and facial expressions and gestures lose much of their significance. This is partly because of the fact that the screen interferes with visual and auditory perception and, in the present case, it was accentuated by the fact that most conversation was addressed to the experimenter across the room. On the other hand, the very wealth of the material which the experimenter within the room is able to observe causes him sometimes to miss the sequence of activities.

The method of synchronization mentioned above made it possible to combine the two specialized records into a much more complete account than any single observer could obtain.

Analysis of the records, units of action, episodes of behavior, and emotional units. Although the intention was to observe each child for 30 minutes on the two occasions, unavoidable variations occurred so that it was necessary to limit the analysis to 24 consecutive minutes.

For purposes of analysis, it is obviously necessary to divide a continuous record of behavior into parts (Allport, 1940; Lewin, 1939). This is a fundamental problem of methodology in psychology. There are many possible ways of dividing the behavioral continuum; the particular problem at hand determining to a considerable extent the particular fractionation to be used. There are, however, some fundamental principles to be considered: In general it may be said that all such divisions must be in terms of psychologically significant units of activity.

Obviously not all possible divisions are psychologically satisfactory. For instance, the fractionation cannot be done in terms of arbitrary physical time units such as seconds or minutes. In dividing a record into physical time units, one might have to separate the sentence, e.g., "Teddy, go and watch Mother iron," into two parts: "Teddy, go and w-" and "atch Mother iron." The letter "w" might be the last letter which falls in the first unit, and the second might start with "atch." Such a cut according to physical time units destroys the psychological meaning of the occurrence. It is inadequate.

In defining psychologically meaningful parts, we may distinguish between actions which are guided to a particular end by a central idea or purpose, the actions being the means to this end, and those which do not involve such "means–end" relations. In the former case, a sequence of behavior which is guided by a common idea or purpose is a psychologically significant unit. Such a sequence may or may not be homogeneous as to the activities or materials involved. Thus the child who places different things on a truck and pushes it across the floor in order to deliver them to a play store incorporates a great diversity of action within one behavior unit. In cases where activities are not guided by a central idea as means to a more or less distant end, the division into behavior units can be made on the basis of the homogeneity of the actions. In this case, the activity is its own end. For instance, when the child is rhythmically swinging the fishing pole, pushing the truck back and forth when no other intention is involved, or walking aimlessly about, a change in the activity is an indication that the psychological unit has changed since the activity and the end are one.

On this basis, divisions of the continuous record have been made. We will designate them as "units of action." These units of action varied in length from 5 seconds to several minutes.

Such behavior units may be at the same time parts of more inclusive units. For instance, the psychological behavior unit of eating lunch may be a part of the larger unit of "going on a picnic," which in turn may be part of the still more inclusive action of "entertaining guests." All such units are psychologically important. Which of them is most significant depends upon the particular problem at hand. For some problems, we have divided the course of events into larger units designated as "episodes of behavior."

To regard a course of events as a sequence of units of actions is not the only way to divide it. Emotional behavior and moods such as crying, being depressed, feeling happy, or restless can also be conceived of as natural psychological units within the course of events. These units are somewhat different from the units of action mentioned above, and frequently the beginning and the end of a unit of action does not coincide with the beginning and the end of an emotional unit. For example, entertaining guests might be divided into the following units of action: calling for friends, riding in the car to the picnic place, ordering lunch, eating lunch, taking a walk, etc. The division in emotional units might be: first, strangeness and formality (if the guests are new acquaintances), then easiness and familiarity, and finally, a tactless remark might lead to a period of uneasiness for the rest of the time. Obviously these units would not necessarily coincide with the units of action.

Sometimes units of action coincide with emotional units, e.g., when a child kicks the barrier. One can look upon this as a unit of action with the purpose of breaking the barrier which hinders locomotion to the desired toys, and also as an emotional unit expressing the anger of the frustrated child.

The course of events, therefore, may be divided into emotional units or into units of action, or both. For some problems the emotional units, the changes in emotional atmosphere are more important than the units of action.

In our experiments, analysis has been made of both units of action and units of emotional mood. However, time has not permitted the treatment of the problem of mood changes in more than a secondary manner.

Additional data. After each experiment, the experimenter recorded his impressions of the children's behavior. The importance of the social aspects of the situation for the child was emphasized in these comments as well as the amount of dependence upon the experimenter, the importance of play for the child, the child's emotional expressiveness, his mood, the extent of his activity, and his talkativeness. These comments were found to be of considerable usefulness in giving a picture of the total impression which the child made upon the experimenter at the time. . . .

V
Constructiveness of Play in the Free Play Situation and Frustration Situation: General Results

We turn now to the experimental results concerning our main problem, namely, the effects of frustration upon the constructiveness of play.

Average Constructiveness of Play in Free Play and Frustration

The mean constructiveness of the play of each child in free play and in frustration is shown in Table 1, together with the difference in constructiveness in the two situations. The same data are presented in the correlation chart, Figure 7. These data include all play, both primary [play which receives the full attention of the child] and secondary [play which occurs simultaneously with another nonplay action]. The mean constructiveness of play in free play is 4.99 constructiveness points and in frustration, 3.94 points. Twenty-five of the subjects regressed in the constructiveness of their play and five increased. The mean of the differences, i.e., constructiveness in frustration minus constructiveness in free play is −1.05 with a standard error of .24. The mean regression is 4.39 times its standard error. Stated in terms of mental age equivalents, i.e., in terms of the regression of constructiveness upon mental age, the mean regression amounts to 17.3 months of mental age.

For the 10 younger subjects, 28 to 41 months of age, the regression is smaller than for the 20 older subjects, aged 42 to 61 months. In the former case, the mean regression is 0.58 constructiveness points, corresponding to a regression of approximately 9.6 months, and in the latter case it is 1.29 points, corresponding to regression of approximately 21.5 months. Proportionately, the amount of regression seems to be quite similar in the younger and the older group.

These data establish rather definitely the fact that a frustrating situation of the kind considered here reduces, on the average, the constructiveness of play below the level upon which it normally occurs in a nonfrustrating, free play situation. Before considering how this reduction in constructiveness is effected, it may be well to stress the fact that these crude results have a great deal of significance.

They show that frustration affects not only actions related to the inaccessible goal, such as attempts to find round-about routes or getting emotional and aggressive against physical or social obstacles, but that frustration may affect behavior in other regions of activity as well. The main expectation of the result of the experiment has been proved correct. More specifically, the result shows the importance of the total situation for promoting or hindering a child's creative achievement. Thus, our second expectation, namely, that constructiveness of play would be a useful instrument for measuring regression, has also been confirmed.

Examples of Play in the Free Play and Frustration Situation

An example is given below to indicate the change of constructiveness of play of the same child (subject 24) with the same toys in the free play situation and the frustration situation. The order of occurrence of the units of play has been changed in order that play with the same or similar material in the free play situation and frustration situation may be placed

Table 1. Mean Constructiveness of Play in Free Play and Frustration, Including Both Primary and Secondary Play

Subject	Free play	Frustration	Difference (*Fru−FPl*)
		Younger subjects	
1	4.21	2.56	−1.65
2	3.34	3.83	+0.49
3	3.08	1.00	−2.08
4	4.68	4.67	−0.01
5	4.34	2.36	−1.98
6	4.16	2.84	−1.32
7	3.06	4.94	+1.88
8	4.01	2.50	−1.51
9	3.72	3.68	−0.04
10	4.04	4.47	+0.43
M	3.87	3.29	−0.58
		Older subjects	
11	5.14	4.17	−0.97
12	5.36	2.00	−3.36
13	6.06	4.32	−1.74
14	4.95	3.78	−1.17
15	5.79	4.65	−1.14
16	4.34	4.30	−0.04
17	5.26	4.56	−0.70
18	4.83	5.76	+0.93
19	5.36	3.48	−1.88
20	6.07	3.03	−3.04
21	4.87	4.76	−0.11
22	6.20	5.33	−0.87
23	5.37	3.60	−1.77
24	6.78	3.79	−2.99
25	6.27	5.27	−1.00
26	5.80	4.14	−1.66
27	4.44	3.65	−0.79
28	6.22	5.56	−0.66
29	4.47	5.06	+0.59
30	7.57	4.11	−3.46
M	5.56	4.27	−1.29
		All subjects	
M	4.99	3.940	−0.053
SD	0.197	0.200	0.240

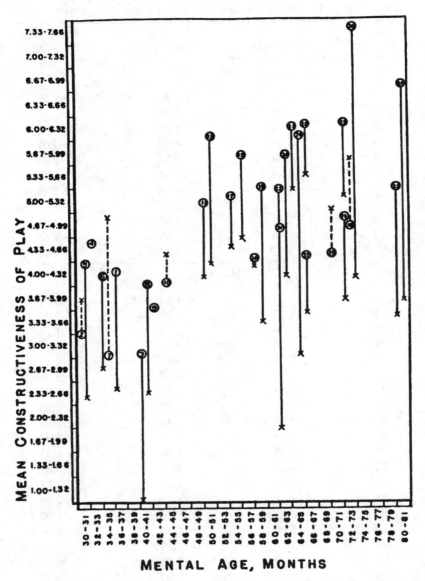

Figure 7. The relation between mean constructiveness of play and mental age and the change of constructiveness in the frustration situation. (1) The mean constructiveness of (primary plus secondary) play in the free play situation is indicated for each child by a circle. The number given is that of the subject as indicated in Table 1. (2) The mean constructiveness of play in the frustration situation is indicated by a cross. (3) Change in constructiveness from the free play to the frustration situation is designated by a solid line when constructiveness decreases in frustration, by a broken line when constructiveness increases. The absence of a cross indicates no change in mean constructiveness for that child.

Exhibit 1.

Free play situation	Frustration situation

Fish pole and boats
(Lower constructiveness in the frustration situation)

6, 7, 8. Child goes to square 3: "Now I'm going out. What's this? (fish pole). I'll let out more string like this. This is the way my daddy fishes. Oh, I caught a fish! Oh, I caught a fish!" Pretends to fish on square paper. "Now I'll take my fish pole home." Goes to square 1. Back to square 3, seizes duck. "Now I catch a duck. Oh, I caught a duck." Sings, takes duck home, to square 1. "Now I'll let the blood run out." Holds duck head downward. Back to square 3. "Why are there two boats?" Makes sailboat go round on lake, makes noise like a boat. "Now I go to the real boat (motorboat)." Makes boat go around the lake while making engine noises. Picks up fish pole. "I'm going	21. Picks up fish pole, swings magnet while looking through barrier. Constructiveness 2; 25 seconds 4. Pushes truck to square 3; examines and manipulates boat, examines wet print it made. Constructiveness 3; 45 seconds 20. Turns to square 3; picks up sailboat and examines it carefully. Tries to put mast into hole. Constructiveness 4; 50 seconds

Peg board
(Lower constructiveness in the frustration situation)

11. Child goes to peg board, contemplates it sometime before beginning to place pegs. Peg in board. Looks at ring-wagon. Puts green pegs in row. "It's too cold," looks out window. "Look at all the green ones," counts them. "I have nine of them." Another in. "No more green ones." Begins with orange pegs on other side. "There are too many orange ones." Begins on purple ones. "What does it say on the paper you are writing on." Continues with purple pegs. "Look, here are the green ones, here the purple, and here the red ones, now I'll do yellow." Puts in red pegs. "There is no room for red." Begins red row parallel to orange. "I'm too hot now. There's too many reds." Constructiveness 7; 550 seconds	12. Goes to peg board. Lies out at full length on stomach, picks up peg board. "The holes go all the way through but the paper is there so you can't see them." Examines peg board, and stirs pegs in box with finger in a dilatory way. Constructiveness 3; 55 seconds 6, 7, 8, 10, 11. Child goes to square 2; sits back to barrier. Draws with crayons. Counts colors to see if she has used them all. Pushes truck over with foot. "Look at my rainbow." Turns about, looks at barrier momentarily. Resumes drawing, taps with foot, crayon in each hand, scribbles in circles. Turns, looks at barrier. Marks on shoe. Dots on paper. Sighs. Constructiveness 4; 265 seconds

Exhibit 1 continues

Exhibit 1. *(Continued)*

Free play situation	Frustration situation

Doll and teapot
(Lower constructiveness in the frustration situation)

5. "I'm going to make some tea now." Takes teapot, puts doll and teddy on chair. "Pours" tea; pretends to drink; has teddy and doll drink. "The bear gets some more. The teddy has to get as full as the baby." Constructiveness 7; 125 seconds	13. Turns and looks through barrier, "That little thing that gives the water (teapot) isn't really hot is it?" Turns to square 1, picks up doll. Constructiveness 2; 15 seconds

Doll and teddy
(Approximately same constructiveness in both situations)

2. Picks up doll and teddy, tries to sit them on truck. "The teddy doesn't sit up very well; I lay the teddy down." They both lie down. Constructiveness 5; 25 seconds	2. Places doll and teddy on truck, pushes to center. Constructiveness 6, 15 seconds
12. Looks about, goes to square 1. Doll and teddy put on truck. "I want my babies to go." Makes noise like engine as truck is pushed around. "Now you stay here." Leaves it in corner. Constructiveness 6; 55 seconds	

Activities which occurred only in the free play situation

1. Shakes phone, laughs, "I forgot which end to talk to. Hello, how are you? You want to come over. I'll be back in a minute." To experimenter, "I'm telephoning my mother. There's a house and all things, even a rolling pin." Constructiveness 6; 85 seconds

4. Examines phone. "Hello, I'm coming back and play with my clay, keep it for me." Constructiveness 6, 55 seconds

9. "I must go and telephone. Hello, how are you; I'm coming home pretty soon, will you save my clay for me?" Constructiveness 6; 30 seconds

3. Takes rolling pin. "I'm making some cookies now for the baby." Rolls with rolling pin. "They'll have them when they're made." Pretends to cut cookies. "Put, put, put." Cookies in oven. Constructiveness 7; 75 seconds

Exhibit 1 continues

Exhibit 1. *(Continued)*

Activities which occurred only in the free play situation *(Continued)*

13. Goes to ironing board, looks underneath. "How do you fold the ironing board up?" Tries. "I can't fold it up again." Tries. Ironing board won't stand up. Constructiveness 4; 125 seconds

Activities which occurred only in the frustration situation

1. Child goes to experimenter's table, "Why can't you have it all the time?" Stands looking about. Looks through barrier. 40 seconds

3. Stands looking at house and pond. 25 seconds

5. Child goes to experimenter's table, "It's too hot." 25 seconds

7. Turns about, looks at house and pond. 10 seconds

9. Turns, looks at house and pond; looks at experimenter; looks at house and pond. 30 seconds

14. Goes to barrier; stands looking through. 30 seconds

15. Comes to experimenter's table singing. Looks at the clock, "There's one too many hands on the clock. That big one's supposed to be little." 45 seconds

16. Goes to barrier, "Looks like Christmas night. Why do you have to put them down?" Holds barrier looking through. 115 seconds

17. Goes to experimenter's table almost whimpering, "I want to go to preschool." 45 seconds

18. Looks at barrier, "Sometime will you have different things?" 15 seconds

19. Looking at the house, "My house is that color." Moves to barrier. "Why will only part of the phone come out?" Holds on to barrier and looks through humming quietly, "Why can't you have everything in the house?" Runs finger over the wire as she talks. Kneels down by barrier looking through intently. 200 seconds

22. Goes to table; takes experimenter's paper. "What is the matter with your pencil? Can't you screw some out?" Leans on table. "It's something like ink isn't it?" Watches experimenter intently. Makes suggestions about dotting i's. Looks about room. 125 seconds

NON-FRUSTRATION   FRUSTRATION

C.A. 4;6

HOUSE WITH A LOT OF WINDOWS

EXPERIMENTER: "WHAT IS THAT?"
SUBJECT: "JUST SOMETHING."

Figure 8.   Drawing by subject 26, C.A. 4;6 in the free play situation and in the frustration situation.

side by side in parallel columns. (The initial number indicates the order in which the units occurred in the record.)

Constructiveness of Play in Consecutive Thirds of the Total Period

It is obvious from the records which have been given that the child does not maintain the same level of constructiveness throughout the experimental period. It will be shown later that the intensity of frustration varies during the experiment. The question arises if there are consistent trends in the level of mean constructiveness throughout the experimental periods, or if the behavior is sufficiently homogeneous in this respect to be considered as a unit.

We have divided the total 24 minute experimental session into three consecutive 8 minute periods and have determined the mean constructiveness of play for each of these shorter intervals. This provides data as to the trends of the constructiveness of play throughout the whole period. The means are given in the following tabulation:

Consecutive Experimental Intervals (8 Minutes in Length)

Session	First	Second	Third
Free play			
M	4.68	5.09	5.03
SD_M	0.29	0.30	0.32
Frustration			
M	4.06	3.83	4.06
SD_M	0.32	0.30	0.29

The differences in the average constructiveness of play in the different intervals of the experimental period are not significant in either the free play situation or the frustration situation sessions. This indicates that we are justified in considering the whole experimental period as a homogeneous unit as far as the average constructiveness of play for the total group is concerned, and that a single measure of the effect of frustration on the constructiveness of play is adequate.

Effect of Frustration on Primary Play

It has been pointed out that secondary play occurs relatively more frequently in the frustration situation than in the free play situation. We have already seen that its constructiveness is lower than the constructiveness of primary play. The question arises as to what part of the decrement in the constructiveness of play in the frustration situation is attributable to the relative increase in the amount of secondary play.

When secondary play is eliminated and only the primary play activities are considered, the data shown in Table 2 result. In computing the statistics for this table, data from subjects 3 and 12 were omitted, inasmuch as they did not engage in primary play in the frustration situation. The mean constructiveness of primary play for the 28 subjects is 5.11 in the free play situation and 4.35 in the frustration situation. The mean of the differences is 0.76 and its standard error is 0.24; i.e., the mean of the differences is 3.18 times its standard error. Twenty-one of the 28 subjects show a decrease in constructiveness of primary play in the frustration situation as against 7 showing an increase.

As before, the regression is greater at the older ages. For the 19 older subjects, aged 42 to 61 months, the regression amounts to 1.00 constructiveness points, and for the 9 younger subjects, the regression amounts to 0.24 constructiveness points.

The position might be taken that by excluding subjects 3 and 12 from the computations we have underestimated the effect of frustration upon creativity; the very fact that these subjects engaged in no primary play indicates that they were severely affected in this respect. However, one is hardly justified in assigning zero constructiveness to their primary play. If they are included by taking the maximal constructiveness of their secondary play as the best available estimate of their highest creativity (constructiveness 1 and 2, respectively), one obtains a mean regression in constructiveness for the whole group amounting to 0.89 constructiveness points.

We may conclude that by the usual statistical tests of significance, it is well established that primary play, i.e., play which is apparently receiving the complete attention of the subject, is pursued, on the average, upon a lower constructiveness level in a frustrating psychological environment than in a nonfrustrating situation.

In seven cases, there is an increase in level of constructiveness in the frustration situation. These exceptions will be considered later.

On the basis of the previously mentioned findings that secondary play is of lower constructiveness than primary play, and that it more frequently

Table 2. Mean Constructiveness of Primary Play in Free Play and Frustration

Subject	Free play	Frustration	Difference (*Fru−FPl*)
Younger subjects			
1	4.21	3.16	−1.06
2	3.36	3.84	+0.49
3	3.10		
4	4.76	4.26	−0.51
5	4.34	2.41	−1.93
6	4.29	3.63	−0.66
7	3.02	5.39	+2.37
8	4.01	2.30	−1.71
9	3.81	4.21	+0.40
10	4.14	4.57	+0.44
M (omitting subject 3)	3.99	3.75	−0.24
Older subjects			
11	5.14	4.94	−0.20
12	5.37		
13	6.06	4.32	−1.73
14	5.01	3.78	−1.24
15	5.79	5.10	−0.69
16	4.44	4.12	−0.32
17	5.26	4.56	−0.70
18	4.83	5.76	+0.93
19	5.36	3.48	−1.88
20	6.07	3.03	−3.04
21	4.87	5.10	+0.23
22	6.45	5.87	−0.58
23	5.45	4.21	−1.24
24	6.78	3.89	−2.90
25	6.27	5.64	−0.63
26	5.80	5.01	−0.79
27	5.31	4.75	−0.56
28	6.22	5.34	−0.88
29	4.47	5.09	+0.62
30	7.57	4.12	−3.46
M (omitting subject 12)	5.64	4.63	−1.00
All subjects			
M (omitting subjects 3 and 12)	5.110	4.352	−0.758
SD	0.275	0.305	+0.239

occurs in the frustration situation than in the free play situation, it is inevitable that the reduction in constructiveness should be less when only primary play is included in the analysis than when both primary and secondary play are involved. This means that a small part of the total regression in the constructiveness of play in frustration is due to an increase in the amount of secondary play, or, in terms of our previous interpretation of secondary play, to an increase in the frequency of overlapping regions of play and nonplay behavior. That there is more frequent overlapping of play and other regions in the frustration situation is understandable by reason of the fact that one more region of nonplay activity, i.e., barrier behavior, is present in the frustration situation than in the free play situation. On a purely chance basis therefore, play should overlap more frequently with nonplay. It may be true, too, that barrier and escape regions are more conducive to the occurrence of overlapping with play than are other regions of free activity.

Although we may conclude that regression in the constructiveness of play in the frustration situation is partly a function of increased overlapping between play and nonplay regions, which according to our assumptions should reduce the maximal degree of constructiveness in either action, still the major portion of the regression is unaccounted for by this factor.

Maximal Constructiveness of Play in Free Play and Frustration

Additional data about the effects of frustration upon play of highest potency is to be found by comparing the maximal constructiveness of play occurring in the free play situation and the frustration situation.

In the following tabulation, the mean of the two highest constructiveness ratings given each child's play are shown. In 17 of the 30 cases this mean constructiveness rating is lower in frustration, in 8 cases it is equal in the free play situation and the frustration situation, and in 5 cases it is higher in frustration. The mean of the differences (frustration situation minus free play situation) is −0.83 constructiveness points, and the standard error of the mean difference is 0.28, i.e., the mean difference is 2.93 times its standard error.

Although these data are in line with those previously given, they do not show the effects of frustration as decisively as did the former data. This may result partly from the lower reliability of high constructiveness ratings. In the case of some subjects the periods of maximal constructiveness involved less than one minute of play and so gave an inadequate basis for making judgments. The reliability of the rating scale for the periods of very high constructiveness is undoubtedly lower than for the medium ranges. As the constructiveness of play increases the behavioral basis for assigning different constructiveness ratings becomes less easily discriminable, and it becomes more and more difficult to record these fine differentiations in the records even when they are observed. In other words, the

Exhibit 3.   Maximal Constructiveness Ratings[3]

Subject	Free play	Frustration	Difference $(Fru-FPl)$
1	5.50	4.00	−1.50
2	4.50	6.00	+1.50
3	4.50	1.00	−3.50
4	7.00	7.00	0.00
5	5.50	4.50	−1.00
6	6.50	5.50	−1.00
7	5.50	6.50	+1.00
8	5.00	2.50	−2.50
9	5.50	5.50	0.00
10	5.50	7.00	+1.50
11	6.50	6.00	−0.50
12	6.50	2.00	−4.50
13	6.50	5.50	−1.00
14	6.50	6.50	0.00
15	4.50	6.50	+2.00
16	6.50	5.00	−1.50
17	6.50	6.50	0.00
18	5.50	4.00	−1.50
19	6.50	4.50	−2.00
20	6.50	4.50	−2.00
21	8.00	5.50	−2.50
22	6.50	6.50	0.00
23	5.00	6.50	+1.50
24	7.50	5.50	−2.00
25	8.00	6.50	−1.50
26	6.50	6.50	0.00
27	6.50	3.50	−3.00
28	6.50	6.50	0.00
29	5.50	5.50	0.00
30	7.00	6.00	−1.00
M	6.13	5.30	−0.83
SD	0.17	0.27	+0.28

[3]Maximal constructiveness is average of two highest constructiveness ratings occurring in each subject's record.

constructiveness scale does not differentiate as satisfactorily at the upper levels as at the lower. These factors may account for the less certain effect of frustration at the upper constructiveness levels.

Nevertheless these results are important, for they suggest that even with play of highest constructiveness, where the probability is smallest that overlapping regions of play and nonplay are involved, there is a tendency for constructiveness of play to be reduced under the influence of frustration. This is further evidence, therefore, that division of the person between two simultaneous actions is not the only cause of the reduction of constructiveness in the frustration situation. . . .

IX
Theoretical Considerations and Summary

Theory in science has two main functions: (1) to open the way to new knowledge and (2) to organize that which is known. The first and probably most essential function determines the fruitfulness of a theory. This function is fulfilled in the following way: The theory, which at first is stated in the form of a hypothesis, envisions unrevealed facts or relations or it denies certain relations, which are believed to hold; in other words, the theory predicts certain facts or relations of facts. This prediction is tested usually through experiments. It is found to be valid or invalid. However, even if it has been found valid, the new data need not be treated in terms of the theory.

It is an essential characteristic of a fruitful empirical theory that it gives birth, as it were, to new knowledge, which is then independent of its theoretical ancestry. In an empirical science, new data, although discovered by theory, are something in themselves which anyone is free to interpret theoretically in his own way or to accept as mere facts. In other words, the fruitful empirical theory is instrumental in establishing new scientific data which should be able to outlive the theory.

The main results which have been presented here have actually been predicted on the basis of a theory or group of theories as indicated in chapters I to III. The experiment has been set up to test the theoretical predictions. In summarizing, we will present two interrelated theoretical considerations, one centered around constructiveness; the other around regression and frustration.

Summary: Experimental Results

Thirty children between 2 and 5 years of age were observed individually while playing with a standardized set of toys in a free play situation and in a frustration situation for half an hour on different days. A record of all behavior was made, and the effect of frustration on the constructiveness of play was determined.

Constructiveness of Play in Free Play Situation

1. A seven-point constructiveness scale was developed on the basis of which each play unit of each child in both the free play and the frustration situation was rated.
2. The constructiveness of play with the same toy varies greatly from child to child.
3. The mean constructiveness of primary play in the free play situation is correlated +.81 with both mental and chronological age.
4. The constructiveness of play is positively related to length of play unit.

5. The constructiveness of play is lower for secondary play (play which occurs simultaneously with another nonplay action) than for primary play (play which receives the full attention of the child).

6. The qualitative analysis indicates that constructiveness of play measured by the scale is related to degree of differentiation, degree of hierarchical organization, originality, and adequacy of play behavior.

The Strength of Frustration in the Frustration Situation and Mood

1. The amount of time spent in attempts to overcome the barrier to the inaccessible toys by physical or social means (amount of barrier behavior) varies greatly from child to child.

2. The amount of time spent in trying to leave the experimental room by physical or social means (escape behavior) is positively related to the amount of barrier behavior.

3. The proportion of the total time occupied with barrier and escape behavior in a situation such as the frustration situation can be used as a measurement of the average strength (potency) of the background of frustration during the experimental period.

4. The potency of a background of frustration can be measured for a given natural "psychological episode" by determining the proportion of the total time occupied with barrier and escape behavior in that episode.

5. In the frustration situation freedom of expression as indicated by play monologue, and friendly conversation with the experimenter, decreases; masking social behavior increases.

6. The frequency of happy actions decreases and of unhappy actions increases in frustration. This change is positively related to strength of frustration.

7. The frequency of restlessness and of aggressive actions is positively related to the strength of frustration.

Regression in Frustration

1. A background of frustration decreases the average constructiveness of play with accessible toys. On the average, the constructiveness regresses by an amount equivalent to 17.3 months mental age. For the younger subjects, 28 to 41 months of age, this average regression is 9.6 months; for the older subjects, 42 to 61 months of age, the average regression is 21.5 months.

2. The maximum constructiveness of play decreases in frustration, although not as much as the average constructiveness of play.

3. The amount of secondary play increases in the frustration situation.

4. The average length of play units decreases in the frustration situation with the strong frustration group.

5. The lowering of the constructiveness of play in frustration is partly due to the increase in the amount of secondary play and to the decrease in the average length of play unit. However, the decrease in constructiveness holds, also, for primary play of the same length of play unit in the free play situation and frustration situation.

6. The amount of regression in constructiveness of play is a function of the strength of frustration. This is shown by the difference in the effect on children showing strong or weak frustration in the experimental setting, and by a comparison of behavior of the same children under different strengths of frustration.

7. In the strong frustration group the regression is equivalent to 24 months, and in the weak group to 4 months mental age.

8. The greater regression in strong frustration holds also for primary play and for play units of the same length.

9. The amount of regression in the constructiveness of primary play of equivalent length of unit in the free play situation and the frustration situation is positively related to the relative strength (potency) of the background of frustration.

10. A background of weak frustration in some cases seems to increase the constructiveness of play.

11. If the play unit with the accessible toys takes on the meaning of a substitute for the inaccessible toys, the mood of the person will under certain conditions be happy and the constructiveness level of play will not indicate regression.

12. Constructiveness of play is not related to the preference for particular toys. The regression in the constructiveness of play is not due to the selection in frustration of toys with a naturally low constructiveness level.

13. The amount of negative emotionality increases with the strength of frustration.

14. The qualitative analysis indicates that the lowering of constructiveness of play is similar in nature to the change in behavior occurring under conditions of high emotionality where restless movements, stereotyped repetition of sentences, and stuttering are frequent. Both changes involve a reduction in degree of differentiation and level of hierarchical organization within a unit of activity, and a certain lack of realism.

Miscellaneous

1. A survey of different types of substitution in play is given.
2. The different ways in which the child tries to control the experimenter are given.

Theory of Constructiveness of Play

Topological and Dynamical Characteristic of Play

Fluidity of Play

According to Sliosberg (1934) and Lewin (1935), play can be represented as an area of activity on the reality level of the life space which has certain specific properties somewhat different from the rest of the reality level. The outstanding dynamic characteristic of the play region seems to be a relatively high degree of fluidity. In this respect, play is similar to levels of irreality. The content of play is also closely related to the content of the irreality level of the person (his wishes and fears). The greater fluidity of the play region holds for limitations set both by physical and by social requirements. In play the meaning of a building block is not restricted to a piece of wood, but may be an engine, a man, a horse, a boat, a telephone, etc. The child is not limited to his own role, but can be his father, his sister, or a dog. He is free to make his own social rules to a much greater extent than in reality. Play is therefore more likely to mirror adequately the state of the child than in the case of an activity which is minutely prescribed for him by someone else. Constructiveness in play is not, however, fundamentally different from constructiveness in other activities.

Play Is an Organized Sequence of Action

The degree of constructiveness of a play action can be understood best by viewing it as a sequence of actions organized as one unit. The degree of constructiveness is expressed in the degree of differentiation of the unit of action (variety and number of its parts) and the degree of hierarchical organization. In highly constructive play (for example, the trip to Chicago), a central idea governs a number of subideas (such as filling the tank with gasoline or following certain streets). Each of the subideas, in turn, rules a number of actions (such as stopping at the gasoline station, talking to the garageman).

Reality and Irreality Levels, Power of Fantasy, Planning

One may distinguish different degrees of reality and irreality (wishes, fears, daydreaming) in the psychological present and in the psychological future (Figure 9). The reality level of the psychological future is defined by the expectations in regard to the future. Planning involves structuring the level of reality in the future by means of action. It is concerned with the discrepancy between the level of irreality and levels of future expectation, i.e., it is an attempt to structure the future life space in a manner which will fulfill certain wishes.

More specifically, we can distinguish planning and hoping. In both cases, the person has not yet reached his goal, i.e., he is outside his goal region on the reality level of the psychological present. The situation does not yet conform to the person's wishes: There is a discrepancy between the structure of the reality and the irreality level at the psychological present. However, in both cases, the person expects that his dream will sometime come true, that he will finally reach his goal. The person sees himself within the goal region on the level of reality in the psychological future ($Ps\ Fu$). To this extent, at least, the structure of the future level of expectation conforms to a level of irreality.

In case a person merely *hopes* to reach his goal without having a definite plan, the structure of the future reality levels ($Ps\ Fu^1$) which lie between the psychological present and that more distant psychological future is rather vague (Figure 10). In case the person has a definite *plan*, he expects to follow a series of steps. In other words, the level of expectation throughout his psychological future ($Ps\ Fu^1$ up to $Ps\ Fu^2$) is structured with sufficient clarity to represent the pathway to the goal.

A fundamental condition for constructive behavior is a close relation between fantasy and action, between the reality and irreality levels of the future (Lewin, 1935). This connection is cut, whenever a goal becomes a mere wish, without plan for realization. In this case the structure of the future reality level is unrelated to that of the irreality level. Such a functional separation may have either of two effects. The wishes (and fears) may become unrestrained by any consideration of what will be realized or the action may become "realistic" in the narrow sense of not being guided by long range planning. In terms of powerfields, this situation can be characterized in the following way. The individual does not believe he has power to form the world according to his wishes.

From this it is understandable that an essential factor for the constructiveness of play is what has been called "power of fantasy." Constructiveness of an activity may be low as a result of a lack of connection with fantasy. On the other hand, constructiveness may be low because of too little realism. Planning involves a mutual influence of the structure of the reality and irreality level on the psychological future. If the potency of the reality level (Escalona, 1939), becomes too small, the plans of the individual become "fantastic." What has been called inadequacy in the treatment of toy material is probably related to this lack of realism.

These considerations make it comprehensible why there is a small and uncertain difference between highly constructive activity and unconstructive, utopian behavior. A constructive plan is a long range plan; its constructiveness tends to increase, at least in certain respects, with the amount of discrepancy between the present and the reality level of the future. If, however, the discrepancy increases beyond a certain limit the plan loses its connection with reality and its constructiveness.

Momentary and Maximal Constructiveness of the Child

The actual constructiveness of the individual's behavior does not always represent his maximal possible constructiveness even in such free situa-

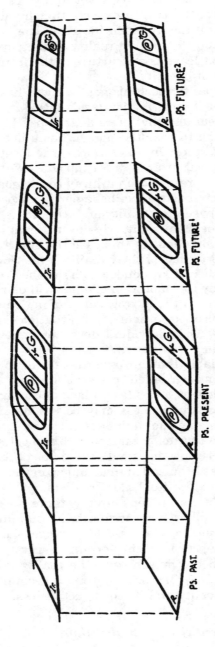

Figure 9. PS. Past, psychological past; PS. Present, psychological present; PS. Future[1], the near future; PS. Future[2], the more distant future. All are represented as seen by the person at time for which the life space is represented. R = level of reality; IR = level of irreality; P = person; G = goal.

Differences in degree of reality and differences in psychological time dimension are conceived of as two different dimensions of the life space existing at a given time. The representation of the psychological time dimension in a discontinuous manner is merely due to the technical difficulty of representing a four-dimensional space on paper.

There is a discrepancy between the structure of the level of irreality and reality in that on the level of wishes (IR), the person sees himself closer to the goal than on the level of reality. However, there is some point in psychological future where the person expects, on the level of reality, to reach the goal. In addition, the intermediate steps on the level of reality are envisaged.

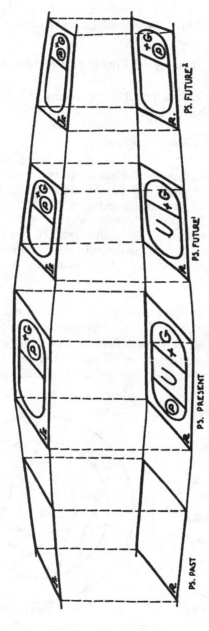

Figure 10.   The meaning of the symbols is the same as in Figure 9.

Also in the case of mere hop, somewhere in the psychological future the person sees himself in the goal region on the level of expectation (R). However, the intermediate regions between the present position and the goal region are unstructured (U) and the position of the person in the near future is undetermined.

tions as play. For a given child, the constructiveness of his behavior seems to vary below the maximum in inverse relation to the degree to which the person is involved in the activity. In other words, the constructiveness of an individual's behavior is a positive function of the proportion of the total personality which enters into it. This proportion in turn depends upon the relative potency of the situation corresponding to the activity.

Simplified Quantitative Theory of Constructiveness

It is possible to derive most of our results respecting the constructiveness of play from the following theorem:

$$cons(A) = F(nc(A)) \tag{1}$$

In this formula $cons(A)$ refers to the constructiveness of an activity A, n to the number of cells (c) involved in the activity A. In view of our discussion of constructiveness, it is not necessary to state that this formula is oversimplified. However, it permits the derivation of the main facts surprisingly well. This may be because of a high correlation between the number of cells of a person involved in an activity and such other factors as the degree of hierarchical organization of the systems involved in the activity.

1.   From this theorem (1) together with the statement concerning the increasing differentiation during development it follows that the *maximum constructiveness of a person* increases with age (Figure 11). For the maximum number of cells involved in an activity is obviously a function of the total number of cells contained in the whole person.

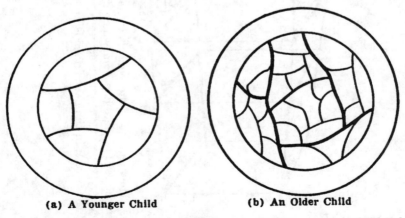

(a) A Younger Child   **(b) An Older Child**

Figure 11.   Degree of differentiation of the person. The younger child is less differentiated than the older. Certain functional parts of the older child show greater independence from each other (indicated by thickness of the boundary line) than corresponding parts of the younger child.

$$cons(P)^{max} = F(MA) \tag{2}$$

$cons(P)^{max}$ means the maximum constructiveness of a person, and *MA* is mental age at the stage where the highest degree of differentiation of the person is reached. This derivation agrees with our results.

2. Formula (1) states that the constructiveness of behavior at a given developmental level is higher the greater the number of *parts of the* person involved in the activity (Figure 12). This implies that:

cons(weak frustration) > *cons*(nonfrustration) in cases

where weak frustration increases the degree of involvement

in the activity over that occurring in nonfrustration.   (3)

Weak frustration actually may increase the general tension level and also the force in the direction of the goal follows from theoretical considerations (Lewin, 1938; Wright, 1937), and is well in line with various experiments (Ach, 1910; Birenbaum, 1930; Wright, 1937) as well as with our observations.

3. Increasing frustration may increase constructiveness by involving more and more regions of the person. If, however, the total person has become involved, further increase in strength of *frustration*

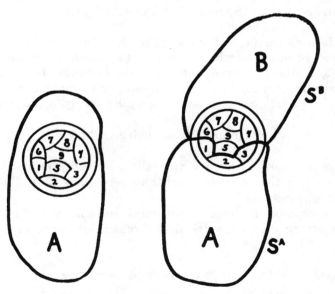

Figure 12.   Areas of the person related to an activity in which the person is (A) fully involved (B) less involved. A and B, different activities; S^A and S^B, situations corresponding to these activities. In case of a non-overlapping situation (Figure 12A), the total person is involved in the activity A; in case of an overlapping situation (Figure 12B), only the peripheral regions 1, 2, 3 of the person are involved in the activity A.

should result in a *lowering of constructiveness*. In cases like ours, where we consider the constructiveness of an activity as play, which is not directed toward the frustrated goal, the increase of frustration should hinder the person from devoting himself fully to this activity. This is equivalent to a decrease in the number of regions involved in play. This decrease should be greater as frustration increases. Therefore it follows from (1) that:

$cons$(play) $= F$(1/strength of frustration) above

a weak level of frustration or if the conditions

indicated in (3) do not hold.   (4)

This is confirmed by the results discussed in VI.*

4. In the same way, it follows that in the frustration situation the constructiveness of play which has the character of a *real substitute* may be higher than that of other play. For, in substitution the total person can again be involved in one activity rather than being split into different activities each involving less than the total person.
5. We can write (4) as a somewhat more general form:

$cons$(A) $= F(Po(S^A))$ where $Po(S^A)$ means the *Potency* (*Po*)

of the *Situation* (*S*) related to the activity (*A*).   (5)

(5) follows from (1). If one applies (5) to "overlapping situations at large" in other words, to the *effect of the background within the life space* on the immediate situation formula (4) results.

6. If one applies (5) to an overlapping immediate situation, for example, to *primary and secondary play* one gets (Figure 12):

$cons$(primary Pl) $> cons$(secondary Pl)   (6)

In other words, primary play should show greater constructiveness (with the same person) than secondary play. This is in line with our results.

7. If frustration increases until *emotional tension* (*et*) becomes high, the person may show the dedifferentiation represented in Figure 12.

$cons(P) = F(1/(et(P)))$ above a certain level of emotionality,

where $cons(P)$ means the constructiveness of a person.   (7)

This follows from the discussion in the Appendix* and agrees with our observations in VII* concerning the relation between construc-

---

Editor's Note. Omitted here.

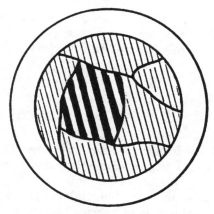

Figure 13. Regression due to high tension. Schematic representation of a person on the developmental level of an older child (corresponding to Figure 11b) in a state of high tension. The degree of differentiation is decreased.

tiveness, frustration, and emotionality; it is also in accord with previous experiments (Dembo, 1931). This is another way of linking the decrease of constructiveness in frustration with (1). The emotional factor may be of particular importance for the explanation of the decrease in constructiveness of actions directed toward an inaccessible goal. In this case the decrease of constructiveness cannot be explained in terms of (5) because the person is fully involved. In our study both factors may have been of importance.

Theory of Regression in Frustration

Regression and Developmental Stages

Regression has been defined here as a change which is opposite to development. Development includes some or all of the following changes: increase in variety of behavior, increase in degree of hierarchical organizations, extension of area of activities and interests including time perspective, and increased weight of organizational dependence relative to simple dependence. Regression, therefore, can be related to some or all of these changes in the opposite direction.

To understand how temporary regression is brought about by situational factors, it is necessary to refer to certain constructs, for example, to those concerning degree of differentiation, organization, and unity of a whole. . . . Originally, our experiment was designed to test the prediction that tension in strong frustration leads to a dedifferentiation of the person and therefore to regression. The regression has been found. However, the experiments have shown that, aside from dedifferentiation, other factors may enter. In other words, there are several possibilities of explaining the observed regression in a situation such as the one studied here. We will leave it open which single factor or which specific constellation of factors has caused the results. Probably different factors were important for different subjects.

Dedifferentiation

One of the best symptoms for the increasing differentiation of the life space (including the person and the psychological environment) during development is the increasing variety of behavior. In the frustration situation the richness of the play activity definitely decreases. Stereotype is increased, particularly in the case of barrier behavior. This indicates a narrowing down and dedifferentiation of the psychological environment.

If the regression is caused by dedifferentiation of the individual, the dedifferentiation is probably brought about by the emotional tension (Dembo, 1931). We will see that the degree of differentiation of a whole is inversely related to the strength of pressure of tension . . . when the tension passes certain limits which are determined by the strength of the boundaries of the natural parts of the whole. Constructiveness in play also decreases with the strength (potency) of frustration.

A decrease in the variety of behavior must also be expected if a part of the whole is kept in a fixed state. This follows from certain properties of a dynamic whole. The amount of decrease depends upon the extent of the fixed areas, their degree of centrality, and their divergence from the normal level. Frustration involving a particular goal keeps a certain area of the person in a state of more or less permanent tension. The variety of pattern should therefore decrease in the case of other activities. This decrease should be greater with the involvement of a larger number of parts of the person with a higher degree of centrality, and with a heightened tension. The experimental results are well in line with these theoretical considerations. It has been shown that emotionality increases with increasing potency of frustration. This would indicate that a decreasing variety of behavior may be due to dedifferentiation of the person as the result of emotional tension, or to the "freezing" of certain parts of the person as a result of preoccupation.

Disorganization

One of the outstanding characteristics of emotionality is the increase in the weight of simple dependence (spreading of tension) relative to organizational processes which are in line with requirements of reality (are adaptive in nature). . . . Such a change can be viewed as one form of regression. Indeed, both the emotionality and the amount of regression change with the potency of frustration.

In a somewhat different way, the disorganization can be derived from the overlapping situation between play and barrier behavior. To be governed by two strong goals is equivalent to the existence of two conflicting heads within the organism. This should lead to a decrease in organizational unity according to our theoretical considerations. . . .

Finally, a certain disorganization should result from the fact that the motor system loses to some degree its character of a good medium because of these conflicting heads. It ceases to be in a state of near equilibrium. The demands on the motor system made by one head have to counteract the influence of the demands of the other head. This is an additional factor which hampers organizational processes.

Lack of Time Perspective: Insecurity

The extension of the life space, particularly in the psychological time dimension, is one of the essential properties of development. We have seen that planning presupposes time perspective. On the average, constructiveness is higher in the long than in the short play units. Therefore a decrease in the extension of time perspective might properly be regarded as a regression.

In the frustration experiment, the experimenter interrupted the elaborate play with the beautiful toys and ordered the child to move to the other side of the partition. In the previous free play situation and in prefrustration, the child had not been interrupted. In some degree the child had probably become confident that his play would not be interfered with, and his security was such that he was able to make relatively long-range plans.

The interference at the end of the prefrustration situation may have shattered the belief of the child in the security and stability of his situation. If the possibility of a superior power, such as that of the experimenter, interfering at any moment continued, it might not seem worthwhile to start a long-range plan. This should lead to a weakening of the connection between the reality and irreality levels and to a narrowing of the life space with respect to the extension of the level of reality (level of expectation) into the psychological future. It is possible to attribute regression in the frustration situation at least partly to the lack of security.

Closely related to this aspect of the situation is the change in "freedom of expression." The child's relation with the experimenter, as well as his other symptoms, indicate that the child in the frustration situation feels more restricted. This is tantamount to saying that the child feels he is not permitted to reconstruct his reality level according to the wish level or to his more intimate needs. We have seen that this should lead to a lowering of the constructiveness level.

The decrease in time perspective during play can be related in part directly to the greater emotionality in frustration. It is known that a strong emotion tends to narrow the extension of the psychological situation.

Regression and Substitution

Freud has linked regression closely to substitution. It may be appropriate therefore to relate the results of our experiments to this theory.[4]

We do not deny the possibility that regression may under certain conditions result from a tendency to substitution. However, this is hardly the cause of regression in this experiment. Of course, it can be maintained that the accessible toys are a substitute for the inaccessible toys. However, even if the accessible toys did have the character of substitute toys, there is nothing to prevent the children from playing on the same constructiveness level as before. Regression, in this case at least, is not an attempt to satisfy a need on a lower level because it cannot be satisfied on a higher level. It is rather the effect of a change of the state of the person resulting from tension or from any of the changes in the life space which we have discussed.[5] When play with the accessible toys had the character of a real substitute for play with the inaccessible toys the constructiveness increased; it did not regress to a lower level.

Methodological Results and Constructs

Methodology

The following methodological points seem to have rather general implications.

1. For studying psychological processes it is important to use psychological rather than physical time units. We have distinguished three units of different length: units of action, episodes of behavior, and total experimental periods.
2. There is a close relationship between the size of the psychological situation and the length of the period which has to be observed, if one wishes to determine the situation at a given moment.
3. It is possible to speak of an overlapping situation not only in regard to the immediate situation but also in regard to the situation at large. The relative potency of the immediate situation and the background situation can be measured. This seems to be of special importance in studying the influence of the background of a situation in the field of personality.
4. Play can be used as an indicator of the developmental level of a person at least between two and six years of age.

---

[4]It should be remembered that the Freudian concept of regression includes retrogression in addition to regression as defined here. The two concepts have somewhat different implications.

[5]This view is somewhat in line with that of McDougall (1922).

Constructs and Theories

It is possible to define the following concepts in rather exact terms: the degree of dependence, the degree of unity and of differentiation of a whole, the concept of natural part and natural whole, central and peripheral layers, and outer and inner layers. On the basis of these concepts, statements can be made concerning the variety of patterns which can be realized by a whole, the conditions of regression, and similar questions. It is important to distinguish simple dependence and organizational dependence, and the different types of unity based on these types of dependence. These concepts may help to determine more adequately the differences between the various levels of development.

A simplified theory concerning constructiveness is brought forth linking constructiveness with the number of interpersonal systems involved in the activity. The relation between constructiveness and the reality and irreality levels of the life space are discussed, particularly the relation to hope and planning.

The regression in our experiment can be linked to any one or all of the following factors: the differentiation and disorganization due to emotional tension; the differentiation and disorganization due to the person's being in an overlapping situation; a decrease in security and a correlated decrease in the extent of time perspective.

References

Ach, N. (1910). *Über den Willensakt und das Temperament: Eine experimentelle Untersuchung.* Leipzig: Quelle und Meyer.

Allport, F. H. (1940). An event–system theory of collective action: With illustrations from economic and political phenomena and production of war. *Journal of Social Psychology, 11,* 417–447.

Birenbaum, G. (1930). Das Vergessen einer Vornahme [On forgetting of an intention]. *Psychologische Forschung, 13,* 218–284.

Dembo, T. (1931). Der Ärger als dynamisches Problem [Anger as a dynamic problem]. *Psychologische Forschung, 15,* 1–144.

Escalona, S. K. (1939). The effect of success and failure upon the level of aspiration and behavior in manic-depressive psychoses. In K. Lewin, R. Lippitt, & S. K. Escalona (Eds.), *Studies in topological and vector psychology I* (Iowa Studies in Child Welfare Vol. 16, No. 3).

Fajans, S. (1933). Die Bedeutung der Entfernung fur die Stärke eines Aufforderungscharakters beim Säugling und Kleinkind [The importance of distance for the strength of a valence in the infant and small child]. *Psychologische Forschung, 17,* 215–267.

Lewin, K. (1935). *A dynamic theory of personality.* (D. K. Adams, Trans.). New York: McGraw-Hill.

Lewin, K. (1938). *The conceptual representation and the measurement of psychological forces* (Duke University Series, Cont. to Psychological Theory, Vol. 1, No. 4).

Lewin, K. (1939). Field theory and experiment in social psychology: Concepts and methods. *American Journal of Sociology, 44,* 868–896.

Lewin, K., Lippitt, R., & White, R. K. (1939). Patterns of aggressive behavior in experimentally created "social climates." *Journal of Social Psychology, 10,* 271–308.

McDougall, W. (1922). *Outline of abnormal psychology*. New York: Macmillan.
Sliosberg, S. (1934). Zur Dynamik des Ersatzes in Spiel und Ernst-situationen [On the dynamics of substitution in play and work]. *Psychologische Forschung, 19*, 122–181.
Wright, H. F. (1937). *The influence of barriers upon strength of motivation* (Duke University Series, Cont. to Psychological Theory, Vol. 1, No. 3).

8

Patterns of Aggressive Behavior in Experimentally Created "Social Climates"

A. Problems and Methods

The present report is a preliminary summary on one phase of a series of experimental studies of group life which has as its aim a scientific approach to such questions as the following: What underlies such differing patterns of group behavior as rebellion against authority, persecution of a scapegoat, apathetic submissiveness to authoritarian domination, or attack upon an outgroup? How may differences in subgroup structure, group stratification, and potency of ego-centered and group-centered goals be utilized as criteria for predicting the social resultants of different group atmospheres? Is not democratic group life more pleasant, but authoritarianism more efficient? These are the sorts of questions to which "opinionated" answers are many and varied today, and to which scientific answers are, on that account, all the more necessary. An experimental approach to the phenomena of group life obviously raises many difficulties of creation and scientific control, but the fruitfulness of the method seems to compensate for the added experimental problems.

In the first experiment Lippitt organized two clubs of 10-year-old children, who engaged in the activity of theatrical mask-making for a period of three months. The same adult leader, changing his philosophy of leadership, led one club in an authoritarian manner and the other club in accordance with democratic techniques, while detailed observations were made by four observers. This study, reported in detail elsewhere (Lippitt, 1939), suggested more hypotheses than answers and led to a second and more extensive series of experiments by White and Lippitt. Four new clubs of 10-year-old boys were organized, on a voluntary basis as before, the variety of club activities was extended, while four different adult leaders participated. To the variables of authoritarian and democratic procedure was added a third, *"laissez-faire"* or group life with adult participation.

With Ronald Lippitt and Ralph K. White. From the *Journal of Social Psychology*, S.P.S.S.I. Bulletin, 1939, *10*, 271–299.

Also, the behavior of each club was studied in different "social climates." Every six weeks each group had a new leader with a different technique of leadership, each club having three leaders during the course of the five months of the experimental series. The data on aggressive behavior summarized in this paper are drawn from both series of experiments.

Some of the techniques used for the equating of groups have been described previously (Lewin & Lippitt, 1938), but will be summarized here with the improvements in method of the second experiment. Before the clubs were organized, the schoolroom group as a whole was studied. Using the sociometric technique developed by Moreno (1934), the interpersonal relations of the children, in terms of rejections, friendships, and leadership, were ascertained. Teacher ratings on relevant items of social behavior (e.g., teasing, showing off, obedience, physical energy) were secured, and observations were made on the playground and in the schoolroom by the investigators. The school records supplied information on intellectual status, physical status, and socio-economic background. From the larger number of eager volunteers in each room, it was then possible to select from each schoolroom two five-member clubs, which were carefully equated on patterns of interpersonal relationships, intellectual, physical, and socio-economic status, in addition to personality characteristics. The attempt was not to equate the boys within a particular club, but to ensure the same pattern in each group as a whole.

In spite of the methods described above to control by selection some of the more elusive social variables, it was essential to use a number of experimental controls which would help to make the results more clearcut. First of all, to check on the "individuality" of the club as a whole, each group was studied in different social atmospheres so that it could be compared with itself. A second question raised by the first experiment was that concerning the personality of the leader as a factor in the creating of social atmospheres. The second experiment, with four leaders, makes possible a comparison of the authoritarianism and democracy of four different leaders and the *"laissez-faire"* method of two different leaders. In two cases it is also possible to compare the same atmosphere created by two different leaders with the same club.

One other type of control seemed very important, the nature of the club activity, and the physical setting. Using the same clubrooms (two clubs met at the same time in adjacent but distinctly separate areas of the same large room) to answer the latter problem, but the question of activity was more complex. The following technique was developed: a list of activities which were of interest to all the children was assembled (e.g., mask-making, mural painting, soap carving, model airplane construction, etc.). Meeting first, in chronological time, the democratic groups used these possibilities as the basis for discussion and voted upon their club activity. The authoritarian leaders were then ready, as their clubs met, to launch the same activity without choice by the members. The *"laissez-faire"* groups were acquainted with the variety of materials which were available, but they were not otherwise influenced in their choice of activity;

in their case, consequently, the activity factor could not be completely controlled.

The contrasting methods of the leaders in creating the three types of group atmosphere may be briefly summarized as in Table 1.

It should be clear that due to the voluntary nature of the group participation, and the cooperation of the parents and school systems, no radically autocratic methods (e.g., use of threats, instilling fear, etc.) were used. Fairly congenial extra-club relationships were maintained with each member by the leader.

The kinds of data collected during the course of the experiments may be classified roughly as (a) pre-club data, described above in relation to the problem of equating the groups; (b) observations of behavior in the experimental situation; and (c) extra-club information.

Table 1

Authoritarian	Democratic	Laissez-faire
1. All determination of policy by the leader	1. All policies a matter of group discussion and decision, encouraged and assisted by the leader.	1. Complete freedom for group or individual decision, without any leader participation.
2. Techniques and activity steps dictated by the authority, one at a time, so that future steps were always uncertain to a large degree.	2. Activity perspective gained during first discussion period. General steps to group goal sketched, and where technical advice was needed the leader suggested two or three alternative procedures from which choice could be made.	2. Various materials supplied by the leader, who made it clear that he would supply information when asked. He took no other part in work discussions.
3. The leader usually dictated the particular work task and work companions of each member.	3. The members were free to work with whomever they chose, and the division of tasks was left up to the group.	3. Complete nonparticipation by leader.
4. The dominator was "personal" in his praise and criticism of the work of each member, but remained aloof from active group participation except when demonstrating. He was friendly or impersonal rather than openly hostile.	4. The leader was "objective" or "fact-minded" in his praise and criticism, and tried to be a regular group member in spirit without doing too much of the work.	4. Very infrequent comments on member activities unless questioned, and no attempt to participate or interfere with the course of events.

Observations of club behavior consisted of:

(a)   A quantitative running account of the social interactions of the five children and the leader, in terms of symbols for directive, compliant, and objective (fact-minded) approaches and responses, including a category of purposeful refusal to respond to a social approach.

(b)   A minute by minute group structure analysis giving a record of: activity subgroupings, the activity goal of each subgroup was initiated by the leader or spontaneously formed by the children, and ratings on degree of unity of each subgrouping.

(c)   An interpretive running account of significant member actions, and changes in dynamics of the group as a whole.

(d)   Continuous stenographic records of all conversation.

(e)   An interpretive running account of inter-club relationships.

(f)   An "impressionistic" write-up by the leader as to what he saw and felt from within the group atmosphere during each meeting.

(g)   Comments by guest observers.

(h)   Movie records of several segments of club life.

All of these observations (except *f*, *g*, and *h*) were synchronized at minute intervals so that side by side they furnish a rather complete cross-sectional picture of the ongoing life of the group. The major purpose of this experiment in methodology of observation was to record as fully and with as much insight as possible the total behavior of the group, a distinct break away from the usual procedure of recording only certain predetermined symptoms of behavior. The second aim was to ascertain whether data collected by this method could be fruitfully analyzed from both a sociological and psychological point of view (Lewin, 1939).

Extra-club information is of the following types:

(a)   Interviews with each child by a friendly "non-club" person during each transition period (from one kind of group atmosphere and leader to another) and at the end of the experiment, concerning such items as comparison of present club leader with previous ones, with the teacher, and with parents; opinions on club activities; how the club could be run better; who were the best and poorest club members; what an ideal club leader would be like, etc.

(b)   Interviews with the parents by the investigators, concentrating on kinds of discipline used in the home, status of the child in the family group (relations with siblings, etc.), personality ratings on the same scale used by the teachers, discussion of child's attitude toward the club, school, and other group activities.

(c)   Talks with the teachers concerning the transfer to the schoolroom of behavior patterns acquired in the club.

(d)   Administration of a Rorschach test to each club member.

(e) Conversations with the children during two summer hikes arranged after the experiment was over.

These data were gathered with a view to correlating the individual pattern of behavior in the club situation with the types of group membership which existed outside the experiment, and with the more or less stable individual personality structure. The individual differences in "social plasticity" seem to be rather striking.

Two other points of experimental technique seem of interest. The first concerns the introduction of observers into the club situation. In Lippitt's first experiment it was found that four observers grouped around a table in a physically separated part of the club room attracted virtually no attention if it was explained at the first meeting that "those are some people interested in learning how a mask-making club goes; they have plenty to do so they won't bother us and we won't bother them." In the second experiment the arrangement was even more advantageous and seemed to make for equally unselfconscious behavior on the part of the clubs. In this set-up the lighting arrangement was such that the observers were grouped behind a low burlap wall in a darkly shaded area, and seemed "not to exist at all" as far as the children and leaders were concerned.

The second point of interest is the development of a number of "group test" situations, which aided greatly in getting at the actual social dynamics of a given group atmosphere. One test used systematically was for the leader to leave the room on business during the course of the club meeting, so that the "social pressure" factor could be analyzed more realistically. Another practice was for the leader to arrive a few minutes late so that the observers could record the individual and "atmospheric" differences in spontaneous work initiation and work perspective. A third fruitful technique was that of having a stranger (a graduate student who played the role of a janitor or electrician) enter the club situation and criticize the group's work efforts. A rather dramatic picture of the results of this type of situation may be seen in Figures 5 and 6. Further variations of such experimental manipulations are being utilized in a research now in progress.

B. Results

The analysis of the results from the second experiment is now proceeding in various directions, following two main trends: (a) interpretation of sociological or "group-centered" data; (b) interpretation of psychological or "individual-centered" data. The sociological approach includes such analyses as differences in volume of social interaction related to social atmosphere, nature of club activity, outgroup relationship, differences in pattern of interaction related to outgroup and ingroup orientation, atmosphere differences in leader–group relationship, effect upon group structure pattern of social atmosphere and types of activity, group differences in language behavior, etc. The psychological approach includes such analyses as relation of home background to pattern of club behavior, range of variation of member behavior in different types of social atmosphere, patterns of individual reaction to atmosphere transitions in relation to case history data, correlation between position in group stratification and pattern of social action, etc. In this paper will be presented only certain data from the partially completed general analysis which are relevant to the dynamics of individual and group aggression.

We might first recall one or two of the most striking results of the first experiment (Lippitt, 1939). As the club meetings progressed the authoritarian club members developed a pattern of aggressive domination toward one another, and their relation to the leader was one of submission or of persistent demands for attention. The interactions in the democratic club were more spontaneous, more fact-minded, and friendly. Relations to the leader were free and on an "equality basis." Comparing the two groups on the one item of overt hostility, the authoritarian group was surprisingly more aggressive, the ratio being 40 to 1. Comparing a constellation of "ego-involved" types of behavior language (e.g., hostile, resistant, demands for attention, hostile criticism, expression of competition) with a group of objective or "nonemotive" behaviors, it was found that in the authoritarian group 73% of the analyzed language behavior was of the "ego-involved" type as compared to 31% in the democratic club. Into the objective category went 69% of the behavior of the democratic group as compared to 37% of the language activities of the authoritarian group.

A second type of data related to the dynamics of aggression as it existed in the first experiment may be seen in Figure 1. Twice during the course of the meetings of the authoritarian club the situation shifted from one of mutual aggression between all members to one of concentrated aggression toward one member by the other four. In both cases the lowered status of a scapegoat position was so acutely unpleasant that the member

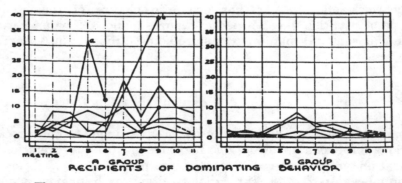

Figure 1. The emergence of scapegoats in an autocratic atmosphere (Lippitt, 1939). The curves (which indicate the amount of aggression directed against each individual) show a much lower general level of dominating behavior in the democratic (D) than in the autocratic (A) group. Twice during the meetings of the authoritarian club the aggression of four members was focused upon the fifth (a and b). In both cases the scapegoat dropped out of the group immediately or soon afterwards.

left the group, rationalizing his break from the club by such remarks as, "The doctor says my eyes are so bad I'll have to play outdoors in the sunshine instead of coming to club meetings." Interestingly enough, the two members who were singled out for persecution had been rated by the teachers as the two leaders in the group, one of them scoring second in popularity by the sociometric technique, as well as being physically the strongest. After the emergence of both scapegoats, there was a rather brief rise in friendly cooperative behavior between the other members of the group.

In the second experiment (see previous discussion, p. 229) there were five democratic, five autocratic, and two "laissez-faire" atmospheres. The fact that the leaders were successful in modifying their behavior to correspond to these three philosophies of leadership is clear on the basis of several quantitative indices. For instance, the ratio of "directive" to "compliant" behavior on the part of the autocratic leaders was 63 to 1; on the part of the democratic leaders it was 1.1 to 1. The total amount of leader participation was less than half as great in "laissez-faire" as in either autocracy or democracy.

The data on aggression averages in these three atmospheres are summarized in Figures 2, 3, and 4. All of them indicate average amounts of aggression per 50-minute, five-member club meeting. They represent behavior records, as recorded by the interaction observer, and include all social actions, both verbal and physical, which he designated as "hostile" or "joking hostile." Figure 2 shows especially the biomodal character of the aggression averages in autocracy; four of the five autocracies had an extremely low level of aggression, and the fifth had an extremely high one. For comparison, a sixth bar had been added to represent aggression in Lippitt's 1937 experiment, computed on the same basis. It is obviously comparable with the single case of exceptionally aggressive behavior in the 1938 experiment. For comparison, also, four lines have been added which indicate the aggression level in the two laissez-faire groups, in the four 1938 democracies, and in Lippitt's 1937 democracy. It can be seen that two of the six autocracies are above the entire range of democracies, and are in this respect comparable with the two laissez-faire groups. The other four autocracies are at the opposite extreme, below the entire range of the democracies.

Figures 3 and 4 show especially the character of the experimental controls. Together, they show how each of four groups was carried through three different periods with three different adult leaders. The relative importance of the deliberately created social atmosphere, as compared with either the personality make-up of the group or the personality of the adult leader, can be estimated from the character of these curves. It is clear that the same group changes markedly, and sometimes to an extreme degree, when it is changed to a new atmosphere under a different leader. In such transitions the factor of group personnel is held relatively constant, while the factors of leader personality and social atmosphere are varied. In addition, the factor of leader personality was systematically varied, as can be seen if the four curves are compared with each other. Each of the four leaders played the role of a democratic leader at least once; also each

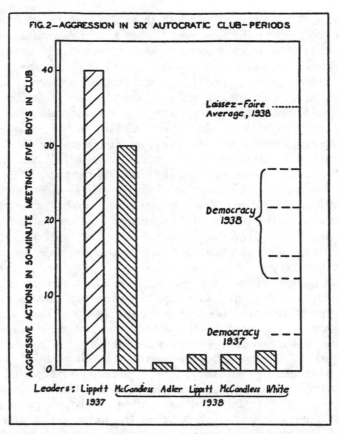

Figure 2. Aggression in autocracy. The amount of aggression is very great or very small compared with aggression in democracy.

played the role of an autocrat at least once; two of them (Adler and White) played in addition the role of bystander in a *"laissez-faire"* group. One leader (Lippitt) was democratic with two different groups; and one (Mc-Candless) was autocratic with two different groups. Through this systematic variation of both club personnel and leader's personality, the effects of the deliberately created social atmosphere (autocracy, democracy, *laissez-faire*) stand out more clearly and more reliably than would otherwise be possible.

In Figure 3, for instance, the two curves both tell the same story: a moderate amount of aggression in democracy and an abnormally small amount in autocracy, regardless of the personality of the leader (note that the roles of Lippitt and McCandless were reversed, with each playing once the role of autocrat and once the role of democratic leader), and regardless of the personnel of the group itself (note that the curves cross once when the atmospheres are reversed, and cross back again when the atmospheres return to what they were at the beginning). In Figure 4, the two *laissez-faire* atmospheres give very high levels of aggression, although different

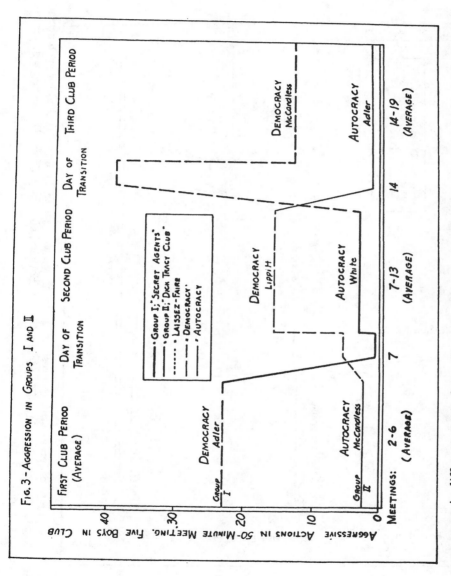

Figure 3. The same group in different atmospheres. In each group, aggression was at a medium level in democracy and at a very low level in autocracy. Note that the leaders in the third period were the same as in the first, but reversed. Note also the sharp rise of aggression in one group on the day of transition to democracy. Group I shows "release of tension" on the first day of freedom (14) after apathetic autocracy. The name of the leader is indicated below that of the atmosphere.

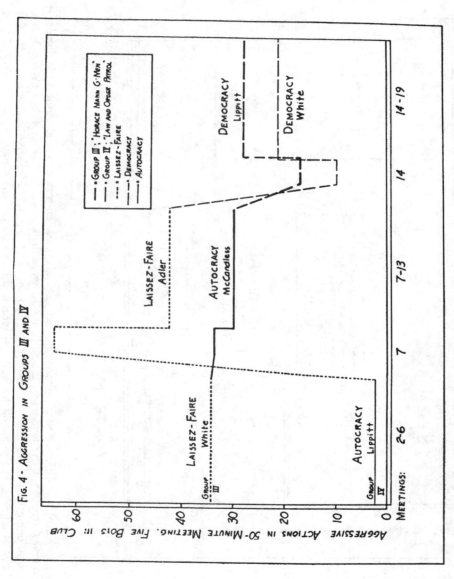

Figure 4. The same group in different atmospheres. Group IV shows changes to the levels typical for each atmosphere. It shows also the "release of tension" on the first day of freedom (7) after apathetic autocracy. Group III seemed resistant to change; it was relatively aggressive even in democracy.

groups and different leaders are involved. The most extreme change of behavior recorded in any group occurred when Group IV was changed from autocracy (in which it had shown the apathetic reaction) to *laissez-faire*. One of the autocratic groups (Figure 4) reacted apathetically, the other very aggressively. The aggressiveness of Group III may be due to the personalities of the boys, or to the fact that they had just previously "run wild" in *laissez-faire*.

The average number of aggressive actions per meeting in the different atmospheres was as follows:

Laissez-faire	38
Autocracy (aggressive reaction)	30
Democracy	20
Autocracy (apathetic reaction)	2

Critical ratios for these comparisons have not yet been computed. The data are comparable, however, with Lippitt's 1937 data, in which the critical ratios for the more important indices ranged between 4.5 and 7.5.

In the interpretation of these data it is natural to ask: Why are the results for autocracy paradoxical? Why is the reaction to autocracy sometimes very aggressive, with much rebellion or persecution of scapegoats, and sometimes very nonaggressive? Are the underlying dynamics in these two cases as different as the surface behavior? The high level of aggression in some autocracies has often been interpreted mainly in terms of tension, which presumably results from frustration of individual goals. Is it, then, an indication of non-frustration when the aggression level in some other autocracies is found to be extremely low?

Four lines of evidence in our experiments indicate that this is not the case, and that the low level of aggression in the apathetic autocracies is not due to lack of frustration.

First of all, there are the sudden outbursts of aggression which occurred on the days of transition from a repressed autocratic atmosphere to the much freer atmosphere of democracy or *laissez-faire*. Two of these are well illustrated in Figure 4. The boys behaved just as if they had previously been in a state of bottled-up tension, which could not show itself overtly as long as the repressive influence of the autocrat was felt, but which burst out unmistakably when that pressure was removed.

A second and very similar type of evidence can be obtained from the records on the days when the leader left the room for 10 or 15 minutes. In the three other atmospheres (*laissez-faire*, aggressive autocracy, and democracy), the aggression level did not rise when the leader left the room. In the apathetic autocracies, however, the level of aggression rises very rapidly to 10 times its former level. These data should not be overstressed, because aggression even then does not rise to a level significantly above that of the other atmospheres. It is so extremely low in the apathetic atmosphere that even multiplication by 10 does not produce what could be called a high level of aggression. (The effect of the leader's absence is shown more significantly in a deterioration of work than in an outburst of aggression.) Nevertheless, the rapid disappearance of apathy when the leader goes out shows clearly that it was due to the repressive influence of the leader rather than to any particular absence of frustration. In this connection it should be added that the autocratic leader never forbade aggression. His "repressive influence" was not a prohibition created by explicit command but a sort of generalized inhibition or restraining force.

In the third place, there are the judgments of observers who found themselves using such terms as "dull," "lifeless," "submissive," "repressed," and "apathetic" in describing the nonaggressive reaction to autocracy. There was little smiling, joking, freedom of movement, freedom of initiating new projects, etc.; talk was largely confined to the immediate activity in progress, and bodily tension was often manifested. Moving pictures tell the same story. The impression created was not one of acute discontent, by any means, and the activities themselves were apparently enjoyable enough so that the net result for most of the boys was more pleasant than unpleasant. Nevertheless, they could not be described as genuinely contented.

The fourth and perhaps the most convincing indication of the existence of frustration in these atmospheres is the testimony of the boys themselves. They were individually interviewed, just before each day of transition to a new atmosphere, and again at the end of the whole experiment. The interviewing was done by an adult who had not served as a leader in the boy's own group. On the whole good rapport was achieved, and the boys talked rather freely, comparing the three leaders under whom their club had been conducted. (For them it was a question of comparing leaders they liked or did not like, as they were unaware of the deliberate change in the behavior of the same leader from one atmosphere to another or of the nature of the experiment.) With surprising unanimity the boys agreed in a relative dislike for their autocratic leader regardless of his individual personality. Nineteen of the 20 boys liked their leader in democracy better than their leader in autocracy. The twentieth boy, as it happened, was the son of an army officer (the only one in the group), and consciously put a high value upon strict discipline. As he expressed it, the autocratic leader *"was the strictest, and I like that a lot."* The other two leaders *"let us go ahead and fight, and that isn't good."* For the other 19, strictness was not necessarily a virtue, their description of the autocrat being that he was *"too strict."* Typical comments about the autocrat were: *"he didn't let us do what we wanted to do"*; *"he wouldn't let us go behind the burlap"*; *"he was all right mostly—sort of dictator-like"*; *"we just had to do things; he wanted us to get it done in a hurry"*; *"he made us make masks, and the boys didn't like that"*; *"the other two guys suggested and we could do it or not, but not with him"*; *"we didn't have any fun with him—we didn't have any fights."* Typical comments about the democratic leader were: *"he was a good sport, worked along with us and thinks of things just like we do"*; *"he never did try to be the boss, but we always had plenty to do"*; *"just the right combination—nothing I didn't like about him"*; *"we all liked him; he let us tear down the burlap and everything."* These comments were almost uniformly dependent upon the role played by the leader, and were exactly reversed when he played a different role.

As between the leaders in autocracy and "*laissez-faire,*" the preference was for the "*laissez-faire*" leader in seven cases out of ten. The three boys who preferred the autocrat made such comments about the "*laissez-faire*" leader as: "*he was too easy-going*"; "*he had too few things for us to do*"; "*he let us figure things out too much*"; in contrast, the autocrat "*told us what to do, and we had something to do all the time.*" For the other seven, even disorder was preferable to rigidity: "*we could do what we pleased with him*"; "*he wasn't strict at all.*"

Another form of aggression was outgroup hostility, as manifested especially in two "wars" between clubs meeting in the same large room at the same time. Both wars seemed to be mainly in a spirit of play. They were much more like snowball fights than serious conflicts. (This is one more reason why in this case one should be cautious in comparing adult political phenomena directly with our data on small groups of children.) Our two small "wars" are interesting in their own right, however, especially since the same general constellation of factors seemed to be operating in both cases.

The curves of rising hostility, computed for five-minute intervals, are shown in Figures 5 and 6. From these curves it can be seen that the first "war" started gradually, with a long period of minor bickering and name calling, followed by a much steeper gradient of increasing hostility. The overt hostilities consisted of throwing water, small pieces of clay (which

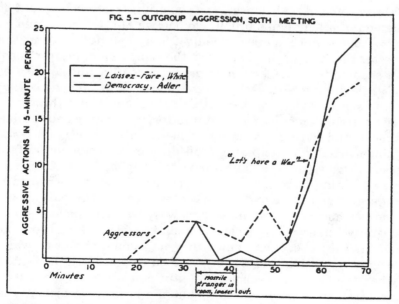

Figure 5. Conflict between groups after intrusion of hostile stranger. After the stranger left, strong hostility developed between the two groups. Before the major conflict, minor hostilities had already occurred, with one or two members of the *laissez-faire* group playing the role of aggressors.

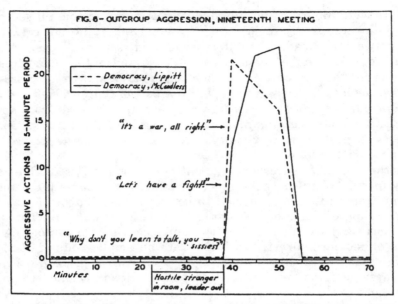

Figure 6. Conflict between groups after intrusion of hostile stranger. The intrusion of a hostile stranger was followed by intergroup conflict (as in Figure 5). In this case the hostilities began suddenly, rising within four minutes almost to their maximum level.

nearly always missed their mark), and sometimes watercolor paint, flicked from the end of a long paint brush. No one was hurt. The second conflict (Figure 6) began much more suddenly. Name calling began in the first minute after the "hostile stranger" left the room, and almost immediately the boys seemed to remember their previous conflict and to wish a repetition of it. Beginning with verbal aggression such as *why don't you learn to talk, you sissies?*" they passed within three minutes to throwing small pieces of soap (small pieces of soap statuettes, which they had carved, were lying about), and within five minutes nearly all the boys on both sides were wholeheartedly participating. This difference in steepness of the hostility gradient was perhaps due in part to a higher level of tension or to weaker restraining forces on the later occasion, but it seemed to be due also to a cognitive difference. On the later occasion the pattern of intergroup conflict had been established; it was, by that time, a part of the boys' "cognitive structure"—a clearly defined region which they could enter or not as they chose; and since they had found the first "war" to be very pleasantly exciting, they readily and quickly entered the same region again when the general psychological situation was conducive to conflict. In this connection it may be noted that the second conflict was labeled verbally almost immediately, while the first one was not labeled until it was already well under way. On the first occasion the shout "*Let's have a war!*" went up long after the minor hostilities had begun; on the second occasion, one boy shouted, "*Let's have a fight*" only two minutes after the name calling began, and another one legalized it two minutes later with the words *"It's a war all right."*

Certain similarities between the two days of conflict suggest some very tentative hypotheses as to the psychological factors conducive to this sort of conflict. In the first place, both occurred on days when, with the adult leader absent, a hostile stranger had been in the room and had criticized the work which the boys were doing. This had been deliberately planned as a "test situation"; a graduate student, playing the role of a janitor or an electrician, was the hostile stranger. It may be doubtful whether or not the term "substitute hate object" is an appropriate one here; but there was no question in the observers' minds that in both cases the intrusion of the stranger tended to disorganize the regular play activities of the clubs and to build up a tense, restless psychological condition which was conducive to intergroup conflict. In the second place, both conflicts started when no respected adult was present. In the first one the main aggressors were unquestionably the *laissez-faire* group (see Figure 5). Their leader was physically present at the time, but he was psychologically unimportant. The second conflict began when the leaders on both sides were out of the room, and by the time the leaders returned, it had gathered great momentum. In the third place, both conflicts occurred at a time when there was no absorbing group activity as an alternative. The first one began at a time when the members of the *laissez-faire* group seemed unusually bored and dissatisfied with their own lack of solid accomplishment. The second one began after the boys had become somewhat bored with their soap carving, and after this individualistic activity had been further disrupted by the criticisms of the stranger.

The free direct expression of aggression by the "wars" following frustration in the *laissez-faire* and democratic situations offers a contrast to several other patterns of expression which were observed in some of the authoritarian situations. These types of behavior might be briefly labeled: (a) a "strike"; (b) rebellious acts; (c) reciprocal aggression among all members; (d) scapegoat attack; (e) release behavior after a decrease in leader pressure; (f) aggression against impersonal "substitute hate objects."

Both the "strike" and symptoms of rebellious action occurred in the aggressive type of autocracy. About the middle of the series of six meetings, the club members went to their teacher with a letter of resignation signed by four of them. They asked their teacher to give this to the leader when he came to get them after school. The teacher refused to act as a go-between, suggesting that the boys go to the leader directly, but when he appeared after school, courage seemed to wane and they all went to the meeting as usual. Overt rebellious acts were of the following nature: breaking a rule by carving on the posts in the clubroom (while casting sidelong glances at the leader), deliberately walking behind the burlap walls of the clubroom without permission (mentioned to an interviewer), leaving the club meeting early, and pretending not to hear when spoken to by the leader. The third and fourth kinds of behavior were also typical of aggressive authoritarianism and have been mentioned in describing the first experiment during which two scapegoats emerged. As has been mentioned, changes in amount of aggression while the leader was out and days of transition to a freer atmosphere were especially good indicators of the existence of unexpressed tension in the apathetic autocracies.

Two very interesting examples of what we have tentatively called "release behavior through an impersonal substitute hate object" are worthy of description. During the eleventh meeting of the first experiment, the authoritarian group was given a chance to indicate by secret ballot whether they would like the club to stop or continue for several more meetings. We may go to an observer's record for further comments:

Peculiar actions follow the leader's announcement that because of the vote there will be no more meetings after today. The leader asks RO and J to put the paper on the floor as usual. They put it down and then run and jump on it time and again in a wild manner. The group masks are divided among the members and J immediately begins to throw his around violently, pretending to jump on it. He throws it down again and again, laughing. R wants to know if it won't break, then starts to throw his down too. Later J and RO chase each other around the room wildly with streamers of toweling. . . .

Rather clearly, the work products of this authoritarian atmosphere seemed to be the objects of aggressive attack rather than prideful ownership.

During a last meeting of the second experiment, a rather similar burst of behavior occurred in one of the democratic groups. The group was highly involved in an activity of making an oil painting on glass. While the leader was out for a short time (by arrangement), a student in the janitor role came in to sweep. From the running accountist's record of the 20-second minute we find,

He is making dirt fly and sweeping it toward the group. They all begin to cough but don't move from their work.

Several minutes later we find the comment,

Janitor has almost swept them away, but still no hostile response. The project seems to have a very high valence.

Five minutes later, the janitor had gotten them out of their chairs in order to sweep; then the janitor accidentally knocks a piece of their glass on the floor. They all yell, and R makes as if to throw something at him. F says that if the leader were here, he would beat up the janitor.

Five minutes later, after a number of comments criticizing the art work of the club, the janitor left. The members dropped their work completely, climbed the rafters and made considerable noise. On the thirty-sixth minute we find,

R comes down from the rafter and begins to complain about the janitor, L joins him and they all complain bitterly and loudly.

Within three minutes the group began to destroy a large wooden sign upon which they had painted the club name. Such comments as this appear in the running account,

F is wielding two hammers at once. . . . R is busy pulling out all the nails. . . . They are excited. . . . F knocks the first hole through it. . . . R tries to caution F for a minute, and then gets busy himself . . . their unexpressed aggression toward the janitor is taking a violent outlet . . . they are all very serious and vicious about the destruction of the sign . . . they seem to be getting a great deal of "pure animal pleasure" of the pillage.

The meeting ended with three or four minutes of pleasant conversation.

C. Interpretive Comments

From the many theoretical problems involved, we should like to discuss but one, namely, the problem of aggression and apathy. Even here, we wish to show the complexity of the problem and its possible attack from a field theoretical point of view rather than to set forth a definite theory.

It is not easy to say what aggression is, that is, if one is not satisfied with mere verbal definition. One important aspect obviously is that one group or an individual within a group turns against another group (or individual). In case these groups are subgroup of one original group, it can be called aggression *within a group*, otherwise aggression *against an out-group*.

Both kinds of aggression occurred in our experiments. All of these aggressions were spontaneous in character. In other words, it was not a situation where a group of people are ordered by a politically dominating power (like the state) to indulge in a certain type of directed activity called war. On the whole the aggression was the outcome of the momentary emotional situation, although in two cases the aggressions had definitely the character of a fight of one group against another group and showed a certain amount of cooperative organization within each group.

It is necessary to mention four points which seem to play a dominant role in the spontaneous aggressions: tension, the space of free movement, rigidity of group structure, and the style of living (culture).

1. Tension

An instance where tension was created by annoying experiences occurred when the group work was criticized by a stranger (janitor). There were two cases where fighting broke out immediately afterwards.

In the autocratic atmosphere the behavior of the leader probably annoyed the children considerably (to judge from the interviews reported above).

In addition, there were six times as many directing approaches to an individual by the leader in autocracy than in democracy (Figure 7). It is probably fair to assume that the bombardment with such frequent ascendant approaches is equivalent to higher *pressure* and that this pressure created a higher tension.

2. Narrow Space of Free Movement as a Source of Tension

On the whole, even more important than this single annoying experience was the general atmosphere of the situation. Experiments in individual

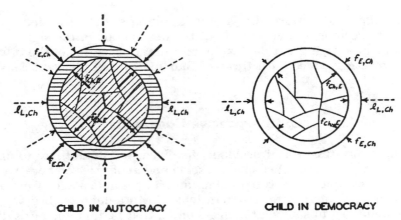

CHILD IN AUTOCRACY   CHILD IN DEMOCRACY

Figure 7. Leader pressure and child tension. In the authoritarian situation the leader makes six times as many directing approaches ($l_{L,Ch}$) to the child member as in the democratic situation. This creates social pressure (equivalent to forces $f_{E,Ch}$ of the environment on the child) and therefore a higher state of tension in the child in the autocratic group: This tension demands some sort of outlet toward the environment (equivalent to forces $f_{Ch,E}$).

psychology (Lewin, 1935) seemed to indicate that lack of space of free movement is equivalent to higher pressure; both conditions seem to create tension. This seemed particularly true if an originally larger space was narrowed down (one is reminded here of the physical tension created by decreasing volume, although one should not overstress the analogy).

Our experiments seemed to indicate that a similar relation between the narrow space of free movement and high tension holds also in regard to groups. The space of free movement in autocracy was smaller in relation to the activities permitted and the social status which could be reached (Figures 8 and 9). In *laissez-faire*, contrary to expectations, the space of free movement was not larger but smaller than in democracy, partly because of the lack of time perspective and partly because of the interference of the work of one individual with the activities of his fellows.

3. Aggression as the Effect of Tension

The annoying occurrences, the pressure applied by the leader, and the lack of space of free movement are three basic facts which brought up a higher tension. Our experiments indicate that this higher tension might suffice to create aggression. This seems to be of theoretical importance; obviously some aggressive acts can be viewed mainly as a kind of "purposive" action (for instance, to destroy a danger), and one might ask whether or not this component is an essential part in the causation of any aggression. In our experiments, the two wars between the two outgroups can hardly be classified in this way. They seemed to be rather clear cases where aggression was "emotional expression" of an underlying tension.

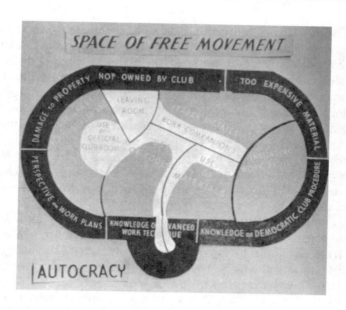

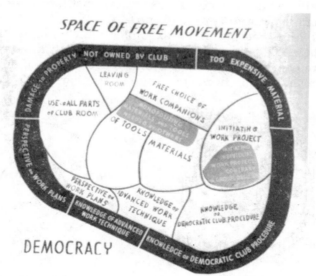

Figure 8 (top) and 9 (bottom).   Space of free movement in autocracy and democracy. In the autocratic situation the space of free movement (white) was originally bounded only by the limitation in ability and knowledge (black) of the members, but was soon limited much further by the social influence of the leader (gray). In democracy the space was increased with the help of the leader.

4. Rigidity of Group Structure

However, to understand aggression one will have to realize that tension is only one of the factors which determine whether or not an aggressive action will take place. The building up of tension can be said to be equivalent to the creation of a certain type of need which might express itself in aggressive action. Tension sets up the driving force (Lewin, 1938) for the aggression (in the two situations with which we are dealing). However, whether these driving forces actually lead to aggression or to some other behavior, for instance, that of leaving the group, depends on additional characteristics of the situation as a whole. One of these seems to be the rigidity of the social position of the person within the group.

Aggression within a group can be viewed as a process by which one part of the group sets itself in opposition to another part of the group, in this way breaking the unity of the group. Of course, this separation is only of a certain degree.

In other words, if M indicates a member or subgroup and Gr the whole group, an aggression involves a force acting on the subgroup in the direction away from the main group ($f_{M,-Gr}$) or other part of the subgroup. From this it should follow theoretically that if a subgroup can easily locomote in the direction away from the group, it will do so in case this force shows any significant strength. In other words, a strong tension and an actual aggression will be built up only in case there exist forces which hinder the subgroup from leaving the group (Figure 10).

Cultural anthropology gives examples which might be interpreted from this angle. The Arapesh (Mead, 1937), for instance, are living in a society where everyone is a member of a great variety of different groups and seems to shift easily from one group to another; it is a society without

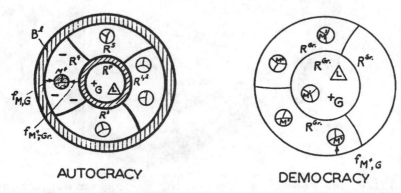

AUTOCRACY   DEMOCRACY

Figure 10. Rigidity of group structure as a tension factor. In autocracy where each member or subgroup (M^1, M^2 ... M^5) has a circumscribed region of activity (R^1, R^2 ... R^5), and especially where the central regions of group life (policy formation R_p) are inaccessible to most members, rigid barriers (B) to own goals (G) continually frustrate member efforts. The member's own position in the group structure (R^4) therefore acquires a negative valence, usually creating a force away from group membership ($f_{M4,-Gr}$). But in rigid group structures a restraining barrier (B^1) keeps members or subgroups from leaving until a very high state of tension develops. In democracy where all group regions (R^{Gr}) are accessible to all members (M^1, M^2 ... M^5), their own goals (G) are more easily attained and no such frustrating situation develops.

rigidly fixed social position. The fact that they show extremely little aggression might well be linked with this lack of rigid social structure.

Another example might be seen in the fact that adolescents who have been kept within the family probably show more aggression; in other words, the more rigid the family structure the more difficult it is for them to move from childhood to adulthood.

An additional example is the well-known fact that narrow family ties which serve to make it difficult for husband and wife to leave each other may make aggression between them particularly violent.

In our experiment, autocracy provided a much more rigid social group than democracy. It was particularly difficult for the members of an autocracy to change their social status (Lewin, 1939). On the other hand, in both groups the member did not like to leave the group as a whole because of the interest in the work project and the feeling of responsibility to the adult leader.

On the whole, then, the rigidity of the group will function as a restraining force (Lewin, 1938) against locomotion away from the group, or from the position within the group. Sufficient strength of this restraining force seems to be one of the conditions for the building up of a tension which is sufficiently high to lead to aggression.

It can be seen easily that the barriers limiting the space of free movement may have a similar function. We mentioned above that a narrow space of free movement seems to be equivalent to pressure, and, in this way, creates tension. At the same time, the barriers prevent locomotion, thus providing the restraining forces necessary for building up higher tension.

It was already mentioned that these restraining forces are particularly strong in our autocratic group (Figure 10).

5. Style of Living (Culture)

Whether or not a given amount of tension and given restraining forces will cause a person to become aggressive depends finally upon the particular patterns of action which are customarily used in the culture in which he lives. The different styles of living can be viewed as different ways a given problem is usually solved. A person living in a culture where a show of dominance is "the thing to do" under certain conditions will hardly think of any other way in which the solution of this problem may be approached. Such social patterns are comparable to "habits." Indeed, individual habits as well as cultural patterns have dynamically the character of restraining forces against leaving the paths determined by these patterns. In addition, they determine the cognitive structure which a given situation is likely to have for a given individual.

For the problem of aggression, this cultural pattern, determined by the group in which an individual lives and by his past history, is of great importance. It determines under what conditions aggression will be, for the individual concerned, the "distinguished path" to the goal (Lewin,

1938). It determines, furthermore, how easily a situation will show for him a cognitive structure where aggression appears to be one possible path for his action (Figure 11).

The factors named are sufficient to warn against any "one-factor" theory of aggression. Here, as in regard to any other behavior, it is the specific constellation of the field as a whole that determines whether or not aggression will occur. In every case, one has to consider both the driving and the restraining forces and the cognitive structure of the field. Such a field theoretical approach seems to be rather arduous. On the other hand, only in this way will one be able to understand, for instance, the paradox of behavior that autocracy may lead either to aggression or to apathy. It was stated that aggression is partly to be viewed as an emotional outbreak due to tension and that this tension, in turn, is due to pressure and restraining forces (lack of space of free movement). We have apathy when the pressure and the restraining forces from without are kept stronger than the forces ($f_{Ch,E}$ in Figure 7) within the person which lead to the emotional expression, and are due to the tension. Whether or not the forces from without or those from within are stronger depends upon the absolute amount of pressure and also on the "willingness" of the person to "accept" the pressure.

The field theoretical approach also provides indications for the circumstances under which one might generalize the results of such experimental group studies. One must be careful of making too hasty generalization, perhaps especially in the field of political science. The varieties of democracies, autocracies, or *"laissez-faire"* atmospheres are, of course, very numerous. Besides, there are always individual differences of character and background to consider. On the other hand, it would be wrong to minimize

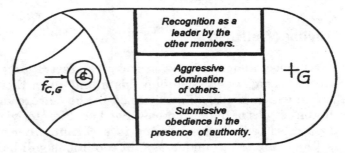

Figure 11. Different styles of living as represented by different distinguished paths (aggressive autocracy). The goal (G) of maximum social status and space of free movement can be reached by one or more of several procedures depending on actual possibilities and the prevailing mode of behavior in that group. In our "experimentally created cultures," the distinguished path to G was for a child (C) in aggressive autocracy that of aggressive domination of other members. In a similar situation the distinguished path for a member of democratic groups seemed to be that of gaining voluntary recognition of the other members as a leader through work and social efforts. In the situation of apathetic authoritarianism the path seemed to be that of submissive obedience to authority, which might win praise from the leader.

the possibility of generalization. The answer in social psychology and sociology has to be the same as in an experiment in any science. The essence
of an experiment is to create a situation which shows a certain pattern.
What happens depends by and large upon this pattern and is largely although not completely independent of the absolute size of the field. This
is one of the reasons why experiments are possible and worthwhile.

The generalization from an experimental situation should, therefore,
go always to those life situations which show the same or sufficiently similar general patterns. This statement includes both the rights and the
limitations of generalization.

D. Summary

1. In a first experiment, Lippitt compared one group of five 10-year-
old children, under autocratic leadership, with a comparable group
under democratic leadership. In a second experiment, Lippitt and
White studied four comparable clubs of 10-year-old boys, each of
which passed successively through three club periods in such a
way that there were altogether five democratic periods, five autocratic periods, and two "laissez-faire" periods.

2. In the second experiment, the factor of personality differences in
the boys was controlled by having each group pass through autocracy and then democracy, or vice versa. The factor of leader's personality was controlled by having each of four leaders play the
role of autocrat and the role of democratic leader at least once.

3. Records on each club meeting include stenographic records of conversation, quantitative symbolic records of group structure, quantitative symbolic records of all social interactions, and a continuous interpretive running account. Parents and teachers were
interviewed; each boy was given the Rorschach ink blots, a Moreno-
type questionnaire, and was interviewed three times. Analysis of
causal relationships between these various types of data is still
far from complete. As a preliminary report, we are giving here a
part of the data bearing upon one specific problem, that of aggression.

4. In the first experiment, hostility was 30 times as frequent in the
autocratic as in the democratic group. Aggression (including both
"hostility" and "joking hostility") was 8 times as frequent. Much
of this aggression was directed toward two successive scapegoats
within the group; none of it was directed toward the autocrat.

5. In the second experiment, one of the five autocracies showed the
same aggressive reaction as was found in the first experiment. In
the other four autocracies, the boys showed an extremely nonaggressive, "apathetic" pattern of behavior.

6. Four types of evidence indicate that this lack of aggression was
probably not caused by lack of frustration, but by the repressive
influence of the autocrat: (a) outbursts of aggression on the days

of transition to a freer atmosphere; (b) a sharp rise of aggression when the autocrat left the room; (c) other indications of generalized apathy, such as an absence of smiling and joking; and (d) the fact that 19 out of 20 boys liked their democratic leader better than their autocratic leader, and 7 out of 10 also liked their "*laissez-faire*" leader better.

7. There were two "wars," more or less playful, and without bodily damage, between clubs meeting in the same room at the same time. The first of these began gradually, the second suddenly. Three factors, present in both cases, seemed conducive to group conflict: (a) irritation and tension produced by a hostile stranger, (b) absence of a respected adult, and (c) a lack of any absorbing alternative activity.

8. There were two striking instances of aggression against impersonal objects.

9. A general interpretation of the above data on aggression can be made in terms of four underlying factors: tension, restricted space of free movement, rigidity of group structure, and style of living (culture).

References

Lewin, K. (1935). *A dynamic theory of personality: Selected papers.* (D. K. Adams & K. E. Zener, Trans.). New York: McGraw-Hill.

Lewin, K. (1938). *The conceptual representation and the measurement of psychological forces* (Vol. 1, No. 4). Durham, N. C.: Duke University Press.

Lewin, K. (1939). Experiments in social space. *Harvard Education Review, 9*(1), 21–32.

Lewin, K., & Lippitt, R. (1938). An experimental approach to the study of autocracy and democracy: A preliminary note. *Sociometry, 1,* 292–300.

Lewin, K., & Lippitt, R. (1939). Field theory and experiment in social psychology. *American Journal of Sociology, 44,* 868–897.

Lippitt, R. (1939). *An experimental study of authoritarian and democratic group atmospheres.* University of Iowa Study, Study of Child Welfare (Vol. 16, No. 3).

Mead, M. (1937). *Cooperation and competition among primitive peoples.* New York: Macmillan.

Moreno, J. L. (1934). Who shall survive? A new approach to the problem of human interrelations. *Monograph of the Nervous and Mental Disease Series, 58.* Washington, D. C.: Nervous & Mental Disease Publishing Company.

Part III

Applied Psychologist

Introduction

Lewin's efforts to apply psychology to the amelioration of social problems, more than any other of his professional activities, most closely identify him with social psychology. His commitment to the idea that the immediate situation is always implicated in behavior inevitably led him to attend closely to the contemporaneous social environment to effect behavioral change. Furthermore, his observations led him to the conclusion that the greatest potential for influencing individuals resided in the social environment of the face-to-face groups to which they belonged. Thus, Lewin's change efforts always involved people in natural groups, and he did no research with groups after the laboratory experiments on democratic leadership, except for applied purposes. It is, of course, impossible to know whether his social psychological research might have taken a more heavily theoretical course had World War II and then his untimely death not intervened. The work of many of his students certainly took that direction under his supervision and later.

Lewin's work in social and applied psychology took the form of action research. As Lewin conceived it, action research is more informed by theory than intended to inform theory. It begins with a social problem. The first step is to describe the nature of the problem not only in the usual terms of its substance, its extent, and so on, but also in field-theoretical terms, such as goal regions, conflicting goals, path to goals, and barriers. Next, relevant theory and extant findings are marshaled to suggest solutions to the problem. Then, practical solutions are designed and tried, in the context of experimental design, as far as is possible under the circumstances. Action research is, in modern terms, formative as well as summative; that is, trial solutions are altered as resultant data or changing circumstances suggest, leading finally to an assessment of whether the experimental intervention effectively ameliorated the problem. Throughout, from the project's planning to its summative evaluation, those who have a stake in the problem participate in the project because their input is likely to limit the range of trial solutions to the realm of practicality, their insights illuminate the data, and their involvement makes the ultimate adoption of promising solutions more likely. Besides, the culture of action research includes a strong commitment to democracy and egalitarianism.

In the first article in this set (Selection 9), Lewin promotes action research. Selection 10 is an example of one of his action research efforts. Selection 11 continues the argument for action research—here, particularly in the field of education—by reviewing completed projects that already had proved useful.

Jewish Education and Reality (Selection 9)

This article does not describe an action research project. Rather, it presents Lewin's rationale for applied psychology, particularly in the form of action research.

Lewin was often called on to address or to write for community leaders and policymakers, especially of the Jewish community in which he earnestly involved himself. The address on which this article is based was supposed to be on how to improve the religious education of Jewish children, an endeavor in chronic difficulty. It was—is—almost always conducted after public school hours and on weekends for restless children, by largely untrained teachers, without much supporting curriculum materials. Lewin was almost certainly recalling his own experiences in a heder in Posen when he wrote his speech.

He eschewed the opportunity to tell his audience specifically what to do. I imagine that that prospect was too daunting. Instead, he prudently advised them to use action research to solve their problems, describing the process in general terms and recounting its early achievements.

Group Decision and Social Change (Selection 10)

Lewin led an action research project on changing the American diet to ameliorate food shortages in the early years of World War II. The project is exemplary action research except that, as far as I know, the effective intervention was not put widely to use.

This report has special interest in addition to its illustrating action research. In his analysis of the problem, the initial phase of the process, Lewin uses field theory to conceptualize not a psychological but a sociological state of affairs. Whereas up to then concepts of regions, forces, and so on were coordinated to psychological states of emotion, motivation, and cognition, here they refer to roles in the social organization of food production and consumption. This analysis pointed in the immediate instance to the most promising participants to enlist in the intervention. Had Lewin lived more than a few years longer, the analysis may have pointed him to sociological applications of field theory.

Dynamics of Group Action (Selection 11)

The value of this article for the purposes of this anthology lies in Lewin's review of the action research in which he was directly involved from 1938 to 1943. Lewin noted that this line in his career began with the studies of modes of leadership. Although they were not, strictly speaking, action research, those studies had demonstrated the feasibility of experimentation with natural groups. Subsequent action research projects, in a wide variety of settings, had since been mounted, and Lewin provided a brief account of them here.

It seems that little if any action research had been used in the field of formal education. In response to a request by the editor of a prominent educational journal, Lewin took the opportunity to encourage educators to join in what had become a virtual movement.

9

Jewish Education and Reality

When I was invited to speak to you who are interested in Jewish education and welfare work, I took it that you did not want me to evaluate what is good and what is bad in present day Jewish education. This is a wide field full of controversy, and many among you, I am sure, are better qualified than I to judge it. You might have expected me, as a social psychologist, to analyze some aspects of Jewish life today and tomorrow. Perhaps you are eager to know whether we can plan Jewish education in America for the next decade with the expectation of a fair degree of democratic freedom; or whether the danger of violence and minority repression is great enough to demand a specific preparation of our children for it.

I will not try to make prophecies which might or might not come true. However a few basic facts about the non-Jew and the Jew are clear, if we consider that period for which our present plans for Jewish education have to be laid out. I mention but one example. In an elementary school, a Jewish boy of eight is approached by a younger non-Jewish girl with the question "Are you Jewish?" The boy answers, "Yes, of course." The girl, "But you don't behave like a Jew." The boy, "How should I behave?" Pointing to the one maladjusted among the well adjusted Jewish boys, she says, "He behaves like a Jew."

This is a good example of the degree to which even the non-Jewish child is guided by certain stereotypes of the Jew and perceives any Jew who is different from this stereotype as the "exception to the rule," although he may meet nothing but exceptions. This fact is not likely to change during the next 10 years.

Neither will certain basic facts of the Jewish psychology change. Like members of other minorities, many Jews will continue to rebel, at some time during their development, against their fate of being born a member of a minority. The period during which this rebellion occurs is very important in determining what attitudes the grown-up will have. For instance, many intermarriages seem to result from a development of this attitude in the late teens.

What Jewish education can do best to bring about a healthy Jewish development, I frankly do not know, and I doubt whether this question can be fully answered, at present. I would like to take the liberty, there-

From *Jewish Education*, 1944, *15*(3).

257

fore, of talking to you about recent developments in social psychology which, in my mind, can be of utmost practical value for Jewish education and Jewish planning in general. I, therefore, hope that you will not mind giving your attention to what may seem at first a rather technical, scientific problem.

In the field of industry, where one deals with physical material, we have become accustomed to the fact that any large-scale undertaking has its own research laboratory whether it deals with glass, with steel, with telephones, or with drugs. It has long since been accepted that efficient, practical work should be based on a full knowledge of the actual properties of the material. The haphazard procedure by trial and error has been abandoned as too expensive and too inefficient. Business has learned that it "pays" to investigate the material it deals with; that the deeper the scientific insight into the nature of the material, the greater is the chance of making use of it successfully.

Why have those undertakings that deal with human beings—like our educational system or the welfare organizations, the YMCA or our government—been so slow to apply similar scientific methods of studying the material with which they deal, namely, people and groups of people? Broadcasting companies were among the first to try it; perhaps, because as a business undertaking they are most eager to be efficient. It is true that many of the large organizations mentioned have so-called "research departments" which give them certain statistical data; for instance, about the number of their members, the duration of their membership. Education has made much progress in using intelligence and achievement tests. It is good and important to have such data. It would be very revealing, for instance, to have achievement tests in Hebrew or Jewish history in every Jewish school in every town. Even such data, however, would hardly give us that measure of understanding of the individual and the group which the organization needs to do an efficient and satisfactory job.

Recently, the demand has been made that Jewish education should prove that it actually serves the purpose which it claims to serve. Doubtless, this demand—right or wrong—will be repeated louder. Can it be met? Time permits but one example to illustrate what I mean.

Take a small town in the United States or Canada with a population, let us say of 120 Jewish families. They are mainly middle-class people feeling Jewish but being otherwise highly assimilated, with little knowledge of things Jewish and only a smattering of religious tradition. Somehow, the Jewish Sunday school has been kept alive in that town; but it proceeds on a low level of attendance and enthusiasm. Every year or two the teacher at the Sunday school changes. If the teacher is able and pedagogically well-trained, attendance is a bit higher and the children like the classes better. If the teacher is not so good, the few children attend because they "have to" rather than because they want to. Now, a new teacher comes and something like a miracle happens. In half a year the attendance doubles. After a year it is tripled. The children become interested in keeping up Jewish rituals and soon they are teaching their parents. Somehow a way is found to overcome that initial resistance against keeping Jewish customs which is so typical for many assimilated parents. Soon the town swings in an amazing way toward a healthy, self-respecting life in the Jewish community.

If we ask why the new teacher was able to bring about a change which previous teachers were unable to accomplish, the usual answer is something like: "He has greater leader abilities. He must be a very gifted teacher. He must have a fine, strong personality."

Perhaps, he *is* an exceptional person; but maybe other teachers actually had the same amount of ability. Only they did not happen to even dream of the possibility of bringing about such a change in the community. It is possible they thought that Jewish community life is determined mainly by the economic and political situation at large, that—at best—it can be changed only by slow processes requiring at least a decade. Therefore, they had resigned themselves to the existing level for the two years they planned to spend in this town.

Perhaps, some of the younger teachers actually were ambitious and wanted to create a better Jewish school and higher attendance. They had tried to reach that goal by offering attractive bribes to the children—plays, cookies, and games. In order not to drive anyone away, they had lowered the requirements of the Jewish school and demanded less and less from the children. By this method of attracting children, they followed a widely accepted idea of what children like and dislike. The teacher felt correctly that this line of action would be quite in tune with the wishes of the parents. He knew they would be pleased to see him uphold only that minimum of observance which is the least common Jewish denominator for the community as a whole. He hoped to best secure the parents' cooperation by keeping the demand for work on the level which interferes least with the children's work in the public school and their many other interests.

If this program which seems reasonable enough did not succeed in having the Sunday school flourish, are we sure that this proves the inability of the teacher? Perhaps, the didactic ability and even the leadership abilities of the two teachers were not different, but their methods of approach differed. Actually, the successful teacher did not follow the principle of the least denominator. He set up a very definite style with definite Jewish demands and customs. The teacher who was trying to cater to the children may be greatly surprised to learn that the children actually liked the seemingly stricter atmosphere better. Was the personality of the successful teacher so attractive that the children liked school "in spite of" the higher demands? But, perhaps, the teacher's personality was not the decisive difference in this case. Perhaps, it is easier to base high morale of a group on stiff goals and the necessity to sacrifice than on soft goals and easy life.

I am sure that every one of you knows many stories of this type. Most of us base our opinion about good and bad methods on such casual observations or on ideas which seem to be "common sense." Actually, however, most of our ideas about good or bad methods are not based on properly analyzed facts, but are the reflection of rather one-sided opinion about what "ought to be" good or bad.

Unfortunately, even if one knows many incidents of successful and unsuccessful conduct, it is by no means easy to make definite conclusions from such everyday examples. Perhaps, the teacher who tried to make the Jewish Sunday school as friendly, nice, and attractive as possible was led to his procedure by the observation that many Jewish schools which demand strict observance and set up high standards do not actually reach the most important of their objectives. By some kind of outside pressure, the school succeeds in holding the Jewish child for quite a number of years. But some of these children break away from Judaism within a few years after leaving the school, in spite of all their Jewish knowledge. These children become a living example of Jewish self-hate and they claim that they have been driven away from Judaism by "too much *heder*."* Perhaps, our unsuccessful teacher had met quite a number of such boys in their late adolescence and may have concluded that there cannot be anything worse than a Jewish school system which sets up in childhood that pattern which is most damaging to the individual Jew and the Jewish group: namely, to be a Jew merely because of outside pressure. Having this picture in mind, our teacher had firmly resolved to avoid all pressure in his Sunday school.

What are our own conclusions? Should we say that the success, after all, shows that we need the pressure? That democracy in education is a nice idea but unfortunately does not work? Or should we say that the most successful path goes along a middle way? Both conclusions would be utterly unrealistic. The experimental studies conducted in clubs, in the laboratory, with the Boy Scouts, and with workers in the factory give, I think, conclusive, quantitative evidence that certain democratic methods are definitely superior in production output and in regard to personality relations and personality development than autocratic methods. However, these studies have taught us, too, that the matter is by no means simple. We have to be rather clear in what we mean by democracy; that we do not mean the wishy washy free-for-all of a *laissez faire* type. It has taught us that democracy is not lack of leadership or weak leadership but a different type of leadership. It has taught us to be careful not to confuse democratic methods of planning and group *decision* with mere group *discussion*. Whereas, democratic group decision was found to be much more effective for group action than a request from outside, mere "group discussion" was found to be highly inefficient in regard to action. This is a result which, perhaps, should be considered by the Anti-defamation League in its methods of combatting anti-Semitism.

These studies have given us deeper insight into the relation between efficiency of group life and the various aspects of democratic and autocratic procedures. They have given us surprising examples of the deep effect which leadership training can have on the leader and on the led. But they have also shown that for any type of conclusions, the specific character of the organization and of the local setting has to be carefully considered.

Editor's Note. Religious school.

The problems of leadership in the Army, in industry, in the Boy Scouts, in a community center, and in a Jewish school, each has its specific characteristics.

What we have learned in recent years of research, and what I should like to emphasize here, is the fact that social psychology has developed instruments which are quite efficient in measuring social atmospheres. It has learned to compare in a concrete way the leadership pattern of Mr. X with that of Mr. Y; to analyze the friendship relations existing in a classroom or in a club at the community center; or the prevailing pattern of social interaction among the children: the degree to which they participate in planning and the form of this participation. These and many other factors which seem so lofty and are so decisive for the success of any group life can be satisfactorily determined in a relatively short time, in a concrete manner.

Instead of taking our own or another person's impression of the reason why children attend or do not attend the Jewish school in a certain community, and instead of using these guesses as a basis for plans, it is quite possible actually to find out the determining forces which make the children come or stay away. It may be the manner in which the Talmud Torah* is conducted, or the relation between the school and the parents, or the organization of the Jewish Board of Education, or certain status relations in the community, or many other reasons. A successful study of the reasons why children join the scout movement, why they stay in, and why they drop out is at present under way in Chicago. It is not conducted by a large staff of scientists and a lot of money but, under the guidance of a scientifically trained person, by the scoutmasters and other volunteer adult members of the scout organization. They enjoy thoroughly this bit of research and at the same time gain a deeper and much more realistic knowledge of the motives of the children with whom they have to deal and of many aspects of the community in which they live. Such a cooperative research not only gives valuable data for efficient planning; it has proved to be a very important means of raising the morale of the organization.

There is no time to go into the various types of studies which have been conducted. They deal with anything from the club life of children, student-cooperatives, change of food habits of housewives, training of volunteer leaders to raising of production in industry by bringing about better team work among workers, better training of beginners, retraining of foremen or management. I can merely point out that social psychology has made very important steps forward. From the highly academic and detached descriptions of social relations and from attitude measurements, it has progressed to highly practical "action research." This action research realizes that it does not suffice to study the individual in isolation. Nor does it suffice to approach the individual through radio and newspaper propaganda as an anonymous member of a mass. The deepest basis of the individual's feelings, values, and action is what the sociologist calls the face-to-face group, that is, the group in which the individual lives—his

---

*Editor's Note. Religious school.

family, his neighbors, his friends, his business or religious groups. We have to study the nature of these groups, their inner organization, their leadership, their atmosphere—if we want to bring about a change in the cultural or social life of an individual or group.

I will not attempt to follow up in detail this idea for the handling of minority problems in general, the fight against anti-Semitism, the handling of Jewish schools in small and large towns, for the Jewish community centers, for the education of the small child in the Jewish family, or of the students in the Jewish fraternities and sororities. More than other people do we Jews live in the dark about our future; we are swept periodically by waves of fear. It is only natural, therefore, that we frequently act intensely, but blindly. This is one of the reasons why we have so many factions in Jewish life and why the fight among them is sometimes so heated. We cannot hope to destroy entirely the fog that surrounds our future. But we can clear up much of the fog about our present. Today, science offers the means to find out the essential facts about ourselves and our environment; to find out whether our methods for pursuing our goals are in line with reality and bring us closer to our objective; or whether our methods are not in tune with reality. We do not need to let things go for decades until a Hitler shows us that our action has led us astray. The scientific instruments, if properly used, are sensitive enough to show us where we and where our children stand and where our actions lead.

Such scientific investigation of facts and of the means of efficient action does not need to get us involved in controversies about the specific goal of Jewish education. One may be inclined to ask: "Do we not have to agree first on the goals of Jewish education before we can discuss means?" In my opinion, research could proceed rather far without waiting for the answer to such questions because of two reasons:

(1) There are after all, some goals on which most Jewish parents and Jewish education agree, namely, to bring up children who will be physically and mentally strong and healthy Jewish adults. We want to educate leaders whose rise and success will not make them drift away or even stab their own people in the back. We know that we need leaders whose belonging to their group is firmly grounded.

(2) Where differences of purpose exist between the Jewish sections, the scientist will not come to criticize but to help. His basic question will be: "What are your troubles? Where do you have difficulties?" The crucial facts about group relations and group dynamics are often hidden and sometimes very different from what they appear to be. Too frequently, the parties are so involved in their "cause," that they are blind to facts. It is in these cases of strong conflicts where scientific fact-finding is likely to be of greatest practical help. Where it has been applied in a spirit of cooperation between the practitioner and the scientist, the results have sometimes been close to a miracle.

The scientific study of human behavior on a group level is gradually emerging from the laboratory and is about to join hands with the practical problems of everyday living. Our political and communal life has been too much guided by emotions, blind forces, and too little rational consideration about whether the means really serve the end. Hitler is said to have made, before the war, experiments in panics. In this country, with a positive goal of character building, of youth education and leadership training, a large national organization is making a decisive effort to apply scientific procedures. Many organizations will doubtlessly follow, because—also in the social field—it pays to base one's action on the knowledge of facts. In the long run, I am convinced that no large-scale organization, whether it has to deal with business, welfare, or education, can afford to follow the more or less blind procedures of today. Action research lies within the scope of many organizations. I like to think of our Jewish organizations as being not among the last but among the first to use it for their own benefit and for the common welfare.

There is more involved in such undertaking than the efficiency of our Jewish organizations. The belief in the rational approach is one of the fundamentals of democracy, as it is of Judaism. The belief in rationality is deeply linked with the belief in the equality of men. It is one of the fundamental issues behind the war today, and the struggle against fascism tomorrow, on which the fate of democracy and of Judaism hangs. A rational, realistic approach should help Jewish education to see its goals in the concrete, rather than in the abstract, without losing its long-range view. Wisely handled, it can be a great consolidating force. I personally do not doubt that the value of Jewish education can be proved scientifically, if the problem is attacked unafraid. Democracy and Judaism have nothing to fear from truth and fact finding, but they have much to gain by them. The love of Torah and research is old in Israel. It can and should be made a living force to link its organizations closer with the facts of reality and in this way help to make Jewish life more normal and strong.

10 _____

Group Decision and Social Change

The following experiments on group decision have been conducted during the last four years. They are not in a state that permits definite conclusions. But they show the nature of the problems and the main factors concerned. They also indicate the type of concepts to which the attempt to integrate cultural anthropology, psychology, and sociology into one social science may lead.

Scientifically, the question of group decision lies at the intersection of many basic problems of group life and individual psychology. It concerns the relation of motivation to action and the effect of a group setting on the individual's readiness to change or to keep certain standards. It is related to one of the fundamental problems of action-research, namely, how to change group conduct so that it would not slide back to the old level within a short time. It is in this wider setting of social processes and social management that group decision should be viewed as one means of social change.

Social Channels and Social Perception

The meaning and the over-all effect of a group decision depends upon the nature of the process itself, and upon the position of the group, within the total social field. In regard to these broader questions we will consider two aspects of social steering, namely, steering through gatekeepers and the function which reality perception should have.

Channels, Gates, and Gatekeepers

Food Habits and Food Channels

The first experiment on group decision was part of a larger study on food habits. Its main objective was a comparison of different ethnic and economic groups in a midwestern town. The favorite family food was studied,

From Newcomb, T. M., & Hartley, E. L., Eds. (1948). *Readings in social psychology* (pp. 330–341). New York: Henry Holt.

what food was considered essential, what main frame of reference and values guided the thinking of these groups about foods, and what authorities were seen as standing behind these standards and values. Children at different ages were included to indicate the process of acculturation of the individual in regard to food. Since this study was part of a larger problem of changing food habits in line with war needs, we were interested in including an attempt to bring about some of the desired changes at least on a small scale.

The data acquired give considerable insight into the existing attitudes and practices of the various groups. However, in this, as in many other cases, such data about a present state of affairs do not permit many conclusions in regard to how to proceed best to bring about a change. Should one use radio, posters, lectures, or what other means and methods for changing efficiently group ideology and group action? Should one approach the total population of men, women, and children who are to change their food habits, or would it suffice and perhaps be more effective to concentrate on a strategic part of the population? Obviously the housewife plays some particular role in food habits. What are the underlying assumptions?

Food which comes to the family table is likely to be eaten by someone in the family since little is thrown away. If this is correct, to consider methods of changing family food habits we have first to ask: How does food come to the table?

Food comes to the table through different channels, such as the Buying Channel or the Gardening Channel (Lewin, 1943). After the food has been bought, it might be placed in the icebox or put in the pantry to be either cooked later or prepared directly for the table (Figure 1). Similarly, the food moves through the garden channel in a step-by-step fashion.

To understand what comes on the table, we have to know the forces which determine what food enters a channel. Whether food enters the channel to the family table or not is determined in the buying situation. The buying situation can be characterized as a conflict situation. Food 1 (Figure 1) might be attractive, that is, the force ($f_{P,EF}$) toward eating is large but at the same time the food might be very expensive and therefore the opposing force ($f_{P,SpM}$) against spending money is large, too. Food 2 might be unattractive but cheap. In this case, the conflict would be small. The force toward buying might be composed of a number of components, such as the buyer's liking for the food, his knowledge of his family likes and dislikes, or his ideas about what food is "essential."

The opposing forces might be due to the lack of readiness to spend a certain amount of money, a dislike of lengthy or disagreeable form of preparation, unattractive taste, lack of fitness for the occasion, etc. Food is bought if the total force toward buying becomes greater than the opposing forces (Food 3) until the food basket is filled. Food of type 1 can be called conflict food.

It is culturally significant that the average conflict rating is considerably higher in the middle group (7.44) than in the high (4.35) or the low economic group (5.62). This conflict is probably the result of the greater

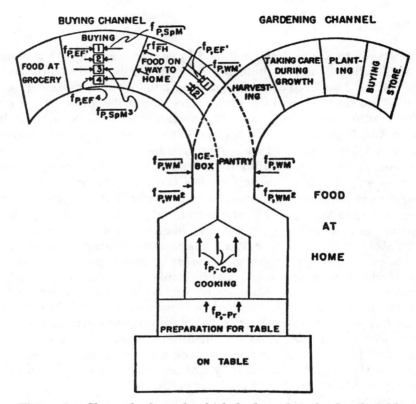

Figure 1.   Channels through which food reaches the family table.

discrepancy between the standards this group would like to keep up and their ability to do so in a situation of rising prices.

In comparing the conflict rating of different foods for the same group, one finds that meat stands highest for the low group, whereas it is second for the middle, and third for the high economic group. That probably means that the conflict between "like" and "expense" in the low group is most outspoken for meat. The high conflict rating of vegetables for the high and middle economic group is probably an expression of the fact that vegetables are desirable as health food but not well liked and not easily prepared. The rates are:

Table 1

Food	High group	Middle group	Low group
Vegetables	.89	1.44	.57
Milk	.70	.89	.33
Meat	.65	1.28	.95
Butter	.30	.94	.67
Fruits	.43	.94	.62
Potatoes	—	.33	.76

The Gate

It is important to know that once food is bought some forces change its direction. Let us assume the housewife has finally decided to buy the high conflict Food 1. The force against spending money, instead of keeping the food out of the channel, will then make the housewife doubly eager not to waste it. In other words, the force ($f_{P,W,M}$) against wasting money will have the same direction as the force toward eating this food or will have the character of a force against leaving the channel.

This example indicates that a certain area within a channel might function as a "gate": The constellation of the forces before and after the gate region are decisively different in such a way that the passing or not passing of a unit through the whole channel depends to a high degree upon what happens in the gate region. This holds not only for food channels but also for the traveling of a news item through certain communication channels in a group, for movements of goods, and the social locomotion of individuals in many organizations. A university, for instance, might be quite strict in its admission policy and might set up strong forces against the passing of weak candidates. Once a student is admitted, however, the university frequently tries to do everything in its power to help everyone along. Many business organizations follow a similar policy. Organizations which discriminate against members of a minority group frequently use the argument that they are not ready to accept individuals whom they would be unable to promote sufficiently.

The Gatekeeper

In case a channel has a gate, the dominant question regarding the movements of materials or persons through the channel is: Who is the gatekeeper and what is his psychology?

The study of the high, middle, and low groups, as well as of a group of Czechs and of Negroes in a midwestern town, revealed that all channels except gardening were definitely controlled by the housewife.

We can conclude from this that changes of food habits in the family finally depend on changes of the psychology of the housewife in the buying situation. Changes of the attitudes and desires of children and husbands will affect actual food habits only to the degree they affect the housewife.

Similar considerations hold for any social constellation which has the character of a channel, a gate, and gatekeepers. Discrimination against minorities will not be changed as long as the forces are not changed which determine the decisions of the gatekeeper. Their decision depends partly on their ideology, that is, the system of values and beliefs which determines what they consider to be "good" or "bad," partly on the way they perceive the particular situation. This latter point will be considered more closely by discussing problems of planning.

Planning, Fact-Finding, and Execution

Planning usually starts with something like a general idea. For one reason or another, it seems desirable to reach a certain objective. Exactly how to circumscribe this objective and how to reach it is frequently not too clear. The first step, then, is to examine the idea carefully in the light of the means available. Frequently, more fact-finding about the situation is required. If this first period of planning is successful, two items emerge: an "over-all plan" of how to reach the objective and a decision in regard to the first step of action. Usually this planning has also somewhat modified the original idea.

The next period is devoted to executing the first step of the over-all plan. In highly developed fields of social management, such as modern factory management or the execution of a war, this second step is followed by certain fact-findings. For example, in the bombing of Germany, a certain factory may have been chosen as the first target after careful consideration of various priorities and of the best means and ways of dealing with this target. The attack is pressed home and immediately a reconnaissance plan follows with the one objective of determining as accurately and objectively as possible the new situation (Figure 2).

This reconnaissance or fact-finding has four functions: It should evaluate the action by showing whether what has been achieved is above or below expectation. It should serve as a basis for correctly planning the next step. It should serve as a basis for modifying the "overall plan." Finally, it gives the planners a chance to learn, that is, to gather new general insight, for instance, regarding the strength and weakness of certain weapons or techniques of action.

The next step again is composed of a circle of planning, executing, and reconnaissance or fact-finding for the purpose of evaluating the results of the second step, for preparing the rational basis for planning the third step, and for perhaps modifying again the over-all plan.

Rational social management, therefore, proceeds in a spiral of steps, each of which is composed of a circle of planning, action, and fact-finding about the result of the action.

In most social areas of management and self-management of groups,

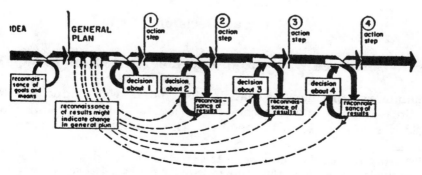

Figure 2. Planning, fact-finding, and execution.

such as conducting a conference and committee meeting, family life, or the improvement of intergroup relations within and between nations, we are still lacking objective standards of achievement. This has two severe effects:

(1) People responsible for social management are frequently deprived of their legitimate desire for reconnaissance on a realistic basis. Under these circumstances, satisfaction or dissatisfaction with achievement becomes mainly a question of temperament.

(2) In a field that lacks objective standards of achievement, no learning can take place. If we cannot judge whether an action has led forward or backward, if we have no criteria for evaluating the relation between effort and achievement, there is nothing to prevent us from coming to the wrong conclusions and encouraging the wrong work habits. Realistic fact-finding and evaluation is a prerequisite for any learning.

Social Channels, Social Perception, and Decision

The relation between social channels, social perception, and decisions is methodologically and practically of considerable significance.

The theory of channels and gatekeepers helps to define in a more precise way how certain "objective" sociological problems of locomotion of goods and persons intersect with certain "subjective" psychological and cultural problems. It points to sociologically characterized places, such as gates in social channels, where attitudes and decisions have a particularly great effect.

The relation between group decision and pre- and post-action diagnosis is two-fold: (1) Group decision depends partly upon how the group views the situation and therefore can be influenced by a change in this perception; (2) A correct perception of the result of social action is essential for the decision of the next step. The measurement of the effect of group decisions is in line with the need for objective evaluation as a prerequisite for making progress in social management and self management of groups.

Group Decision

Lecture Compared With Group Decision (Red Cross Groups)

A preliminary experiment in changing food habits[1] was conducted with six Red Cross groups of volunteers organized for home nursing. Groups ranged in size from 13 to 17 members. The objective was to increase the

_____

[1]The studies on nutrition discussed in this article were conducted at the Child Welfare Research Station of the State University of Iowa for the Food Habits Committee of the National Research Council (Executive Secretary, Margaret Mead).

use of beef hearts, sweetbreads, and kidneys. If one considers the psychological forces which kept housewives from using these intestinal meats, one is tempted to think of rather deep-seated aversions requiring something like psychoanalytical treatment. Doubtless a change in this respect is a much more difficult task than, for instance, the introduction of a new vegetable such as escarole. There were, however, only 45 minutes available.

In three of the groups attractive lectures were given which linked the problem of nutrition with the war effort, emphasized the vitamin and mineral value of the three meats, giving detailed explanations with the aid of charts. Both the health and economic aspects were stressed. The preparation of these meats was discussed in detail as well as techniques for avoiding those characteristics to which aversions were oriented (odor, texture, appearance, etc.). Mimeographed recipes were distributed. The lecturer was able to arouse the interest of the groups by giving hints of her own methods for preparing these "delicious dishes" and her success with her own family.

For the other three groups, Mr. Alex Bavelas developed the following procedure of group decision. Again the problem of nutrition was linked with that of the war effort and general health. After a few minutes, a discussion was started to see whether housewives could be induced to participate in a program of change without attempting any high-pressure salesmanship. The group discussion about "housewives like themselves" led to an elaboration of the obstacles which a change in general and particularly change toward sweetbreads, beef hearts, and kidneys would encounter, such as the dislike of the husband, the smell during cooking, etc. The nutrition expert offered the same remedies and recipes for preparation which were presented in the lectures to the other groups. But in these groups, preparation techniques were offered after the groups had become sufficiently involved to be interested in knowing whether certain obstacles could be removed.

In the earlier part of the meeting, a census was taken on how many women had served any of these foods in the past. At the end of the meeting, the women were asked by a showing of hands who was willing to try one of these meats within the next week.

A follow-up showed that only 3% of the women who heard the lectures served one of the meats never served before, whereas after group decision 32% served one of them (Figure 3).

If one is to understand the basis of this striking difference, several factors may have to be considered.

Degree of Involvement

Lecturing is a procedure by which the audience is chiefly passive. The discussion, if conducted correctly, is likely to lead to a much higher degree of involvement. The procedure of group decision in this experiment follows a step-by-step method designed (a) to secure high involvement and (b) not

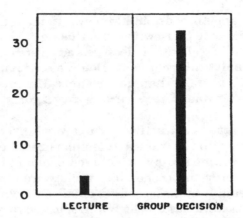

Figure 3. Percentage of individuals serving type of food never served before, after lecture and after group decision.

to impede freedom of decision. The problem of food changes was discussed in regard to "housewives like yourselves" rather than in regard to themselves. This minimized resistance to considering the problems and possibilities in an objective, unprejudiced manner, in much the same way as such resistance has been minimized in interviews which use projective techniques, or in a sociodrama which uses an assumed situation of role playing rather than a real situation.

Motivation and Decision

The prevalent theory in psychology assumes action to be the direct result of motivation. I am inclined to think that we will have to modify this theory. We will have to study the particular conditions under which a motivating constellation leads or does not lead to a decision or to an equivalent process through which a state of "considerations" (indecisiveness) is changed into a state where the individual has "made up his mind" and is ready for action, although he may not act at that moment.

The act of decision is one of those transitions. A change from a situation of undecided conflict to decision does not mean merely that the forces toward one alternative become stronger than those toward the other alternative. If this were the case, the resultant force should frequently be extremely small. A decision, rather, means that the potency of one alternative has become zero or is so decidedly diminished that the other alternative and the corresponding forces dominate the situation. This alternative itself might be a compromise. After the decision, people may feel sorry and change their decision. We cannot speak of a real decision, however, before one alternative has become dominant so far as action is concerned. If the opposing forces in a conflict merely change so that the forces in one direction become slightly greater than in the other direction, a state of blockage or extremely inhibited action results rather than that clear one-sided action which follows a real decision.

Lecturing May Lead to a High Degree of Interest

It may affect the motivation of the listener. But it seldom brings about a definite decision on the part of the listener to take a certain action at a specific time. A lecture is not often conducive to decision.

Evidence from everyday experience and from some preliminary experiments by Bavelas in a factory indicate that even group discussions, although usually leading to a higher degree of involvement, as a rule do not lead to a decision. It is very important to emphasize this point. Although group discussion is in many respects different from lectures, it shows no fundamental difference on this point.

Of course, there is a great difference in asking for a decision after a lecture or after a discussion. Since discussion involves active participation of the audience and a chance to express motivations corresponding to different alternatives, the audience might be more ready "to make up its mind," that is, to make a decision after a group discussion than after a lecture. A group discussion gives the leader a better indication of where the audience stands and what particular obstacles have to be overcome.

In the experiment on hand, we are dealing with a group decision after discussion. The decision, itself, takes but a minute or two. (It was done through raising of hands as an answer to the question: Who would like to serve kidney, sweetbreads, or beef hearts next week?) The act of decision, however, should be viewed as a very important process of giving dominance to one of the alternatives, serving or not serving. It has an effect of freezing this motivational constellation for action. We will return to this point later.

Individual Versus Group

The experiment does not try to bring about change of food habits by an approach to the individual, as such. Nor does it use the "mass approach" characteristic of radio and newspaper propaganda. Closer scrutiny shows that both the mass approach and the individual approach place the individual in a quasi private, psychologically isolated situation with himself and his own ideas. Although he may, physically, be part of a group listening to a lecture, for example, he finds himself, psychologically speaking, in an "individual situation."

The present experiment approaches the individual as a member of a face-to-face group. We know, for instance, from experiments in level of aspiration (Lewin, 1946) that goal setting is strongly dependent on group standards. Experience in leadership training and in many areas of re-education, such as re-education regarding alcoholism or delinquency (Lewin & Grabbe, 1945), indicates that it is easier to change the ideology and social practice of a small group handled together than of single individuals. One of the reasons why "group carried changes" are more readily brought about seems to be the unwillingness of the individual to depart too far from group standards; he is likely to change only if the group changes. We will return to this problem.

One may try to link the greater effectiveness of group decision procedures to the fact that the lecture reaches the individual in a more individualistic fashion than group discussion. If a change of sentiment of the
group becomes apparent during the discussion, the individual will be more
ready to come along.

It should be stressed that in our case, the decision which follows the
group discussion does not have the character of a decision in regard to a
group goal; it is, rather, a decision about individual goals in a group
setting.

Expectation

The difference between the results of the lectures and the group decision
may be due to the fact that only after group decision did the discussion
leader mention that an inquiry would be made later as to whether a new
food was introduced into the family diet.

Leader Personality

The difference in effectiveness may be due to differences in leader personality. The nutritionist and the housewife who did the lecturing were persons of recognized ability, experience, and success. Still, Mr. Bavelas, who
led the discussion and subsequent decision, is an experienced group
worker and doubtless of unusual ability in this field.

To determine which of these or other factors are important, a number
of systematic variations have to be carried out. To determine, for instance,
the role of the decision as such, one can compare the effect of group discussion with and without decision. To study the role of group involvement
and the possibility of sensing the changing group sentiment, one could
introduce decisions after both, lecture and discussion, and compare their
effects.

The following experiments represent partly analytical variations,
partly repetitions with somewhat different material.

Lecture Versus Group Decision (Neighborhood Groups)

Dana Klisurich, under the direction of Marian Radke, conducted experiments with 6 groups of housewives composed of 6 to 9 members per group.
She compared the effect of a lecture with that of group decision. The topic
for these groups was increasing home consumption of milk, in the form of
fresh or evaporated milk or both (Radke & Klisurich, unpublished
manuscript).

The procedure followed closely that described above. Again there was
no attempt at high-pressure salesmanship. The group discussion proceeded in a step-by-step way, starting again with "what housewives in
general might do" and only then leading to the individuals present. The

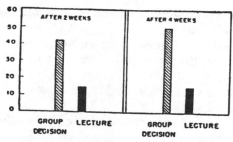

Figure 4. Percentage of mothers reporting an increase in the consumption of fresh milk.

lecture was kept as interesting as possible. The knowledge transmitted was the same for lecture and group decision.

A check-up was made after two weeks and after four weeks. As in the previous experiments, group decision showed considerably greater effectiveness, both after two weeks and after four weeks and for both fresh and evaporated milk (Figures 4 and 5). This experiment permits the following conclusions:

1. It shows that the greater effectiveness of the group decision in the first experiment is not merely the result of the personality or training of the leader. The leader was a lively person, interested in people, but she did not have particular training in group work. She had been carefully advised and had had a try-out in the group decision procedure. As mentioned above, the leader in lecture and group decision was the same person.
2. The experiment shows that the different effectiveness of the two procedures is not limited to the foods considered in the first experiment.
3. It is interesting that the greater effectiveness of group decision was observable not only after one week but after two and four weeks. Consumption after group decision kept constant during that period. After the lecture, it showed an insignificant increase from the second to the fourth week. The degree of permanency is

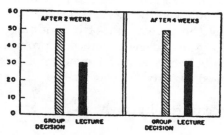

Figure 5. Percentage of mothers reporting an increase in the consumption of evaporated milk.

obviously a very important aspect of any changes in group life. We will come back to this point.

4. As in the first experiment, the subjects were informed about a future check-up after group decision but not after the lecture. After the second week, however, both groups knew that a check-up had been made and neither of them was informed that a second check-up would follow.

5. It is important to know whether group decision is effective only with tightly knit groups. It should be noticed that in the second experiment the groups were composed of housewives who either lived in the same neighborhood or visited the nutrition information service of the community center. They were not members of a club meeting regularly as were the Red Cross groups in the first experiment. On the other hand, a good proportion of these housewives knew each other. This indicates that decision in a group setting seems to be effective even if the group is not a permanent organization.

Individual Instruction Versus Group Decision

For a number of years, the state hospital in Iowa City has given advice to mothers on feeding of their babies. Under this program, farm mothers who have their first child at the hospital meet with a nutritionist for from 20–25 minutes before discharge from the hospital to discuss feeding. The mother receives printed advice on the composition of the formula and is instructed in the importance of orange juice and cod liver oil.

There had been indication that the effect of this nutrition program was not very satisfactory. An experiment was carried out by Dana Klisurich under the direction of Marian Radke to compare the effectiveness of this procedure with that of group decision (Radke & Klisurich, n.d.).

With some mothers, individual instruction was used as before. Others were divided into groups of six for instruction on and discussion of baby feeding. The manner of reaching a decision at the end of this group meeting was similar to that used in the previous experiments. The time for the six mothers together was the same as for one individual, about 25 minutes.

After two weeks and after four weeks, a check was made on the degree to which each mother followed the advice on cod liver oil and orange juice. Figures 6 and 7 show the percentage of individuals who completely followed the advice. The group decision method proved far superior to the individual instruction. After four weeks, every mother who participated in group decision followed exactly the prescribed diet in regard to orange juice.

The following specific results might be mentioned:

1. The greater effect of group decision in this experiment is particularly interesting. Individual instruction is a setting in which the

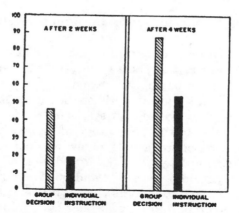

Figure 6. Percentage of mothers following completely group decision or individual instruction in giving cod liver oil.

individual gets more attention from the instructor. Therefore, one might expect the individual to become more deeply involved and the instruction to be fitted more adequately to the need and sentiment of each individual. After all, the instructor devotes the same amount of time to one individual as he does to six in group decision. The result can be interpreted to mean either that the amount of individual involvement is greater in group decision or that the decision in the group setting is itself the decisive factor.

2. Most of the mothers were not acquainted with each other. They returned to farms which were widely separated. Most of them had no contact with each other during the following four weeks. The previous experiment had already indicated that the effectiveness of group decision did not seem to be limited to well-established groups. In this experiment, the absence of social relations among

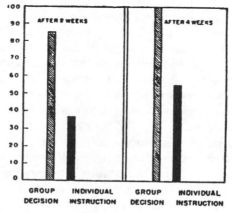

Figure 7. Percentage of mothers following completely group decision or individual instruction in giving orange juice.

the mothers before and after the group meeting is even more clearcut.

3. The data thus far do not permit reliable quantitative, over-all comparisons. However, they point to certain interesting problems and possibilities. In comparing the various experiments concerning the data two weeks after group decision, one finds that the percentage of housewives who served kidneys, beef hearts, or sweetbreads is relatively similar to the percentage of housewives who increased the consumption of fresh milk or evaporated milk or of mothers who followed completely the diet of cod liver oil with their babies. The percentages lie between 32 and 50. The percentage in regard to orange juice for the baby is clearly higher, namely, 85%. These results are surprising in several respects. Mothers are usually eager to do all they can for their babies. This may explain why a group decision in regard to orange juice had such a strong effect. Why, however, was this effect not equally strong on cod liver oil? Perhaps, giving the baby cod liver oil is hampered by the mothers' own dislike of this food. Kidneys, beef hearts, and sweetbreads are foods for which the dislike seems to be particularly deep-seated. If the amount of dislike is the main resistance to change, one would expect probably a greater difference between these foods and, for instance, a change in regard to fresh milk. Of course, these meats are particularly cheap and the group decision leader was particularly qualified.

4. The change after lectures is in all cases smaller than after group decision. However, the rank order of the percentage of change after lectures follows the rank order after group decision, namely (from low to high), glandular meat, fresh milk, cod liver oil for the baby, evaporated milk for the family, orange juice for the baby.

   The constancy of this rank order may be interpreted to mean that one can ascribe to each of these foods—under the given circumstances and for these particular populations—a specific degree of "resistance to change." The "force toward change" resulting from group decision is greater than the force resulting from lecture. This leads to a difference in the amount (or frequency) of change for the same food without changing the rank order of the various foods. The rank order is determined by the relative strength of their resistance to change.

5. Comparing the second and the fourth week, we notice that the level of consumption remains the same or increases insignificantly after group decision and lecture regarding evaporated or fresh milk. A pronounced increase occurs after group decision and after individual instruction on cod liver oil and orange juice, that is, in all cases regarding infant feeding. This seems to be a perplexing phenomenon if one considers that no additional instruction or group decision was introduced. On the whole, one may be inclined to expect weakening effect of group decision with time and therefore a decrease rather than an increase of the curve. To under-

stand the problems involved, it is essential to formulate the question of condition of social change on a more theoretical level.

Quasi-Stationary Social Equilibria and the Problem of Permanent Change

The Objective of Change

The objective of social change might concern the nutritional standard of consumption, the economic standard of living, the type of group relation, the output of a factory, the productivity of an educational team. It is important that a social standard to be changed does not have the nature of a "thing" but of a "process." A certain standard of consumption, for instance, means that a certain action—such as making certain decisions, buying, preparing, and canning certain food in a family—occurs with a certain frequency within a given period. Similarly, a certain type of group relations means that within a given period, certain friendly and hostile actions and reactions of a certain degree of severity occur between the members of two groups. Changing group relations or changing consumption means changing the level at which these multitudes of events proceed. In other words, the "level" of consumption, of friendliness, or of productivity is to be characterized as the aspect of an ongoing social process.

Any planned social change will have to consider a multitude of factors characteristic for the particular case. The change may require a more or less unique combination of educational and organizational measures; it may depend upon quite different treatments or ideology, expectation, and organization. Still, certain general formal principles always have to be considered.

The Conditions of a Stable Quasi-Stationary Equilibrium

The study of the conditions for change begins appropriately with an analysis of the conditions for "no change," that is, for the state of equilibrium.

From what has been just discussed, it is clear that by a state of "no social change" we do not refer to a stationary but to a quasi-stationary equilibrium, that is, to a state comparable to that of a river which flows with a given velocity in a given direction during a certain time interval. A social change is comparable to a change in the velocity or direction of that river.

A number of statements can be made in regard to the conditions of quasi-stationary equilibrium. (These conditions are treated more elaborately elsewhere [Lewin, 1947]).

(a)   The strength of forces which tend to lower that standard of social life should be equal and opposite to the strength of forces which tend to raise its level. The resultant of forces on the line of equilibrium should therefore be zero.

(b) Since we have to assume that the strength of social forces always shows variations, a quasi-stationary equilibrium presupposes that the forces against raising the standard increase with the amount of raising and that the forces against lowering increase (or remain constant) with the amount of lowering. This type of gradient which is characteristic for a "positive central force field" has to hold a least in the neighborhood of the present level (Figure 8).

(c) It is possible to change the strength of the opposing forces without changing the level of social conduct. In this case the tension (degree of conflict) increases.

Two Basic Methods of Changing Levels of Conduct

For any type of social management, it is of great practical importance that levels of quasi-stationary equilibria can be changed in either of two ways: by adding forces in the desired direction or by diminishing opposing forces. If a change from the level L1 to L2 is brought about by increasing the forces toward L2, the secondary effects should be different from the case where the same change of level is brought about by diminishing the opposing forces.

In both cases, the equilibrium might change to the same new level. The secondary effect should, however, be quite different. In the first case, the process on the new level would be accompanied by a state of relatively high tension, in the second case, by a state of relatively low tension. Since increase of tension above a certain degree is likely to be paralleled by

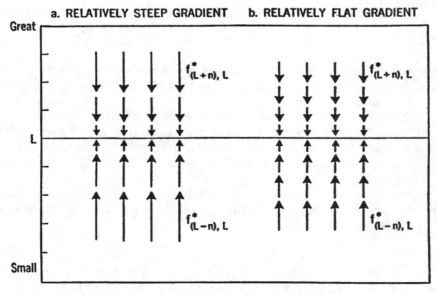

Figure 8. Gradients of resultant forces (f*).

higher aggressiveness, higher emotionality, and lower constructiveness, it is clear that as a rule, the second method will be preferable to the high pressure method.

The group decision procedure which is used here attempts to avoid high pressure methods and is sensitive to resistance to change. In the experiment by Bavelas on changing production in factory work (as noted below), for instance, no attempt was made to set the new production goal by majority vote because a majority vote forces some group members to produce more than they consider appropriate. These individuals are likely to have some inner resistance. Instead, a procedure was followed by which a goal was chosen on which everyone could agree fully.

It is possible that the success of group decision and particularly the permanency of the effect is, in part, due to the attempt to bring about a favorable decision by removing counterforces within the individuals rather than by applying outside pressure.

The surprising increase from the second to the fourth week in the number of mothers giving cod liver oil and orange juice to the baby can probably be explained by such a decrease of counterforces. Mothers are likely to handle their first baby during the first weeks of life somewhat cautiously and become more ready for action as the child grows stronger.

Social Habits and Group Standards

Viewing a social stationary process as the result of a quasi-stationary equilibrium, one may expect that any added force will change the level of the process. The idea of "social habit" seems to imply that, in spite of the application of a force, the level of the social process will not change because of some type of "inner resistance" to change. To overcome the inner resistance, an additional force seems to be required, a force sufficient to "break the habit," to "unfreeze" the custom.

Many social habits are anchored in the relation between the individuals and certain group standards. An individual may differ in his personal level of conduct (Lp) from the level which represents group standards (LGr) by a certain amount. If the individual should try to diverge "too much" from group standards, he would find himself in increasing difficulties. He would be ridiculed, treated severely, and finally ousted from the group. Most individuals, therefore, stay pretty close to the standard of the group they belong to or wish to belong to. In other words, the group level itself acquires value. It becomes a positive valence corresponding to a central force field with the force fP,L keeping the individual in line with the standards of the group.

Individual Procedures and Group Procedures of Changing
Social Conduct

If the resistance to change depends partly on the value which the group standard has for the individual, the resistance to change should diminish if one diminishes the strength of the value of the group standard or changes the level perceived by the individual as having social value.

This second point is one of the reasons for the effectiveness of "group carried" changes resulting from procedures which approach the individuals as part of face-to-face groups (Maier, 1946). Perhaps, one might expect single individuals to be more pliable than groups of like-minded individuals. However, experience in leadership training, in changing of food habits, work production criminality, alcoholism, prejudices, all indicate that it is usually easier to change individuals formed into a group than to change any one of them separately (Lewin & Grabbe, 1945). As long as group standards are unchanged, the individual will resist changes more strongly the farther he is to depart from group standards. If the group standard itself is changed, the resistance which is due to the relation between individual and group standard is eliminated.

Changing as a Three-Step Procedure: Unfreezing, Moving, and Freezing of a Level

A change toward a higher level of group performance is frequently short lived: After a "shot in the arm," group life soon returns to the previous level. This indicates that it does not suffice to define the objective of a planned change in group performance as the reaching of a different level. Permanency of the new level, or permanency for a desired period, should be included in the objective. A successful change includes therefore three aspects: unfreezing (if necessary) the present level L1, moving to the new level L2, and freezing group life on the new level. Since any level is determined by a force field, permanency implies that the new force field is made relatively secure against change.

The "unfreezing" of the present level may involve quite different problems in different cases. Allport (1945) has described the "catharsis" which seems to be necessary before prejudices can be removed. To break open the shell of complacency and self-righteousness, it is sometimes necessary to bring about deliberately an emotional stir-up.

Figure 9 presents an example of the effect of three group decisions of a team in a factory reported by Bavelas, which illustrates an unusually good case of permanency of change measured over nine months (Maier, 1946).

The experiments on group decision reported here cover but a few of the necessary variations. Although in some cases the procedure is relatively easily executed, in others it requires skill and presupposes certain general conditions. Managers rushing into a factory to raise production by group decisions are likely to encounter failure. In social management, as in medicine, there are no patent medicines and each case demands careful diagnosis.

One reason why group decision facilitates change is illustrated by Willerman. Figure 10 shows the degree of eagerness to have the members of a students' eating cooperative change from the consumption of white

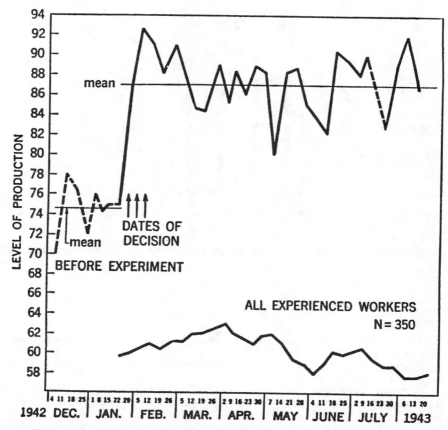

Figure 9.   Effect of group decision on sewing-machine operators.

bread to whole wheat. When the change was simply requested, the degree of eagerness varied greatly with the degree of personal preference for whole wheat. In case of group decision, the eagerness seems to be relatively independent of personal preference; the individual seems to act mainly as a "group member."

Summary

Group decision is a process of social management or self management of groups. It is related to social channels, gates, and gatekeepers; to the problem of social perception and planning; and to the relation between motivation and action, and between the individual and the group.

Experiments are reported in which certain methods of group decision prove to be superior to lecturing and individual treatment as means of changing social conduct.

The effect of group decision can probably be best understood by relating it to a theory of quasi-stationary social equilibria, to social habits and

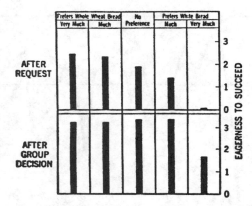

Figure 10.   Relation between own food preferences and eagerness to succeed.

resistance to change, and to the various problems of unfreezing, changing, and freezing social levels.

References

Allport, G. W. (1945). Catharsis and the reduction of prejudice. *Journal of Social Issues, 1,* 3–10.

Lewin, K. (1943). Forces behind food habits and methods of change. *Journal of National Research Council, 58,* 35–65.

Lewin, K. (1946). Behavior and development as a function of the total situation. In L. Carmichael (Ed.), *Manual of child psychology* (pp. 791–844). New York: John Wiley.

Lewin, K. (1947). Frontiers in group dynamics: Concept, method and reality in social science; Social equilibria and social change. *Journal of Human Relations, 1,* 5–41.

Lewin, K., & Grabbe, P. (1945). Problems of re-education. *Journal of Social Issues, 1*(3), 1–66.

Maier, N. R. F. (1946). *Psychology in industry.* Boston: Houghton Mifflin.

Radke, M., & Klisurich, D. (n.d.). *Experiments in changing food habits.* Unpublished manuscript.

11 _____

The Dynamics of Group Action

It is less than ten years ago that, defying hosts of prejudices, the attempt was made to proceed from *descriptive* studies of social relations and attitudes to what may be called "action research" on groups. It is not merely the nearness to problems of the practice which lies behind this particular interest in changes, but the fact that the study of experimentally created changes gives a deeper insight into the dynamics of group life. Even the most exact measurement of food consumption or attitudes toward food, for instance, does not tell how strong the food habits are, how great the resistance would be against changes, or how changes could be brought about effectively. Only experiments in changes can, finally, lay open the deeper layers of group dynamics.

Such action research started as a mere trickle with studying children's clubs. It has spread to the study of such groups as the Boy Scouts, college students, housewives, and to the fields of nutrition and industry. No university seems yet to have realized the deep implications which a resolute promotion of research in group dynamics would have for every aspect of social life. But the trickle has become a creek and will become a river: We are moving toward a full-fledged experimental science of group dynamics which will include the problems of leadership and leadership training, ideology and culture, group morale and group production, discipline and group organization, in short, all phases of group life.

The various aspects of group dynamics are the most important determinants for our life, including our character, our happiness, and productivity. If someone should have failed to notice this fact, the experiments should help to make it clear. Any experimental research in a new field at first seems to accomplish not more than "proving scientifically" what the well-experienced practitioner has known. Although it is equally true that in a field as full of words as the discussion of group and leadership problems, one can be sure to have equally experienced practitioners express opposite views. Without trying to make direct applications to education, I should like to select a few experimental findings which might be of interest to the teacher.

_____

From *Educational Leadership*, 4, 195–200.

Autocracy, Democracy, and Laissez Faire

One of the outstanding facts which has been known but which is not sufficiently recognized by teachers, parents, or other persons connected with
education concerns the relation between autocracy, democracy, and individualistic freedom (laissez faire). The average Sunday school teacher,
foreman, or university professor alike is accustomed to perceive problems
of discipline or leadership as lying on one continuum, on which lack of
discipline and maximum individual freedom represent the one end and
strict authoritarian discipline the other end. This conception, however, is
basically incorrect. Autocracy, democracy, and laissez faire should be perceived as a triangle (Figure 1). In many respects, autocracy and democracy
are similar: They both mean leadership as against the lack of leadership
of laissez faire; they both mean discipline and organization as against
chaos. Along other lines of comparison, democracy and laissez faire are
similar: They both give freedom to the group members in so far as they
create a situation where the members are acting on their own motivation
rather than being moved by forces induced by an authority in which they
have no part.

The person who thinks in terms of one continuum has no choice but
to consider democracy as something *between* autocratic discipline and law-
lessness; he sees it as a soft type of autocracy or frequently as a kind of
sugar-coated or refined method to induce the group member to accept the
leader's will.

It is a prerequisite to democratic education that this concept be destroyed. The democratic leader is no less a leader and, in a way, has not
less power than the autocratic leader. There are soft and tough democracies as well as soft and tough autocracies; and a tough democracy is likely
to be more rather than less democratic. The difference between autocracy
and democracy is an honest, deep difference, and an autocracy with a
democratic front is still an autocracy.

The experiments help in many ways to substantiate this triangular
relation and to clarify the rather disturbing complexity of problems by

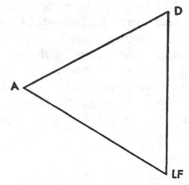

Figure 1. The relations of similarity and difference between autocracy (A), democracy (D) and laissez-faire (LF) cannot be represented by one continuum.

showing where the differences lie, why differences in group procedures which might look important actually are unimportant and others which look unimportant are important. It is particularly interesting to consider what might be called an efficient "tough democracy."

The gospel of inefficiency of democracies has been preached and believed not only in Nazi Germany. We ourselves are somehow surprised to see the democratic countries execute this war rather efficiently. When Lippitt's first study (1940) showed the beneficial effects which the democratic atmosphere has on the overt character of the member, how it changes his behavior from hostility to friendliness, from egocentricism to we-feeling and to an objective, matter-of-fact attitude, the argument was frequently presented that these results may hold in the friendly settings of a boys' club, but that the advantages of the democratic atmosphere would not stand up in a tough situation such as an industry requiring high efficiency.

For studying these aspects of democracy experiments were conducted in the fields of nutrition and industry.

Discussion, Decision, and Action

In school as well as in industry, certain standards exist concerning the rate of learning or production. These standards are set up by the teacher or the management and are upheld by these authorities with a certain amount of pressure. It is assumed that relaxing the standards will slow down the work of the group members.

This assumption is probably true, but it has little to do with the problem of democracy. Lowering the standards or relaxing the pressure to keep up the standards in an autocratic atmosphere means shifting to a softer form of autocracy. It means a shift from autocracy (A) toward laissez faire (LF) in Figure 1. It does not mean a shift in the direction of democracy (D). Such a shift would involve a positive change of the type of motivation behind the action, a shift from imposed goals to goals which the group has set for itself.

It is by no means certain that production goals set for themselves by work teams, or learning goals set by groups of students, would be higher than those ordered by an authority. However, it is by no means certain that they would be lower. Whether the standards will be set higher or lower depends on the specific social atmosphere and the type of democracy created. Experiments in industry under controlled conditions show a substantial permanent increase of production created in a short time by certain methods of "team decision," an increase in production which was not accomplished by many months of the usual factory pressure (Figure 2). (The money incentive remained unchanged.) This demonstrates that democratic procedures may raise group efficiency.

Only a few details of the problems, which are by no means simple, can be discussed here.

1. One should be careful to distinguish discussion and decision. A discussion might be better than a lecture for clarifying issues and

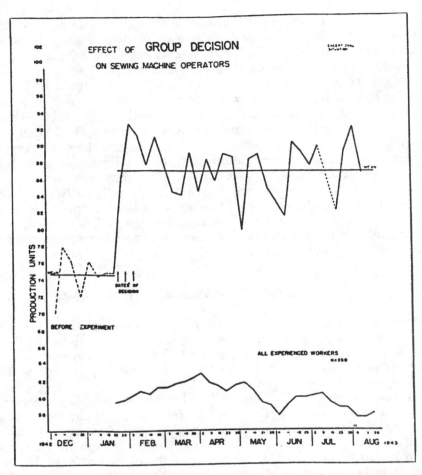

Figure 2. The effect of team decision on production in a sewing factory. An experiment by Alex Bavelas shows a marked permanent rise in production after decision. As comparison, the production level of experienced workers is given during the same months.

bringing about motivation. However, it is one thing to be motivated, another to transform motivation into concrete goals and into stabilizing these goals in a way which would carry the individual through to the actual completion of the work. Controlled experiments under comparable conditions show that a discussion without decision did not lead to a parallel increase in production. There are indications that, even if the discussion leads to the *general* decision of raising production without setting *definite* production goals to be reached in a definite time, the effect is much less marked. Experiments with groups of housewives (Lewin, 1943) and students' eating-cooperatives (Willerman, 1943) show that lectures as well as requests are less efficient to bring about changes in food habits than group decision. Discussions without decisions do not make for efficient democracy. On the other hand, democratic methods, if properly handled, are superior to requests in bringing about changes.

2. One of the reasons why democratic methods are superior is illustrated in the study of the students' cooperatives. The students were to change from the consumption of white to whole wheat bread. From each student was obtained a rating of his eagerness to reach the goal and of his like or dislike of whole wheat as compared with white bread. The result shows that after request, the eagerness to succeed was lowest in the individuals who disliked whole wheat bread and that it increased with the degree of liking. After group decision, however, the eagerness to reach the group goal was largely independent of personal like or dislike. In other words, group decision provides a background of motivation where the individual is ready to cooperate as a member of the group more or less independent of his personal inclinations.

3. It is important to realize that these methods of changing group goals and obtaining group efficiency are not based on dealing with the individual as an individual but as a group member. The goals were set for the group as a whole or for individuals in a group setting. The experimental studies indicate that it is easier to change ideology or cultural habits by dealing with groups than with individuals. In addition, the anchorage of the motivation of the individual in a group decision goes far in achieving the execution of the decision and in establishing certain self-regulatory processes of the group life on the new level of ideology and action (see Lewin, 1944).

Democratic Leadership

In all the experiments mentioned, the problem of leadership plays an important role. As the earlier experiments show (Lippitt, 1940, 1943), a group atmosphere can be changed radically in a relatively short time by introducing new leadership techniques. The paradoxes of democratic leadership are by no means solved; however, the studies on leadership and particularly on leadership training (Bavelas, 1942) give some information.

1. Autocratic as well as democratic leadership consists in playing a certain role. These roles of the leader cannot be carried through without the followers playing certain complementary roles, namely, those of an autocratic or of a democratic follower. Educating a group of people in democracy or re-educating them from either autocracy or laissez faire cannot be accomplished by a passive behavior of the democratic leader. It is a fallacy to assume that individuals, if left alone, will form themselves naturally into democratic groups; it is much more likely that chaos or a primitive pattern of organization through autocratic dominance will result.

Establishing democracy in a group implies an active education: The democratic follower has to learn to play a role which implies, among other points, a fair share of responsibility toward the group and a sensitivity to other peoples' feelings.

Sometimes, particularly in the beginning of the process of re-education, individuals may have to be made aware in a rather forceful manner of the two-way interdependence which exists between themselves and others within a democratic group. To create such a change, the leader has to be in power and has to be able to hold his power. As the followers learn democracy, other aspects of the democratic leader's power and function become prevalent.

What holds for the education of democratic followers holds true also for the education of democratic leaders. In fact, it seems to be the same process through which persons learn to play either of these roles, and it seems that both roles have to be learned if either one is to be played well.

2. It is important to realize that democratic behavior cannot be learned by autocratic methods. This does not mean that democratic education or democratic leadership has to diminish the power aspect of group organization in a way which would place the group life on the laissez faire point of the triangle (Figure 1). Efficient democracy means organization, but it means organization and leadership on different principles than autocracy.

These principles might be clarified by lectures, but they can be learned, finally, only by democratic living. The "training on the job" of the democratic leaders (Bavelas, 1942) is but one example for the fact that teaching democracy presupposes the establishing of a democratic atmosphere.

One should be slow in generalizing experimental findings. Any type of organization like a factory, a business enterprise, a community center, a school system, or the Army has characteristics of its own. What democracy means technically has to be determined in each organization in line with its particular objective. The objective of our educational system is customarily defined as twofold. It is to give knowledge and skills to the coming generation and to build the character of the citizens-to-be. The experiments indicate that democratic education does not need to impede the efficiency in regard to the first objective but can be used as a powerful instrument toward this end. The experiment also indicates that, for educating future citizens, no talk about democratic ideals can substitute for a democratic atmosphere in the school. The character and the cultural habits of the growing citizen are not so much determined by what he says as by what he lives.

Today, research institutes on physics and chemistry are common in industry. The time is approaching when research institutes on group dynamics will be just as common for any large organization dealing with people. It is essential that a democratic commonwealth and its educational system apply the rational procedures of scientific investigation also to its own process of group living.

References

Bavelas, A. (1942). Morale and the training of leaders. In G. Watson, (Ed.), *Civilian morale* (pp. 143–165). New York: Reynal and Hichcock.

Lewin, K. (1943). *The relative effectiveness of a lecture method and a method of group decision for changing food habits.* Washington, DC: National Research Council, Committee on Food Habits.

Lewin, K. (1943). The special case of Germany. *Public Opinion Quarterly, 7,* 553–566.*

Lippitt, R. (1940). An experimental study of the effect of democratic and authoritarian group atmospheres. *University of Iowa Studies in Child Welfare, 16*(3), 44–195.

Lippitt, R. (1943). From domination to leadership. *Journal of the National Association of the Deans of Women, 7,* 147–152.

Willerman, B. (1943). *Group decision and request as means of changing food habits.* Washington, DC: National Research Council, Committee on Food Habits.

Editor's Note. Lewin provided a different reference: Changing the cultural atmosphere in Germany. *Public Opinion Quarterly,* 1944. However, I have not been able to locate any such article. Probably the title and publication date of the article in press were changed after the present article went to press.

Part IV

Sage

Introduction

There is a fine line between Lewin's contributions as an applied psychologist and as a sage. Perhaps it would be better to speak of the broad range of Lewin's intellect rather than of its many facets. It is quite clear that Lewin thought of his professional activities as a piece, seamless and integrated. However, such an image is not so easily conveyed in the organization of an anthology. Partitioning a body of work into sections is a useful sort of organization if one is mindful not to overemphasize the divisions implied.

In contrast to his writings as an applied psychologist, the four articles in this section display Lewin in a more discursive mode, drawing generally on the resources of social science—particularly those that he and his colleagues had created—to help various publics solve their problems. Although he alluded to specific research, mostly action research, he did not dwell on specifics. None of the problems addressed in these articles had at the time been subject to the rigorous sort of applied research that Lewin advocated. These are thoughtful, more general but not less careful articles.

Socializing the Taylor System (Selection 12)

Lewin began offering sagacious advice early in his career but, as always seems to have been the case, only when asked. In this instance, his close friend Karl Korsch asked Lewin for his comments on the Taylor System of industrial management. *Taylorism*, or time-and-motion study, was at the height of its popularity in the United States in the 1920s and was attracting favorable attention in Europe (Lears, 1997). This system was touted to increase productivity dramatically, and European industry was desperately trying to recover from the dreadful aftermath of World War I, not least of which was the shortage of labor. The socialist Korsch was anxious about the implications of Taylorism for the welfare of workers, and he realized that the scientific rationale for it was an important source of its appeal. So he asked Lewin, already a respected social scientist, to comment on Taylorism, confident that Lewin would also view the system from a social democratic perspective.

As the article reveals, Lewin was sympathetic to the application of scientific methods for improving industrial management. However, his intuition told him that advocates of the Taylor System were not taking adequate account of important factors—namely, the needs of the workers. This was well before his research on modes of leadership and participative management, so he had no data directly relevant to cite. There were only the holistic principles of his kind of Gestalt psychology and the initial data in hand on the significance for behavior of people's needs, motives, and intentions.

Another revealing aspect of this article is that already in the 1920s, Lewin was writing insightfully about social organization and was eager to construct a useful psychology. This article demonstrates that his later article on "channeling" (Selection 10) was neither Lewin's first essay on the sociological side of social psychology nor his first about applied social science. This earlier article actually gives short shrift to the Taylor System itself; it is mostly addressed to a social organizational analysis of how people come to occupy certain occupations and the ways that applied psychology can bring that process closer to the ideals of a social democratic society.

Democracy and the School (Selection 13)

In this article, Lewis and his wife, Gertrud, integrate child development and group dynamics to advise educators about inculcating democratic values and teaching the skills of democratic participation.

Personal Adjustment and Group Belongingness (Selection 14)

Lewin invoked what today is called "social identity" to counsel people working in Jewish agencies on the treatment of maladjustment in their Jewish clients. He observed that one's sense of self-integration is often grounded in the role one plays as a member of a recognized social category. Hence, one's psychological well-being is contingent on the nature of that social category and is vulnerable to maladjustment if that social category is the object of prejudice and discrimination.

Uncharacteristically, Lewin did not, therefore, advise intervention to change the social situation. Rather, he urged a highly individualistic solution.

Psychology and the Process of Group Living (Selection 15)

Lewin displayed all the facets of his professional self in this article, his presidential address to the Society for the Study of Social Issues (which he had helped found). Here, he drew on his philosophy of science, basic psychological research, and action research to suggest to his colleagues the various ways they could contribute both to the victory of his adopted country in a war in which it had just become an active combatant and to the establishment of a stable and just peace afterward.

Reference

Lears, J. (1997). Man the machine [Review of the book *The one best way*]. *New Republic, 311,* 25–32.

12 _____

Socializing the Taylor System

I. Applied Psychology as a Mere Means and the Necessity for External Goal Specification

The following comments are not intended to address the totality of the questions of economic psychology in all of their utmost importance to society. They are not intended to explore the psychology of advertising, educational or medical psychology, such as the treatment of war casualties, nor are they intended to discuss the broad field of problems of applied psychology that are important for social welfare, such as the elimination of unsuitable persons from the jobs of locomotive engineer or chauffeur in the interest of public safety. Rather, I will confine myself to the question of how, from the standpoint of a just communal life, from the standpoint of socialism, the methods and goals of applied psychology should be regarded.

Applying psychology to work processes and to the allocation of individuals to occupations[1] initially means nothing more than that it is an aid to their general *rationalization*, as is the aim of other technical and social measures as well. It is a path to knowledge and control of the social world, toward an organized, deliberate shaping of material which up to now has grown wildly, and has, under the pressure of various circumstances, indeed inevitably developed, although not at all lawfully. Neither intrinsic destiny nor even chance have thus far been the decisive forces in the allocation of individuals to the different occupations, but rather, first of all, the individual's membership in particular economic classes; next, society's vocational ideology and the occupation's economic status; and only in third or fourth place, after chance, the individual's inclination on the one hand and the vocation's needs on the other. The employment of psychological methods means, under these circumstances, merely a decrease of chance, rationalization. It is not the task of applied psychology to decide in which *direction* such deliberate shaping should go; it can just as easily adapt to the social class structure as it can serve to break it. It is, like all tech-

---

Die Sozialisierung des Taylor systems, *Praktischer Sozialismus*, 1920, *4*, 3–36 (translated for this volume by Anja Spindler).

[1]Those unfamiliar with the application of psychology to vocational problems will find some references in Section VII of this paper.

niques, nothing but a *means*, a means which does not itself set new aims but is applicable to many kinds of even contrary aims.

Thus, before one can ask: What may psychology contribute so that that occupation is chosen that really "wants to" or "should" be chosen, so that work processes are shaped in a sensible and good way? The question must be answered according to what ultimate aims should the allocation of individuals be managed, and by what standard should improvements in work be evaluated. Vocational psychology can, as an *applied* science, only fulfill a task which it is *given* but cannot set a task for itself.

Regarding the *question of the goal*, an answer now appears to applied psychology as "self-evident" that seems to eliminate the need to set a particular purpose: Everyone chooses the occupation for which he or she is relatively best suited, and improving work should of course be oriented toward increasing output, that is, to increase productivity without simultaneously increasing work effort. The problem of vocational allocation in society appears to be no different from the one of vocational allocation within an industry. An industry needs a number of workers for its different departments. How should the available workers be distributed to the different departments?

With "unskilled" and apprentice workers, one considers the individual's physical strength: One assigns rougher work to stronger individuals, lighter work to the weaker ones. Selection thus takes place, insofar as the industry has a say in it, no doubt according to the principle of aptitude. As far as "skilled" work is concerned, allocation is on the whole prescribed by the respective worker's type of education. In reality, however, the allocation function is in this case only transposed; specifically, it is placed prior to and into the apprentices' period of training. It would be only consistent with and represent merely a refinement of imperfect selection methods if, in the recruitment of apprentices and workers, the psychological characteristics of an applicant are also taken into consideration alongside physical ones in assignment. In each part of the organization, it emerges repeatedly that certain individuals are particularly talented at different tasks and that talented unskilled workers soon excel over even skilled ones. Since it can be demonstrated that many of the "clumsy" or otherwise "untalented" workers could perform relatively better in a different position, the obvious necessity is to assign, with a better allocation of workers, "every person to the right place," that is, *the* place at which he or she performs better. This is required by the productivity of the entire industry as well as by the interest of the individual worker: In the position in which the worker performs better, he or she will earn more and will also feel more comfortable. The company's and the worker's interests therefore likewise encourage the introduction of vocational psychology's assistance; and particularly, the more the socialization of production progresses, the less likely becomes any conflict between the two interests regarding the question of improving work processes, specifically, increasing work *performance without* increasing work *effort*.

It is therefore not quite comprehensible and must in the first instance appear unfounded if, particularly from the socialist side, fundamental apprehensions about the application of the psychology of economics are raised repeatedly, objections which not only give voice to foregone socio-political conclusions, but which are directed at obvious abuses like the individual's exploitation in the interest of private capital and the excessive intensification of labor that actually constitutes continuous overexertion, with the consequence of premature aging. It is striking that a number of socialists go beyond the disapproval of such phenomena, which of course will always be uneconomical in terms of political economy, and attack fundamentally the use of applied psychology. There apparently exists the feeling that the application of psychology to labor and vocational choice would represent another step on the way toward the mechanization of life, toward excessive specialization, and toward a depersonalization of work. Although selecting individuals based purely on aptitude and work processes based on performance is undoubtedly economical by guaranteeing maximum productivity—largely by eliminating uneconomical job changes and training people to avoid redundant motions—it nevertheless also carries with it a general narrowing, contributes to an impoverishment of life for the individual.

Guiding everyone toward his or her special field without "detours" also takes away all detours and some richness and breadth. On this way toward "perfection," the human appears bound to become a machine. And not only does the goal of applying psychology apparently amount to the degradation of the human being, but so do the psychological methods of experimenting and interviewing. The notion prevails that human beings are valued only as "subjects," as material, as mere objects. The way in which human beings are regarded here, not as persons but as ciphers equivalent to machines, appears to harbor something distinctly capitalistic. The disposition to confront a form of *exploitation* is the main motive that makes not only "Taylorism" but also any application of psychology suspect to socialism.

It should be emphasized at this point that the demand for vocational selection of individuals based on aptitude and the improving work processes based on the principle of increasing productivity do not in reality stem from vocational psychology itself. For example, in order to accommodate as many of the unemployed in a company as possible, applied psychology could just as well opt for the goal of decreasing output. The seemingly "self-evident" contrary task definition contains in reality a stated goal that is dictated by highly particular interests.

II. Socializing Individual Abilities and Work Processes as a Requirement of Production

Furthermore, one must realize that those interests that establish the principles of aptitude and productivity do not emerge from the specific economic form of *capitalism*, but that it is the position of economic *production in general* which leads to these principles. Vocational allocation of individuals based on their aptitude and improving work processes in order to

increase productivity is merely a consequent elaboration, a technical refinement that is required in the interest of production as such, independent of the particular social form of production. The principle of allocation
based on aptitude is independent of whether the goal of the economy is
profit for private capital or production to satisfy the needs of the aggregate
of consumers, of whether the economic goal is profitability or productivity,
even if in each case very different occupations exist because of the different
problems inherent in the two economic arrangements. As soon as one generally takes the industry or economic production as given, the principle of
aptitude follows necessarily as *the* sensible Gestalt principle for the
person–job relationship and increasing productivity as the only principle
for improving work. Even in a pure communal economy, each industry and
department must have the propensity to seek *the* worker and *the* work
method that would accomplish the work that has to be done as best as
possible, meaning as economically as possible. From the perspective of
production, the "position" seeks its "person," and the allocation of workers
that the political economy inherently demands is therefore vocational allocation according to optimal suitability, no matter which form of economy
prevails.

The *socialist* form of economy especially requires individual vocational
choice according to his or her aptitude and, undoubtedly, the more emphatically, the more it is a genuine communal economy. Behind the demand for the socialization of industry stands *the socialization of labor*, and
along with the "ability to work," the demand for *socialization* of the individual's *talents and abilities*. For abilities and talents are after all the most
essential "means of production"; and their significance for economic stratification must inevitably emerge the stronger, the further the socialization
of the rest of the means of production progresses. The more the differences
in private ownership of the means of production disappear, through the
shift toward a communal economy, the more crass must appear the character of individual abilities as private property and must the possibility
emerge to exploit these personal "monopolies" in the individual interest
against the interest of the community. It is also true that if an individual
does not make use of his or her abilities and talents, the community can
be severely harmed, no less than by the use of individual abilities against
the communal interest.

Contained in the demand to convert the means of production into communal property is the fundamental requirement to expropriate the individual's "property" in terms of his or her abilities and talents. Free disposition over his or her talents and abilities is wrested away; a right of
the community to have a voice in deciding on their use is established.[2]

_____

[2]The idea that one's own abilities are not personal property, that is, that they should
not be subject merely to one's own personal discretion, is not only a socialist idea; monarchs
and power figures have always readily stressed that *all* personal abilities and power, including their own, should be considered the property of the people, which they are obliged
to use in the interest of the people, even contrary to their own inclinations. Just as much,
nationalism has always regarded it a self-evident duty of the individual to offer his or her

An analogous case is the right of the individual under communal production to shape the work process at his or her free discretion or convenience. The worker must use the work process that is prescribed in the interest of production, that is, a process with the highest possible output. The unpleasantness of an operation should therefore be considered only insofar as it directly in turn reduces its productivity; but the dissatisfaction of the worker, the *degradation* of a task, is itself not limited by the principle of communal production.

The community's interest in superior productivity requires therefore that the training and use of an individual's talents, particularly in occupational assignment and work processes, are not left to chance, the individual's descent, limitation, or discretion but are determined according to the best appropriate methods of science. Hence, controlled, practical psychological studies and surveys should currently certainly be called upon to determine vocational aptitude, and output should be increased by psychotechnical means. From the viewpoint of communal production, the job's sovereignty in selecting its individual is limited only by consideration of other production sites, that is, the condition of the "labor market." In the pure socialist communal production economy, the totality of available positions ultimately and unconditionally determines the vocational assignment of the individual members of the community, depending on their training as well as its application; and the only recognized criterion for vocational allocation is the "aptitude" of the individual in question for the job in question, and the only criterion for a work process, its output. Occupational choices must be made according to such aptitude, and work processes have to be shaped according to such output, if necessary, even contrary to the individual's or others' inclinations or wishes.

The degradation which can be perceived in the scientific assessment of aptitude of those choosing a vocation, their appraisal as material equivalent to any machine, should therefore not be regarded as a specifically "capitalistic" exploitation. The requirement to take up a vocation according to one's aptitude and to perform in it as best as possible, rather, is a requirement of production as such. If in the place of individual gain, common welfare becomes the goal of the production process, subordination to the demands of production thus loses part of its degradation but not at all the character of being used passively. What was exploitation under capitalism now appears sanctioned. The requirement particularly of *communal* production also *provides grounds* for the *force* of exclusive consideration of vocational aptitude, and no doubt in sharper form, the more radical the community's interest is pressed.

The demand for training and vocational choice according to the principle of pure aptitude, and hence the most vigorous use of all of applied psychology's methods, should therefore appear as a self-evident consequence of socialist thinking. Nevertheless, as mentioned, the employment of applied psychology for this purpose is severely challenged, particularly

life for the national community. Philosophers and moralists have demanded, instead of the community, control by objective values like art, science, and religion over these abilities.

by some of the socialist wing. Undoubtedly, this struggle signals partly a residue of the feeling that such improvements in production benefit primarily the entrepreneur; partly a bit of liberalism, that is, a desire for freedom in the sense of personal discretion; and finally also superstition about property where it resides most deeply: concerning *those* means of production that are felt most strongly to be "natural" private property with exclusive "disposal power," "one's own" talents and abilities.

III. Working and Occupation as Production and as Consumption

Along with these shortcomings and contradictions of socialism, there exists certainly a valid principle, even for the socialist, that denies "aptitude" its status as the exclusive criterion for vocational choice: It is the viewpoint of consumption.

Occupation as well as working confront the individual with two different faces.

On the one hand, working is effort, burden, exertion of energy. Whoever is not provided for by pensions or power or love must inevitably work to earn his or her living. Working is an indispensable prerequisite for life, yet it is not actually life itself. It is nothing but a means, a thing without independent life value that has weight only because it creates the possibility for life, and should be affirmed only if it creates it. As one does not live in order to eat but eats in order to live, one thus inevitably works in order to live and does not live in order to work. (Whoever would want to work for the sake of working is no better than one who lives in order to eat, a philistine or creature of habit.) Hence, work as little and as conveniently as possible! Therefore the most efficient organization of the work process! All progress in respect to working aims at easing work effort and increasing its output; its goals would be as much freedom as possible from the compulsion to work by reducing its duration and its importance relative to other aspects of life. It does not matter if working must become more monotonous and unvarying for this purpose as long as productivity remains unimpaired. All the incentives to work like this are only indirect, only for the economic advantages that working offers to the worker. It is a burden without its own value, nothing but a means.

On the other hand, the other face of working:

Working is indispensable to the human being in a completely different sense. Not because the necessities of life compel it, but because life without working is hollow and incomplete. Even when freed from the force of necessity, every human being who is not sick or old seeks work, some field of activity. This need to work, the flight from continual idleness, which, if working time is too brief, drives one toward working outside the job, does not depend on the mere habit of working but is based on the "life value" of working. It is the same "super-individual" quality of working that induces the worker to perform clean, solid, "good" work, even when less good work would not result in material or personal disadvantage. This capacity of work to endow each life with meaning and importance is somehow innate to any work, whether it is difficult or easy, varied or monotonous, as long as it does not generate senseless activity such as the meaningless piling of wood to and fro in prison yards. Of course, it is found in different tasks to very different degrees. Because working itself is life, one also wants to invest all one's life strength in it and be proficient at it. Therefore one wants working to be rich and broad, diversified, and not confining. As a result, there would be love for the product, delight at creating, vitality, and beauty. Working would not inhibit the opportunity for personal development but rather bring it to full flower. Progress in work processes therefore does not aim at the greatest possible attenuation of work time but at increasing work's life value, to make it richer and more humane. Progress creates the opportunity for work of any desired duration and intensity. For if work time could be limited to a minimum at the price of its impoverishment, it would still be a shame even for this slice of life. The requirement would remain to make even this minimum worth living. Should one, because of this requirement, lengthen the minimal work time again, even revoke time limits in general, even this would not necessarily be regarded as evil.

Working carries this dual face only if one approaches it from a particular standpoint: the workers' standpoint on their work, which will be denoted here as the standpoint of the *work consumer*.[3]

Production itself does not distinguish between these two kinds of working. Whether it concerns burdensome work or enjoyable work, production always measures work by the same super-individual standard of work performance. If it sometimes contrasts positive and negative incentives, the contrast is of making and destroying. From the perspective of production, however, evaluation remains consistently neutral and unaffected by the attitude of the individual worker toward his or her work. Only from the standpoint of the worker as a work consumer does the distinction between taxing and enjoyable work appear.

It is an essential realization on the path toward the enrichment and humanization of work that the degree of its power to provide meaning—that the life value of working—depends not only on the kind of work itself but is also based on a relationship between the specific work and the character of the human being who carries it out. Whereas production measures work by the "objective" standard of performance, which is independent of the personality of the individual working, the worker's individual characteristics of course play a role in the degree of pleasure in working, although this personal factor carries different weights in the different types of work.

The same dual face is displayed by the occupation. The concern here

---

[3]The concept of the work consumer should not be mistaken for the one of the performance consumer, the "consumer" in the general sense of the word in economics. In the socialist communal economy, the interest of the aggregate of performance consumers is synonymous with the interest in production.

is the occupation as a way of making a living by leading a working life that is only in part euphemistically called life—an occupation chosen at best on account of its utility, an occupation that has its own "morality," which means it stands detached from morality, just as working may be without dignity. It is the occupation with which the individual has no inner, personal relationship apart from the economic, one that is a milk cow to him or her. This is occupation in the sense of production. It has only negative value as "consumer goods" or is at best a matter of indifference.

In contrast stands the occupation as life's task, to which an individual is internally "called." It is the occupation to which human beings aspire even though the path is open to what would for them be economically or socially more advantageous occupations. It usually, but not necessarily, corresponds to the occupation to which the person concerned is best suited by his or her abilities, if one considers past performances as a measure of suitability. The genuine occupation of an individual is characterized by the fact that through it the person concerned experiences "fulfillment." It is essential for such a consumption occupation that it does not inhibit but promotes personal development, brings to flower all the powers of the human being concerned. Therefore, educator can be considered more of such an occupation than teacher, craftsman more than most types of factory workers. A great number of occupations, in the usual sense of the word and in particular the purely economically choice occupations, can therefore not at all or only in rare exceptions be considered a genuine human occupation. Similarly, the majority of people have by no means one particular occupation, in this sense, but can find their fulfillment in a whole series of different occupations; also, to many, an occupation in the usual sense of the word may not in any way offer essential fulfillment in their lives (here, I am disregarding vocations such as lay-about, Don Juan, etc.). Moreover, regarding occupation there is, in any case, besides its evaluation as a "production job," the question of its positive or negative incentives as a "consumption vocation." As with work processes, consumption value does not depend exclusively on the occupation itself but also on the relationship between the individual and his or her occupation.

IV. Producer and Consumer Capitalism in Working and Occupation, and the Demand for Socialist Reconciliation

Thus, there is in fact a principle, which should be acknowledged from the standpoint of socialism as well, that limits the demand for production in relation to working and occupation. The interests of production should be set against those of consumption. Only a genuine reconciliation of both, an avoidance of both single-minded production as well as consumer capitalism, constitutes socialism.

Now, what do the producers' and consumers' interests require, at what points do they coincide, and where are they opposed?

The interest of production, which in a communal economy is analogous with that of the aggregate of consumers of the products, can be unequivocally and generally stated: With regard to the labor market, it requires the allocation of individuals to occupations according to their optimal aptitude, and the configuration of work according to the principle of profitability. The work *consumer's* interests are determined, on the one hand, by the fact that for him or her, working constitutes in any case only a part of life whose domain should somehow be kept from encroaching on recreation and other aspects of life, whereas from the point of view of production, working is the essence of all productive activities and should therefore be considered exclusively. Furthermore, the type of work is decisive for the worker. From the perspective of production, every productive activity is equally work, to be measured by the same standard of economic performance. Consumption, however, distinguishes two different classes of work activity: work with a negative and with a positive consumption value—the unpleasant, reluctant work, "work" in the stricter sense—and operations that are performed with pleasure and love, those enjoyable activities that are not really "working." In between lies the entire range of work activity that offers hardship and enjoyment in different combinations.

Regarding unpleasant work activity, the work consumers' interest demands extensive reconfiguration or reduction of work time to a minimum; regarding "enjoyable work," however, the demand is for unlimited work time. Regarding their occupation, the work consumer interest demands: avoidance of every constraint. Everybody chooses and changes occupations according to his or her inner calling, freed from the force of necessity.

Thus, the interests of production and consumption undoubtedly run, in many respects, in opposite directions. Their ideal reconciliation from the standpoint of socialism would be easier if all unpleasant work could be transformed completely into work with its life value, without neglecting production interests, and if furthermore every human being possessed an inner calling for an occupation, whose validity one could not dispute, even from the standpoint of production itself. But since this cannot be achieved at all or at least only with an endless process, thus, since for the present one has to assume the existence of unpleasant work, on the one hand, and the vocations of lay-about and bon vivant, on the other hand, one is dependent on compromise solutions. There are several paths to such solutions (which are "compromises" only from the standpoint of pure production or consumption, but they do not have the character of compromise from the standpoint of socialism, since it is this very position that requires a just reconciliation of both standpoints).

One can either demand that everybody *uniformly* takes on a certain quantum of this unpleasant work, or one can try to create compensations for the less pleasant work by providing more leisure time or in other ways. Such attempts to reconcile the opposing interests of production and consumption in the work process and in an occupation will not occupy us further here. Up for discussion is only the question of whether *applied psychology* should be enlisted for improving work and for improving the allocation of individuals to occupations and how it should be used (i.e., how the interests of production and consumption should be reconciled through the use of psychotechnical methods).

V. The Socialist Reconciliation in Applying Psychology to Work Methods

A) The Common Interests of Consumption and Production

First of all, it should be noted that in very many cases concerning psychotechnical improvement in *work processes*, conflict does not exist between the interests of production and consumption. If the locksmith is instructed to replace his files twice as often as he is accustomed to, if pieces are counted in batches of 50 instead of batches of 100, if a switchboard is more clearly configured, if a handle is attached and shaped more manageably, if a crude task is assigned to the foot instead of the hand, such improvements do make work both more economical and more pleasant. In all those cases where unpleasant or, at least from the standpoint of consumption, unattractive work is shortened without requiring more intense effort by the simple avoidance of superfluous motion, production and consumption interests equally require psychotechnical rationalization. Also, both interests run parallel in the great number of cases that involve facilitation of physically strenuous work. Stubborn adherence to outdated methods of work, which too often unduly favor methods that can be quickly learned over methods that are better but more difficult to learn, should on no account be justified. It is not even a valid objection that all improvements of this kind benefit only, or at least mostly, management and not the worker or that such an improvement always results in some economic damage to the worker, be it direct, by depressing wages, or be it indirect, by making fellow workers redundant and thus increasing the number of unemployed; for this is not an argument against psychotechnical improvements in particular but a question that arises with every improvement in the work process, for example, with each new machine, and which should therefore by all means be solved, whether psychotechnique is introduced or not. Settling the question of how to proceed regarding improvements in the management of production must in any case be pursued generally, and a general solution will always readily include psychotechnical improvements.

In all those cases where psychotechnique can configure a work process to be both more pleasant and more economical, its application should be demanded immediately. Such a "two-sided" improvement is now possible for most tasks. The significance of this for the elevation of all of economic *and* cultural life is so fundamental that this knowledge obviously entails the unconditional demand for the most intensive, broadly based study of all work processes to find such dual improvements, as well as for rapid general implementation of the improvements found. In the implementation of all such improvements in work processes, sufficient control of production, on the one hand, and of the work consumers, on the other hand, should be required so that, in fact, only those improvements are introduced that make the work more economical as well as more pleasant. Before going into the possibilities of such control, the question should be briefly discussed, To what extent should one limit oneself to the introduction of such *dual* improvements?

B) Protecting the Consumption Interests of the Operators

It happens that a certain improvement in work methods indeed constitutes economic improvement but at the same time erodes the life value of working. Here, one should be mindful primarily of that arrangement that is usually denoted with the catchword "Taylorism." This refers to relentless exploitation of the individual in the service of production, with the consequence of rapid aging; setting the barely achievable performance level as the normal level; whipping the workers to the most intense effort by all available means; degradation of work by driving it to the most extreme division of labor without regard for the worker's psyche, in short, an "expenditure" of the worker in the service of production according to calculations of wear and tear and amortization that are applied to machines.

In all those cases where the erosion of labor's consumption value goes as far as to bring with it, for example, direct, medically detectable bodily harm to the worker through premature aging, such a work process should certainly be abandoned on the grounds of human welfare. Such an "improvement" should be regarded as a throwback, if only from a purely political *economic* perspective—as exploitation, advantageous at most from the standpoint of the individual entrepreneur. That such improvements in work that are detrimental in terms of political *economy* are not acceptable is after all sociopolitically self-evident. Nevertheless, it remains conceivable perhaps that, from the viewpoint of the production *community*, an "exploitation," an "expenditure" of human beings, might somehow still be economical. In most such instances, one should point to the principle that the human being does not exist for production but production for the human being. Taylorism, in the meaning indicated, is a method which cannot be justified socialistically, even if a community interested in high production figures takes the place of the individual entrepreneur, because an arrangement of this kind would have to be rated as a one-sided exaggeration of the interests of the consumers of labor, thus as consumer capitalism.[4]

From the standpoint of socialism, one must demand, in the interest of the work consumers, that those economic improvements be abandoned which, although they do not result in medically detectable harm, substantially reduce the consumption value of work.

The number of these cases is, by the way, limited by the fact that a decrease in labor's consumption value is accompanied by a decrease in

---

[4]See Korsch, K. (1919). Was ist Sozialisierung? (What is socialism?) *Sozialistich Schriftenreihe, Vol. 1.* Hannover: Verlag Freies Deutschland.

work satisfaction. As applied psychology has known for a long time, work satisfaction is in turn a very essential factor in the profitability of work; hence such improvements often only amount to apparent improvements and should certainly be avoided for the sake of production.

Nevertheless, there doubtlessly remain cases where an actual improvement in production coincides with actual damage to the consumption value of labor.

It has already been remarked at the beginning that the type of application which is denoted as Taylorism is not necessarily characteristic of the psychotechnical management of industry. Applied psychology could just as well put itself one-sidedly into the service of the humanization of labor, consider only beauty and convenience, and completely disregard the profitability of work. It is by nature merely a method that could serve *any* goal in changing work processes. All that matters is to assign it the correct task and to exert control over whether it indeed pursues this task. It is therefore necessary to provide opportunities for the consumers of work to protect their interests at the introduction of psychotechnical changes in work. In whatever way it is done, one may determine in detail the line between acceptable methods of work and those that should be rejected, despite their productivity, on the basis of their negative consumption value—if one wants to introduce only those work changes which simultaneously yield higher profitability and a higher consumption value, or if one wants also to permit those work changes whose increased unpleasantness, caused by increased production, is compensated by a reduction in working time. In any case, the work consumer must in some form be given a voice in whether a change of work processes should be introduced or not. The existing council rules already designate to work councils the right to take part in decisions on work processes. A specific institution expressly for cases of psychotechnical changes in operations that evade the political-economic protection of work consumers' interests—protection which should be required generally—seems therefore unnecessary, even more so because even without such protections, psychological changes in processes cannot be carried out by going over the workers' heads or even against their will.

Certainly, *examining* which work process is the more economical cannot, in the majority of cases, be done in the remote laboratory with just any subject but must take place in the factory itself with the skilled workers concerned. Psychologists in Germany who, by the way, have for sociopolitical reasons always greeted Taylorism with suspicion, have begun to realize that a fruitful investigation of the work process needs the support, even direct *cooperation* of the workers. As is generally the case in psychological experiments, one of the "subject's" essential tasks here is to be a "self-observer," that is, to be able to provide information on the more detailed characteristics of his or her work process under particular experimental conditions. Therefore the worker need not fear being abused as a guinea pig in a harmful or degrading way. Whoever has been a subject once will confirm that these studies usually involve not uninteresting procedures from which one can sometimes learn something for one's personal method of work.

The fact that management, the worker, and the psychologist, as a rule, have to work together if psychological studies are to turn out fruitfully, and the absolute necessity for publicity about such investigations in connection with the worker's legal right to take part in proposing work processes do, in my opinion, sufficiently ensure the protection of the work consumers' interest in this matter.

Enough here on the cases of economical—that is, in the interest of productivity—psychotechnical improvements in work and guarding against concomitant damage to the work consumers' interests.

C) Protecting the Interests of Performance Consumers in Production

On the other side stand those cases of psychotechnical improvements in work that indeed organize work to be more pleasant but also hurt productivity. I have already mentioned that psychotechnique could just as well be used in the service of increasing work's consumption value as its production value. The demand of socialist justice, in the work consumers' interest, for unlimited joy, culture, and life-enhancing tasks of transcendent significance—this demand has both profound and extensive implications because it encompasses both the most enduring and the most important domain of life: human labor; and because it could prompt direct intervention where human misery at labor is the greatest.

Actually, one could submit this task to technology, generally. But more than any other branch, psychological technology, which is most relevant to mental factors, appears capable of substantially improving labor's consumption value. Where workers are particularly dissatisfied with their operations, one can examine with which features of the work the dissatisfaction is chiefly linked. Certainly, wages and physical exertion play a very essential role. But still they do not necessarily constitute the only decisive factors, to which they are elevated by that fanciful theory of labor which supposes itself to be particularly close to practical life and believes that it comes closer to reality the more "materialistically" it comports itself. Theories of this kind, as much superficial as external, can by no means do justice to different kinds of work: Seemingly monotonous tasks often are not monotonous at all to the worker concerned, and, vice versa, seemingly varied ones are extremely boring. Only when a close examination of the mental factors involved in the different tasks identifies in detail the concrete operations and goals that enhance labor's life value will such problems be solved, whether directly by psychological means or by general technical improvements.

One could demand that first of all, *particularly unpleasant* tasks should be examined in order to enhance their consumption value, and if the opportunity arises, the improvements developed should be introduced generally, like workers' safety devices, even if they added a certain economic burden to production. One should be permitted to demand at least that all of those improvements in consumption should be introduced which do not impose direct damage on production. One should not assume that workers of their own accord do everything possible in this direction. For aside from other limitations, workers' freedom of movement here is dependent on factors which for *them* are "given," factors which in themselves are quite alterable, as, for example, tools, but are factors currently unilaterally governed by production and therefore take the worker as consumer into consideration, at most, incidentally. Furthermore, from a scientific—that is, a systematic—investigation that specifically targets this question, one may expect far more, at the least by way of summarization and utilization for the general public, than from the accidental discoveries of the individual that are made only incidentally. At the same time, one may hope that the scientific, especially the psychological, investigation of work processes would sometimes demonstrate ways to increase the consumption value of labor that would allow doing justice to the work consumers' interests without harming the interests of production, as can be the case in a simple reduction in working time.

Nevertheless, from the standpoint of socialism, it would be unreasonable to demand that such improvements in work should be introduced without *any* consideration for production, that is, for the interests of the fellow members of the community, the "consumers" in the usual sense of the word, who here are called performance consumers in contrast to the work consumer. It is to the benefit of production capitalism based on the overlap of operators and work consumers to leave such uneconomical relief to the discretion of the individual industry or its branch. From the standpoint of socialism, the introduction of such operational changes has to take into consideration the particular situation in the totality of the other occupations. As, in the opposite case, the work consumer must be able to protect his or her interests, the performance consumer must take part in decisions about eroding the economic value of work for the purpose of increasing its consumption value, whether participation be direct or by governmental mediation.

Here, too, we are dealing with a question of a general economic nature, which, for example, plays a role in every wage calculation and which hence should at any rate be resolved, no matter whether one aims at a systematic enhancement of working life by psychological means or not.

The route toward increasing consumption value by way of improving the psychological conditions of work would in any case allow, to a much greater extent than a simple cut in work time, a concomitant consideration of its profitability, resulting, in a given economic situation, in a much more extensive enhancement of consumption value. It would moreover achieve what a mere reduction in work time never promotes, the reconfiguration of the inner value of work itself. Although even this cannot readily change every unpleasant job into a desirable one, it can in very many cases increase its level of pleasantness, its consumption value, to a significant, even decisive extent.

Accordingly, with regard to the question of using applied psychology for the improvement of *work processes*, it should be noted in summary:

1. Proposed work processes must be unobjectionable from the standpoint of the common economy. Improvement should thus aim at productivity (and not at profitability as such) and should protect the interest of human resources and of the people's vitality (social hygiene).

2. Applied psychology should not place itself one-sidedly in the service of production, even though in a socialist community the interests of production are synonymous with those of the aggregate of performance consumers. Rather, it should also recognize the elevation of work's consumption value as an independent, equally privileged task in the interest of workers as work consumers.

3. There is a great number of cases where both interests run parallel, hence, where greater profitability coincides with the greater pleasantness of work.

4. Considering the amount of success that should be achieved according to previous experiences (there have been increases in productivity of 50% and more), the investigation of work by means of applied psychology and the introduction of validated improvements should therefore be most vigorously implemented in the twofold interest of the community.

5. In order, on the one hand, to protect the life value of work from diminution and, on the other, from a decline in profitability, work consumers as well as performance consumers must have a guaranteed right to take part in decisions about the introduction of changes in work methods. Currently, there is hardly a need for special institutions that serve this purpose exclusively. For the time being, it is sufficient if the interested parties, above all the worker councils, become aware of the importance of this question.

6. The problems of relative wage reduction and unemployment due to psychotechnical improvements in work are general problems of social policy, which arise in the exact same way from other industrial improvements and can be resolved only by integration with them.

VI. The Socialist Reconciliation of the Application of Psychology to Vocational Allocation

From the standpoint of socialism, the assistance of applied psychology should be sought to achieve a reconciliation of production and consumption interests by influencing *occupational choice* as well as work processes.

Whereas psychological modification of work processes involves an operational problem, in the occupational question we are dealing essentially with a problem of distribution.

As noted, the interest of *production* clearly aims at vocational assign-

ment of individuals on the basis of their aptitude for maximal performance, that is, at an allocation in line with the respective person's ability
to attain in the occupation what for him or her is the optimum of economically satisfying work, taking into consideration the entire labor market.
This principle is not less valid even when one extends the concept of production beyond economic production. Considering the paramount significance of economic factors in contemporary social structure, I will confine
myself in the following to economic production. Production limits the number of occupations that it recognizes as such to activities that produce
economically, in the sense of a sufficient amount of value-added productivity. Because from the viewpoint of production, individual "abilities" are
a means of production just like any other means for accomplishing tasks,
production, as far as it involves a production *community*, feels justified in
ignoring the individual's preferences and hence justified in principle to
ensure, by economic or other means of coercion, the use of individual abilities in the service of the community.

The interest of work *consumption*, on the other hand, aims at vocational allocation in line with inner calling, that is, at perhaps liberation
from every occupation in the sense of productivity. For occupations in the
sense of consumption also include the unprofitable occupations of artist
and scientist, of parent, and even the lay-about. The consumers' interests
essentially demand an equality of these occupations with productive occupations, even in an economic respect. For freedom of occupational choice
exists only where the necessities of life do not force one to choose a profitable occupation.

No doubt there exists at present a deep current within the proletariat
to emphasize the interests of work and vocational consumption more
strongly than those of production. Consistent with this, the right of the
individual, even the unemployed, to subsistence is acknowledged through
unemployment benefits; furthermore, a certain adjustment in the consumption value of the various profitable vocations is being prepared based
on the principle that for particularly strenuous occupations, such as the
miner, compensation should be arranged, with greater leisure time or
higher wages. The issue at hand here is not to examine how, in regard to
vocational allocation, a socialistically just general reconciliation of the interests of consumption and production might be achieved; rather, this
question is discussed only insofar as it involves the participation of applied
psychology.

When one distinguishes the positive force to choose a particular occupation from the negative force of exclusion from a particular occupation,
the present relationship between force and freedom in vocational choice is
so situated that, *strictly legally*, vocational choice remains free of any *positive* force—formally, no one is forced into a particular occupation by society, we have no "castes"—and the individual's free discretion is limited
negatively only by qualifying examinations for certain occupations. *Actually*, however, going far beyond this, freedom of vocational choice is extremely limited for the vast majority of individuals.

First of all, the necessities of life force all those who are not provided for by inheritance or because of some other dominating social position to limit their choice to profitable occupations in the sense of production. This pressure to choose a profitable occupation is in general stronger and applies to a greater degree to women, juveniles, and the elderly, the worse the economic condition of their particular family. But even in economically better-off strata, the social and subjective reality of the idea of the necessities of life and of being provided for, on the one hand, and on the other, the social disrespect for the lay-about and for the majority of the "consumption vocations," which are not utilitarian, results in an, albeit moderated, force in this direction. Development tends in this respect to limit even further the number of the consumption occupations that are not disparaged, such as the part-time *au pair*, or to suspend the earlier social encouragement of such occupations.

Beyond this pressure for a utilitarian occupation, generally, there is in reality a positive force on the individual toward a particular *group* of occupations, consistent with the individual's membership in a particular social class. This social differentiation of occupations is generally correlated with their economic advantage for the individual concerned. Again, the positive force is the stronger, the realm of choice the smaller, the worse the condition of the social class to which those choosing an occupation belong.

The economic opportunity for personal *training* in a particular occupation thus plays a crucial role. The fact that training is predominantly an economic monopoly immediately precludes an entire set of occupations for the vast majority of people, regardless of individual aptitude and inclination. For members of economically better-situated classes, the number of socially acceptable occupations is not necessarily larger under all circumstances; but this limitation is experienced subjectively as less of a constraint because these occupations, relative to inferior occupations, are also the ones which are better paid or at least economically more promising, owing to opportunities for promotion; moreover, because they have, apart from their economic advantage, greater consumption value, because they are thus usually more pleasant, and finally because the individual, as a result of the prevailing occupational ideology, is inclined to choose a "superior" occupation even if, taking account of aptitude and inner calling, the consumption value of an "inferior" vocation would actually be greater for him or her.[5]

Since the introduction of the freedom to practice a trade, individual vocational choice is indeed, in a formal sense, free of any positive force.

---

[5] The effect of social ideology about vocation in all strata is the greater since, in the majority of cases, the one choosing a vocation knows nothing about potential occupations from direct experience and is therefore inevitably influenced very strongly by any ideologies. Because the social ideology of vocation conceals the true consumption value of an occupation for a particular individual through the occupation's social standing and economic remuneration, social pressure in vocational choice is felt as such only by very few individuals in the economically better-off strata. The lack of the subjective feeling of pressure should not, however, mask the fact that here, too, social pressure in principle opposes the individual's genuine consumption interest in vocational choice consistent with inner calling.

Factually, though, for the vast majority of individuals there exists an economic or other social force that in all social strata runs counter to vocational allocation of individuals consistent with their inclinations and inner calling, hence counter to individuals' actual consumption interest; and its effect is the stronger, the worse off the social class to which the individual concerned belongs.

The positive force to vocational choice is opposed by the *negative* force that originates in the occupational position through the selection of applicants by means of certain entrance conditions that the individual must satisfy. This selection by the occupation is conducted mainly in the service of production and accordingly is guided by aptitude for maximal performance, generally by employing some tests. This principle of selection based on the interests of production is currently decisively violated by the actual monopolies of education and training that prevail as a result of the economic class structure. Contrary to the interests of production, in the sense of communal production, selection for a large number of vocations is actually based, primarily, not on the aptitude of the applicant but on the parents' economic situation, while the occupation itself has to rely on *post*-selection training to satisfy its requirements.

It is known that selection is further distorted in that entrance examinations generally place too much weight on knowledge and too little on actual abilities.

Furthermore, for the majority of vocations, no *preliminary* selection by aptitude takes place at all. As far as individual aptitude is concerned, whether someone becomes a locksmith or carpenter, steelworker or glazier is mostly left to chance. And yet, in the inferior occupations no less obvious than in the superior ones, not only does the level of talent vary among individuals, but, more important, so does the bent of talent that makes an individual suitable for one occupation and unsuitable for another. In the majority of occupations, selection of suitable individuals currently occurs only when those who are unfit lose their jobs as a result of poor performance, hence through a process that is as much inefficient in the sense of production as it is inappropriate for the economic interest of the vocation consumer and his or her need for inner gratification.

The current social means of vocational allocation can therefore on the whole be characterized as follows: Assignment to the various productive occupations is divided according to their economic status; differentially directed to certain social strata of individuals among whom, in a small number of occupations, post hoc selection is made often by inadequate means; while for the majority of occupations, selection is left completely to chance. In the vast majority of cases, individuals for their part are faced with the impossibility of choosing an occupation consistent with their inner calling. Beyond the pressure to take up a profitable vocation, they are, in general, extremely limited in their choice of a vocation that is suitable to them by the social situation of their class.

Allocation of individuals to particular occupational groups thus occurs mainly on the basis of factors which consider neither inclination nor aptitude. Above all, the assignment of an individual to a specific occupation *at the beginning* of employment is, with few exceptions, in a thoroughly chaotic, disorganized state.

To counter this situation, the interest of production, in the sense of a socialist communal economy, unequivocally aims at promoting aptitude as the sole principle of allocation. Therefore, it has to oppose (1) vocational selection based on the individual's membership in a particular economic class and (2) the power of mere chance in determining assignment, in favor of a useful design for determining an individual's aptitude.

Applied psychology is indispensable for accomplishing the second task. First of all, it has to determine which abilities are necessary for the different occupations and their subtypes, since the person who works in the job usually cannot answer this question. It should group occupations according to their requisite abilities into psychologically defined occupational categories, which usually requires completely different distinctions from economic definitions. Furthermore, and definitely in the province of applied psychology, means should be created that permit the determination of the respective individual's vocational aptitude, if possible, before beginning employment itself. Finally, an organization should be created that ensures optimal allocation of individuals based on their aptitude and takes into account the particular situation of the labor market. Such allocation is partly the task of the school, in the broadest sense of the word, and partly the task of the work sites, especially at present, since the school does not yet function adequately in this respect.

The creation of special precautions against vocational allocation that is in the interest of the production community in order to protect the interests of vocational consumers appears unnecessary for the time being. Although one can conceive of a case in which an individual's aptitude and inner calling do not coincide, such a case very seldom occurs, however, as long as one actually applies, as a criterion for the interest of the vocational consumer, the individual's *general* need for choice consistent with an inner calling rather than the opportunity of the few to exploit social conditions in order to gain especially favorable economic advantage.

In the vast majority of cases, assignment of individuals based on their aptitude leads at the same time to greater satisfaction and improvement in the individual's economic situation. Even regarding the question of change in occupation, where productivity seems to require that the number of changes be kept as low as possible, while the consumption interest of a number of individuals encourages a more than infrequent change in the type of occupation, these interests conflict only in part. For occupational shifts of this kind are not always entirely inefficient in the sense of productivity, as long as the occupations involved are only economically different but presuppose the same individual skills.

The requirement of production for optimum economic performance and the need of consumption for an occupation as worthy of living as possible thus come into conflict so rarely that *assignment of individuals based solely on their aptitude is not only in the interest of production but, in contrast with the distortion of vocational allocation by economic or social forces, it would also have an effect today like a tremendous liberation of*

*the human drive to choose one's own occupation according to an inner call-
ing and for the potential of inner gratification.*

Therefore, the interests of production and consumption currently run
in the same direction with regard to occupational allocation. Allocation
based on aptitude would increase overall output greatly, first by limiting
the frequently uneconomical effects of chance and by deliberately utilizing
the fact of varying bents of talent; second, by eliminating the inadequate
social sorting, primarily in the so-called superior occupations that, as a
result of economic class monopoly of the high schools, rely on about 5% of
the population.[6] Such occupational allocation would at the same time
mean a crucial, real cultural improvement in living arrangements for the
vast majority, even in the economically better-off classes.

Applied psychology can provide very essential, in part, indispensable
means for such an allocation. One should be aware, though, that even with
all the importance accorded already to the utilization of psychological procedures for measuring vocational aptitude, its effect must remain essentially limited as long as no change occurs in the social *ideology* of vocation
and its economic consequences. As long as it is more honorable to be a bad
officer, scholar, or merchant than a good laborer, that is, as long as social
approbation focuses more on affiliation with a particular occupation than
on performance in it, then every positive and negative selection factor will
remain insufficient, because the individual's "natural" inclination for a
particular occupation will inevitably be distorted by the social status of
the occupation.

The interest of production in finding the most suitable human being
for each position, as well as the interest of the individual in finding the
vocation that corresponds to his or her inner calling, therefore require an
essentially equal social evaluation of all occupations.[7]

Social discrimination among occupations should take into account primarily their different consumption values by creating some compensation
for those cases with particularly pronounced negative values. In today's
bourgeois economic structure, such a change in vocational ideology is, in
turn, dependent essentially on the wages paid for working at the different
occupations, hence on economic calculations of a general nature, which lie
outside the scope of the questions of social organization that are considered by applied psychology.

---

[6] Before the war, there were ten million primary school children in Germany compared
with about half a million in high schools.

[7] Differences between occupations themselves are also highly conceivable, and particularly intrinsic value differences should be commonly acknowledged, for example, evaluation based on the degree to which an occupation serves the culture. But even besides the
fact that it is questionable whether such an evaluation can justifiably be applied to the
entire "occupation" as a social fact and not just to the quality of its realization by a particular
individual, an evaluation of this kind would in any case not lend support to the *current*
standard and would no less strictly require a change in the prevailing, specifically bourgeois
ideology of vocations, even though the ideology extends far beyond bourgeois circles. At least
as matters stand today, it should be required that all occupations basically should be regarded from the perspective of production as equally privileged.

With respect to the question of employing applied psychology for vocational allocation, it can be noted:

1. Vocational allocation of members of the community should be guided by the principles of aptitude and inner calling.
2. Production's interest in allocation based on aptitude, and individuals' interest in an occupation consistent with an inner calling and opportunities for personal development run mostly in the same direction today.
3. Concerning the decisive significance of the prevailing economic and social impact of occupation by way of determining the individual's class, the issue at hand is therefore above all to mandate the strict application of the principle of selection by aptitude in the allocation of occupations.
4. An indispensable aid in this matter is vocational psychology.
5. A prerequisite for the unimpeded effect of all the positive and negative means of selection in vocational allocation consists in the elimination of the prevailing vocational ideology and its ranking of occupations based on social classes.

Summary

Regarding the position of socialism, the idea of a just community life, the expressed aims of vocational psychology, as well as their significance for the improvement of work methods and vocational allocation, it can be generally concluded:

Economic psychology as an applied science is a means that has no goal of its own and can thus be put in the service of different purposes. The socialist society needs its services and specifically requires it to work on two tasks: (1) on increasing *the productivity* of working and of occupations and (2) on increasing their *consumption value* for the worker. From the standpoint of socialism, both tasks stand equally privileged.

That this analysis deals perhaps in greater detail with the idea of increasing consumption value as an independent goal of psychology than would seem appropriate for an equal emphasis on the interests of production and consumption is related to the fact that we are dealing here to a greater extent with new territory. For, in the task of increasing production by psychological means, the task at hand is, after all, only to shift the goal, replacing the interests of private economy with those of communal economy; that is, a step that is already anticipated, particularly in Germany, by the emphasis on aggregate aspects of the economy in contrast to private economic interests. With regard to the work consumer, however, the issue at hand is to move beyond merely indirect consideration of the consumption value of labor, given so far mainly with the aim of protecting the people's vitality and the workers' safety. Increasing the consumption value of work itself must be recognized as an independent goal of psychotechnique. Economic psychology should be freed entirely of its one-sided emphasis on the interests of production and be directed toward an equally intensive consideration of work and vocational consumption.

Nevertheless, it should not be overlooked that not less than this transition from sociopolitical to socialist thinking, the transition from the profitability principle to the productivity principle also constitutes an essential and practically meaningful leap. Frequently, and in fact particularly often in the question of vocational allocation, it is of utmost importance to respect the viewpoint of production pure and simple and to emphasize the rights of the community as a production community. The goal of productivity therefore should be protected from faulty attitudes and emphasis given to the interest of the common economy in suspending the prevailing vocational ideology, which ranks occupations based on social classes.

With regard to the differentiation between production and consumption interests, it has emerged that: There are many improvements of work methods that are in the interest of both. For now, in the current legal and actual situation, protection against an unjust preference for either interest does not seem to require special institutions, since both interests are legitimized in the regulations implementing general economic policy.

Regarding vocational allocation, ensuring the communal interest in production does not lead, in the vast majority of cases, to the suppression of individual interests, but, rather, in comparison with the current situation, would constitute at the same time tremendous progress toward *autonomy of vocational choice*, that is, its liberation from social pressure.

VII. On the Organization of Psychological Improvement of Work Processes and Occupational Allocation, and on the Current Status of Applied Psychology

Among psychological methods for determining individuals' vocational aptitudes, the following should be noted: (1) systematic and practical psychological studies. Here, a number of tasks are presented to the individuals concerned, so-called tests, that are judged typical of the requirements of the respective occupations. Based on the objective evidence of the applicants' responses, their quality and duration, as well as on simultaneous observation of the applicant, his or her degree of aptitude is determined so that it can be compared numerically with the aptitude of other persons with a certain precision.

In addition to these observations, there exists (2) a method for determining aptitude with the help of psychological *questionnaires*. Every year, for example, teachers should complete a questionnaire on the strength and direction of each of their children's specific talents. Thus, one obtains a series of assessments from several persons and across several years, and can gain from their totality an image of each individual's abilities, for example, for the purpose of vocational counseling after graduation.

While observation provides a current cross-section of abilities, the questionnaire reveals general development. The systematic observation can better assess "abilities" in a narrower sense: manual dexterity; the quality of vision and hearing; the ability to judge distances, thickness, and other dimensions or to notice other specific differences between objects; intelligence; the type of concentration; nervousness; consistency of work; short-term stamina; etc. The questionnaire, on the other hand, permits to a greater extent the assessment of the individual's "characterological dispositions"; his or her industriousness, tidiness, honesty, inclination and ability to lead others or to be led, persistence in carrying out decisions, suggestibility, etc. Hence, both methods should be used in tandem, if possible, because they complement each other and also compensate for error due to a single source.

The methods of psychological vocational counseling and industrial development will not be dealt with here in greater detail. Only a few points on their present status and the question of their organization that are essential for their application will be mentioned.

Applied psychology still stands at the beginning of its task on both the matter of vocational counseling as well as of improving work. Therefore one should not harbor exaggerated hopes for the scope of what can be achieved immediately. Considering the intrusive significance that decisions made on the basis of psychological tests have for the particular individual as well as for the community, one should in each case proceed with the greatest caution and apply only carefully "calibrated" psychological instruments, that is, those which have been shown to be accurate through comprehensive comparison with work experiences. Psychological methods for the study of occupations and work processes and for expanding ways to make and test improvements have, on the other hand, developed sufficiently to permit, with the prospect of relatively quick success, comprehensive, systematic investigation covering a great number of occupations and work processes. It is in the interest of the political economy that investigations of this kind are not left only to the initiative and inclination of independent investigators or industries but rather come under the controlling influence of central institutions in order to avoid unnecessarily fragmented effort.

No doubt, valid psychological study of occupations and work processes will often have to take place on the spot, hence, not in some psychological laboratory, where genuine psychological similarity of circumstances would have to be proven every time anew, but at the work site itself—so for industrial work, in the factory. It is necessary that the specific industry, both as a work site as well as the aggregate of those who work in it, be made closely involved in the psychological studies. Only in this way can one count on sufficient cooperation from the members of the industry and at the same time guarantee their protection from abusive exploitation.[8] On the other hand, it is not permissible to limit validated improvements in work and aptitude tests to the one company. The general public has a right to the universal introduction of such improvements in work, whether they increase productivity or consumption value. Therefore, should com-

---

[8] Under certain circumstances, groups of companies may be combined that would have to share the relatively low costs of investigation and implementation.

panies be short-sighted enough to reject such improvements, the community should try to effect their introduction. As for vocational counseling, a fruitful arrangement is ultimately hardly feasible without general access to psychological analyses of occupations and the creation of a central office. Such a central office would have to ensure systematic review and scientific control of results and prohibit their exploitation, as well as any dilettantism, which in this particular domain could easily become dangerous. Furthermore, it would have the essential task of adjusting psychological selection of occupations to the particular condition of the labor market.

Psychological aptitude tests do not distinguish simply between two categories, between individuals who are suited and unsuited for the occupation; rather, they assign the individual to a particular place on, for example, a hundred-point, normally distributed scale, depending on his or her degree of aptitude. The greater the supply of labor in comparison to the demand for a particular position, the higher the individual aptitude score required for acceptance, as long as open positions are not left vacant. The central office would now have the responsibility of regulating the labor market by determining different standards of minimal degrees of aptitude for the separate occupations, depending on the economic situation. When there are more job openings in an occupation, the minimum aptitude score required for it would have to be lowered and, conversely, for occupations with fewer openings, the score would have to be raised. In this way, a sensible and rapidly effective mechanism could be readied for adjusting the labor market to minor changes in the employment situation as well as to long-term upheavals. This would be both the most economically sound way to regulate occupational allocation and to fight unnecessary unemployment, as well as one that is most satisfying for the work consumer.[9]

The organization of vocational psychology must therefore, on the one hand, consider broad decentralization of both research and testing in the various occupations. This should encourage the cooperation of the companies and the work consumers, protect the work consumers from exploitation, and grant the companies the opportunity to reject applicants or assign them within each industry. On the other hand, tight central management is necessary: a central office that would oversee the scientific aspects of the research, organize its findings, and assess them scientifically. The composition of this central office would have to prevent bias in favor of production or consumption interests. In regard to administrative-technical matters, it would have to ensure the general introduction of validated improvements and to regulate the labor market by determining the respective minimal aptitude for the different occupations.

---

[9]This suggestion is put forward jointly with Dr. O. Lipmann.

13 _____

Democracy and the School

Nations need generations to learn the democratic way of living and to develop the democratic way of political procedure. We admire the English people, who manage to maintain freedom of speech and of parliamentary discussion and criticism in the midst of their deadly struggle. We are aware of the mistakes which the German democrats made after 1918 when they tried to build up a democratic government with a people who were without democratic tradition and without adequately trained leadership. In part, their mistakes have been the same ones that are made within a smaller frame in the field of education.

Begin Democratic Practices Early

Democracy in education has to clarify its goals, its possibilities, and its procedure; it has to analyze typical mistakes and misconceptions. One of the reasons why so much uncertainty and confusion still exist in this field seems to be the fact that here, we deal with immature persons who are to be prepared for a future citizenship. One day they will be participating in a government of the people, by the people, and for the people. But now they are under the autocratic rule of the all-powerful adult generation. Yet, to organize education so that the democratic rights and responsibilities of the child conform to his level of maturity should be a challenging task to the educator.

Obviously, no full self-determination can be entrusted to the newborn baby. Yet, from the first day, various cultures (Mead, 1935) and various homes within one culture differ widely in the degree to which the nursing and handling of the baby follow the baby's needs or proceed according to a rigid authoritarian pattern dictated by parents, pediatrician, hospital routine, or tribal ritual. A toddler can be dragged along at the hand of the mother or nurse or be pushed by the shoulders in front of her to greet some adults who may be visiting in the living room. Yet you can introduce a small child to your guests just as graciously and respectfully as you would introduce an adult newcomer, without condescension or without the use of force. Such a procedure, giving the child the position of a person in

_____
With Gertrud Lewin. From *Understanding the Child*, 1941, *10*, 1–7.

his own right, can frequently be observed in the United States, but is rare in most of the European countries. The basis of democracy is not universal suffrage, decisions by majority vote, and other organizational procedure. This is the technically necessary superstructure on the ground of a democratic atmosphere, its consequence and expression. The atmosphere is produced by very subtle ways of demonstrating that human beings are basically equal and all entitled to the same respect and consideration.

Treat Child as Thinking Person

A child in a democratic atmosphere from his earliest days is not treated as an object but, as a person, is given explanations and reasons for the events in his surroundings and especially for necessary limitations of his freedom; he is given the right to make himself understood, to ask questions, and to tell "his side of the story." He is given a chance to make a choice and to make his own decisions wherever this is reasonably possible. Such a child will develop a better emotional basis for social living and will be prepared to shoulder responsibilities when he becomes mature enough to play with other children of his age.

Limits of Individual Freedom

Freedom of the individuality is only one side of the democratic way of life. If unlimited, it will lead to *laissez-faire*, to anarchy. Democracy demands limitations of individual freedom for the sake of the group. The child who grows into such a group will naturally be led to a democratic discipline for the "common good of all," be it among playmates where he learns to take turns with favorite toys or to avoid hurting his companions (Murphy, 1937), or be it within a family where he learns not to disturb a sleeping member of the household, not to interfere with the parents' work, and to respect the toys and products of brothers and sisters. Children are able to accept quite willingly such "infringements on their rights as individuals" if these are not imposed on them as by a ruling class on an underprivileged minority but rather are evolved during a process of cooperation and "give and take." Thus, a child before school age may well have experiences of being in a group, of identifying himself with group goals and cooperating in group projects. What the school adds to this is essentially that living and learning how are more planned and more formally organized.

The school which the child enters can be more or less democratic. The principal can be a dictator to his staff or he can build the staff as a democratic group with everybody, including the typists in the office and the janitors, cooperating. But the question which puzzles many is: Can the immature citizen of this school community have a share in this self-determination? Can there be a student self-government?

Successful Student Self-Government

The Educational Policies Commission (1940) in an inquiry of 90 American secondary schools shows that this has been done successfully for high-school-age children. In concrete instances are shown the fallacies and typical misunderstandings found in such endeavor. But also shown are the many promising efforts and beginnings of true democratic school teaching: democratic in the determination of policy (goal setting); democratic as to content of what is being taught; democratic in methods of teaching by allowing planning ahead, free discussion, investigation of sources, and criticism; democratic in matters of discipline and administration by giving the students privileges as well as responsibilities. Very convincingly, it shows how in a pseudo-democratic discussion, criticism and arguing are permitted but the real goals are always set in advance by the administration and the students know what they have to discuss until they hit the "right thing."

The study of Lippitt and White (Lewin, Lippitt, & White, 1939; Lewin, 1940) deals with the same problem of democratic group leadership with children of a younger age in clubs. It demonstrates with the exact methods of experimental social psychology the difference between a benevolent autocracy and a truly democratic leadership. It also shows the difference between democracy and the anarchic individualism of *laissez-faire*. Its "freedom" proved to be very unsatisfactory from the standpoint both of work output and of the children's feelings.

Efficiency of Democratic Schools

Probably the two types of aberration from democratic procedure, "pseudo-democracy" and "*laissez-faire*," are the causes of the low esteem in which "progressive" schools are held among some sections of the public and of the reputation of inefficiency that they carry.

Both studies agree well as to the much discussed point of efficiency. The Educational Policies Commission concludes that democratic school teaching can be just as efficient, and more lastingly so, as an autocratic one. They describe many instances of courses of study, study units, and extracurricular projects in various schools all over the country where efficient democratic work is being done. The social-psychological experiments show that with proper leadership, a democratic group can be just as efficient in its work as the autocratic one, that a democratic organization gives better promise of a steady work output and lasting results (the work goes on in the absence of the leader, cleaning up is done without the leader's command), and, moreover, that a general atmosphere of friendliness prevails as against a tense and hostile one under autocracy. The quantitative results of this study concerning friendliness versus hostility and tension and the analysis of the development of a scape-goat situation in autocracy are so impressive that these features alone seem to make it worthwhile for every teacher to understand and develop educational democracy to its fullest possible extent.

Democratic Organization Among Young Children

Democratic organization means that the policy of goal setting and of methods is to be determined by a majority vote. This has been demonstrated to be possible and successful in the upper grades of high school to quite a surprising degree. We cannot expect a first grade, though, to plan its own course of study successfully because the life-space at that level is still too narrow; neither in time nor in social space can these children be expected to show the necessary foresight or knowledge of possibilities. But within the planned course, a good number of items can be kept flexible; there can be choice between two or more projects to be worked out. The teacher may be alert for spontaneous suggestions that the pupils may contribute. The unit of action that a group of first or second graders can plan and pursue will be small, but within this narrow unit a planning by majority, an acceptance of the group decision, and cooperative work for the common goal will train for more comprehensive democratic procedure. After all, we should not forget that even the most democratic action of the adults is also limited to relatively small units of space and time by physical nature and the social conditions of the world.

Democratic Organization Among Older Children

As the children mature they will plan larger units, they will learn to know and appreciate each other better, and will be able to use judgment in delegating special powers and responsibilities to certain children. The unit of democratic learning will grow not only quantitatively but will also be more structured and complicated, with subgroups responsible for certain tasks. Children will have to prove their skills and knowledge in the jobs assigned to them; they will have to report to the group and will learn to take the group's criticism. A democratic work organization may be possible at an earlier level of maturity than democratic forms of self-government. Making first graders elect a class president and hall monitors may not be as democratic as it seems to be at first glance. Its effects on the emotional state of some children can be quite undesirable from the viewpoint of a democratic philosophy. On the other hand, the fact of a successful work organization, the objective, friendly, unemotional attitude it tends to produce, may eliminate the need for many disciplinarian measures that are unavoidable in an autocratic school (Educational Policies Commission, 1940).

The successful attempts toward a more democratic education show how much the school can contribute. However, these attempts also show that the degree to which education for and through democracy can be realized is related to the degree to which the adults are able to realize democracy in their world.

Summary

In summary: Democracy is opposed to both autocracy and *laissez-faire*; it includes long-range planning by the group on the basis of self-responsibility; it recognizes the importance of leadership, but this leadership remains responsible to the group as a whole and does not interfere with the basic equality of rights of every member. The safeguard of this equality of status is the emphasis on reason and fairness rather than personal willfulness. The right to influence group policy must have as its counterpart the willingness to accept majority decisions.

Democratic education has proved to be highly satisfactory both from the point of view of the group and its efficiency and from the point of view of the individual and his personality development. Democratic education cannot start with an autocratic treatment of the baby and then slowly shift to democratic methods. It should, rather, apply the full spirit of democracy from the beginning, but it should take into account realistically the size and the organization of the psychological and sociological world which exists for the child. It should create a democratic atmosphere for and within the actual world of the child.

References

Educational Policies Commission. (1940). *Learning the ways of democracy*. Washington, DC: National Education Association.

Lewin, K., Lippitt, R., & White, R. K. (1939). Patterns of aggressive behavior in experimentally created "social climates." *Journal of Social Psychology, 10*, 217–299.

Lippitt, R. (1940). An experimental study of authoritarian and democratic group atmospheres. *University of Iowa Studies in Child Welfare, 16*(3), 44–195.

Mead, M. (1935). *Sex and temperament*. New York: Morrow.

Murphy, L. B. (1937). *Social behavior and child personality*. New York: Columbia University Press.

_____

14

Personal Adjustment and Group Belongingness

If the social worker who deals with problems of personal adjustment of Jewish clients is himself Jewish, he may be able to understand his clients better and to be more sympathetic with them. On the other hand, this fact may distort his analysis in the direction either of over- or under-emphasizing the degree to which problems specifically Jewish enter his case. An objective, impartial judgment of this degree presupposes that the social worker is well adjusted as a Jew. Otherwise, the conclusions he reaches about the client will be fallacious.

What is a well-adjusted person? The term "adjustment" is as vague as it is popular. To give this term a useful meaning, one should set out from the fact that human conduct can be viewed as a sequence of an individual's "playing" certain "roles." The individual will behave differently at a swimming pool and at a formal dinner, at home and at his business. Any one of those roles are guided by certain ideologies in respect to what is appropriate and what is not. Practically the whole waking life of the individual, including his relaxed "private" behavior and his more formal "public" behavior, is guided by such ideologies, which are the mirror of the values and taboos of the various groups in which the individual acts as a member. A person is maladjusted if he behaves at a formal dinner as he might at a swimming pool, and at the swimming pool as he might at a formal dinner. In other words, an individual behaves as a member of many groups. He is well adjusted if, at a given time, that group belongingness which is ruling his behavior is "natural" for that situation. The typically maladjusted behavior of the adolescent or the marginal man, for instance, a marginal Jew, is based on the fact that that person does not react as a Jew when he should react in that fashion and does react as a Jew when he should not.

Individual Maladjustment and "Jewishness"

A discussion of the problems of personal adjustment in Jews is very much hampered by the fact that research in this field is extremely meager. Mere

_____

From *The Jewish Social Service Quarterly*, 1941, *17*, 362–366.

statistics on employment or occupational distribution or number of children do not give us the information we must have—namely, the psychological situation of the individual case. The interest in psychoanalysis
which has recently become so widespread among social workers has done
a great deal to make them conscious of this need. On the other hand, the
psychoanalytical aspect, at least in its classical form, has misled many
into viewing the client only as an "individual human being," governed by
common innate drives, and to minimizing the extent to which the psychology of the individual is only a reflection of his social relations.

It is clear that not all maladjustments of Jewish individuals stem from
their being Jewish. Jewish maladjustment has the same source as that of
non-Jews. However, it would be difficult to find a maladjusted Jew for
whom being Jewish has not influenced the type and degree of maladjustment. Modern psychology is increasingly realizing how much the "general
atmosphere," its state of tension, security, friendliness, and time perspective, means for the determination of the behavior of the individual in every
concrete action, and how much it determines the character of the growing
child. In a situation of relatively mild discrimination, such as exists in the
United States, any single difficult situation which an individual has to
face as a Jew is usually less severe, and seldom more severe, than some
of the difficulties *any* normal person has to meet in a normal life. This
might easily lead to the conclusion that specific Jewish difficulties may be
very essential for maladjustment of the Jewish individual in Hitler's Germany, but may be of very little importance in the United States. Actually,
however, the latter is not the case.

The Larger Psychological "Field" for the Problem

In a recent study on prisons (Farber, 1940), it was shown that the amount
of suffering the inmate experiences is not correlated with the agreeable-
ness or disagreeableness of his momentary prison job. It is, however,
greatly affected by whether or not he expected a fair deal in the matter of
a parole four or five years in the future, or his feeling of having been
treated fairly or unfairly during his trial. In other words, human beings
live by hope; their mood is a product of how they see their future and their
past, as recent experimental studies of frustration show clearly (Barker,
Dembo, & Lewin, 1941).

Field theory teaches us that the immediate situation must always be
viewed with reference to its larger background, and that even a slight
change in the degree of security or in the rate of progress toward the goal
may deeply affect the behavior of the individual. Psychology brings out
more and more clearly that the social aspects of this larger psychological
field, the position of the individual within a group and his attitude toward
the group, are of prime importance. Experiments with groups have shown
that the amount of aggressiveness, friendliness, objectivity, etc., can be
very quickly changed within an individual through a change of the social

atmosphere within the group (Lewin, Lippitt, & White, 1939; French, 1940).

It is an obvious fact that the expectations of the individual for his future life, his estimate of the possibility of success, the degree and type of possible danger he sees ahead are greatly influenced by his Jewishness. This alone would make psychologists anticipate that the relation to the Jewish group has a great influence on the adjustment of the individual Jew. Add the fact that this individual has grown up in a home where the conduct of the parents and the atmosphere of his family and friends have again been part and parcel of the same or similar background. Then the scientist will readily expect that, for the overwhelming majority of Jewish individuals, their Jewishness should have, for good or for bad, a decisive influence on their personality and conduct.

Indeed, I do not personally remember any case of maladjustment in a Jewish person in which I would judge that his being a Jew had not been important. More specifically, in most cases the maladjusted individual was not adjusted to his being a Jew. Whether we have to deal with a severely maladjusted Jewish refugee who shows extreme anti-Semitism and makes the Jews responsible for Hitler and for his personal difficulties or whether we deal with the common over-sensitivity of the Jew to things Jewish, everywhere we find the impact of the relation between the Jew and the Jewish group as an important factor.

Specific Roots of Maladjustment Among Jews

If I were to enumerate briefly some of the specific roots of lack of adjustment among Jews, I would mention the following:

a) *Unclearness* as to whether, in a given case, a set-back is due to the individual's lack of ability or due to anti-Semitism. If the young Jew is refused a job, is not invited to a birthday party, is not asked to join a club, he is usually not fully clear as to whether he himself is to blame or whether he is being discriminated against. A person who knows that his own shortcomings have caused his failure may do something to overcome them, or, if that is not possible, he can decide to apply his efforts in other directions.

If he knows that his being refused has nothing to do with his own abilities he will not blame himself, and instead may try to change the social reality. However, if he is in doubt whether or not his own shortcomings are the cause of his experience, he will be disoriented. He will intermittently blame himself and refuse responsibility, blame the others and be apologetic. In other words, this unclearness necessarily leads to a disorganized emotional behavior in the area of self-esteem which is so important for adjustment and personality development.

I frankly confess that I do not know how this unclearness can be prevented under the given circumstances. I know that its irritating effect sometimes spreads even to the benevolent Gentile who, for instance, as a professor judging Jewish students may lean over backwards and pass a student of low ability because of his fear of treating him unfairly. A partial remedy might be the strengthening within the Jewish individual of those factors which lead to objective evaluation of the situation.

b) A second fundamental source of maladjustment are those factors which underlie what has been called self-hatred or *Jewish anti-Semitism*. This old and well-known phenomenon has recently been interpreted as an expression of the "death instinct." But why is this drive stronger in Jews who have survived through thousands of years than in other people? Actually, a similar, even stronger self-hatred is evident in the Negro and among the members of many underprivileged groups. This self-hatred is the direct result of the position of an individual in an underprivileged group, of a membership which he has not fully accepted. It can be shown (Lewin, 1940; Kallen, 1940) that the tendency to leave the underprivileged group, the hatred against its cultural symbols, the enmity between certain subgroups within this group, and the self-hatred of its members in various forms, are all but different expressions of the same basic constellation of forces which lead to a "negative chauvinism." Basically we find the same behavioral symptoms (overaggressiveness, sensitivity, a quick shift from dominance to submission and back, generalized uneasiness) in the maladjusted adolescent who does not want to be a child any longer but knows that he is not fully accepted as an adult, and in the maladjusted Jew who does not want to be a Jew but knows that he is not fully accepted by the Gentile. Also in respect to this point, the adolescent, the Jew, and the maladjusted member of any other underprivileged group are alike in that they have accepted the standards and views of the more privileged majority to such an extent that they judge the qualities and values of their own group with the hostile or deriding attitude of this majority.

It is not the place here to discuss why those members of the underprivileged group who actually want to leave are forced to stay in the group. It is clear, however, that an individual cannot be well adjusted without being clearly adjusted to his own group, because the group is the ground on which the individual stands socially and without firm ground and clear orientation no one can act in an organized way.

Educational Accomplishment and Emotional Tension

c) The third point I wish to mention as a source of maladjustment among Jews is connected with *education*. Jewish parents would like to believe in the statement that "well-educated people are not anti-Semites." In other words, they present anti-Semitism to their children as the result of certain bad individuals among the Gentiles. In addition, they frequently have accepted the common rationalization of the non-Jew who attributes anti-Semitism to the bad behavior of Jews. They preach to their children, therefore, that they must behave well. If we recall the common and entirely correct statement of the Jewish father to his son that he must show much higher accomplishment than the non-Jew if he hopes to achieve success, we have a picture of a child kept in a state of tension which is above the normal. Probably this parental advice is one of the causes for special achievements among Jews. From the point of view of mental hygiene, however, it has a bad effect of heightening the level of emotional tension.

Emphasizing the private, *individualistic*, in matters of anti-Semitism rather than the social, group aspects, actually puts the individual under a heavier burden. It is, moreover, an attitude which is so *unrealistic* that it is prone to lead to a shocking awakening sooner or later, particularly for those individuals who had nothing but pleasant experiences with non-Jewish friends during childhood.

As in all cases of maladjustment, Jewish maladjustment leads to a vicious circle. The maladjusted individual creates for himself an unfavorable setting—which heightens his tension and makes him still less able to see things realistically. In this way the less fitted person has to live in the more difficult situation.

Courage to Face Danger Is Required

What are the possibilities to forestall or cure Jewish personality difficulties? Here I can merely mention a few facts which would need much elaboration. To help a person adjust himself means helping him to face reality. No insight into any kind of so-called "psychological mechanism" will be of any avail if the basic relations to one's own group cannot be established on a realistic and sound basis. The particular question of the psychology of Jewish adjustment can very simply be described: It is the problem of how to make the individual face that additional *danger*, present and potential, which is embodied in his being a Jew. A strong reaction to this, as to any other danger, is the impulse to fly. In our case that means the tendency to leave the group, to sever or minimize one's connection with it, and all the consequences of self-hatred and maladjustment which go with it. There is only one adjusted way to meet unavoidable danger—that is courage. Horace Kallen (1940) in a recent address recalled "Plato's definition of courage as wisdom concerning dangers." He continues, "Life today is dangerous enough, spiritually and physically, for all races and conditions of men the world over, but especially it confronts the Jews with dangers. And what other equipment for meeting this danger can serve them better than wisdom concerning it? . . . More than a condition of the body, disaster is a state of mind. Judaism is disaster only if you choose to think it thus, and you choose only as you flee the knowledge of its inner quality and outer values, of its nature and significance to the Jew and its role in the orchestration of the cultures of mankind."

What is true for Jews as a group is equally true for the individual Jew who has to face those additional dangers. Being maladjusted means not having the courage to face danger. An individual who is in the state of flight from a group is unable to face the dangers which are the result of his group membership in an organized form of courage. Only if the individual can be led to take his full share of active responsibility for his group and do that in a positive and realistic way is there any hope for him to have his just share of happiness as an individual.

References

Barker, R., Dembo, T., & Lewin, K. (1941). Frustration and regression: An experiment with young children. *Studies in Topological and Vector Psychology II, University of Iowa Studies: Child Welfare, 18*(1).

Farber, M. (1940). *Imprisonment as a psychological situation*. Unpublished doctoral dissertation, State University of Iowa.

French, J. R. (1940). *Behavior in organized and unorganized groups under conditions of frustration and fear*. Unpublished doctoral dissertation, Harvard University.

Kallen, H. (May, 1940). *Judaism as disaster*. Address to National Association of Jewish Community Center Workers, Pittsburgh, PA.

Lewin, K. (June 1940). Jewish self-hatred. *Contemporary Jewish Record*.

Lewin, K., Lippitt, R., & White, R. K. (1939). Patterns of aggressive behavior in experimentally created social climates. *Journal of Social Psychology, 10*, 271–299.

15

Psychology and the Process of Group Living

This is an unusual *SPSSI* meeting, the result of a last-minute decision to discuss the pressing problems of war psychology in spite of the difficulties of coming together. There was no time to prepare a survey of recent research work and to evaluate it fairly. I suppose people are able to get along anyway without the well-balanced words of approval and criticism with which presidential addresses feel themselves entitled to reward the good and to punish the bad colleagues.

However, I would like to discuss with you in a more informal manner some problems which are connected with the work of this society and the progress of psychology in that field to which this society is devoted. These problems and ideas are connected with *practice* and with *theory* in more than one way.

Psychology and Group Work

. . . The desperate struggle in which we are involved has made it clear to an increasing number of people how vital socio-psychological problems are, and how imperative it is to approach them in a much more radical and earnestly scientific way. Many of those who have been well aware of this fact, as for instance the members of this society, still have found few channels for such work and have been frustrated in this desire to make a more intensive use of their psychological knowledge for the improvement of social life today.

. . . Although the scientific investigations of group work are but a few years old, I don't hesitate to predict that group work—that is, the handling of human beings not as isolated individuals, but in the social setting of groups—will soon be one of the most important theoretical and practical fields. It is commonplace knowledge today that science has failed most in making us understand group life, group structure, and group movements.

From *The Journal of Social Psychology, SPSSI Bulletin,* 1943, *17,* 113–131. It is Lewin's edited version of the presidential address he gave to the *Society for the Psychological Study of Social Issues* in Washington, DC, in September, 1942.

There is no hope for creating a better world without a deeper scientific insight into the function of leadership, of culture, and of the other essentials of group life. Social life will have to be managed much more consciously than before if man shall not destroy man.

There are many indications that group work will not be limited to the problems of group management as such. Some of the recent studies indicate the importance of a fact which has always guided the practice of revival meetings or the gatherings of their forerunners; namely, that it is easier to affect deeply the personality of 10 people if they can be melted into a group than to affect the personality of any one individual treated separately. I am looking forward to the time when more than a few psychopathologists will seriously face the implications of the fact that a dominant factor in psychopathology is the social situation of the patient. A temporary psychological isolation of the patient from the social world in which he suffers will probably always be one of the decisive tools for a beginning treatment. That does not mean, however, that the psychological treatment should be performed in a situation which approaches a social vacuum as closely as possible. The group of two—composed of patient and doctor—is only one of many groups of different types, size, character, and composition which should be considered. What group is best fitted for different patients and for different periods of the treatment is a question wide open for investigation.

We are slowly coming to realize that all education is group work. Education of children and adults, education in families and schools never deals with the individual on the one hand and the subject to be taught on the other. It is common knowledge that the success of a teacher of French depends as much on the social atmosphere he creates as on his mastering the French language or the laws of learning. Probably in no country have the schools been as much aware of the importance of group management for education as in the United States. Still, the psychologist who has spent an immense amount of time studying learning curves has left the problems of social management in education almost entirely to the practitioner, who is forced to base his procedure on the primitive method of trial and error, or upon a peculiar mixture of philosophy and instinct.

The situation is not much different in regard to the problems of group management in family life, in the factory, or in the army. Everywhere science has made but feeble beginnings toward studying the psychological result of different group organizations, group atmosphere, or different types of leadership for the productivity of groups in reaching their group goal; for the stability or instability of the group; for the happiness or tension among their members and for the thousand and one effects which the group has on the well-being, the development, and the character of the individual member. Yet, the manipulation of groups will be able to fulfill its immense function in education or in any other field of human endeavor only if it can be based on a scientific foundation. Throughout history, political geniuses have arisen who have been masters in group management, such as Napoleon or Hitler. The only hope, however, for a permanent foundation of successful social management, and particularly for a permanent democratic society of the common man, is a social management based to a high degree on a scientific insight which is to be accessible to the many.

Cultural Differences and Human Nature

That American public opinion has been so slow in grasping the real world situation, that we started so late to arm, is, to a very considerable degree, due to the fact that everyone considers as "human nature" what actually is the character of his own specific culture. That a German news reporter could send from the front the dispatch (March 22, 1942) "much more than for wife and security are our soldiers longing for a new, a more beautiful, and a more bloody war" is hard for an American to realize. The people of this country flatly refuse to believe the existence of a culture which considers peace to be an unavoidable, but unattractive, pause between wars; a culture where, for generation after generation, the military caste has had the highest status in the social hierarchy; a culture which does not know the concept or the term "fairness"; a culture which, as Gregory Bateson has pointed out, is thinking mainly in terms of "rule or obey." We will have to pay a frightful price for the lack of understanding foreign cultures, and there seems to be little hope for a better world organization after the war unless we learn these facts.

This understanding of the effect of culture upon the group life and upon the conduct of the individual has been much hampered by an incorrect formulation of the problem. Usually the question is raised: *Are human beings everywhere essentially alike or are they essentially different?* The democratic tradition favors the answers which sustain the essential quality of man. This sentiment has become still stronger and more determinant since the all-out war of Nazism to establish, philosophically and practically, an all-out inequality of man. However, let us not forget that the democratic belief in the equality of man means—as you well know—the granting of equal rights to individuals of *different* character, race, or creed. This principle acknowledges essential differences between individuals and between groups; indeed, it encourages and safeguards these differences by promising tolerance for all but the intolerant. In other words, the democratic equality of man means the right of individuals or groups to be different.

This political credo, of course, does not prove that cultural differences are actually of great consequence for human conduct. One might say that many facts suggest that human nature is essentially the same everywhere. Are not all people given to love and jealousy? Is it not correct that "All people love peace"? Can we seriously doubt that the German solider, too, would like to be out of the bloody mess in spite of the Nazi reporter?

To clarify the issue, let us turn to an experimental example. Studies of the ideology of children show that the 8-year-old child is frequently dominated by the ideal of "generosity." If he has to distribute four good and four not-so-good toys between himself and another child, he is likely to give all four good toys to the other child and keep the poor ones. If one asks the child which toys he would "like" to have, he of course answers, "the four good toys." But in spite of his wishes and likes, his action is dominated by his ideals. Similarly, the Nazi soldier might "like" peace. I feel sure, however, that at least 95% of them are unable to conceive of a pacifist in any other way than of a disgusting coward and deserter.

Wishes and ideology are both important for the conduct of men. Which of these factors "is more important," that is, which factor wins in a case of conflict, or which deserves more consideration, depends upon the particular situation and the problem on hand. In comparing modern cultures, it might be correct to say that—by and large—the level of wishes shows a similar pattern and the same dynamics everywhere and that the differences within one culture are greater than between cultures.

This level of wishes and individual temperament is important. However, instead of insisting on an "either–or" statement about the effect of culture, we should realize that ideology, too, is an important determinant of conduct and that for certain problems ideological differences are decisive.

It would be a tragic mistake if the organization of the peace-to-come should be based on a misconception which has blinded American opinion in a most unfortunate way during the whole period leading to this war: namely, that satisfying the hunger of a nation for food and raw material suffices to make that nation peace loving and democratic. If we want to establish a basis for permanent peace, we should be very clear that satisfying needs without changing culture will lead us nowhere.

What progress science will make in understanding the effect of culture on conduct and character will depend greatly on the ability of the psychologist to deal with these problems and to cooperate theoretically and practically with the group workers, the cultural anthropologist, and the sociologist.

Application and Theory

Why have we psychologists not done more in this important field? As it happens frequently in the development of sciences, objective difficulties and certain sentiments have converged to block the way. The psychological study of groups may be viewed as closely related to problems of "applied psychology." There was a period in psychology when theoretical and applied problems had equal status among psychologists. It may be that psychologists were a bit too bold or too naive or too commercial in their endeavors in the field of application. Anyway, a period seems to have followed where the scientifically-minded psychologist did not look with much favor upon applied problems.

Today, it seems to me that a new type of synthesis is needed. We should be aware of the value of theory. A businessman once stated that "there is nothing as practical as a good theory." During the last decade, psychologists in this country have increasingly realized the importance of theory for psychology at large. That this recognition comes slowly is, to my mind, all to the good. Although we need theory, we will have to watch out that theory never breaks loose from its proper place as a servant, as a tool for human beings. In some European cultures, science, together with religion, politics, or the state, has been considered for generations one of those superhuman entities which are supposed to rule rather than to serve man. In such a culture, the wife of the professor is addressed as "Mrs. Professor" and the wife of the mail carrier is addressed as "Mrs. Mail Carrier." This is only one of the many daily symptoms of the character of a culture which conceives of happiness as a mere biological fact and where participation in superhuman values is considered the only way to elevate man from the level of the animal. It may be that in such a culture, theory progresses faster and the soldier is more ready to die for the state. It has been an outstanding characteristic of the culture of our country to see culture as the servant of man. I can conceive of permanent peace only in an atmosphere where equity and the dignity of man as man are fundaments of human relations and of cultural values; where man is not conceived of as a tool for other men nor for the supposedly superhuman values of the state, of economics, the arts, or sciences.

In a democratic culture, the attitude of the man of action toward science and of the scientist toward theory should be similar to that of the public toward government. It should contain a great deal of distrust and an eternal vigilance against an overextension of power. Given this as the foundation, however, we should be clear that neither the problem of government nor of theory can be solved by a negative attitude of neglect or hostility. A positive treatment is necessary; it is a question of "how" rather than of "whether or not." The weight of the government in politics and the weight of theory in science has to be great if they are to fulfill that function of leadership without which no democracy or science can live.

That research in the psychological problems of group life has not been more bold and more extensive is, of course, not only the result of the attitudes of the psychologist. There are very essential methodological difficulties which have to be overcome.

The first task of science is to register objectively and describe reliably the material one wishes to study. We have learned to register fairly accurately the *physical* aspects of behavior. But in regard to the *social* aspects of behavior, the task of objective scientific description seemed for a long time insoluble. Not many years ago, a methodological study of this problem in one of our leading universities came to the following pessimistic conclusion: observing the interrelation of a group of individuals, it was possible to collect reliable data about such items as who moved his arm, turned his head, or moved from one place to another. However, no reliable data could be obtained about friendliness or unfriendliness or many other social characteristics of behavior. The study seemed to lead to the unfortunate conclusion that what can be observed reliably is socially meaningless and what is socially meaningful cannot be observed reliably.

Fortunately, during the last years, a number of studies have shown that, after all, the social aspect of interpersonal behavior can be observed with high accuracy and with a degree of reliability which satisfies fully the scientific requirements. It may be worthwhile to pause a moment and consider how this methodological step forward has been accomplished.

Social Perception and Interpretation

One of the fundamental difficulties is related to the distinction between "observation" and "interpretation." In all sciences, it is important to keep observation as free as possible from theories and subjective interpretation. In psychology, too, the observer has to learn to use his eyes and ears and to report what happened rather than what he thinks should have happened according to his preconceived ideas. That is not an easy task. Can it be accomplished at all in social psychology? Can a friendly or an aggressive act be observed without interpretation in the same sense as the movement of an arm can be observed?

Until recently, the majority of psychologists were inclined to answer with an emphatic "no," and even today they may give that answer. Actually such an answer implies the impossibility of a scientific social psychology. If we ask the same psychologist, not as a "psychologist" but as an ordinary human being, how he gets along with his wife, he will probably be eager to tell us that—with few exceptions—he and his wife are well able to understand the social meaning of each other's behavior. If we were unable to perceive adequately and objectively the majority of social interactions with our colleagues and students, we would hardly be permitted to remain on the campus for long. Child psychology has established beyond doubt that within the first year of life, social perception is well under way. Within three or four years, the child can perceive rather complicated social actions. He is not likely to be fooled by the superficial friendliness of a hostile or uninterested aunt. He is able to "see through" such a surface. Frequently he seems to perceive more clearly than an adult the character of certain social interrelations in his surroundings. This social perception has to be adequate in most of the essential cases if the child is to survive socially. Therefore, objective social observation must be possible, and the psychologist should find a way to do in science what any normal 3-year-old child does in life.

I think we would have sooner found our way, if we had not been blinded by philosophical considerations. For more than 50 years, psychology has grown up in an atmosphere which recognizes only physical facts as "existent" in the scientific meaning of that term. The effect of this atmosphere can be observed in every psychological school, in the classical form of Gestalt theory as well as in behaviorism. As usual, the conservative power of philosophy—this time in the form of physicalistic positivism—did its part to keep alive an attitude which once had a function for the progress of science, but which now has outlived its usefulness.

What is needed in social psychology today is to free its methodology from speculative limitations. We do well to start again with the simple facts of everyday life for which the possibility of an adequate social observation never could be in doubt because community life is unthinkable without it. Such an empirical basis should be one basis of the methodology of social psychology. The other should be a progressively deeper understanding of the laws of "social perception."

I would like to mention a few aspects of the problems of social perception. How is it possible today to get reliable observations of social action which could not be recorded reliably yesterday?

If a biologist is to observe the growth of a leaf during a fortnight, he will never finish his job if he tries to follow the movement of the ions contained in that leaf; nor will he succeed if he watches only the tree as a whole on which this leaf grows. The first prerequisite of a successful observation in any science is a definite understanding about *what size of unit* one is going to observe at a given occasion.

This problem is of fundamental importance for social psychology. For a long time, we have misinterpreted the scientific requirements of analysis and have tried to observe under all circumstances as *small* units as possible. It is true that sometimes a twinkle of the eye means the difference between acceptance or refusal of marriage. But that meaning is the result of a defined and specific setting. An observation which approaches the movement of the arm or head in isolation is missing the social meaning of the events. In other words, social observation should look toward units of sufficient size.

In addition, the observer should perceive the units in their particular setting. This again is by no means a problem specific for psychology. A physician who would cut up the X-ray picture of the broken bone into small pieces and classify these pieces according to their shades of gray would have destroyed all that he wanted to observe. To give another example, if two persons, A and B, are running one behind the other, it may mean that the first is leading and the second following, or it may mean that the first is being chased by the second. There is frequently no way to distinguish between these possibilities if the observation lasts only a few seconds. One has to observe a sufficiently extended period before the meaning of an act becomes definitely clear. One does not need to be a Gestalt psychologist or be interested in field theory to recognize these facts which are well established in the psychology of perception. All that is necessary is to acknowledge that the same laws which rule the perception of physical entities also rule social perception.

Like the physician who has to read an X-ray picture, the social psychologist has to be *educated* to know what he can report as an *observation* and what he might add as a more or less valuable *interpretation*. A transition exists between observation and interpretation in the case of the X-ray picture as well as in regard to social data. But that does not weaken the importance of this distinction. Observers have to be trained; then they are able to give reliable observations where the untrained person has to resort to guesswork or interpretation. That holds for the flyer who has to learn to recognize enemy planes even under adverse conditions, for the physician studying the X-ray picture, and also for the social psychologist.

All observation, finally, means classifying certain events under certain categories. Scientific reliability depends upon correct perception *and* correct classification. Here again, the observers have to be trained and trained correctly.

There has to be agreement among observers as to what is to be called a "question" and what a "suggestion," where the boundary lies between "suggestion" and a "command." Exactly where the boundary is drawn between two such categories is, to a certain degree, a matter of convention. However, there are certain basic facts to be learned that are not a matter of arbitrary conventions. If the teacher says to the child in a harsh, commanding voice, *"Would you close the door?"* this should not be classified under the category "question" but under the category "command." The statement of one of our native Nazis that the President's neck is well fitted for a rope is definitely not to be classified under the category "statement of facts" nor under the category "expression of opinion," in spite of its grammatical form. In the attempt to be objective, the psychologist too frequently has made the grammatical form of a sentence, or the physical form of behavior rather than its social meaning, the criterion for classification. We can no longer permit ourselves to be fooled by such superficialities, and will have to recognize that the social meaning of an act is no less objective than its grammatical meaning. There are, of course, also in psychology boundary cases which are difficult to classify; however, experience shows that the observer who is well trained to look for the social meaning of the action is able to perceive correctly and to classify reliably his data.

We should be aware that the problem of social perception has very broad theoretical and practical implications. To name but a few examples: The development of better methods for psychologically correct classifications of social actions and expressions could be of great value for the legal and political aspects of free speech.

Recent experiments have shown that the training of leaders is to a high degree dependent upon the sensitizing of their social perception. The good leader is able and ready to perceive more subtle changes in social atmosphere and is more correct in observing social meaning. The good scout master knows that a joking remark or a scuffle during the ceremony of the raising of the flag is something different than the same scuffle during a teaching period or during a period of games; that it has a different meaning if the group is full of pep or all tired out; if it occurs between intimate friends or between two individuals who are enemies.

Social Units of Different Size

Observation of social behavior is usually of little value if it doesn't include an adequate description of the character of the social atmosphere or the *larger unit* of *activity* within which the specific social act occurs. A running account of such larger units of activity should record whether the situation as a whole has the meaning of "discussing plans" or of "working," of "playing around," or of a "free-for-all fight." It has been shown that a reliable description of the larger units of social events is possible and that the beginning and end of such periods can be determined with an astonishing degree of accuracy. The statistical treatment of the data and their evaluation must carefully take into account the position of a social action within that unit to which it actually belongs. This is as important theoretically as practically. For instance, on the average, the democratic leader will give less direct commands and will more frequently place the responsibility for decision on the members of the group. That does not mean, however, that whenever a leader gives a command, he turns autocrat.

In matters of routine, even an extremely democratic group might gladly accept a leader or a parliamentary whip who has to see to it that certain objectives are reached efficiently and with a minimum of bother for the members. The democratic leaders who may have to be careful to avoid commands in his first contacts might be much freer in the form of his behavior after the social character of the group and his position within it is clearly established. The social meaning and the effect of a command depends upon whether this command deals with an unessential question of "execution" or an essential problem of "policy determination"; whether it is an isolated event, which as Fritz Redl says is "antiseptically" imbedded in the general social atmosphere or whether it is one of the normal elements of this social setting. It is not the amount of power which distinguishes the democratic and the autocratic leader. The president of the United States always had more political power than the kaiser in Germany. What counts is how this power is imbedded in the larger social unit and particularly whether in the long run the leader is responsible to the people below him. In Hitlerism, the leader on any level of the organizational hierarchy has no responsibility whatever to the people below. The leader above him is his only judge and his only source of power.

Of course, much is a question of degree. However, two points should be clear; first, that a democratic leader is neither a man without power nor a traffic policeman nor an expert who does not affect group goals and group decisions; secondly, that the evaluation of any social atmosphere or organization has to take into account the full special and temporal size of the social unit which is actually determining the social events in that group.

It is clear that observation and theory in social psychology face here a number of problems which we have barely started to attack. In physics, we are accustomed to recognize that an ion has different properties than the atom of which it is a part, that the larger molecule again has specific properties of its own and that a macroscopic object like a bridge, too, has its specific properties as a whole. A symmetrical bridge might be composed of unsymmetrical molecules and the stability of the bridge is not identical with the stability of its molecules. These are simple facts beyond dispute. In social psychology the same facts hold: The organization of a group is not the same as the organization of the individuals of which it is composed. The strength of a group composed of very strong personalities is not necessarily greater but frequently weaker than the strength of a group containing a variety of personalities. The goal of the group is not identical with the goal of its members. Frequently, in a well-organized group, the goals of the members are different. For instance, in a good marriage, the husband should be concerned with the happiness of the wife and the wife with happiness of the husband rather than the husband and wife both being concerned only with the happiness of the husband.

That a social unit of a certain size has properties of its own should be accepted as a simple empirical fact. If we refuse to see any magic into it, we will be better prepared to perceive these units correctly and to develop methods for their scientific description.

The greatest recent progress in methodology has been made in the study of relatively small units: of the single social acts and of face-to-face groups. Some of the characteristics of group structure, for instance, the degree of subgrouping for work, can frequently be recorded with rather simple means. Sometimes a filming of a recording of the physical grouping of the members gives a fairly accurate picture. Beyond that, methods have been developed which, I think, are able to secure a pretty adequate and reliable picture of the social atmosphere and the social organizations of the group. The leaders and sub-leaders within the group can be determined, and their form of leadership can be measured accurately in a rather short time in many face-to-face groups. Such measurement makes it possible, for instance, to determine typical forms of social management of the good leader and compare these with the typical forms of group management of the poor leader in the same organization. Such measurement is obviously of greatest importance for the training of good leaders. We should be aware of the fact that good leadership in one organization is not necessarily good leadership in another organization. Leadership should be tailor-made for the specific organization. Even the symptoms, for instance, for an autocratic leader are fairly different in different types of activities. They are different in teaching, in dancing, or playing football. They are different in recreation, in the factory, or in the army, although they all are parts of one democratic culture.

In studying and evaluating problems of leadership or other social actions, we should be careful to determine how much in that social setting is *imposed* on the life of the group by the rules of the organization or other social powers which limit the freedom of action by the members of the group. There is not much chance of distinguishing the democratic from the autocratic scout master within the opening ceremony of flag raising. The way a foreman in a factory treats his workers might be determined by a fight between union and management to such a degree that no training of the foreman in social management could affect the social relations between the foreman and the worker to any considerable degree. In this case, a change in the relation between management and union would be a prerequisite to any essential change in the foreman's behavior. Such an example shows clearly that the size of the social unit which has to be taken into account for the theoretical or practical solution of a social problem is not an arbitrary matter which can be decided by the social psychologist in one way or the other. What social unit is decisive for a given social behavior is an objective question and a problem which has to receive much consideration in any social study.

For instance, the interest which the church or the school which sponsors a Boy Scout troop has in scouting and the status which scouting has in the community might be more important for the membership and the group life of a scout troop than the behavior of the scout master. It is of prime importance in studying morale in the army to know whether the loyalty of the soldier is preliminarily directed toward his squad, his platoon, his regiment, his corps, or to the army as a whole.

In studying the relatively small face-to-face groups we are, I think, well on the way to measuring even such more dynamic properties of a group as the degree of group tension, the degree of cohesiveness, and, of course, its ideology. It is possible to conduct experiments, with a group as a whole, which fulfill the requirements of standardized settings to a degree not much different from what we are accustomed to require of an experiment with individuals. It is possible, also, to study empirically the question to what degree group life, in a given case, depends upon the specific personality of its individual members.

Some properties of groups such as the degree of homogeneity of its ideology can be measured on all sizes of groups. On the whole, however, we are at present much less able to deal adequately with the properties of the social units beyond the size of a face-to-face group. One of the reasons seems to be that the time period which has to be taken into consideration for one unit of events within this larger social group is frequently of considerable extent. The action within a smaller unit—particularly if one deals with children—lies usually within the grasp of an observer who spends an hour or two watching the group. This provides him with a sufficient background to perceive the meaning of the social acts he wishes to study. However, to determine the social meaning of a foreman's conversation with a worker, a continuous observation of the foreman alone, even for weeks, might not suffice. It might be necessary for adequate observation of the foreman to attend a number of meetings of the workers, of certain committees which include management and workers, and to attend some meetings of the management.

In studying such larger units, the interview of certain persons is one of the most essential means of investigation. It is very important to know in what position within the group one is likely to find the best "informants." The psychologist can learn much in this respect from the cultural anthropologist. The questionnaire which has been somewhat in disgrace in psychology may come back in a slightly different form for the study of group life and particularly of the ideology of a group. We are gradually giving up the idea that the answer to the questionnaires or interviews is an expression of facts. We are slowly learning to treat them as reactions to a situation which is partly determined by the question, partly by the general situation of that individual. We have to learn to treat questionnaires as we are accustomed to treat a projective technique. In short, we need most urgently a real theory of questionnairing and interviewing which offers more than a few technical rules.

The difficulties which lie ahead should not discourage us. I think social psychologists have every reason to be confident and somewhat proud about what has been accomplished within the last years. After all, who would have been bold enough to predict five years ago that we would be able today to measure social atmospheres, measure and train leaders, to study group tension and the process of group decision in the way in which we can do it today.

One technical point seems to hold practical promise for the future: Although groups of different sizes have their specific problems, nevertheless certain dynamic characteristics seem to depend more on the structural properties than on the absolute size of the group. Therefore, we might be able to investigate the properties of large groups on relatively small scale models. We don't need, for instance, to study whole nations to find out to what degree our perception of the ideals of other persons depends on our own culture. We can study the same phenomenon in the 8- and 11-year-old child who perceives the degree of egoism, generosity, or fairness of his surroundings according to his own degree of egoism, generosity, or fairness.

To mention another example: The morale of a group of any size seems to be stronger if its action is based on its own decision and on "accepting" its own situation. For instance, the ability of an individual to "take it" in a shock situation is much greater—according to a recent study of the Harvard Psychology Clinic—in persons who create this situation themselves than in persons who are pushed into the situation from without. A comparison of a lecture method with a method of group decision for changes of food habits in housewives shows that the method of group decision is much more effective.

The success of the fight for equality of an underprivileged group seems to depend greatly on finding leaders who have fully accepted, for better or for worse, their own belonging to this minority or who have joined spontaneously the underprivileged group, as it happened in the French Revolution.

Cooperative Research

There is one last point I would like to mention. The scientific study of group life is frequently beyond the scope of the work of a single psychologist or those small research cooperatives which are customary. We will have to resort to research cooperation on a much larger scale. This is an important and by no means easy problem, the solution of which will greatly depend on the way in which we psychologists ourselves act as a group.

This brings us back to a problem which is of basic importance to the *Society for the Psychological Study of Social Issues* and to its members. Science and research is not a product of isolated individuals called "scientific geniuses" but is a cooperative endeavor deeply connected with the culture of the people in which it occurs. There is no country anywhere in the world where the social status granted to psychology as a science and the opportunities given to the psychologist as teacher and research worker approaches that opportunity which is granted to him by the public and the government in these United States. Whether we will live up to this opportunity and responsibility will depend largely on the degree to which we see the problem of psychological research as a part of a group process. In other words, it will depend upon the way in which the psychologists organize themselves as a group and the degree to which they apply scientific insight and democratic principles to their own organization.

. . . For a decade or two, psychologists have been dreaming of getting "close to life." The progress in scientific methods of the last years has brought us closer to the "real" problems of life than we have ever been before. As long as our experiments dealt with the individual in the laboratory, our troubles were rarely worse than persuading a reluctant colleague to use his students as subjects or persuading a hard-boiled superintendent to permit our using the children in his schools.

Today, things look a bit different. The boss of a powerful organization might be eager to have certain problems of his organization studied, but he might be as eager to prevent the appearance of any data which, to his mind, would be detrimental to the prestige of his organization. We might be dealing with such highly organized, at the same time, rigid and extremely sensitive social bodies, as the army or a factory. In such, and in many other "hot" situations, the psychologist is bound to wonder whether he has not stretched out his hand a bit too far into the "real social life." After all, he had planned to make science and not politics his work.

. . . We might as well be clear that the psychologist is caught, for better or for worse, in a situation which is unavoidable. The study of social relations, of groups and of their culture will, of necessity, bring us in close contact with all the social forces which are ruling the life of these groups. We might be able to handle these problems more or less cautiously and more or less wisely. But we will have to be prepared for occasional attacks by local or national politicians. Goodwin Watson . . . has been honored by such an attack. We were happy when this affair was finished victoriously for him by a unanimous vote of the Senate. It is clear that no one can face such problems single-handed.

The *Society for the Psychological Study of Social Issues* can help to organize and to facilitate the study of social problems by providing certain channels of research. However, an organizational framework means little in itself, particularly in a democracy. The success of the *SPSSI* and the success of the psychologist at large will depend on the same factors which determine the success of other group endeavors in a democracy: namely, on the courage and the determination of its members and on the vision and the wisdom of its leaders.

Index

About the Editor

Martin Gold, PhD, is a Senior Research Scientist at the Research Center for Group Dynamics of the Institute for Social Research and Professor Emeritus of Psychology at the University of Michigan. His research includes national surveys and field experiments on juvenile delinquency and studies of suicide, mother–daughter–friend relationships, sociometric structure of classroom groups, and effects of social status on family functioning. His most recent book is *A New Outline of Social Psychology*. He has also published articles on social psychological theory, particularly on the field theory of Kurt Lewin.